DISCOVERING MUSIC

A Course in Music Appreciation

DISCOVERING MUSIC

A Course in Music Appreciation

—

THIRD EDITION

Howard D. McKinney

Professor of Music, Rutgers University

and

W. R. Anderson

Critic and Reviewer for *The Gramophone, Musical Times,*
and other English publications

AMERICAN BOOK COMPANY

PRELUDE

This book has been written with a double purpose: (1) to guide the uninitiated traveler who would embark upon a journey into the complex land of music; and (2) to be a Good Companion to those who, having already set sail, have made some discoveries for themselves and are eager to shape their course towards wider worlds.

The ability to "listen" to music rather than merely to "hear" it is not, as such, a natural capacity, but one that has to be acquired and developed by active, continual, and highly pleasurable observation. The power to cultivate this listening skill varies as does any other human accomplishment, but no cultivation is possible without guidance.

The principles used in the preparation of this guidebook have been shaped out of extended experience rather than fashioned out of theories. We believe that the greatest incentive for embarking upon voyages of artistic discovery should be the pleasure that one can derive from them. Housman has said that the nature of such arts as poetry and music is more physical than intellectual; it is the sense of delight that can be obtained from reading a poem, or looking at a picture, or listening to good music that attracts and holds us. It is this yielding of delight that will lead us on in a search for other wonders. Art educates in the proportion that it gives pleasure. We have shaped our treatment along sound pedagogical lines, and have proceeded from the known to the unknown; it will be found that we have placed the points of departure in familiar and interesting territory.

Some books of this nature are based upon the traditional educational process of starting at the earliest times and working up to the present. Others begin at the present and work as faithfully backwards. In the course of the treatment, they too often give historical and technical information as to how music has been put together and how it can best be listened to so as to recognize its formal structure, but pay insufficient attention to the actual cultivation of the reader's enjoyment and enthusiasm. Our method is to begin with the everyday musical experiences that are both real and satisfying, and use these as stimuli and points of departure for further artistic development. That is why we have not kept to strict chronological order. This arrangement of material has been found useful in giving students, in a year's work, a realization of their own capacity for participating in the world's heritage of musical experience. The authors believe it will prove equally useful in the hands of the general reader who has had no formal musical training.

We have felt that a book planned along these lines must be more than just a history of music or a dictionary, although it should contain much historical material and include a glossary of musical terms in common use. Impressed by the cultural value of music, still insufficiently recognized, we have constantly associated musical ideas with those of other arts. Though it is impossible, in a book of reasonable size, fully to develop these comprehensive ideas, enough has been given, it is hoped, to show how music can take its proper place in civilized life. As part of the life of its period, music, like everything that has contributed to growth, can be analyzed and reasoned about and its existence justified. Through such processes its nature and influence can be understood.

We think that most books try to do too much, and especially to tell too much. Telling does not go far in music — doing and discovering are so much more important. Talking about music is of very little value unless one hears it, too; so we have discussed musical works that are constantly to be listened to, these progressing from the easily understood compositions to the more abstract — a logical outcome of the emphasis on enjoyment as the chief end of listening. We have taken most of the illustrations from the repertoire of phonographically recorded music. Thus laymen, teachers, and students will have in their hands lists of the finest material upon which to build a good library of records.

In our discussions, we have used ordinary technical terms, as far as they were necessary; surprisingly few of them are needed. When they are necessary, however, it seems foolish to go out of the way to avoid them. If anyone is interested enough in a subject to study a book of this sort, he will learn its vocabulary quickly enough, and be pleased to call a thing by its right name. We have not tried to make this a critical book, though we hope that its readers will get out of it a great deal that will broaden and strengthen their critical judgment. If all of the music mentioned herein is not immediately liked, the student will find out why this is so, and thus gain valuable knowledge.

The subject matter has been arranged in a manner suitable for presentation in class form, and appropriate topics for further discussion along similar lines have been furnished at the end of each chapter. Suggestions for further reading have likewise been made, and the reader who follows these will find himself possessed of a great fund of information which will be of inestimable value in the development of his listening powers.

Acknowledgment must be made of the help that has been received from various sources, especially the members of the "music-appreciation" courses who have proved the value of this material in actual use over a period of years. F. Austin Walter has helped in preparing and copying different sections; Wilbert B. Hitchner and the teachers who co-operated with him have shown the effectiveness of this method of treatment for high-school pupils. A word of appreciation is also due those authors and publishers who have given permission to quote from their works.

PRELUDE TO THE SECOND EDITION

The use of this book over a period of some years and in widely varying circumstances has suggested the changes and additions made in this new edition. A number of new chapters containing additional information and musical examples have been added; but the fundamental method of approach to the subject, a method that has proved itself time and time again in practice, has not been altered.

Owing to the exigencies of war, the cordial co-operation and constant consultation that made the first edition of *Discovering Music* so successful have not been possible in preparing this second edition. While I must be held responsible for most of the changes and additions that have been made, this new volume goes forth on its mission with the fond hopes of both authors for its continued usefulness in its important field.

Howard D. McKinney

PRELUDE TO THE THIRD EDITION

In this third edition the authors are happy to have resumed again full co-operation, incorporating the results of further experience through using the book in daily teaching.

A great deal of fresh matter has been added, and the contents have been re-arranged so as to make the work still more effective. The basic course material consists of the numbered chapters; from time to time will be found "Interchapters" containing supplementary information which will be valuable for study by those readers who wish for still further enlightenment.

Howard D. McKinney
W. R. Anderson

ACKNOWLEDGMENTS

The authors and publishers herewith offer thanks to the following, who have kindly given permission to reproduce copyrighted material:

The American Mercury for permission to quote from Winthrop Sargent's article of September, 1941.

D. Appleton-Century Co. for a passage from Sacheverell Sitwell's *Mozart*.

Percy Buck, author, and Ernest Benn, Ltd., for the passages from *History of Music*.

The John Day Co. for quotations from *What Is American?* by Ernest Hill.

Alban Dobson and the Oxford University Press for the poem, "Love Comes Back to His Vacant Dwelling," by Austin Dobson.

J. Fischer & Bro. for the poem by George Ashdowne Audsley.

Lawrence Gilman for several quotations.

Dr. Grace, editor of the London *Musical Times,* for the passage by him from the *Musical Times.*

W. J. Henderson for the passage from one of his articles in the *New York Sun.*

Hubbard Hutchinson for the passage from one of his articles in the *New York Times.*

John Lane The Bodley Head Ltd. for the quotation from Philip Heseltine's *Frederick Delius.*

John Lomax for permission to quote the passage from *Cowboy Songs.*

Longmans, Green & Co. for the quotation from Dean Inge's *Personal Idealism and Mysticism.*

Lincoln MacVeagh, The Dial Press, Inc., for the sentences from Olin Downes's *Symphonic Broadcasts.*

Edward B. Marks Music Co. for twelve measures from their score of *L'Après-midi d'un faune* by Debussy.

Modern Music for permission to quote from Roger Sessions and Grigori Schneerson.

New York Times for permission to reprint an excerpt from "Reaching the Man in the Street," *New York Times,* July 27, 1941.

The New Yorker Magazine and Dr. Irwin Edman for quotations from "Varieties of Musical Experience."

Ernest Newman and the London *Sunday Times* for permission to quote from Newman's critical articles.

Oxford University Press for the passage from Mowat's *History of Europe,* selections from Cobbett's *Cyclopedic Survey of Chamber Music* (articles by Cobbett and Hadow), selection from Hannam's *On Church Cantatas of J. S. Bach,* and the poem by Austin Dobson.

George Sampson for the quotation from his works.

The *Saturday Review* (London) for the poem by "F.E."

G. Schirmer, Inc., for the passages from Rimsky-Korsakoff's *Scheherazade* Suite, Dvořák's *New World Symphony,* and Tchaikovsky's *Andante cantabile.* These passages as used in this book were taken from the Schirmer editions. To G. Schirmer, Inc., also, for permission to quote from Stanford's article "Some Thoughts Concerning Folk Song and Nationality" in the *Musical Quarterly,* April, 1915.

Charles Scribner's Sons for the passages from Edward Dickinson's *Spirit of Music,* and from Augustine Birrell's *Collected Essays and Addresses;* for Gosse's paraphrase of Mallarmé's *Eclogue,* and the selection from the poem, *Arabian Nights Entertainments,* by William Ernest Henley.

Basil de Sélincourt for an extract from his notes written for concert programs.

George Bernard Shaw and Constable and Co. for the passage from Mr. Shaw's *Music in London, 1890–1894.*

Simon and Schuster for the quotations from Durant's *Story of Philosophy,* Dimnet's *Art of Thinking,* and *The Victor Book of the Opera* by Charles O'Connell.

H. Royer Smith Co. for permission to quote parts of the article "Has the Organ a Place in Our Present-day Musical Sun?" from *Disques.*

The eight measures from Křenek's *Toccata und Chaconne* are used by permission of the Universal Edition of Vienna, Copyright, 1923.

CONTENTS

ART AND LIFE

BEAUTY IN THE LIFE OF TODAY

In an article which appeared on the feature page of a pragmatic American newspaper, a thoughtful reporter who has spent considerable time wandering about the Old World, enjoying and admiring the beauty left behind by the genius of the past, asked the practical question: "Of what use is beauty in the world?" In a period which has been inclined to see beauty in the machinery that performs its daily work, in factories that provide its money, or in skyscrapers that house thousands of its workers, of what use is an understanding and appreciation of the beauty of paintings, statues, mosaics, churches, palaces, or of the literature and the music of the past? A number of years ago John Ruskin made the statement that the most beautiful things in the world are the most useless, a statement which stands the test of time better than do some of his other pronouncements. The modern reaction to this would probably be the ingenuous question asked by the modern factory manager: "Well, if beautiful things haven't any use, what good are they?"

Our newspaper writer answers this question by saying that the only use that he can see for beauty in this world is for developing taste. The more one learns to appreciate the beautiful, the more he will avoid and despise the ugly. A man cannot learn really to like Shelley and Keats, Goethe and Shakespeare, and at the same time continue to enjoy reading pulp-paper confession magazines. If a man becomes enthusiastic about the music of Beethoven or Brahms, he loses his taste for the products of the Tin Pan Alley fabricators. An understanding of and liking for the works of Michelangelo and Rembrandt, Da Vinci, or El Greco is the best possible antidote for the cheapness and vulgarity of so many of the present-day movies and modern paintings.

All right, you may say. Granted all this, what then? Is the person who spends his time cultivating his taste any better off than the one who is concerned only with the useful things in life? Does the man who can see the beauty in a field of daffodils or in an Alpine sunrise or in that "loveliest of trees, the cherry hung with bloom along the bough," get more out of life than he who derives his pleasures from reading the favorable reports received from the management of the company in which he has been shrewd enough to invest his money, or from scanning the financial pages of his newspaper during a rising market? The hard-headed newspaper writer says that he does, for the observing reporter has noticed that the people who have taken the trouble to develop their taste derive more happiness from life than those who have not. He wonders whether the modern concern with usefulness is not thoroughly idiotic and suicidal, and if the world would not be much better off by cultivating a sense of abstract beauty and giving *usefulness* a good rest. If the admiration — he goes so far as to say the adoration — of beauty can develop our taste to the point where we can learn to appreciate it to the full, he is sure that the avenues of life's enjoyment will become wider and more spacious; that we will find more joy in life, and with no additional expense.

LASTING BEAUTY IN ART

What the reporter should have realized, if he had been more of a philosopher, is that what he called the cultivation of a sense of beauty is only one of a number of possible "useless" human activities contributing toward a better and more satisfactory life, to what he called "more joy in life." The most general of these is a study of philosophy, that attempt to apprehend reality through the consideration of broad relationships like the function of art, the place of education in life, the meaning of experience, etc. Another is the cultivation of one's spiritual and imaginative powers through religion — the adoration and service of a Higher Power of some sort and an attempt at obeying His commandments as we understand them. A third, unfortunately developed today at the expense of the others, is the study of science; that is, the apprehension of accuracy, the investigation of physical laws, and the development of practical apparatus for living. All these are necessary for the development of the complete, social man, ready to undertake his responsibilities in life and equipped for enjoying this life as he lives it.

Not the least of these varied activities necessary for the complete life in a difficult world is the understanding of art, that activity by which man, in all the years which he has lived in the world, has communicated his experiences and transformed the things he used into what we call *beauty*, thus making the world a better place in which to live. Indeed, there are good reasons for maintaining that the knowledge and experience gained from a study of the art activities of man is really superior to any other kind of historical knowledge.[1] For it alone, in its highest manifestations, is universal:

All passes; Art alone
Enduring stays to us.

In its widest and most significant conception, art has not been concerned with merely the skillful making of things or their creation for practical use. The artist — that is, the man who creates these manifestations of beauty that have no seeming practical value — produces a building, a piece of furniture, a ceramic plate, a poem, or a symphony as a means of expression through which he is trying to tell us something. Something, perhaps, that concerns nature, or man, or simply something about the artist himself. And this that he is trying to tell us, if we but learn to understand it, may be as valuable as, or indeed more valuable than, that which we learn from the fields of philosophy or science. It is only when we begin to recognize this function of art as a kind of knowledge equal to and parallel with the other means by which man learns to understand his place in the world that we realize its importance.

This has all been summed up in the age-old aphorism: "Art is long and time is fleeting." Which is simply a terse way of saying not only that art endures far beyond the confines of any single human existence and contains within itself the real meaning of such an existence, but also that, because it has endured beyond any other accomplishment of mankind — systems of religion, social and economic societies, scientific theories and achievements — it has a very

[1] Herbert Read, in his *Art and Society* (New York: Macmillan), has an excellent treatment of this.

special value. And that which it would communicate to us is of particular and unusual significance.

> All things return to dust
>> Save beauties fashioned well.
> The bust
>> Outlives the citadel.
>
> The gods, too, die, alas!
>> But deathless and more strong
> Than brass
>> Remains the sovereign song.
>> *— Théophile Gautier*
>> TRANSLATED BY SANTAYANA

ONE

THE CO-OPERATING BEGINNER

WHAT IS ART?

A recent book published on the interrelation of the various activities that we call the arts [1] — music, literature, painting, as well as the more practical arts of wood carving, furniture designing, and the like — observes that it is possible to distinguish at least twenty-two different meanings of the term "art." Most of these are based, according to this account, on the concept of skill. This is no place to attempt a clarification of such distinctions, for we are not writing a book on aesthetics outlining the theory and practice of the arts. It will not even be necessary for our purpose to attempt a definition of what art is other than suggesting that it *is* a skilled way of making or doing something, thereby resulting in the creation of beauty and order, and that it likewise serves as a kind of language, a form of communication between the artist and his fellow man. This language is not of the ordinary variety by means of which we talk with each other, but one able to express feeling, sentiment, and emotion, as well as to communicate personal and social experience.

What happens when the creator produces what we call "art" is that he undergoes some experience which he feels to be of concern to his fellow men or apprehends some truth which seems to him of general interest to mankind. This may be of such universal stature that it produces a Goethe's *Faust* or a symphony of the quality of Beethoven's *Eroica;* or it may be of such limited and local nature that it results in nothing more significant than a homespun quilt or a newspaper editorial. With whatever technical powers the artist is

---

[1] *The Arts and Their Interrelations* by Thomas Monroe (New York: The Liberal Arts Press).

endowed or has acquired, he reports these experiences and expresses these ideals so as to make them comprehensible to his fellows. The better his technic, the more orderly and beautiful his expression and, usually, the clearer his communication. By means of brush and pen, sculptor's tool or architect's square, as well as the more humble wood carver's chisel or the potter's wheel, the creator's ideas of form and his emotional concepts or personal experiences are communicated to us.

Thus there are many differing forms which this created communication of the artist takes. Generally speaking, they may be classified into the Useful Arts, serving purposes outside themselves, such as the arts of carpentry, cooking, organ building, etc.; and the Fine Arts — architecture, sculpture, painting, literature, and music, distinguished by generally self-sufficient powers of expression. The philosophers have had a wonderful time all down through the ages in attempting to classify these different kinds of art. Without seeking to follow them or make any invidious comparisons, we may say that of all the arts, fine or useful, the one that is most universally appealing and most readily apprehended by the average man is music. For it speaks to us in a language that is entirely its own — a universal language which does not need to be translated into the medium of any of the other arts and which can hint to us of concepts that are quite beyond the range of painting, literature, sculpture, and architecture. Not needing to deal exactly with thoughts and ideas, music can speak to us with a force and a power that are readily felt by all who have learned to listen. Concerning itself so very largely with emotion, it is the ideal means for transmitting the experiences of a sensitive artist directly to a responsive listener.

MUSIC FOR ITS OWN SAKE

These resources for communicating beauty we are too apt to take for granted. We have become so accustomed to presuming that music is an essential part of our everyday lives that only in moments of reflection and introspection do we become fully conscious of its tremendous power. The average person seems to think of music always as a means to something else — to reading, to relaxation, perhaps to nothing more important than passing away the time. Music is generally considered as an amenity rather than as something that is satisfying in its own right, something that can dominate our whole lives, possess our whole beings. There is nothing in listening to music, according to popular conception, other than placing ourselves under its sway — sitting quietly and letting it flow through our consciousness. We may receive some vague sort of emotional thrill from it, or we may be interested in the mannerisms of the orchestral conductor as he interprets the music for us or of the pianist as he forges his way through some intricately difficult passage. We may be entertained by this bit of music because it reminds us of an army on the march, or because it suggests a May morning in the country, the wind in the trees, a rippling brook, a crowded square in an Oriental city, or whatever our imagination may be able to suggest. But we are not greatly concerned if we do not like what we have heard, for there is plenty of music with pleasing tunes and vigorous rhythms, without bothering about this difficult music of the classics.

There seems to be little need for considering music otherwise than as something to be enjoyed — and by "enjoyed" the average person means something to be whistled, hummed, or danced to. It may be used as a means for putting in the time when there is nothing better to do, or as a background for some other activity. What could be better than some music on the radio as an accompaniment for luncheon, a bridge game, or for the few quiet moments available to the businessman as he peruses his evening paper?

Perhaps our average hearer may be inveigled into going to a concert because some internationally known star is to sing or play, or (if he is honest enough to admit it) for no more serious reason than that it has become the fashionable thing to do. But he rarely thinks of music as a thing to be listened to seriously and enjoyed for its own sake.

Granted that there is a type of music so light and "recreational" that we need have no compunction in talking or playing bridge through it, and that concert-going may have certain pleasures other than purely musical ones; nevertheless, it hardly seems possible to some people that there are others to whom music is life's chief interest and joy, people to whom the hearing of a great piece of music means as much as does the reading of Shakespeare, Goethe, or Dante to a lover of literature. Lawrence Gilman tells of a philosopher who, during the time he was occupied in reading his favorite subject, became white as a sheet. Are there listeners who feel as intensely about music? We often make the statement that a person is "passionately fond of music." Is he really? As Gilman pointedly asks, what does such an individual do with his music, or for it? "Will he forgo leisure, forget his meals, face poverty? Will the blood leave his face after he has spent an hour with Beethoven's *Appassionata*?"

HOW LISTENERS DEVELOP

The reader of this book, because of the very fact that he has enough interest in music to want to know how to get more out of it than he does at present, knows that there are people, plenty of them, who realize the tremendous potential powers of music. In the lives of these people music is an important factor far above that of mere social amenity, even though perhaps an hour with Beethoven does not make any great disturbance in their vasomotor system. These fortunate ones seem to have acquired a technic by means of which they are able to get something from music that is not perceptible to the average person. They seem to have found some sort of touchstone that brings them closer to the infinite. What is this technic that enables the individual to train himself so that he can hear things which otherwise would be missed entirely? Is there really a means by which the initiate into the mysterious art of listening gets more out of music than does the man in the street, who knows nothing about it except "what he likes"?

If there is any doubt in the reader's mind as to the answers to such questions, let him talk to someone to whom the art of music has become indispensable, overpowering, imperative — some person who has learned to enjoy intelligently such music as the Bach *Passacaglia,* or the *First Symphony* of Brahms, or Debussy's *Pelléas et Mélisande.* Such a music lover will tell the inquiring listener that his appreciation of such music is a treasure which he values the more because he has not always possessed it; that he has come through the gradual, cumulative process of learning to understand what the composer has put into such music, a process of acquiring ears to hear. In cases where the man who possesses these great treasures of music is honest, he will admit that the music of Bach and Brahms and Debussy has not always meant to him what it means to him now; that at one time in his listening career he preferred the romantic harmonies and colorful suggestiveness of Tchaikovsky's *1812 Overture* or Grieg's *Peer Gynt.*

THE ADVENTURER'S CONQUESTS

Then he will go on to tell how, when this more obvious kind of music had yielded him everything it possessed, when he had learned to recognize the reasons for its popular appeal and to realize its special weaknesses, he of necessity passed on to works of greater scope and more general significance. New composers were taken up, men whose music was somewhat more reticent in revealing the secrets of its beauty but which possessed greater universality of content and emotion and was more skillfully constructed. This music was in turn enjoyed, its particular excellencies recognized, its unique shortcomings noted. The process was again repeated and the conquest extended to type after type of music until the music lover came into the realm of the immortal composers. Here, no matter how much he may hear of their music or how eagerly he may try to solve the riddle of their beauty of utterance, no matter how often he reacts to the intellectual and emotional stimuli of their music or how great is the satisfaction he obtains from it, there is always something in reserve. There is something beyond the reaches of his searching, an inexhaustible supply of beauty ready to satisfy any demands which may be made upon it. He has at last arrived and is ready to understand the finest things in music, fully equipped to share the spiritual contributions of its greatest composers.

All this is not to say that a process such as this has necessarily been consciously directed. Hearing a great deal of music, the student has subconsciously chosen what happened to be best suited to his particular stage of development at the time, letting the rest go by. The process has of necessity been a slow one, and there have been many "blind spots" — things which have not been clear to him as he progressed. Some of these may always remain, for nobody can appreciate everything; it is not often worth while to try, though we can always enlarge our range of sympathy and understanding if we want to. Any man can improve his taste; and that, as we have said, is the important thing — the thing that will bring joy into our lives. We should lay ourselves open to *quality* in general and give all reputable composers a good trial. Frank Roscoe has a good saying: "Education is more a matter of infection than injection"; and if we expose ourselves to the infection of great music, we are bound to catch it. Some may start with an enthusiasm for music of the jazz type, but they cannot go far there, for jazz is peculiarly of an inbred, feeble-stock race, incapable of development. An American educator has gone so far as to allege that all "popular music" is really for the adolescent who does not use it as an art at all, but rather as a sex stimulant. Granted that there is more to it than this — there are, for instance, the quite legitimate uses of such music for relaxation or as a mild anodyne, like tobacco — we shall all agree that "popular music" does not reach down very far or last for very long. Even small children, he goes on to remark, have more significant experiences with music chosen for its interest at their level than with the "popular" kind. Its lack of rhythmical variety (necessitated by its special purpose), its brevity, its repetitiveness and lack of sustained development, together with the fact that commercial reasons prevent its being, as a rule, very well written, all mark this as a side issue, having next to nothing to do with serious music; and consequently it has proved itself entirely useless as a basis for developing the taste of the amateur.

The ambitious listener might better start from the level of Chopin's melodious piano music, or Grieg's northern elegiacs, or Tchaikovsky's gorgeous colorfulness. Given certain native ability and a willingness to keep his ears open and his mind free, the problems of his musical evolution will quickly solve themselves. All that is necessary is the opportunity of hearing a great many good performances of fine music, together with some hints as to how he can cooperate in the process of listening to them.

LIST OF SUGGESTED MUSIC

If you would see how easy it is to begin the adventure, listen to the following works:

Fantaisie impromptu, Op. 66   Frédéric Chopin

Berceuse in D Flat Major, Op. 57   Frédéric Chopin

Peer Gynt, Suite No. 1   Edvard Grieg
  Morning; Anitra's Dance; Death of Ase;
  In the Hall of the Mountain King

Elegiac Melodies (String Orchestra)   Edvard Grieg

These different selections show the great Norwegian composer in various moods: the *Peer Gynt* music (written for Ibsen's play of the same name) is full of the spirit of the North; the lovely lyrics for strings contain some of his most concentrated sentiment.

The Nutcracker (Suite)   Peter I. Tchaikovsky

The last number of this popular and delightful ballet suite gives the enterprising listener an excellent chance of realizing how a simple piece of music is put together.

First Movement from *Symphony in
B Minor* (Unfinished)   Franz Schubert

Kaiserwalzer   Johann Strauss II

Since, as someone has said, Strauss is what you make him, we have chosen these waltzes for the reason that Bruno Walter and the Vienna Philharmonic Orchestra have played them in what many experts believe to be the finest performance of Strauss on records.

Overture to *The Magic Flute*   Wolfgang Mozart

This is deservedly one of the most popular short pieces of great music available for the listener.

Last Movement from *First Symphony*   Johannes Brahms

Listen to this, just to hear what the biggest music sounds like. An ardent admirer of this composer characterizes him as follows: "Brahms does not dazzle, but is true and lasting; he stands like a rock in the welter of strife, of problems and experiments, and holds out his hands to all those who strive towards what is great and noble, regardless of sensation."

TOPICS FOR FURTHER DISCUSSION

What place should music hold in a scheme for a liberal education?

Is it your experience that familiarity breeds contempt in the case of music? of any grade of music — *classical* as well as *jazz*?

Is there any circumstance in which it may be legitimate to have music going on without attending to it?

Discuss the dictum of Arnot Robertson, the novelist, who speaks of "Thinbrows" as "the pests of the literary world, who have not the courage to be either highbrows or lowbrows, according to their own tastes, but who keep always on the safe side by admiring only what it is fashionable to admire." Do these exist in music?

Comment on the statement made by a music critic to the effect that "consistently with all the inescapable tasks and sacrifices, there will be no truer deed than that which propagates the art of music, that we may not forget, in the midst of evil, the truth for which men die."

[TWO]

WHY WE LIKE MUSIC

The best reason in the world for undertaking the study of a subject is the natural liking and aptitude that we may have for it. And, although we may not be able to explain why, most of us are conscious of the fact that we do have a liking and a certain amount of aptitude for music. Someone has well called it the most universal avocation, meaning that it is the thing we most naturally turn to for a hobby, when we would have our attention diverted from our usual pursuits. Most people think of music in this way and are quite indifferent to the great role which it might play in their lives; even so, they react instinctively and naturally to this art in ways that are different from their ordinary experiences. Why?

In an attempt to account for this affection, a well-known psychologist [1] who spent the most fruitful years of his long professional career in the study of music and its action upon the human consciousness wrote a little book which he called *Why We Love Music*. In it he gives a sort of natural history of the psychological origin and development of our love for music in terms of its objects and motives. We can profitably study what Seashore says in this respect, for he probably knew as much about the subject as anyone today. Put into simple terms, the reasons for our liking music are these:

MORALE: PHYSICAL AND SPIRITUAL

1. We like music because it instills in us a sense of well-being; it sets us up, so to speak, both physically and emotionally. We seem to be endowed with some sort of mechanism that reacts and responds to *sounds* without any conscious effort on our part. This

[1] Carl E. Seashore, late Professor of Psychology at the University of Iowa.

mechanism involves not only the central nervous system, which controls the actions of our muscles and the functions of our internal organs, but also the so-called autonomic nervous system, with its regulation of the internal secretions which are thought to be the physical bases of all our emotional reactions. Experiments have shown that sound can directly affect such physical functions as the circulation of the blood, digestion, hunger, and thirst, as well as the psychological backgrounds of pleasure and pain.

Thus do the scientists explain our instinctive physical and emotional response to such sounds as the blare of trumpets or the sweetness of violins. Other considerations quite aside, the purely physical effect of the hundred members of an orchestra playing in full accord and the stirring strains of a good military band as it leads a regiment in parade are important factors in our lives. We may be aroused and enlivened by some sound combinations, quieted and dispirited by others. This natural reaction of our organism to sound underlies all our musical experience; we are not capable of controlling these responses, but without them music would lose a great deal of its natural appeal.

FROM ANOTHER WORLD

2. Another, and a very important, reason for our liking music is the fact that its domain is so largely outside our ordinary world, its field of operation so entirely beyond these sensory impressions and physical reactions. We may not be able to help reacting to music physically, but our greatest enjoyment of it comes from the fact that its world is so largely one of memory, imagination, and feeling. In the midst of a humdrum, practical, pressing world, one which badgers and confuses, music takes us outside ourselves, transports us, as nothing else can, into another existence. In listening to such intricate and refined manipulation of tonal resources as we find in Delius's *Over the Hills and Far Away*, we do respond, certainly, to physical sensuousness and tonal allure; but what haunts our minds and captures our spirits is this music's imaginative, otherworldly atmosphere, its peculiar blend of a reminder of things that exist best in the memory, and its suggestion of things that have never really existed at all.

In this way, music possesses us as does a dream; it lives within us, something entirely apart from material and tangible experiences, its appeal heightened by the fortunate necessity of this art's indefiniteness. All the arts are conditioned by the physical means which they employ: the writer is naturally limited by the meaning of the words he must use, the painter by certain exterior associations connected with the objects he represents on his canvas; music, based as it is on sound, has no need for any exact connotation or literal significance outside itself. And so it exists as the ideal means for communicating inward and subjective concepts.

MUSIC AS PLAY

3. We like music also because it is an ideal form of play. Seashore reminds us that we are all really of the same age — born millions of years ago, and that, in spite of inhibitions and restraints developed through the centuries, we delight in play. For it is in play that we get a definite and liberating sense of freedom, a feeling of creative power, of doing things purely for the joy of achievement, without ulterior motive or designed effect. Moreover, play is a positive force, and one whose success, in strong contradistinction to the world about us, depends upon our accepting its fictitious nature: "It rests upon make-believe; liberated from realities, it accepts the ideal and lives it as real."

All art is play, of course; but none of the other arts lends itself so ideally to fulfilling these psychological needs as does music. The man singing lustily in his bath, somehow stimulated by the sound of running water to do his noisy best; a group of listeners under the sway of a great interpretation of a forceful piece of music; the dancer, stirred by the rhythmical excitement of the music, or perhaps lulled by its dreamy flow into an ecstasy of pleasure — all these are playing in the ideal sense. Music furnishes them with a medium for expressing themselves, for exhibiting their joy in living, their aspirations for the future, their nostalgia for the past, their desire for freedom, their love for action. This is one of the simplest and most direct of the charms which music possesses, and one of the reasons people turn instinctively to it for recreation.

THE ATTRACTION OF RHYTHM

4. We are also strongly attracted to music because of its rhythm. By "rhythm" in music most of us mean but one thing — that regular pulse which we all feel in the flow of the music, the pulse that is

marked by a regular recurrence of what we call a "beat." Unless this is present we cannot sense music at all. All of us, even though we are hardly able to distinguish one tune from another, seem to be able to learn to "hear with our feet" — to beat out the underlying rhythmic impulses inherent in music.

Using the term in its wider sense, however, as meaning movement marked by a regular recurrence of certain features or elements, we find that there are plenty of other rhythmic attributes of music to which we react. The human ear seems to demand some sense of "grouping" in what it hears. So we find the composer grouping the musical ideas he uses — measures into phrases, phrases into sentences, sentences into still larger units, all being gathered together to make a unified yet varied rhythmic whole. We likewise demand certain dynamic rhythms (alternations of loud and soft) and timbre rhythms (alternations in the various tonal qualities) in the music we enjoy. All this gives us, without our being aware of it, perhaps, great listening pleasure and increases the satisfaction we derive from music.

The psychologist explains this by showing us what this rhythmic grouping does: it enables us to perceive more easily what we hear; it brings into relationship certain features that give a sense of balance and expanse to what we hear; there is an alternation of stimulating and soothing influences which enriches and objectifies our associations and tones up our whole organism. Seashore expresses it well when he says that rhythm in music is a play within a play: the composer realizes the need for it; the performer makes us aware of it; and we, the listeners, react to it.

AN EXPRESSION OF EMOTION

5. Music has often been called the language of the emotions; and certainly, while aestheticians may question the complete validity of such a statement, a great deal of our pleasure and enjoyment in music comes from the fact that in its essence it expresses and embodies emotion.[2] In its truest sense, art is an "objectification or expression in a communicable form, of an artist's actual reaction to some stimulation or of his 'experience.' "[3] In the case of music, this

[2] The psychologist defines an emotion as "any one of the states designated as fear, anger, disgust, joy, grief, surprise, yearning, etc."

[3] From F. R. O'Neill's definition of art in The Relation of Art to Life (London: Routledge).

stimulation or experience is likely to have been an emotional one, and thus one readily understood by us all. A great artist — Beethoven, for example — is moved by some profound personal experience; he reacts keenly to the sorrows and sufferings of humanity or to the personal awareness of a limitation of his physical powers. Through his ability, first as a sensitive human individual to feel these emotions, and then as an artist to grasp their essence and objectify it in a medium by which it can be communicated to others, he produces great works of art — the *Eroica Symphony* and the *Symphony in C Minor*.

It is a demonstrable fact that of all the sensory mediums, tone is most closely associated with the emotions: thus music becomes the ideal communicative medium for artists, and the most purely emotional of all the arts. When we add to this the fact that music, in order to be intelligible to us, must be re-created for us by an interpreter — a third person who comes between us and the composer, and this interpreter must of necessity add his own emotional significance to what he plays — we realize the secret of music's great human appeal and its power in the lives of men.

In this sense we can say that music is a language of the emotions, for it is at once both a message and a means of communication which, for the moment at least, puts creator, interpreter, and listener in the same world of experience.

MUSIC AND INTELLIGENCE

6. Intelligence also plays a strong role in music. We like music because we can learn to understand it as a thing in itself, can recognize how it is put together, how it proceeds from point to point and reaches a climactic finish. Such pride in intellectual achievement is very human and lies directly at the base of all artistic interest. The ability to understand different art forms, to analyze the ways by which the artist achieves his effects, to see the relationships between the different elements that go to make up the whole, to sense the affinity between the different arts — all these deepen our insight and increase our understanding of music, or painting, or architecture. Then, too, there is the joy of acquiring interpretative skill in music, of learning to read those symbols left behind by the composers (the notes), of securing sufficient physical and mental agility to be able to play an instrument or to sing. These "glimpses into the

vistas of unexplored resources" cannot but intensify our love for music, our awe and admiration for it as an art that, no matter how ardently we may try, can never fully be mastered.

THE POWERS OF SUGGESTION

7. A final reason, and one of the most potent of all reasons why we love music, is that it tends to give some form of realization to our inmost dreams and longings, because it stands as a sort of symbolic suggestion of everything we desire, or believe in, or hope for. The listener tends, as Seashore says, "to live himself concretely into the feeling" suggested by the music. Most of us, as we listen, live realistically within the music, in so far as the realm of our interests allows us. Such associations and suggestions may be enjoyed for their own sake; the listener often tends to forget the music entirely in the imaginative associations it stirs in his mind. But the truest enjoyment comes when these symbolic suggestions are somehow fused in their general meaning with the music which calls them to mind.

To make this clear, let us take a concrete example, one of the most significant pieces of music ever written, a work that stands up magnificently through the years because of its quality as *music*, and yet which probably has as powerful, direct, and human an appeal as any other music in existence: Beethoven's *Fifth Symphony*. Anyone who is at all sensitive to music will come under the spell of this work; for there is evident in it a titanic struggle, a wrestling with some of life's greatest problems, together with a decision as to some of its deepest meanings. At once, without being aware of the mechanics of the process, we are apt to be diverted, when listening to this music, by all sorts of symbolic suggestions — the harshness and ruthlessness of life, the necessity for human struggle, the consolation that beauty brings, the ominous precariousness of our existence, the exalted happiness that comes from surmounting difficulties. All these, and many more like suggestions, may come to our minds as the music progresses. We realize that all the diverse forces of our lives are present in this music, for it shows us as well as anything ever created by the mind of man that "we ourselves are our own Heaven and Hell." We can, and probably do, enjoy these associations for what they are themselves, as a sort of work of art deserving of separate consideration. But not until they have become blended and fused in their general meaning with Beethoven's music do we realize their full impact. Not until we are conscious of how inextricably they are woven into the warp and woof of Beethoven's glowing fabric (a realization which comes only after study: see Chapter Twenty-nine) do we really "enjoy" this symphony.

So it is with all other types of music, whether they sound the note of joyous exaltation, religious fervor, or consuming passion. Sacred oratorios, dramatic operas, moving symphonies, even the small piano pieces, all make use of this fundamental power of music to "seize the individual for some form of dreamlike realization of the subjects of his longing." The professional musician tends to frown upon this enjoyment of associations and images; to him music exists for its own meaning and beauty, and he hears it as a combination of note patterns, colors, rhythms, and so on. He consciously tends to suppress any of his own feelings, associations, and characterizations that the music might evoke, and assumes a critical, analytical viewpoint, from which he surveys the materials of which it is composed and the way it is put together. In so doing he may easily miss the real significance of the music, just as does the untrained listener, for whom music's only appeal is through the associations it arouses.

The wise music lover avoids both extremes. But he must never forget, as Henri Bergson puts it, that "beneath the thousand rudimentary actions which are the outward and visible signs of an emotion, behind the commonplace conventional expression that both reveals and conceals our individual mental state," it is the emotion, the original mood, that composers attain and wish to communicate to us. "Beneath their joys and sorrows . . . they grasp something that has nothing in common with language, certain rhythms of life and breath that are closer to man than his inmost feelings, being the living law — varying with each individual — of his enthusiasm and despair, his hopes and regrets." To miss these aspects of the reality of human experience as revealed to us by a composer is to miss the greatest significance of his music.

We will soon show that the fullest understanding of music depends on something more than natural tastes and aptitudes. One must always remember that there are many degrees and levels of musical understanding, and that we are not all capable of liking music to the same extent and in the same way. The individual's attainments in music depend not only upon his natural, innate capacity (which, of course, differs greatly with different people) but also upon his musical experience and training. This accounts for the wide divergences of opinion that we hear expressed on every hand. Not many people are so honest as Mark Twain about this:

Huge crowd out tonight to hear the band play the *Fremersberg!* I suppose it is very low-grade music — I know it must be low-grade — because it so delighted me, moved me, stirred me, uplifted me, enraptured me, that at times I could have cried, and at others split my throat with shouting. The great crowd was another evidence that it was low-grade music, for only the few are educated up to a point where high-class music gives pleasure. I have never heard enough classic music to be able to enjoy it, and the simple truth is I detest it. Not mildly, but with all my heart.

What a poor lot we human beings are anyway! If base music gives me wings, why should I want any other? But I do. I want to like the higher music because the higher and better like it. But you see I want to like it without taking the necessary trouble, and giving the thing the necessary amount of time and attention. The natural suggestion is to get into that upper tier, that dress circle, by a lie — we will *pretend* we like it.

LIST OF SUGGESTED MUSIC

Here is a short list of recordings of well-known musical compositions. Listen to each one carefully and then, referring to the reasons given in this chapter for our liking music, try to decide why *you* like the music.

Gaîté Parisienne   Offenbach

España Rapsodie   Chabrier

Last Movement from *Sixth Symphony*   Tchaikovsky

The Water Music   Handel

The Washington Post   Sousa

Fugue in G Minor ("Little")   Bach

First Movement from *Concerto in E Flat*
  (Piano and Orchestra) K.482   Mozart

Valse triste   Sibelius

TOPICS FOR FURTHER DISCUSSION

Imagine yourself at a gala concert of a world-famous orchestra. In looking over the festive and well-dressed audience, try to determine the percentage of those present who came (*a*) because it was the thing to do; (*b*) so as to be included in the social and intellectual elite; (*c*) to satisfy their curiosity; (*d*) so as to be able to say they had heard the orchestra under its famous conductor; (*e*) to learn something about music; (*f*) really to enjoy the music.

Which inherited traits do you consider most helpful in the development of a love for good music? Which would make such development difficult?

THREE

HOW WE LIKE MUSIC

It has been shown that it is natural for us to like music; practical experience has proved, on the other hand, that there are people who do not like it and probably never will. In general it may be said that this is perhaps due to some deficiency in training. We have just made the statement that a full response to music is the result of native capacity *plus* experience and training; it is this experience and training that are so often wanting, and any device (such, for example, as this book) that will increase our musical experience and train our musical reactions cannot but add to our enjoyment.

There are comparatively few individuals (Charles Lamb, the English essayist of the Romantic period, seems to have been one) who are completely incapable of ever liking music. Most of those who do not like it simply beg the entire question and protest: "It is all away beyond me: music is too full of technicalities that I cannot understand. I know what I like, so why should I bother with trying to learn any more about it?"

To which the reasonable answer is, as Edwin Alden Jewell has said in an article on "Reaching the Man in the Street" [1]:

> Art is beyond nobody who cares. Technicalities are but means employed by the artist in expressing what he has to say, and it is the expression that counts. Besides, once you have really *heard* what the artist has expressed, it is simple — and fascinating — to work back, step by step, through the technique. Thus may one share in the task of creation. And no one who has learned really to share in that can be thenceforth indifferent. Learning to share and learning critically to discriminate may well end in learning to love.

[1] In *The New York Times*, Sunday, July 27, 1941.

Here is the crux of the whole matter. This is what we mean by learning to appreciate music. This expression has been criticized for its ambiguity, for the fact that it can mean so many different things to so many different people. But until a better one is invented, we must continue to use it; *appreciate* means, Webster says, "to set a just value on; to esteem to the full the worth of; to approve of; to be grateful for; to be sensitive to the aesthetic values of." These are exactly the meanings we give to this phrase in connection with music.

VARIOUS APPROACHES TO APPRECIATION

In this sense an appreciation of music covers a number of different factors and can be gained in a number of different ways:

1. One of the commonest ways is through learning to do something in music — to play an instrument or to sing. No one in his proper senses would wish to deny the importance of the performing amateur. Active participation in music gives a kind of interest that can come in no other way; it fosters an admiration for and an understanding of the skill of a composer that can hardly be gained through hearing alone. It is one of the most pleasant and beneficial means of occupying leisure time, this amateur playing and singing, and it often leads, of course, to a real knowledge and understanding of music. But there are obvious dangers which have to be considered; anyone who has observed at all carefully will have noticed that sometimes the process of acquiring mental and physical dexterity and powers of co-ordination sufficient to perform music with any degree of facility weakens the very thing which should above all else be developed — a love for the music itself. What is more, this faculty of performing, once acquired, often occupies the interest and attention of the player or singer to the exclusion of attention to what he is playing or singing. Too few singers, for instance, after they have spent years in acquiring a technic, know or care about the finest things in vocal literature — the songs of Schubert, Franz, or Wolf. Too few pianists pay much attention to the supreme things in piano literature unless these happen to provide an abundant opportunity for exhibiting technical prowess. There have been many movements for stimulating active participation in music in recent years — massed singing movements, choral and instrumental contests, and such. But the net results of all these activities, in so far as

concrete gains in musical knowledge and consequent improvement in taste are concerned, are often dubious. A stimulation of activity does not always mean an attainment of worth-while results; it is not unknown for localities which have shown the greatest activity to exhibit the poorest taste in the music they have chosen to perform.

No, the ability to perform music does not provide an open sesame to an awareness of its beauty or understanding of its message. If cultivated properly, performance is assuredly a stimulating and fructifying influence; but we must not confuse our issues here. The ability to perform music and a knowledge of and love for the best music are individual attainments, the second by no means always the consequent of the first.

2. The most natural approach to music is through its rhythmic appeal. As we will see later, rhythm is one of the most fundamental aspects of music, and even the unmusical person can usually feel the essential power of repeated rhythms — witness the present-day appeal of the drumbeats of the African savage or their more sophisticated modern counterparts, the rhythms of American jazz. Learning to "hear with our feet" is easy; but it does not lead us very far into the beauties which music possesses.

3. Another approach is through the development of the physical capacities by which we receive musical stimuli. Music is physically a matter of *sound;* and until we can learn to recognize clearly its physical attributes, we are certain to be more or less in the condition of the man who is blind and to whom any appreciation of painting is impossible. We have to learn to *listen,* in the literal sense: to hear accurately and acutely, to differentiate between the various pitch levels, to recognize various rhythmic patterns, melodic ideas, and so on. This is not easy but requires real concentration from the listener. It cannot be emphasized too strongly from the very beginning that *one cannot learn to listen to music when he is doing something else.* The fact that there is so much music readily available today on records, radio, and television makes it almost inevitable that it is usually heard rather than listened to; it is used as a background for reading, study, etc., without the hearer's being aware of it other than as a sort of accompaniment to various kinds of personal activity. No real listening can ever be done under such circumstances.

4. The listener should try to develop habits that will enable him to retain these stimuli as meaningful musical ideas. That is, once he

has started to develop the powers of pitch discrimination, rhythmic recognition, and so forth, he must learn to relate them to the musical apparatus used by composers. He must be able to realize how these creators of music combine various pitches into groups called chords and out of these invoke the mysterious magic of harmony; how they weave complex musical fabrics out of a number of separate themes; how they relate various parts of their compositions to the whole. In short, the listener must learn how to recognize the simple facts of musical construction, its grammar, structure, and form.

In doing this, his greatest help will come from the development of his musical memory. Music is unlike any other art in that it goes past us like a flash, and not every particular piece may be immediately available again. (Here, obviously, is the advantage of the phonograph.) One may stand before a piece of sculpture, before the Parthenon or a painting, and take one's time in enjoying its details. Even if a piece of music be played over many times, one may not remember all its fine detail; and from one hearing the less-experienced listener, however eagerly he may desire to take it in, may well come away baffled. Patience and time are needed, and the cultivation of the memory — not only for tunes, but for what the composer does with them — for the structural logic of a musical work. A symphonic movement may last a quarter of an hour or more; symphonies oftentimes go on for fifty minutes, some of them for an even longer time. It is obvious that only the impatient and thoughtless listener would expect to understand all that such a work had to tell him even after two or three hearings. The best resource of all, undoubtedly, is the power to read the printed score; but that power we shall not presume to exist in our readers, while congratulating those who have cultivated it or are cultivating it, and offering them every encouragement to persevere in this valuable exercise, in which the beginner can soon begin to make headway if he starts with simple enough scores. One of the best mottoes that a group of musical amateurs could adopt would be: *Poco a poco*. Little by little is the right way to tackle any study; and if music is worth our attention at all, it is worth being taken seriously, like any other study in which we seek to educate ourselves and by which we wish to make of ourselves whole and balanced citizens of the world.

5. We must learn to recognize and apperceive the different emotional and mood reactions engendered by music and to evaluate these in comparison to their other elements. This is a matter of nice

discrimination and avoids the extremes of being completely swept away in a state of emotional hysteria on the one hand, and of entirely abjuring the emotional significance of music on the other. What the music does to us is one of its important powers and should be neither overemphasized nor neglected.

6. The listener should try to make the composer's experience his own, crystallizing it as definitely as possible so that he can seize it, reflect upon it, and even, perhaps, use it as the basis for an imaginative creativeness of his own. We have said that all art is communicative; we should prepare ourselves so that we stand ready on the receiving end, qualified to make part of our own experience whatever the music can give. The development of a certain ability to describe such experiences in words may help in this respect. When Charles O'Connell writes in this vein of the first movement of Beethoven's *Fifth Symphony*, we know that he has made the music's experience his own:

> The bitterness and violence of this movement have no parallel in music. The sheer power that moves it, the utter logic and inevitableness and finality of this music almost remove it from the manipulations of the conductor; given instruments and knowing hands, it plays itself. Many a conductor has found that there is but one interpretation — Beethoven's — and *that* one speaks, rudely and clamorously and sufficiently, for itself. This is an utterance of the supreme and ruthless ego, momentarily frustrated but unconquered, and it does not brook interference.[2]

7. In music, sounds often have other-than-ordinary significance; we should try to realize these special meanings; in other words, learn to relate music to other experiences. This involves the understanding of such things as national idioms in music, certain qualities of musical "atmosphere" (the aesthetic tone or mood of, or harmony of effects in, a work of art), and the like. When we argue whether Tchaikovsky's symphonies are or are not Russian in character; when we demonstrate, to our own satisfaction at least, that Dvořák's *New World Symphony* has more of a Bohemian than an American [3] flavor; or when we speak of Debussy's music as being impressionistic, we are relating music to experiences and ideas outside itself.

[2] From *The Victor Book of the Symphony* by Charles O'Connell (New York: Simon & Schuster).
[3] See Chapter Eighteen.

As we progress we shall see how really important is this single phase of musical understanding.

8. And finally we must relate music to other values of life. We should realize how it has developed historically, how it parallels other phases of man's development, what it stands for now, and what are its possibilities for the future. This historical aspect of music's development is a lengthy study in itself and involves plenty of careful reading and patient listening. But it is absolutely necessary if we are to obtain anything like a proper perspective in listening. To know why and how Palestrina's *Missa Brevis* differs from Beethoven's *Missa Solemnis* is an essential factor and fundamental necessity in our appreciation of the qualities of these two different works. If we are to take any reasonable view of present-day developments in music, we must know how these have grown out of the past and how they point towards the future. Otherwise we may become confused and lose our way altogether.

GOALS

These then should be our goals. The process of Discovering Music, we shall find, is nothing more or less than the process of becoming aware of these various aspects of music's rich and complex structure. The more we can make them a part of our intellectual and artistic experience, the deeper will be our understanding and the fuller our enjoyment of the music we hear.

Into all appreciation some degree of criticism must come. We shall not attempt to make a specialty of that; but the real meaning of appreciation is to sum up, to strike a balance. There is a world of amusement, and much profit not yet gained, in the study of bad music; but, mercifully, we shall not pursue that — we are already overtaken by too much bad music every day, willy-nilly. We suggest that stern criticism may well be left to mature with time and experience. As to "knowing what we like," we do our readers the courtesy of presuming that they are too wide-awake to mistake that for criticism. In the right man, it may be; but for Everyman it is usually no more a manifestation of artistic appreciation than is his preference for mustard over ketchup, or his enjoyment of or dislike for olives or tomatoes.

It is a commonplace among music lovers that, in distinguishing among qualities — in even the most mild form of criticism — it is essential that we do not decry a work for failing to do what its composer did not set out to do. We do not blame the lightweight boxer for failing to stand up to the heavyweight champion, or the butterfly for being apparently less industrious than the bee. Each works according to his nature and his build. But an essential question must not be omitted here: Is what the composer is striving to do worth doing?

George Sampson, a discerning critic of literature, has a wise word on this: The good student is "not to be taken in by novelties, or to be put off with accidentals. Confronted by the mass of Walt Whitman's work, with all its disconcerting irregularities and inequalities, he does not waste time by asking painfully and fruitlessly, Is this poetry? Is this prose? Is it both, or neither? He asks what is, after all, the real question for critics: Does this succeed artistically? In days when religion was decisively a part of life, there came suddenly to certain men rare moments when they felt strangely uplifted in spirit and moved beyond themselves. Such moments of ecstasy come also from the great creative arts of poetry and music. The moments that make you catch your breath, the moments in which you are carried beyond space and time, and feel as if the powers from afar had touched you with their wings — these supreme moments of beauty are, in plain terms, the moments of artistic success. To create such moments is the prerogative of the artist; to share them is a privilege of the humble receiver." Could we have a better ideal than that in our search for significance in the beauty of music?

LIST OF SUGGESTED MUSIC

Handel in the Strand   Grainger

Some of the best "light music" ever written is by this Australian-born, English-influenced, American pianist and composer. Here he is in his most light-hearted mood, with a strong rhythmic appeal that is constantly maintained throughout; and there is a flavor of national idiom in the music suggestive of the style of writing inaugurated by the great Handel in England during the first half of the eighteenth century, lightened and popularized for the delight of today's throngs on London's great thoroughfare, the Strand. Grainger takes his theme actually from Handel's *Fifth Harpsichord Suite.*

London Suite   Coates
London Again Suite   Coates

Another who has skillfully explored the possibilities of good light music is the Englishman Eric Coates. These two suites describing various London scenes are great favorites and may be listened to with real pleasure by any musician.

Slow Movement from the *Surprise Symphony*   Haydn

Here is an idea presented in its simplest form and then differently shaped in a series of *variations* without losing its essential meaning. In following the different presentations of this idea, we learn to look with concentration to details and to develop the power of memory as we constantly compare the new form to the old.

Last Movement from *Suite*, Op. 19   Dohnányi

Again good popular music in the best sense, this time by a Hungarian composer. There is good practice in following the reappearances of the one main theme and in appreciating a first-class craftsman's use of the orchestra.

Prelude to *Lohengrin*   Wagner

Notice how the whole of this music grows from a single theme heard high on the strings near its beginning. Wagner is one of the greatest masters of Romantic writing.

Romeo and Juliet Overture   Tchaikovsky

This splendid piece can be appreciated in a great many ways. The first thing that will be recognized is its various emotional and mood reactions. There are three great sections: the first, starting with the beginning of the piece, quiet, sustained, almost religious in nature; the second, making up the body of the piece, agitated and calm by turn; and the third, towards the end, again sustained and reflective. It certainly is not difficult to make this composer's experiences our own, for he is telling musically one of the great love stories of all time, and in so doing arouses in the hearer all the imaginative creativeness he may possess. There is likewise a certain Russian color in this telling of Shakespeare's story, a warm intensity of emotion, a tremendous working-up of feeling, and a strong contrast of moods, all of them characteristic of the art of this nation.

Note, too, that the main part of the piece — the middle section — is worked up out of two musical germs, or *themes;* one impulsive, eager, suggestive of Romeo; the other gracious, lovely, feminine, suggesting Juliet. These are elaborated and "developed" and then are again heard as at first. Thus the composer makes his musical apparatus correspond to the poetic idea — the program — of his piece.

First Movement from *Symphony No. 5*   Beethoven

Reread O'Connell's paragraph on this and see how well his description fits the music. Again this movement is built up out of two main contrasting themes, followed by a "development" section and then their restatement as at first. We shall have more to say about this particular type of "form" later on.

TOPICS FOR FURTHER DISCUSSION

Which aspect of musical appreciation mentioned in this chapter seems most difficult to you? Which is most attractive? Why?

In your experience, why are so many people uninterested in serious music? Is this due to defects in temperament, or in training?

Why is the criticism of music, taken in bulk, generally poorer than the criticism of literature?

As an aid to remembering music heard, prepare a small card index or loose-leaf notebook, and alphabetically record therein each composition that you hear, either on phonograph, radio, or in actual concert. A few comments on the characteristics of the music and on the composer may well be added. Information regarding the latter will be found in *Grove's Dictionary of Music and Musicians,* or in any standard history of music, such as Pratt's or Dickinson's.

MUSIC AS AN ART

In what we have said about music so far, we have referred to it as an individual experience, a matter of personal enjoyment. Its significance reaches far beyond this, however. Because of its peculiar nature, the art of music is a factor of tremendous importance in our modern social and educational development. Let us see why.

We have said that music's appeal must always be primarily to the senses; we have to realize that it need not tarry within such bounds. Cutting through them, it addresses itself directly to man's spiritual nature, acquainting him with those great realities that are too far-reaching to be expressed in mere words. Someone has put this poetically by saying that while "speech is but broken light on the depths of the unspoken, music is a mystical illumination of these depths, which the rays of language are too feeble to reach." We feel this time and time again when listening to great music.

Poets and essayists, novelists and playwrights, painters and sculptors have left us clearly formulated and carefully articulated thoughts and ideas cast into permanent and tangible form. These constitute one of our great cultural heritages as well as one of the most important factors in our educative process. For it is this enhancement of the qualities which make ordinary experiences appealing, appropriable (capable of full assimilation), and enjoyable that makes art an important factor in education, as John Dewey tells us. Since the great artists have been men possessed of special, what might be called *intuitional,* powers, the experiences which they have revealed and communicated cannot but deepen our understanding of human life in relation to the universe in which it is lived. No better definition of real education could be formulated: the study of art is thus not the educational luxury that so many would have us believe; it gives emphatic expression to that which makes all life worth while.

MUSIC AS A HUMANITY

Music is of special importance in such an educational development. For its mission is to give expression to such passions and inspirations, such imageries and realities as are too mighty or subtle, too suggestive or spiritual, to be imprisoned within the meanings of words or the bounds of canvas or stone. Of necessity less precise than literature, less definite than painting or sculpture, music's very vagueness gives it a vastness of meaning that thereby becomes more powerful and significant. With the other arts we somehow have a feeling of a crystallization of emotions from which the vital essence has escaped; by defining, they necessarily limit. It is only music which can reveal to us the "illimitable which lies behind the barriers of time." If properly understood, music can tell us more of life than living itself.

To be more exact: the material of which music is made is tone, just as the material out of which poetry is fashioned is words, or the material of painting is spatial shape and color. Words, however, are associated with things, for they are ordinarily used to symbolize and communicate ideas. So, too, shapes and colors are associated with such external objects as houses, rocks, trees, sky, and so on, and have comparatively little to do with spiritual qualities. The elements of which a building is composed — the pillars, pediments, openings, and so on — are so closely associated in our minds with their functional purposes that we cannot see them separately without immediately associating them with building.

All of which is decidedly limiting to the artist who would work with general ideas and convey universal concepts — who would deal in what the artists call abstractions.[1] Such a generic word as "house" suggests to us a definite material concept, even though it has different associations for different people living in different lands: in even such a poetic phrase as "house of many mansions," it is difficult for us to remove the ordinary connotations of the term. This makes the language of words a difficult one for the transference of ideas that go beyond ordinary experience. The painters are similarly limited. The representations of flowers, landscapes, human

[1] *Abstract:* "considered apart from any application to a particular object."

figures, and the like which they put into their pictures are so closely associated with things in the natural world that it is difficult to make them "mean" anything but what they represent externally. And when a painter tries to get away from this idea of natural association and convey his thoughts and feelings by using what to the ordinary person are meaningless shapes and patterns, he is likely to be thought unintelligible.

PARTICULAR POSSIBILITIES

With the musician it is different. The tonal material which he uses has, with the exception of a direct imitation of a few sounds which occur in nature, no association with anything outside itself. Moreover, these tones can reach directly any hearer who has ears to hear; they do not have to be translated into any other language, and they constitute what is, in every real sense, the only universal language in the world, one supremely capable of conveying emotions and feelings. This makes music the ideal means for the communication of those abstract ideals and imaginative concepts that so exalt the mind and lift the spirit. The musician is envied by all other creative artists; he does not have to mean anything and therefore can mean everything. And so his medium is capable of giving expression to that which has no counterpart in the external world and which belongs only to the inner world of the spirit and imagination.

A concrete example will make this clear. From time immemorial artists of all kinds have been concerned with the fundamental problem of man's existence — from whence he came, why he is here in the midst of so great tribulation, and whence he is going. The struggles of man against his manifest fate, his feeble attempts to live nobly in the midst of a tempestuous and unfriendly world, the question of his perishing so that he might continue existence in another life — these have been some of the universal themes of art. Such questionings have concerned man from the earliest days of his history. The great sacred writings — the Bible, the Veda, the Koran — are full of them. The great national epics — the *Iliad* and the *Odyssey*, the *Eddas*, the *Nibelungenlied*, the *Kalevala* — deal with little else. Dramatists from Euripides to O'Neill have tried valiantly to answer them. Painters as widely different in time and spirit as the fifteenth-century Piero della Francesca (in his *Resurrection*)

Adolph Lewisohn Collection

PIERO DELLA FRANCESCA: *Resurrection*   PAUL GAUGUIN: *I Greet You, Maria*

Two Painters' Concern with the Fundamental Problems of Man's Existence

and the nineteenth-century Paul Gauguin (in his *Ia Orana Maria*) have tried to express, with poignant and impressive means, their understanding of this inner need of man for quieting such challenges of his spirit.

A comparison of these art works, great as they may be, with such pieces of music as Beethoven's *Fifth Symphony,* Brahms's *First Symphony,* or even Tchaikovsky's *Fifth Symphony* will show the peculiar properties of music in this respect. For all attempts on the part of writers and painters to solve this problem of man's eternal struggle between life and death, between hope and despair, have had to deal with particularities. Figurative some of them are, of course; but our imagination, even in such great works as the *Iliad,* or Shakespeare's *King Lear,* is limited because of the necessity of using meaningful words and interpretable symbols. The treatment of special ideas and concepts makes anything like a universal application of them difficult. Whereas the significance of Beethoven's *Fifth Symphony* (The "Fate" Symphony), to take one of many possible examples, may be said to lie in the fact that it is an expression of his own personal defiance of fate and struggle against despair; or in that it is the "utterance of a tormented and puzzled and cynical and hopeful — and finally triumphant humanity"; or in that it embodies, as those engaged in the second great World War interpreted it, the spirit of man's triumphant victory over the forces of evil and despair. Any of these interpretations fit this comprehensible and human music; many others might be read into it. Being absolute art in the real sense of that term, Beethoven's music is not bound to anything outside itself; so it does not need to mean anything and can mean many things to different people. To realize something of this particular potentiality of music is to sense its peculiar significance as an art and its importance as a factor in our everyday life.

LIST OF SUGGESTED MUSIC

First Movement from *First Symphony*   Brahms

Fifth Symphony   Tchaikovsky

Listen to these works, mentioned in the chapter. What does the music mean to you? Look up some of the interpretations given to this music by more experienced listeners and see how yours agrees or differs. O'Connell's *Victor Book of the Symphony* and Philip Hale's *Boston Symphony Programme Notes* are excellent books to use for such references.

FOUR

GETTING BEHIND THE MUSIC

ENJOYMENT, EMOTIONAL AND INTELLECTUAL

If one were rash enough to begin a catechetical inquiry into the subject of aesthetics, his first question might well be, "What is the chief end of art?" and the answer, "To be enjoyed — in the literal sense of the term, to give pleasure, to be delighted in." A painter plans his canvas or distributes the elements of his mural decoration so as to produce a design, appealing in its proportion, balance, rhythm, use of color. The writer produces his prose or poetry so as to give pleasure to the reader, either an intellectual satisfaction in the ideas conveyed, or an aesthetic one through the beauty of their expression. Even the most practical of the fine arts, architecture, if it is true to its principles, must formulate its designs so that they are structurally proportioned, and thus pleasing to the eye, as well as practically useful.

So it is with music; unless it provides us with a sense of enjoyment it will be of very little value to the listener. There are, of course, various ways of enjoying music, just as there are of enjoying life. We may approach it through the senses, in the manner of those who seem to feel that sensual enjoyment is the great end of all existence. Music possesses tremendous powers of sensual appeal through its rhythms, its melodies, its charm of sound. Even the most unmusical person feels the essential appeal of the repeated rhythms in the nervous drumbeats of savages. We all react to the appeal of a sentimentally turned tune, as well as to the trumpet's wild blare or the seductive strains of muted strings. On the other hand, we may enjoy our music primarily from the intellectual standpoint through realizing how it is constructed, how logically it develops through various stages to a final climax, how well it succeeds in varying its constituent parts so as to provide variety and achieve unity. This sort of enjoyment is like that of the intellectual who derives his greatest pleasure in life through the processes of his mind and who distrusts the pleasures of his senses.

Both these ways of enjoying music are legitimate and need to be cultivated. But after all they are but the means through which we come in the end to the fullest sort of enjoyment, that which comes through sharing the feelings that impelled the creation of the music in the first place. Our greatest art productions are obviously the result of their creator's overwhelming enjoyment of an idea, a formal design or color pattern, a state of mind or a feeling. Something takes possession of the creator which he cannot resist, and we feel that the music or the painting or the poem which he produces forms itself without conscious effort, the creative artist being a mere instrument in the hands of some power outside himself. Every great work of art is born in such a glow of creative enthusiasm, whether the result happens to have been an immediate one, as in the case of a Schubert song or a Mozart symphony, or whether the creative effort was spread over a long period of time, as in the *First Symphony* of Brahms, or in Goethe's *Faust*. Perhaps even centuries may have elapsed between the beginning and the finishing of a work of art, as was the case of the medieval cathedrals. But the delight in each case is the same, a delight so keenly felt that the artist is driven to share it with posterity through the mysterious powers of creation. Through his abilities as a craftsman he has been able to communicate his delight to others; and the greatest enjoyment that can come to us as listeners or readers or beholders of the work he has created is in sharing this delight, in experiencing a glow similar to that of the creator, even if necessarily a much feebler one. Aldous Huxley has reminded us that of all the arts, music is that which has the least connection with what we call reality, and that, like mathematics, it is an almost unadulterated product of man's inner world. And it is this inner world that will best understand it and derive the greatest pleasure from it. We should be able to experience such a sense of pleasure in hearing music that we go out from it with "joy in our hearts and like the poor cripple in the story, walking the streets like a god," as Mr. Edward Dickinson tells us in his fine book, *The Spirit of Music*.

Our study of the technic of musical construction, necessary as it is to the full comprehension of what we hear, must be used as a means to help this spiritual understanding. The full meaning of music and the pleasure to be derived from it are gained only when to analytic dissection of its structure we add the evaluation of it as an expression of human experience. To paraphrase William Blake, we must learn to hear *through*, not *with* our ears. Lewis Mumford has observed that painting is an organization of human experience in terms of the image, as literature is in terms of the word; and we might justly add, as music is in terms of sound. And music, because of its essential characteristics, is able to communicate this experience even more significantly than do its sister arts.

ADVANTAGES AND DANGERS TODAY

One of the chief reasons why music has been so long in reaching the height of its development, as compared with the other arts, has been the peculiar necessity for the interpolation of a third person — the performer — in order to establish contact between the minds of the composer and the hearer, while a poem or a painting or a building is in itself the contact between its creator and ourselves. The fact that music has to be re-created each time it is to be enjoyed has given the re-creator a prestige out of all proportion to his real importance in the scheme of musical things. To make matters still more complicated, a poor interpretation can, of course, change the whole complexion of the music and completely distort the composer's intentions. So a great deal of the effect which music has upon the listener is due to the manner of its interpretation. Things have changed for the better in this respect, however. Much of the dominance of the interpreter has gone with the advent of present-day conditions in the reproduction of music through means such as the phonograph. Music has now really a better chance to speak for itself.

Any study of music that has any other purpose than that of leading the student directly to the music itself is, of course, valueless. As someone has put it: to talk of music without hearing it is about as fruitful as to sit in an Eveless desert discussing the beauty of women. Until recently, however, unless one were a Maecenas and able to possess his own musical establishment, the only way of approach to music was through the means of an occasional concert, or through one's own efforts or one's friends' efforts at reproduction. Now what have been called the miracles of science have changed such conditions. The phonograph and the radio give us invaluable means for providing repeated hearings of music whenever we desire them. Even in the present stage of their development, admittedly far from perfection, these products of the machine age are able to give us a repertoire of the greatest music, interpreted by the world's greatest artists, with rather startling fidelity of reproduction. And the experts tell us that within a few years the recorded reproductions of music will be even finer. Thus, in so far as the listener is concerned, the performer in a personal sense is no longer the necessity he once was.

THE LISTENER'S PITFALLS

All of the foregoing is true enough, and we should be ready to take every advantage of these marvelous opportunities offered to our generation for the study of music and for increasing our appreciation of it. But there are very obvious dangers to be avoided in the process. Even in the case of such an art as music, an art which is above all things to be enjoyed, as we have already insisted, its full glories are revealed only to those who have shown some proof of their worthiness to comprehend it. And by worthiness to comprehend we mean a willingness to exert some active desire. The idea of "mere hearing" suggests a superficial and passive process, rather than the necessary personal effort in learning to hear what is in the music. The old idea of "appreciation" of an art was largely that of exposing oneself to it, of perhaps putting oneself in the same room with it, and then daring it to exert some influence upon us. And, of course, in the great majority of cases, nothing happened. Music, because of its blessed ability to dispense with the aids of reality and fact, especially tempts us to enjoy it in passive and sensual ways. As a recent writer in the London *Musical Times* says, "We love to sit dozing in a symphony just as we sit dozing and bathing in the warmth of the sun. And when an art that is both too difficult (because of its spiritual qualities) and too easy is made suddenly accessible to everybody by the pressing of a switch, it is likely to lose at least as much as it gains. That is the danger of music today; there is so much of it and it is so promiscuous that it is being heard rather than listened to. And there are ninety passive listeners to ten live (participative) ones, because listening calls for knowledge as well as effort, and only ten (or even less) have been given the knowledge. Since taste is largely dependent upon knowledge, it follows that the ninety either prefer bad music, or don't know the difference between good and bad."

If you are inclined to doubt the truth of such a statement, consider the parallel case of the art of literature. Never before in the history of the world have there been so many books published; they are spread far and wide by the activities of both author and publisher. And yet there is probably less reading today — that is, reading with real understanding — than in the times when books and magazines were less easily available. The mere presence of such a bulk of literature and music may act as a deterrent from putting forth personal effort in trying to understand them. Probably the very extent of the flood does some good, but the proportion of value, of virtue absorbed into the reader, is apparently small in most cases. Things these days seem to be just turned on like a tap — reading, seeing, hearing — and the senses become completely dazed. In art appreciation, as in all phases of human activity, the truth holds that we get just as much out of our efforts as we put into them.

Another danger that we must guard against as we take advantage of these mechanical devices in the reproduction of music is that such processes are liable to short-circuit our experiences. When we seem to be transported at once where we desire to be, we are likely to forget that we may not be really there, that we can really get there only by the slower process of going around. Basil de Sélincourt puts it well: "Our first impression when music is delivered over to us in these mechanical fetters is that this most difficult of arts has been made easy at last. What a dangerous illusion! Within a few years we find our opportunities for hearing it multiplied a thousandfold. Everybody now can have all he wants; but curiously enough, this does not mean that it is easier to be musical. It is in the nature of music to provide experiences of an exceptional and critical kind, and if the critical comes too often, it ceases to be critical.

"The danger of these mechanical facilities is that they make music customary, they produce a bad habit and spoil our freshness of attention before we know what they would be at. This we can correct only by allowing for it, and being for that reason more careful. Wireless and gramophone can train us for direct, personal contact with music, for which there is no substitute. Just as most people read stupid books and only a few find out the good ones, so in a little while when music is everywhere, avoiding bad music will be as difficult as crossing a crowded traffic intersection, and the good will be available only if we care to climb for it and accustom ourselves to high altitudes and the vigor and splendor in which it lives."

While discussing musical mechanisms, we may note that music when reproduced can never be expected to sound as true as when heard in a concert hall. Consider but a few of the possibilities of distortion. The process of making records requires the intervention of an engineer who controls the volume, and to some extent the timbre, of the recording. Then we have to consider the nature of the substance of which the records are made; and, when we come to the reproduction which transforms the impressions in the record grooves into music, the quality and efficiency of our apparatus — and even the nature of the needle employed.

If, in addition, records are broadcast, as so often they are, yet further possibilities of distortion enter. The cumulative effect finally achieved in this chain of cause and effect would run: the production of the sound, its recording, the record itself, the reproducing machine, the radiobroadcasting apparatus (controlled by engineers), the receiving set, and the listener.

TYPES OF LISTENERS

Psychologists who have made a careful study of the subject tell us that there are in general four different ways in which music affects listeners:

1. To many people music appeals largely as a sensory, emotional, or conative experience; [1] in listening to such a work as Tchaikovsky's *Symphonie pathétique*, these listeners are apt to follow the differing aspects of the composer's inner experience, to suffer and rejoice with him, to be moved first to hope and finally to despair, the while they are thrilled with the colorful sonorities and the appealing charm of his melodies.

2. For others music arouses all sorts of associations, many of them having little or nothing to do with music itself. A certain phrase or rhythm may remind such listeners of a day in the country or a trip to the mountains, and awaken some very intimate, personal associations connected with such events. One thing leads to another,

[1] The psychologists are careful to distinguish here: *conation* means "the power or act of striving with or without a conscious goal." *Joy* and *sorrow* are "emotional states"; *hope* and *despair* are "conative attitudes."

and often the listener reflectively connects these personal associations and experiences with universal moods and feelings, thus giving the music a larger, more human significance.

3. There is likewise an objective method of enjoying music, by considering its value *per se,* without reference to anything else. Those who enjoy music in this fashion refrain from an individual response to music; to them matters of form and technic are of paramount importance, and they criticize music largely, if not entirely, from this viewpoint.

4. Perhaps the simplest response to music — in this case the listener does not "get behind the music" at all — is through personifying its character; that is, thinking of it as morbid, joyful, light, heavy, and so forth. Very little discrimination is needed for this kind of listening, and, of course, comparatively little satisfaction results from it.

One listener may, and often does, react in all these different ways to music, according to his mood and to the type of music he is hearing. Generally speaking, however, listeners fall naturally into such classifications as are mentioned above.

LIST OF SUGGESTED MUSIC

In order to ascertain the ways in which you listen to music, hear the following pieces, trying to determine whether your reactions are those of type 1, 2, 3, or 4 mentioned above.

L'Après-midi d'un faune   Claude Debussy

Here is a fine illustration of the possibility of "getting behind" music and sensing it as poetic experience in terms of sound. Before listening to this, read Chapter Twenty-one of this book and also Aldous Huxley's translation of Mallarmé's poem upon which the selection is based, in *An Anthology of World Poetry,* edited by Mark Van Doren.

Theme and Variations from *Quartet in D Minor,* No. 14   Schubert

This is the second movement from the *Death and the Maiden* quartet, one of Franz Schubert's finest chamber-music works.

Suite No. 2 in B Minor   J. S. Bach

Here is a delightful set of eighteenth-century dances, put into an exhilarating piece of music by one of the greatest composers.

TOPICS FOR FURTHER DISCUSSION

Do you think any amount of technical knowledge, however great, can spoil enjoyment? Compare music, in this respect, with sport as seen by an onlooker.

Can too much talk about music harm a work of art or weaken the hearer's appreciation of it?

Is it possible for a listener's appreciative faculty to outstrip his technical facility — in other words, can a person learn to appreciate music that it would be impossible for him to produce? And is the reverse possible, or likely — a performer becoming highly skilled, and not understanding what he performs?

Discuss the belief that "the great composers always held their art as an open one," without anything mysterious about it. Is the cult of the mysterious a modern development? How does art fare in the present-day craze for publicity and stunting?

DEFINITE SUGGESTIONS FOR READING

The Spirit of Music, Dickinson (New York: Scribner's), Chapter II: "How to Find the Spirit of Music." This should be read and reread by teachers and students of music appreciation.

FIVE

THE COMPOSER'S MATERIALS

BUILDING A BACKGROUND

"An accurate taste in poetry, as in all the other arts, is an acquired talent, which can only be produced by severe thought and a long continued intercourse with the best models of composition."

We have already indicated our belief in this opinion of Wordsworth and suggested that it is as true of music as he says it is of poetry; there are no short cuts to culture. Augustine Birrell puts this truth in lighter phrase when he says that "you may as well expect to be born with a silk hat on your head as with good taste. To go wrong is natural. To go right is discipline. . . ." It is well to keep this in mind when we hear people question the sincerity of those who would improve their taste by asking whether such subjects as the appreciation of music, or of poetry or of painting, can actually be taught. Some advice may be acceptable as to where lie the most desirable destinations, and some suggestions for help in reaching them. The listener's early concern should be the acquiring of enough musical background to make his listening as intelligent as possible from the very beginning. This does not imply the superficial sort of knowledge that is so often evidenced in the persons who *know* practically nothing about music, yet who *talk* about it with an authority quite astonishing to the professional musician. Rather does it mean that the listener should so direct his musical education that he may know what music actually is, how to distinguish the materials of which it is composed, how these are used, and what aims they seek to accomplish. If we stop for a moment to consider the relationship of music to the other arts, of how it is like them in some respects and how utterly unlike in many others, we will find a starting point from which this approach can be made.

THE RAW MATERIALS OF MUSIC

All the arts, of course, make use of materials of one sort or another, materials which the artist selects, organizes, and interprets for his particular purpose. The heaven-soaring ideals of the medieval architect were carried out through the organization of such simple materials as wood and stone, materials that were shaped into forms relating mass to mass through the genius of the builders. Our masterpieces of literature were formed from words used in ordinary speech, shaped through the power of poet or novelist. The raw materials of sculpture consist of certain three-dimensional blocks of various materials — stone, wood, clay, and so on — capable of assuming, under the skilled hand of the artist, the shapes he desires. The world's greatest paintings, in so far as their materials are concerned, are simply colored pigments applied to canvas, wood, or plaster.

But there is something beyond these purely physical substances which we must consider when we think of materials with which artists work, something that is all the more important because it cannot be seen, something upon which the real quality of any work of art depends. For example, we cannot truthfully say that the materials of architecture are merely the wood and stone, the bricks or concrete that have gone into the building we know. Beyond these and thĕ physical laws which enable man to use them as he wishes are all those necessities and inducements that have led him to plan and erect buildings — such necessities as those of providing shelter from the elements, or depositories for his goods, or temples for the worship and glorification of his gods. Without these spiritual and social necessities the art of architecture as we know it could never have come into being.

Similarly we realize that what we call "literature" would never have been created if man had not been impelled to use words in a manner that far transcends their ordinary purpose of communicating simple ideas. We can say that the desire of man to acquaint his fellows with his reactions to the world about him or his reflections on his own inner and personal experiences constitutes as important a material of literature as the significance and symbolism of the words he uses.

So it is with music. The physicists tell us that the raw material of music is auditory sound [1] having variations of pitch, intensity,

[1] They mean sound that is produced by some sort of vibrating medium, transferred

timbre, and duration. And to a certain extent they are right. These musical materials can be studied as laboratory phenomena; that is, the structure of sound can be analyzed and stated in terms of scientific and mathematical formulas. And it is important that the listener, if he aspires to anything like a real understanding of music, be familiar with them in a general way. But he must always remember that in themselves these physical materials do not necessarily constitute music; that there are certain spiritual concepts and ideas without which music is merely an interesting physical phenomenon, a dead series of tonal relationships and mathematical ratios, with no power to stir the imagination or move the hearts of men. It is necessary that we consider both these aspects of music's materials; let us take the physical ones first.

THE PHYSICAL CHARACTERISTICS OF TONE

The physical material of which music is composed is, as we have just said, sound,[2] — tones, vocables, and noises — together with an occasional use of silence, what the musicians speak of as a "rest." For systematic purposes, and in order to account fully for certain of their characteristics, the physicists are careful to describe these variations of auditory sound — pitch, intensity, timbre, and duration — as being both physical phenomena (pulsations in the ear) and psychological effects (sensations) perceived by the listener. This careful reasoning need not concern us too much as practical musicians, for we naturally assume that the one implies and causes the other.

Long and detailed experimentation has shown that the vibratory motion producing sound has four important characteristics:

1. *Frequency;* that is, it occurs a certain number of times a second. The term *cycle* is used to designate one of these complete vibrations.

2. *Amplitude;* that is, it has a certain extent or range.

3. *Form.* The series of pulsations which transmits sound through the air is called a "train" of sound waves and consists of longitudinal vibrations of the air molecules. The physicists have devised machines which graphically represent these linear motions of the sound waves,

through alternate compressions and rarefactions of the atmosphere and registered in the auditory centers of the brain through the human ear mechanism.

[2] As one writer puts it, "Sound is the auditory experience, the stimulus for which is the vibratory motions of some elastic body." (Schoen: *The Psychology of Music*).

and these graphs show that the vibratory motion has definite form that is sometimes simple and sometimes complex.

4. *Duration;* that is, the vibratory motion lasts a certain definite length of time.

The sound waves produced by any single tone possess all four of these characteristics; and, since any two waves may differ in one or more of them, we can readily see how complex is the matter of producing even a single tone on any one of the musical instruments.

Now each of these physical properties produces a certain psychological effect upon us, and it is these psychological concepts with which we as listeners are concerned. What we have come to know as the *pitch* of a tone depends largely upon the frequency of the sound wave it generates.[3] That quality in a tone that we recognize as *loudness* depends upon its amplitude.[3] *Timbre* or *tone quality* depends upon the form or overtone structure of the sound wave.[3] And the existence of a tone in time, its persistence as an auditory experience, depends upon the objective factor of duration.[3]

A change in any of the physical characteristics of a tone thus produces a reciprocal change in that which we hear; which is simply another way of saying that the experience of listening to music is an exceedingly complex one, made up of a number of experiences that unite to form a single impression.

These properties of tone are not merely of theoretical interest: they underlie the most fundamental concepts of music. For, as we shall see, the scales which are at the base of our present-day musical structures are simply expressions of certain intrinsic arrangements of pitch relationships. The dynamic quality in music, upon which so much of its beauty depends, is a matter of degrees of loudness and softness. The specific tone qualities of the various instruments, qualities that color and condition all the music we hear, are a matter of overtone arrangement. And rhythm, that "life force of music," depends to a great extent upon the relationships of tonal durations. All these factors, then, are basic to musical organization of even the simplest sort.

[3] Also, to a much less degree, upon other physical characteristics. Certain changes in the form of a sound wave produce definite changes in pitch; the intensity of a tone likewise affects its pitch to some extent. Experiments have shown that the loudness of a tone depends upon the frequency and form of its sound wave as well as upon its intensity. But in general the statements given above are true.

PITCH

By pitch we mean the relative highness and lowness of a tone; [4] though, strictly speaking, the terms are incorrect, since there are no such space relationships in music. What we call high and low pitches are in reality differences in frequency of vibrations; but for practical reasons these attributes of space are applied to music, the art which exists only in time. Around 550 B.C. the Greek philosopher Pythagoras showed that the pitch of any tone depends upon the number of vibrations per unit of time set up by the vibrating body which produces the tone. Every body capable of being set in vibration — be it string, reed, elastic membrane, or air column such as an organ pipe or tin whistle — has its own frequency of vibration (number of vibrations per second), depending on the materials of which it is made, its size, its density, or the degree of its tension, and its shape. Experiments have shown that the human ear at its best is capable of hearing anything from deep bass rumbles of about twenty cycles per second to high treble overtones of around eighteen to twenty thousand cycles per second. The frequency range of the fundamental tones on the piano keyboard is shown below for comparison; ordinary spoken language occupies a still more limited range — from about three hundred to four thousand cycles.

RANGE OF HUMAN SPEECH

20   50   100   300   1,000   4,000   10,000   20,000

On the following page is a chart which shows the vibration frequencies (fundamental tones and overtones) of the principal musical instruments and the human voice.

Man has come nearer agreement on the matter of pitch than he has in most other fields of his endeavor, for most countries using the European system of music have finally agreed on a uniform standard of pitch for their music-producing instruments. According to this standard, A when sounded in a temperature of 68 degrees

[4] Technically, tone is sound that is produced by regular periodic vibrations and having fixed pitch; it is thus distinguished from "noise," which is produced by vibrations that are scattered and irregular. "Vocables" are the sounds we use in speech, and they occupy, according to the theorists, a sort of intermediate position between tones and noises.

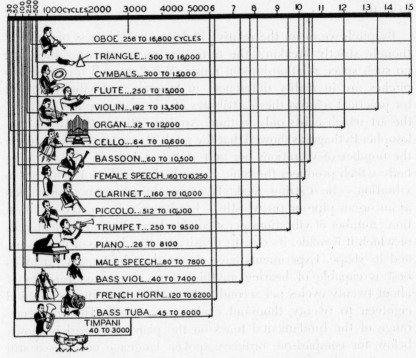

Chart Showing the Complete Frequency Range (Fundamentals and Overtones) of the Principal Musical Instruments and the Human Voice

Fahrenheit has 440 cycles of vibration per second. This has not always been agreed: a standard reference book on the subject, Helmholtz's *Sensations of Tone,* gives a seventeen-page compilation of the listing of pitches throughout Europe and the United States from 1360 to 1880, showing that during that time the range of A was from 373.3 to 567 cycles — an enormous difference.

Several factors have operated to resolve such wide differences. The human voice, by holding pitch to the usual ranges of the respective voices — soprano, alto, tenor, and bass — has had a great influence. In 1711 an English musician, John Stone, invented the tuning fork having a pitch of 419.9 cycles per second for A; this gave a dependable and easily determinable source of pitch. So that, while there was a difference ranging from about 415 to 428 cycles for A during the two centuries that comprise what we call the Classic Age, when so many of the foundations of music were laid by the great masters, there was a sort of mean-pitch agreement at a level considerably below that of today.

During the nineteenth century this was gradually raised, largely by the makers and players of wind instruments in order to secure a more brilliant tone, greatly handicapping singers who had to produce their music at a pitch considerably above that for which it was originally composed. In general it may be said that all music of this classic period is being produced today about a half tone higher than the pitch for which it was written.

Without trying to trace in detail the long list of governmental commissions appointed to regulate and standardize this matter of pitch, the Department of Commerce in Washington says that the present standard was first adopted in Germany in 1834 but was rejected by the rest of the world in favor of A–435, which the French favored and which was established in France as the official pitch in 1859. The fact that the Allies of the First World War captured so many good German instruments having A–440 pitch is credited by the Commerce Department with having started a movement which has since resulted in the establishment of A–440 as standard. In Europe the governments have had power to fix pitch by refusing to subsidize conservatoires and theaters which would not adopt the pitch ordered. In other parts of the world, the standards were obtained by the mutual consent of instrument makers and users. The present influence of the National and International Associations of Standards is very great; and this has been used to give recognition to 440 cycles for A. For those interested it will be important to know that the Bureau of Standards in Washington, as well as the BBC in London, broadcasts this note, produced by an electric tone-generator, in order to ensure absolute accuracy. This A–440 is what is called middle A, the one represented on the second space of the treble staff.

The important thing for the listener, however, is what happens when an instrumentalist or a singer uses a scale from any tone such as A, going up a tone at a time. As the pitches become higher and higher, their wave lengths become shorter and shorter, and the number of waves which reach his ear per second becomes greater and greater. Finally he will recognize a tone which bears a strong resemblance to the original tone from which the player started; this relative of the first tone, the physicist will show him, has a wave length that is exactly half that of the original and whose frequency is exactly twice that of the starting note. This second tone we call the "octave" of the first. To make this more concrete, if the length of the sound wave set up by an oboe sounding A is 31.02 inches, measured from the crest of one wave to that of the next, the wave length of the A above will measure exactly 15.51 inches; if the frequency of vibration of the first is 440 cycles per second, that of the second will be 880.

This relationship between a tone and its octave, discovered by Pythagoras, is one of the most important phenomena in all music. For it is easy to see that there would be absolute chaos in a world in which such a great number of vibrations is capable of being recognized by the ear, were it not for this happy relationship of the octave. The fact that doubling or halving the number of vibrations set up by any tone produces another tone so like the first that we can immediately recognize it as its twin brother reduces the vast range of sound waves at our disposal (from about 16 to 18,000, remember) to a workable unit that is repeated over and over again at various pitch levels. The 88 different tones represented on the modern piano keyboard, giving vibrations from 27½ to 4186 and covering only a part of the entire range of audibility, is thus con-

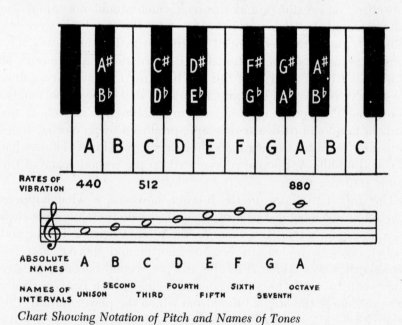

Chart Showing Notation of Pitch and Names of Tones

veniently divided into a seven-octave system (with a few notes over).[5] How much more difficult would the recognition of pitch relationships be, were there no such interrelationships in which a cycle is completed and then started all over again, and we had to learn to relate each tone directly to all the others!

It is possible, even within the octave, to obtain an indeterminate number of pitch variations, and we should be little better off in our attempts to avoid confusion had not musicians agreed upon the necessity for using only a certain few of these pitches for their musical systems. The number and character of these within-the-octave pitch relationships have varied in different parts of the world and at different times in history. Our present-day usage employs twelve pitches within each octave — count them on your piano keyboard. Out of these pitches we form certain basic tonal relationships called scales (see page 94); and in speaking of them we use two kinds of names:

(a) Absolute, based on the number of vibrations per second — A, B, C, D, E, F, G

(b) Relative, based on the relationship of one tone to another, such as that of octave, second, third, fourth, fifth, sixth, seventh. (These terms refer to the interval or ratio of vibration-frequencies between the tones.)

These relationships, common to all Western music, may be expressed in mathematical-physical ratios. For reference, here is a complete table of the frequency ratios corresponding to the most commonly used intervals; that is, pitch-distance between tones:

Octave, for example from c to c^1	$2 : 1$
Fifth, for example from c to g	$3 : 2$
Fourth, for example from c to f	$4 : 3$
Third (major), for example from c to e	$5 : 4$
Third (minor), for example from c to e flat	$6 : 5$
Sixth (major), for example from c to a	$5 : 3$
Second, for example from c to d	$9 : 8$
Seventh (major), for example from c to b	$15 : 8$

[5] This can readily be realized by playing through this piano range, taking note of the number of times the same tone is repeated in octave relationships.

LOUDNESS

As the arc of the swing of a vibrating body increases (that is, the extent to which it moves away from its normal state of rest), the energy of a tone increases, and it becomes louder to our ears. If we pluck a violin string or strike a piano string lightly, a certain number (say, 256) of slight vibrations per second will be set in motion; if we strike harder, the same number of vibrations per second will result, but their amplitude will be wider, and thus the tone will be louder.

The relationship between physical cause and psychological effect here is a peculiar one; for it has been shown by experiment that the sensation of loudness does not vary directly as the intensity of the vibrations but as the logarithm of the intensity. For example, if we increase the intensity of a vibrating sound-producing body from ten to a hundred times, the resulting loudness which we hear is increased only from one to two times.[6] In nonmathematical terms, doubling the intensity of a sound does not double its loudness. The practical results of this scientific formula are important: two flutes playing together are not twice as loud as one flute; ten pianos played at the same time are not ten times as loud as one. It has been estimated that twenty players would have to be added to an eighty-piece orchestra to produce a difference in loudness that would be appreciably noticeable.

These facts suggest the reason why comparatively few degrees of dynamic intensity are needed by musicians: it has been argued[7] that seven different degrees of dynamic intensity are all that are necessary to cover the extremes of *fortissimo* and *pianissimo* used by a pianist in interpreting ordinary music written for his instrument. Other theorists would insist that there are more; but in any event, compare this with the eighty-eight different degrees of pitch relationships that are at the disposal of the pianist.

TIMBRE

The scientist can take us into his laboratory and show us that it is entirely a matter of vibrations that determines the characteristic quality of a tone, or its *timbre*. By means of his specially con-

[6] Since the logarithm of 10 to the base 10 is 1, and that of 100 is 2.
[7] By Guy Montrose in *The Journal of Applied Psychology*, April, 1928.

structed instruments he obtains graphs which tell us strange things. A tuning fork, which gives the simplest of all musical tones, forms this sort of graph:

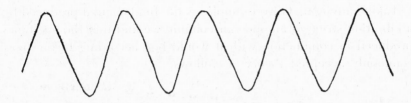

Most elastic bodies (including all the musical instruments) produce, on the other hand, complex sound waves, resulting in graphs like this one, representing clarinet tone pulsations:

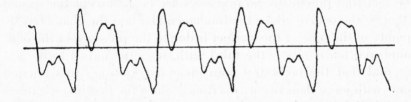

Being properly interpreted, this means that a body which produces this sort of wave vibrates not only as a whole but also in parts or segments; and that it therefore produces not only a fundamental tone but also a number of supplementary or "partial" tones. The vibration of the body as a whole is the strongest and loudest of the compound tones we hear when a note is produced; this is what we call its *fundamental*, and when we speak of the pitch of a tone we refer to the number of vibrations of this fundamental. The tones produced by the fractional vibrations of the body are called *overtones* or *harmonics*. These stand in simple ratio to the vibration of the whole (producing the fundamental) — namely, $1 : 2 : 3 : 4 : 5 : 6$, and so on — and vary in intensity and number according to the composition of the vibrating body, the manner in which it is sounded, and so forth. It is the number and relative intensities of the overtones which determine the quality of any musical tone. When we hear such a tone as is produced by a piano or an orchestral instrument, we may think that we are hearing only one tone — the fundamental; in reality, we are hearing also many other tones of lower intensity, and it is the presence or absence of these in combination with the fundamental which determines the *timbre* of the instrument. As we will see in the next chapter, the recognition of *timbre* is one of the keenest pleasures in learning to listen.

Taking any note, G for example, as the fundamental produced by a vibrating string of an open-air column, we find that the overtones produced in conjunction with it would be,[8] according to the most commonly accepted theory, as follows:

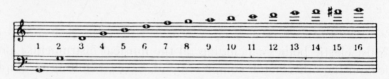

The pure qualities of the upper tones of the flute are caused by the fact that practically no overtones are heard except the second (that is, the octave above the fundamental); and the characteristic quality of the tone of the clarinet is due to the presence of the odd-numbered harmonics — the third, fifth, seventh, and so forth; and we find that the orchestral horn gives out a strong fundamental tone, with more than twenty overtones. Since the first investigations of Helmholtz (1821–1894) regarding these physical bases of tone quality, a great deal of research has been done, and we know that there are other factors that help to determine timbre. But in the main, his theories are still considered correct.

DURATION

The duration of a musical tone is obviously the time which elapses between the commencement and the cessation of vibrations. It has been estimated that the shortest possible lasting period, if it is to give rise to any consciousness of existence, is about ½₀ of a second. It is customary to measure the duration of tones not by any absolute units but by making relationships between the relative time value of different tones or groups of tones. We say, for example, that the duration of a whole note (○) is twice that of a half (♩) and four times that of a quarter note (♩). Here are the relationships in general use now:

[8] The overtones present in any tone depend partly upon the instrument producing the tone and partly on the manner in which the tone is produced.

Whole Note o
Semibreve [9]

Half Note ♩
Minim [9]

Quarter Note ♩
Crotchet [9]

Eighth Note ♪
Quaver [9]

Sixteenth Note ♪
Semiquaver [9]

Thirty-second Note ♪
Demisemiquaver [9]

Sixty-fourth Note ♪
Hemidemisemiquaver [9]

In practical use, the sense of duration includes such a related capacity as *tempo*, the rate of speed at which a piece of music moves. Its indication may be made either by means of some Italian adjective like *adagio, andante,* or *presto* affixed to the music, or by means of a definite reference to the metronome, an instrument devised for marking exact speeds.

The system of *notation* which has been developed in Western music during the centuries is really a system of written signs which indicates to the interpreter of the music the prescribed pitches and duration values of the tones. The pitch is graphically represented by the vertical pattern of the note-signs on a horizontal indicator (called a staff or stave) consisting of five parallel lines, each of which signifies a certain pitch. The pitch of the various lines and the spaces between them is determined by a *clef* sign, placed at the left-hand edge of each staff, denoting high (treble, 𝄞), medium (the C clef, which can be placed on several different lines, 𝄡), and low (bass, 𝄢) pitches, thus:

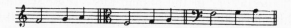

Duration is indicated by the character of the notehead used (whether open or closed), and that of the stem (see above).

This common alphabet came into use in European music around 1600; and every listener who wishes to come into close contact with great music should at least learn to read it. It is no more difficult to learn than the multiplication table and opens, like the learning of the alphabet, the gateway to an entirely new and wonderful world.

[9] These are the names given to these notes by the English.

THE SPIRITUAL FACTOR IN MUSIC

It was Beethoven who defined music as the "link which connects the spiritual with the sensuous life"; what he meant was that in addition to its existence as sound, music is a means of communication by which something of the processes of a man's inner life is revealed to his fellow men. The composer expresses not what lies outside him but what goes on inside him: through the external physical means which we have just outlined he communicates his inner feelings and spiritual concepts in such a way that they can be perceived through the senses of those who listen. As someone has said, "The musical composition which a composer makes is the expression in musical tones of his inner life."

On the afternoon of the day before this was written, the authors met with an experience which should furnish sufficient proof, if such be needed, of the validity of the statements just made. In a large metropolitan concert hall an audience that taxed the capacity of the auditorium had gathered to hear one of the world's great orchestras interpret the music of one of its greatest composers. As the program progressed, it was evident that the audience came more and more under the spell of the music; forgotten were the immediate surroundings, the discomfort of the crowded hall, the technical perfection of the playing, even the sympathetic interpretation of the orchestra, in the emotional significance of the music. Here was a great man speaking simply, out of the depths of his spirit, with a direct vigor and forcefulness of utterance that could not be denied, of things that matter today just as they mattered in the time they were first put on paper and as they always will throughout the history of the human race. There was a great deal more to this music than "auditory sound organized with variations of pitch, timbre, intensity, and duration." Something was being communicated from composer to listener so forcefully, so directly that, to quote a poetic observer of the occasion, when the finale of the last symphony came and the "portals of the skies swung asunder and the great chant of victory and defiance was heard," the audience crashed into applause and wild cheers.

This is what we mean when we say that there are spiritual as well as physical materials to be reckoned with in music. An audience listening to the Boston Symphony Orchestra playing a program of Sibelius's music would never have received the impressions it did at the concert described above had it not been for the physical means used to convey the ideas of the composer — the superb timbre of orchestral tone, the carefully adjusted matters of pitch relationship, intensity of tone, correct relations of tempo, and so on. Had there been nothing else, however, the music would have been but sounding brass and tinkling cymbal; what made it memorable was the fact that the conductor and the orchestra were able to convey, through these physical means, what the composer had so evidently put into the music — "the full expression of his inner life." To paraphrase St. Paul: music is an art not only of the letter, but also of the spirit; and he said, "The letter killeth, but the spirit giveth life."

SIX

INSTRUMENTS:

THE MEANS FOR MAKING MUSIC

> Some to the lute, some to the viol went,
> And others chose the cornet eloquent.
> — *Marvell*

Even though the skill of the composer enables him to write down his ideas by means of black notes on a white sheet of paper, music does not exist, practically speaking, until it has been "produced" by some sort of physical means. Before they have any value for the average person, these ideas must be brought to life through the medium of some instrument which, be it lute, viol, or "cornet eloquent," is but a machine for producing sound by putting air into vibratory motion. For sound is produced, as we have just seen, through but one means, the setting up in various ways of air pulsations which are communicated to our ears through the ability of the air particles to transmit motion. If these pulsations strike upon our sensitive hearing mechanism irregularly, at varying periods of time, we call the sensation they give us "noise"; if they come at regular intervals, we say we hear musical tones. The means for setting the air particles in vibration are many and vary from the simple banging on the stretched skin of a primitive drum, through the vibrating strings and reeds of the orchestral instruments, to the elaborate electrical vibratory mechanisms of our time. Instruments are the means by which sound impinges upon the consciousness of the average music lover.

THE INTERACTION OF GROWTH: INSTRUMENTS AND EMOTION

Once music outgrew its early savage state, its development has been surprisingly conditioned by the instruments available for its production. Up to the beginning of the seventeenth century it was produced largely by the human voice; as soon as the possibilities of music made by instruments were thoroughly understood, a new art, that of instrumental music, arose, and the most glorious period in the whole development of the art began. The reasons for the choice of a particular instrument for the expression of the thoughts of a composer have always been a source of interesting speculation for the musical amateur, for in listening to great music we must realize that a great deal of its poignance and effect is due to the choice of instrumentation made by the composer. (In this connection it is important to realize that the composer of serious music, in contradistinction to most of the writers of popular music, writes his own orchestration, which is never changed in interpretation.) In writing his immortal *Fifth Symphony*, it is difficult to imagine Beethoven choosing any other instrument than the orchestra for depicting this noble revelation of his soul; a string quartet would have been inadequate and the piano almost ridiculous. On the other hand, many of the best compositions of Haydn and Mozart belong inherently to the string quartet and would lose their essence if transposed to any other instrument. In this connection, we must remember that the symphony orchestra, although composed of a large group of individual instruments, is really an instrument itself, coordinated and played upon by the will of the conductor, and that a trio or a string quartet — combinations of violin, viola, and violoncello, or two violins, viola, and violoncello — are likewise instruments in an individual sense. A great deal of Schumann's and almost all of Chopin's music sprang directly from their love for and understanding of the piano, as we shall see. The majestic dignity and architectural splendor of Bach's organ works are due to his careful cultivation of the resources of that huge instrument and are unthinkable on any other, unless it be the modern orchestra. Furthermore, each age seems to have selected its own particular instrument, one which definitely expressed its own characteristics and which was developed for its needs. The lute suggests the romantic spirit

The Boston Symphony Orchestra

of the sixteenth century; the organ, in spite of many modern improvements which have made it more easily playable, is a quiescent instrument today — its period of great glory extended from the latter part of the seventeenth century to the early eighteenth.

THE INFLUENCE OF POLITICS

The eighteenth century was the great period of the string quartet and other "chamber" (or room) music. The nineteenth was the century of the piano — an age of individualism, of star performers demanding a solo instrument capable of complete, single mastery, and suitable for great displays of virtuosity. The choice of these instruments for the varying periods was no haphazard one; political changes and economic conditions had a great deal to do with it. The organ reached its dominance and achieved its importance during the seventeenth century because Germany at the time (immediately following the Thirty Years' War, 1618–1648) was a poverty-stricken country, unable to support the elaborate and costly court music to which France and Italy were accustomed, and looked to the stimulating influence of the strong Protestant Church to satisfy its love for music. Opera had its genesis (the first opera was written in 1600 for the celebration of the marriage of Henry IV and Maria de' Medici in Florence) and largely developed during the following years through the demands of the luxurious European courts for amusement. The division of eighteenth-century Europe into various petty courts, each with its own prince and its royal establishment, made possible the system by which chamber-music organizations flourished so widely. The democratic idea in government swept away the petty prince, and with him the string quartet and chamber-music organizations maintained for his court concerts. The passing of nineteenth-century Romanticism with its great individualistic figures — Liszt and Chopin — (the last of the interpretive giants, Paderewski, died in June, 1941) sounded the death knell of the piano as the deified deliverer of self-conscious soul-strivings.

It is no accident that the great bulk of the music that we have chosen for illustrating these chapters has been orchestral music; the symphony orchestra is the instrument of our time, and its music, although almost incredibly complex in many instances, is better understood and more easily appreciated than music written for instruments of another period. Not so many years ago it was thought to be a mark of cultural distinction to be a regular attendant at symphony concerts; now, rather unfortunately in some ways, orchestral enthusiasts are only too common. The orchestra, because of its size, its capacity for varying tone color and all shades of dynamics, appeals to all types of listeners, to the musically trained and the musically ignorant. As someone has well said, it is as modern as present-day industry — one big thing made up of many parts — and it suits our age as the simpler instruments suited handicraft times.

THE GROWTH OF THE ORCHESTRA

Most of us are hardly aware of how new an instrument the modern symphony orchestra is. We are so accustomed to the fine orchestras of today, with their almost unbelievable perfection of technic, that it seems as if they must have been in existence for many centuries. As a matter of fact, the first real attempt at developing an orchestra in the present-day sense must be credited to a German prince, Karl Theodore, Elector Palatine in 1743, whose band at Mannheim developed a beauty of tone, a unanimity of playing, and a degree of dynamic shading that had been entirely unknown before; in this sense, as well as in the type of music it played, this orchestra can be said to have been the first "symphony orchestra" according to our modern way of thinking. Most historians credit this band of players with being the experimental laboratory out of which came our present ideas of symphonic music. Charles Burney, the most famous musical traveler of the eighteenth century, gives an interesting account of this orchestra of Karl Theodore: [1]

I found it to be all that its fame had made me expect: power will naturally arise from a great number of hands; but the judicious use of this power, on all occasions, must be the consequence of good discipline; indeed there are more solo players and good composers in this than perhaps in any other orchestra in Europe; it is an army of generals, equally fit to plan a battle, as to fight it. [We cannot help wondering what Burney might have said of the Boston, the Philadelphia, or the London Philharmonic orchestras!]

But it has not been merely at the Elector's great opera that instru-

[1] *Present State of Music in Germany, Netherlands, and United Provinces* — Charles Burney (London, 1773).

mental music has been so much cultivated and refined, but at his concerts, where this extraordinary band has "ample room and verge enough" to display all its powers, and to produce great effects without the impropriety of destroying the grandeur and more delicate beauties peculiar to vocal music; it was here that Stamitz . . . first surpassed the bounds of common opera overtures, which had hitherto only served in the theatre as a kind of court crier, with an "O Yes" in order to awaken attention and bespeak silence at the entrance of the singers. Since the discovery which the genius of Stamitz first made, every effect has been tried which such an aggregate of sound can produce; it was here that *Crescendo* and *Diminuendo* had birth; and the *Piano*, which had before chiefly been used as an echo, with which it was generally synonymous, as well as the *Forte*, were found to be musical colours which had their shades as much as red or blue in painting.

I found, however, an imperfection in this band, common to all others that I have ever yet heard, but which I was in hopes would be removed by men so attentive and so able; the defect I mean is the want of truth in the wind instruments. I know it is natural to those instruments to be out of tune, but some of that art and diligence which these great performers have manifested in vanquishing difficulties of other kinds, would surely be well employed in correcting this leaven which so sours and corrupts all harmony. This was too plainly the case tonight, with the bassoons and hautbois [oboes], which were rather too sharp at the beginning, and continued growing sharper to the end of the opera.

My ears were unable to discover any other imperfection in the orchestra throughout the whole performance; and this imperfection is so common to orchestras in general that the censure will not be very severe upon this, or afford much matter for triumph to the performers of any other orchestra in Europe.

The Elector, who is himself a very good performer upon the German flute, and who can, occasionally, play his part upon the violoncello, has a concert in his palace every evening when there is no public exhibition at the theatre; but when that happens, not only his own subjects, but all foreigners have admission gratis.

The going out from the opera at Schwetzingen, during the summer, into the electoral gardens, which, in the French style, are extremely beautiful, affords one of the gayest and most splendid sights imaginable; the country here is flat and naked, and therefore would be less favorable to the free and open manner of laying out grounds in English horticulture, than to that which has been adopted.

His electoral highness' suite at Schwetzingen during summer amounts to fifteen hundred persons, who are all lodged in this little village at his expense. To a stranger walking through the streets of Schwetzingen during summer, this place must seem inhabited only by a colony of musicians, who are constantly exercising their profession: at one house a fine player on the violin is heard; at another, a German flute; here an excellent hautbois; there a bassoon, a clarinet, a violoncello, or a concert of several instruments together. Music seems to be the chief and the most constant of his electoral highness' amusements; and the operas and concerts, to which all his subjects have admission, form the judgment and establish the taste for music throughout the electorate.

THE ORCHESTRAL FAMILIES

The four great divisions of the orchestra are: the strings, which produce their tone by setting into vibration stretched strings, by means of bows; the wood winds, instruments in which the wind vibrates in a hollow tube, or in which the vibrations are caused by reeds; the brass winds, in which the players' lips act as the vibrating medium; and the percussion — drums, cymbals, gongs, and so on. We may best remind ourselves of the qualities which these instruments give to the orchestra by dividing them into "families":

String	Wood Wind	Brass	Percussion
Violin	Flute (piccolo)	Trumpet	Kettledrums
Viola	Clarinet	French horn	Bass drum
Violoncello	Oboe	Trombone	Side drum
Contrabass	English horn	Tuba	Bells
	Bassoon		Cymbals
	Bass clarinet		Celesta, and so on
	Contrabassoon		

These are combined in various ways and in differing proportions. In an orchestra adapted to playing the symphonies of Haydn and Mozart (Haydn died in 1809 and Mozart in 1791) we would have about the following proportion of musical instruments:

8 first violins
8 second violins
5 violas   to balance
5 cellos
4 double basses

2 flutes
2 clarinets (occasionally)
2 oboes (occasionally)
2 bassoons
2 horns
2 trumpets
2 kettledrums
(sometimes only four to six wind instruments)

For a Beethoven symphony two extra horns would be added, together with more strings to balance the increased use of brass and wood wind, giving a total of about forty-five strings in an orchestra of sixty. Since the reforms of Berlioz (who died in 1869) and Wagner (who died in 1883), the brass group has mightily increased in importance, both as to numbers and as to quality; naturally this in turn demands more strings for balance, so that properly to interpret modern works with well-balanced forces, an orchestra of approximately a hundred players is necessary. Wagner's last work, *Parsifal*, for instance, calls for the following instrumentation: 3 flutes, 3 oboes, 1 English horn, 3 clarinets, 3 bassoons, 1 contrabassoon, 4 horns, 3 trumpets, 3 trombones, 1 tuba, kettledrums and strings to balance.

One of the legitimate pleasures of concert-going is the ability to recognize the different instruments of the orchestra by both sight and sound. To do this, it is useful to know how an orchestra is seated. Different conductors have different ideas as to the best seating plan for their orchestra, but all give those instruments which have the smaller tone opportunities for being heard to the best advantage. Thus the strings are usually placed in front, with the first violins generally to the conductor's left; the wood winds are directly behind the strings, and the brass and percussion bring up the rear. Because of the necessity for securing a good foundation tone for the whole orchestra, the double basses are placed in the rear or to one side, upon an elevation, so that their voices can penetrate the whole tonal mass.

THE IDEAL CONDUCTOR

The conductor's function is, of course, to keep the whole band together, securing unanimity through his signals; he is likewise responsible for obtaining the effects intended by the composer and marked in the score — interpreting the music, as we say. It is hardly necessary to add that this interpretation is a tremendously important factor in the impressions received by the listener, so important that very often the interpreter gets more credit for the effects produced than does the composer. Music is a unique art in that, as we have already said, a third person must be interpolated between the composer and the listener in order that the latter may receive the impressions desired by the former. This fact has made

The Score as Used by the Conductor

possible the present-day overemphasis on the conductor as a musical influence, especially as most hearers of orchestral music do not know what the real functions of the conductor are. Some listeners seem to think that through some occult means, while the performance is in progress, the conductor is presented with brilliant inspirations which he transmits to his men as they are playing. And the show-man-like gyrations of many of our conductors do not help in dis-illusioning the public!

A good conductor studies his score carefully, decides just what effects are to be desired in various places, the proportions and balance of tonal effects desired, and the shaping of the various musical phrases. Then in long and very often laborious rehearsals, he impresses these ideas upon his men so that they know exactly how they are expected to play each phrase, how their parts are to balance with the others, and so forth. Henderson tells us how he once asked Arthur Nikisch, one of the world's greatest conductors, if he was ac-customed to making changes in the reading of an orchestral work during the course of its performance. He replied that if he realized that the music was going rather heavily, he might increase the pace, but otherwise he made no attempt to change details or general outlines. At the concert performance the conductor can work his men into a frenzy of inspired playing, but to do this he has to build upon the solid foundation of careful advance preparation. Today's magnificent orchestral performances are the result of constant and painstaking rehearsals and are in strong contrast to the conditions at the time when Beethoven conducted the first performance of his *Fifth Symphony* in Vienna, which was then (1808) the musical capital of the world. Not one full rehearsal for the program had been held; Beethoven had to stop the orchestra in

Gilbert Friedberg

Rehearsing the Orchestra

A photographer for the *Boston Globe* concealed himself among the players at a Boston Symphony rehearsal and obtained a number of unposed action pictures of Charles Munch as he was drilling the orchestra in Ravel's *Daphnis and Chloë* suite.

the middle of a passage when a player lost his cue, and the response of the few auditors in the unheated hall, Beethoven tells us, was anything but enthusiastic, owing to the wretched performance his music received.

With the coming of radio another factor intrudes between conductor and audience — the volume controller, a musician-engineer who can alter the dynamics at will, so that there shall not be inaudibility or "blasting" in the listener's receiving set. He has to legislate for average sets, of course. This is just another of the many reasons why we must not forsake the concert room for the radio set if we want to hear music as nearly as possible as the composer conceived it. In phonograph recording, too, there is "control." No reproducing machine gives the truth, the whole truth, and nothing but the truth.

GETTING ACQUAINTED

How can we listen so that we may obtain the most from the complexities of this wonderful modern instrument, the orchestra? We have already suggested in the previous chapter that the recognition of the *timbre* of the different instruments, played singly as well as in combination, is one of the most obvious pleasures that we can derive from listening. The most practical manner of learning to recognize timbres is through observing what the various classes of tone

Seating Plan of the Philadelphia Orchestra

sound like — what massed string tone is like, or the beauties of the wood-wind ensemble, or the sonorous glories of the brass choir. This may easily be done at orchestral concerts where we may see as well as listen, or rather, see while we listen. The seating plan of the Philadelphia Orchestra, one of the best orchestras in the world, shows where in general to look for the various choirs, although other orchestras may vary it somewhat.

Recognition of the various orchestral timbres may be aided by a study of the many fine recordings now available. Take such a familiar composition as Wagner's *Tannhäuser* Overture, for example; before the music has run the course of fifty measures, the listener has obtained the essential color of the different orchestral choirs. In the first fifteen measures the wood winds are heard alone; the French horn is often counted as a wood-wind instrument because of its peculiarly smooth tone. Then for some twenty measures more we have the wood winds blending with the strings, and finally some of the brass choir sounding the melody of the Pilgrims. The beginning of the Waltz from *The Nutcracker* suite is also a good tonal illustration of the wood-wind ensemble. There is a flowing background here supplied by the harp, an instrument that belongs to none of the regular orchestral classifications but is used for occasional effects.

Then there is the beginning of the second movement of Brahms's *Third Symphony*. Certainly we can hardly find a better illustration of the richness possible from the wood-wind ensemble; there is an occasional interpolation of one or two measures from the strings in order to set off the peculiar wood-wind timbre desired by the composer. In fact this whole lovely movement is given over almost entirely to a combining of the wood winds and the strings; only occasionally a trombone enters to help sustain the whole and tie it together. This is music worthy of many hearings; in trying to realize just how the composer used these two groups of orchestral instruments, the hearer will incidentally become familiar with some of the world's noblest music.

Another place for recognizing the contrasting colors of strings and wood winds is at the very beginning of Tchaikovsky's *Symphonie pathétique*. After a slow introductory melody on the bassoon accompanied by low-toned strings, the whole string section suddenly bursts into animated action, followed immediately by the wood winds taking up the same phrase.

The Orchestral Strings

INSTRUMENTAL CHARACTERISTICS

The strings are the foundational group of the orchestra; they take up its main burden and are helped and relieved by the other choirs. Here, as we found to be true in the case of the wood winds, there is a diversity of duties: the violins are divided into two groups, firsts and seconds, and generally take the melody; the violas take an alto part, the cellos a broad flowing tenor or baritone part, and the basses supply the foundation tones for the whole. Listen to the beginning measures of Beethoven's *First Symphony;* the strings have the main say, the violins on top sounding the melody. They are joined occasionally by the wood winds, but the chief color is that of the strings, forming a background for the characteristic qualities of the other groups. What a portentous beginning the deep-toned strings (cello and bass) give to Schubert's *Unfinished Symphony!* There is a lightening of the mood when the violas and the violins are added a few measures later, and the whole section forms a background for the melody sung by the blended oboe and clarinet. In all orchestral compositions the strings are heard much alone: sometimes the composer writes a whole composition for them, as Mozart did in his *Eine kleine Nachtmusik,* composed for some special occasion in Vienna. Here from the four movements of this serenade we can gain a good idea of the varied possibilities of the string choir, ranging from the introspective rendering of sentiment to a light, fleet celerity of which no other instruments in the orchestra are capable.

The brass with its impressive choir of trumpets and trombones can on occasion "roll up the heavens like a scroll." Witness the opening measures of the last movement of Beethoven's *Fifth Symphony,* or the Introduction to the last movement of Brahms's *First Symphony* (measures 30–60), where the effect of the whole is determined by the golden weight of this important family of instruments. But this brass group can also speak eloquently with a still, small voice; what more suitable opening can possibly be imagined than the beginning measures of Weber's *Oberon* Overture, with its faint "horns of elfland, softly blowing"? Wagner uses the brass choir for tremendous, resounding effects, as well as for some delicate, imaginative ones. The Funeral March from *Götterdämmerung,* for instance, gains its almost overpowering poignancy through the inexorable way in which Wagner uses the brass, here including 4 horns, 3 trumpets,

The Orchestral Wood Winds

The Orchestral Brass

a bass trumpet, 4 trombones, a tenor tuba, 2 bass tubas, and a contrabass tuba. The effect of all these sounding together is unforgettable, cataclysmic, a fit prelude to the destruction of the gods. On the other hand, the composer's delicate use of the horns at the beginning of the second act of *Tristan und Isolde* gives exactly the proper mood for the moonlit scene that follows in the lovers' garden.

A fact which the orchestral listener is likely to forget is that, because of difficulties inherent in their construction and mechanism, wind instruments (both brass and wood-wind) have to be kept in tune with one another and with the rest of the orchestra by "main force." Every note on all the wind instruments used in the orchestra must be tempered by the use of the breath and the lips of the player if it is to sound in tune with the rest of the ensemble.[2] And this is true today, even after considerable improvements which the makers (particularly the Belgian C. J. and A. J. Sax and the German Theobald Boehm) have made in the methods used in constructing instruments. No wonder that Bach, Haydn, and Mozart used the oboes, bassoons, flutes, trumpets, and horns of their day so sparingly; or that it was not until Beethoven's scores that the clarinet became a regularly functioning member of the symphony orchestra. The problems — adjustment of valve lengths, proper breath and lip pressure, the correction of deflection from pitch due to temperature changes — connected with the playing of wind instruments are so complicated that they have never been completely solved. And the mechanical imperfections of these instruments are still so great as to make necessary a great deal of lip and breath control on the part of the player. It is this fact that makes these sections the most temperamental departments of the orchestra; even in the best of ensembles occasional out-of-tune playing by these instruments is sometimes noticeable.

The percussion family is probably the oldest of all the orchestral divisions in actual point of time; most of its members contribute to the rhythmic, coloristic, or dynamic qualities of the ensemble rather than to its harmonic or melodic enrichment. Such instruments of indefinite pitch as the side or snare drum, the bass drum, the tambourine, cymbals, and so on, are used entirely for special dynamic effects. The kettledrum, bells, celesta, glockenspiel, and

[2] The slide trombone, however, because of the infinite number of positions possible with the slide, can be played in perfect tune, without the need of tempering by use of lip and breath, with any instrument or combination of instruments.

The Timpani

xylophone are instruments capable of producing definite pitch and are often used by composers for special instrumental effects; of them all, the kettledrums are the most consistently used by post-eighteenth-century writers.

Every opportunity should be taken for observing these and other similar tonal groupings, for it is in this way that the listener is brought to realize the part that is played by the orchestral voices in combination. After he has familiarized himself with the sound of these groups, he will be interested to notice the individual timbres of the various instruments.

SPECIFIC ILLUSTRATIONS

Benjamin Britten has given us what has been well called a "painlessly educative" method of doing this in his piece *The Young Person's Guide to the Orchestra*. Originally written for a film produced for educational purposes, this music introduces the listener first to the sounds of the various choirs, and then he hears the different instruments one at a time. Britten uses as a theme a tune from music written for a play by an earlier English composer (Purcell's rondeau from *Abdelàzer*) and lets us hear it first played by the whole orchestra:

Then he repeats it played by the various choirs in turn: first the wood winds, then the brass, followed by the strings, and finally, very cleverly, by the percussive instruments. Then, just to remind us, he gives it to us again by the whole orchestra.

There follows a series of variants of the tune, thirteen in all, each emphasizing one of the instruments. Here is the scheme:

Variation 1. For the highest of the wood-wind group, the clear, sweet Flute and its rather shrill brother, the Piccolo, with a background of first and second violins.

Variation 2. For the plaintive Oboe, which, as the music shows us, can be likewise forceful. This slow variation has an accompaniment of strings playing an unmistakable rhythm.

Variation 3. Two Clarinets, beautifully smooth and mellow, over an accompaniment of strings and (of all things) a tuba!

Variation 4. Here the tune is given to two deep-voiced Bassoons, again with a very distinctive string accompaniment.

Variation 5. First and Second Violins, soaring above a polonaise rhythm on the brass.

Variation 6. The Violas are heard next against short, repeated chords in the wood winds and brasses.

Variation 7. Warm, rich, smooth Cello tones with clarinet and viola accompaniment.

Variation 8. The score here calls the Double Basses the "grandfathers of the string family, with heavy, grumbling voices." Here they are heard against a wood-wind background.

Variation 9. The Harp, with its 46 strings and seven foot-pedals, shows what it can do; it is heard above a soft string *tremolo.*

Variation 10. The four Horns, rich and full, played in harmony.

Variation 11. For two Trumpets with a military-like section, accentuated by a strong drumbeat.

Variation 12. Displays the heavy, brassy voice of the Trombone and the still heavier tones of the Tuba.

Variation 13. Includes parts for the most familiar Percussion instruments: Timpani or Kettledrums; Bass Drum; Cymbals; Tambourine; Triangle; the Side Drum; Chinese Block; Xylophone; Castanets; Gong; Whip.

Having taken the orchestra apart in this fashion, Britten then proceeds to put it together again in a fugue, adding instrument after instrument in the same order as before, starting with the piccolo, which has the theme first. At the very end there comes the original theme thundered out on the brass, with the rest of the orchestra whirling madly about it. This makes a most exciting and original finish to the whole piece.

Another good practice piece for the same purpose is Ravel's famous and overplayed *Bolero.* Written as a sort of stunt, this employs a two-part Spanish dance tune as a theme, repeating it over and over again throughout the course of the piece, the only change, except at the very ending, being in orchestration. Here is the plan of the various solo instruments as they bring out this rhythmic tune:

(a) *refers to the first part of the tune;* (b) *to the second.*

1. (a) Flute
2. (a) Clarinet
3. (b) Bassoon
4. (b) E-flat Clarinet
5. (a) Oboe d'amour (an obsolete type of oboe, tuned a little lower than the usual one used in the orchestra. Not in general use since Bach's day.)
6. (a) Flute and Trumpet
7. (b) Tenor Saxophone (saxophones, wind instruments made of brass with wood-wind characteristics, were invented by Adolphe Sax in 1840; because of their peculiar nonblending quality, they are not usually used in orchestras but are members of military bands and jazz and swing orchestras.)
8. (b) Soprano Saxophone
9. (a) Horn, Celesta, Piccolos
10. (a) Oboes, English Horn, Clarinet
11. (b) Trombone
12. (b) Same as 10 plus Flutes and Piccolo
13. (a) Same plus First Violins
14. (a) Same plus Second Violins
15. (b) Same minus Clarinets and plus Trumpet
16. (b) Same plus Clarinets, Soprano Sax, Violas
17. (a) Wood Winds, Saxes, Trumpets, High Trumpet, First Violins
18. (b) Incomplete, modulating into a great, loud explosion, with Trombone

IN CONCLUSION

We all have our favorites, and learning to recognize their voices gives an added refinement of pleasure to orchestral listening. Perhaps we are particularly enamored of the horn; Gilman has called it the romantic poet of the tonal world and said that, like Blake's Evening Star, it can "bid the wind sleep on the lake and wash the dark with silver." Or the cello, eloquent amorist and imposing rhapsodist of the orchestra; how like the voice of a friend bringing comfort in trouble is the cello passage at the beginning of the second movement of Beethoven's *Fifth Symphony!* And yet the same instrument, if not treated with respect and given music suited to its inherent capabilities, may sound like a Hebrew prophet doing handsprings, as someone has put it. The crystal clearness of the clarinet melody in the *Oberon* Overture, the pastoral sweetness of the oboe and the flute in the third section of Liszt's *Les Préludes,* the nostalgic longing of the English-horn melody in the second movement of the César Franck *Symphony,* and its prophetic sadness in the shepherd's tune at the beginning of the third act of *Tristan und Isolde,* all these are highlights of unforgettable beauty. The violin is a universal favorite, for it can "dance and mock and flirt like Columbine, as well as sigh and glow like Juliet"; it is an instrument equally capable of light-hearted gaiety, empty-headed brilliance, or soulful discourse on things of mighty import. It can be the means of suggesting playful badinage, as in the first measures of the last movement of Beethoven's *First Symphony,* or of conveying such grave commitments as are entrusted to it by Brahms in the second movement of his *First Symphony.*

LIST OF SUGGESTED MUSIC

Tannhäuser Overture   Wagner

Funeral March from *Götterdämmerung*   Wagner

Prelude to Act II of *Tristan und Isolde*   Wagner

Shepherd's Tune, beginning of Act III of *Tristan*   Wagner

Waltz from *The Nutcracker* Suite   Tchaikovsky

First Movement of *Symphonie pathétique*   Tchaikovsky

Second Movement of *First Symphony*   Brahms

Second Movement of *Third Symphony*   Brahms

First and Last Movements of *First Symphony*   Beethoven

Second Movement of *Fifth Symphony*   Beethoven

First Movement of *Unfinished Symphony*   Schubert

Eine kleine Nachtmusik   Mozart

Oberon Overture   Weber

Pastoral section of *Les Préludes*   Liszt

The Young Person's Guide to the Orchestra   Britten

Bolero   Ravel

Instruments of the Orchestra

Examples compiled by various recording companies, demonstrating the characteristics of the principal instruments that comprise the modern symphony orchestra.

TOPICS FOR FURTHER DISCUSSION

A book has been written claiming that almost all instruments are defective, even the violin. Discuss, according to your knowledge, this general charge.

One able musician has suggested that saxophones may take the place of clarinets in the symphony orchestra. Would that be an advantage?

What factors must we remember when considering even the best phonograph records as representative of the effects produced by the orchestra?

Discuss the instrumentation used by the following composers: Stravinsky, Richard Strauss, Wagner, Berlioz, Beethoven, Haydn, Bach, Monteverdi.

SEVEN

MEANS BY WHICH MATERIALS

ARE MADE INTO MUSIC

As we listen to a piece of music, there are certain factors which organize the raw materials of physical sound in ways that heighten our understanding and increase our enjoyment. Although we may not realize it, our interest in a composition is dependent upon one or more, perhaps all, of these factors: we may not be conscious of the presence of a single one of them, but, nevertheless, it is their combined effect that makes music capable of being apprehended. So one of the first needs in learning to listen to music is that of training our ears to recognize these fundamental factors by means of which its raw materials are organized: *rhythm, melody,* and *harmony.* These might well be called the elements of the language of music, and a complete understanding of them demands much study and belongs to the higher intricacies of the art. But even if the music lover is enabled to hear how their use helps to shape the composition to which he is listening, his appreciation of it will be tremendously advanced. These factors are present in all music; and the importance of great masterworks results partly from the significant ways in which a composer employs them.

RHYTHM

Rhythm is the most easily perceived of these fundamental factors of music. There is good reason for this, for rhythm is one of the most fundamental elements in nature. A famous musician is quoted as saying that "in the beginning there was rhythm," and if we stop to consider the universe in general we will see that this is true in other things besides music. Our life is being sustained constantly by the rhythmic beating of our heart, the beats occurring in pairs, one accented and the other one unaccented. Our breathing is likewise rhythmical, the inhalations corresponding to unaccented beats, the exhalations to accented ones. Our walking and running are rhythmical, as is, indeed, the natural pace of all animals. The larger operations of nature occur in rhythmical sequence — the succession of the seasons, the movements of the stars and planets, the ebb and flow of the tides, the beating of the waves on the shore, and so on.

So an art is merely conforming to a universal truth in insisting that the elements of which it is composed be arranged in some sort of harmonious correlation. The rhythmic schemes of the space arts — architecture, sculpture, and painting — are rather easily discernible to the eye, just as those of the time arts — music and literature — are to the ear. Every work of art worthy of the name is arranged according to some succession of weak and strong units that gives it interest and makes it intelligible to the mind of the beholder or listener. The façade of a building, the arrangement of details in a painting, the distribution of the elements of a piece of sculpture, all these give grace and serve to stimulate the interest; they are among the most important means which serve to make the art work intelligible to the beholder. In music and poetry there is need for even more careful organization of rhythmic elements if we are to have a sense of order and balance. We do not have to listen to a piece of poetry or music long before we realize that its constant flow is marked by a succession of beats or pulses, arranged into definite groups by means of heavier stress coming every so often. For instance, in the nursery rhyme that begins:

Bobby Shafto's gone to sea
Silver buckles on his knee

there are four periods of stress or accent in each line. In the first line they fall at the first syllable of "Bobby" and of "Shafto," and on "gone" and "sea." This point of stress we call an accented (strong) beat, as opposed to the others, which are unaccented (weak). We can diagram the above lines thus, letting ↓ represent a strong beat, and ᴜ a weak beat:

$$\downarrow \cup \downarrow \cup \downarrow \cup \downarrow \ (\cup)$$
$$\downarrow \cup \downarrow \cup \downarrow \cup \downarrow \ (\cup)$$

Such a tune as this one has exactly the same general rhythmic scheme, one which we may call duple, since the meter consists of two beats or pulses, a heavy and a light, with the first one in each group accented:

On the other hand, such lines as these will be found to have quite a different scheme:

Spotted and veinèd with various hues
Through the clear realms of azure drift

↓ ∪∪ ↓ ∪∪ ↓∪∪ ↓ (∪∪)

and a tune like this famous one represents the same pattern:

This is what we call triple meter, consisting of three beats or pulses, with the first one in each group accented.

Practically, it will be found that most of the more complicated regular rhythmic schemes may be resolved into these two elemental ones, duple and triple. For example, such a line as this:

Sandy cat by the Farmer's chair

↓ ∪ ↓ ⌣ ↓ ∪ ↓ (∪)

where the heavy accent really comes on the first beat of each group of four, with something of a secondary accent halfway between, is obviously an elaboration of duple rhythm. In music we have this well illustrated by such a tune as the old round "Frère Jacques":

Such a scheme as the following is clearly a modified triple meter, with the main accent coming on the first beat of each group of six and a secondary accent midway between:

Often I think of the beautiful town

↓∪∪ ↓ ∪ ∪ ↓∪∪ ↓ (∪∪)

The old French folk tune illustrates this well:

The fundamental time units which occur in music are called *measures;* they are assumed, in ordinary music, to be of equal length and to be made up of a certain number of beats, organized and bound together by the principal accent with which they begin. Thus, in duple time we speak of two beats in a measure; in triple, of three; in quadruple, of four. The vertical lines which are placed on the music score to designate its division are called *bars* or *bar lines,* while the divisions themselves bear the name *measure.* When writing or printing music, the general rhythmic scheme is indicated at the very beginning by means of a fraction placed before the first note, the numerator of which indicates the number of beats that there are to be in each measure, and the denominator, the kind of note which represents each beat. Thus, 2/4 has two quarter beats to a measure; 4/4, four quarter beats to a measure; 6/8, six eighth beats to a measure; 9/8, nine eighth beats to a measure, and so on.

MUSIC'S METER

This aspect of music's rhythmic structure may be called its *meter* [1] (or measure), since it is concerned with its division into units, called *measures,* each of which consists of a certain number of beats or pulses. The principal meters used in present-day music are:

2/4 meter: two beats to a measure, each a quarter note

2/2 meter: two beats to a measure, each a half note

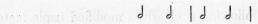

4/4 meter: four beats to a measure, each a quarter note, the accent

[1] This is often erroneously spoken of as *time;* the latter is not a musical term at all, but refers to "that which elapses while music is being played."

coming on the first and third beats, with the third-beat accent slightly
weaker than the first

3/4 meter: three beats to a measure, each a quarter note

♩ ♩ ♩ | ♩ ♩ ♩ |

3/2 meter: three beats to a measure, each a half note

𝅗𝅥 𝅗𝅥 𝅗𝅥 | 𝅗𝅥 𝅗𝅥 𝅗𝅥 |

3/8 meter: three beats to a measure, each an eighth note

♪ ♪ ♪ | ♪ ♪ ♪|

6/8 meter: six beats to a measure, each an eighth note, the accent
coming on the first and fourth beats, the fourth being slightly less accented than the first

♫♫ ♫♫ | ♫♫ ♫♫ |

9/8 meter: nine beats to a measure, each an eighth note, dividing itself into three groups of three eighth notes each

♫♫ ♫♫ ♫♫ | ♫♫ ♫♫ ♫♫ |

12/8 meter: twelve beats to a measure, each an eighth note, dividing
itself into four groups of three eighth notes each

♫♫ ♫♫ ♫♫ ♫♫ | ♫♫ ♫♫ ♫♫ ♫♫ |

It is possible, of course, to have 2, 3, or 4 beats in a measure with
any length of note as the unit; this note length may be simple
(divided into halves) or compound (divided into thirds). As can
readily be seen, the 6/8, 9/8, and 12/8 meters are illustrations of
this — multiples of simple meters with 2, 3, and 4 units in measures
that have internal divisions of thirds.

Such regular patterns of meter, when used with invariable regularity, lay the music open to the charge of being monotonous. So composers are apt to use various means for avoiding this monotony incurred by an overdose of regularly recurring down beats. One of the most popular of these is syncopation — the shifting of an accent in a measure, so that it does not come where we expect it naturally. For example, instead of having the accents in a measure occur according to the usual scheme, $\downarrow \smile \downarrow \smile | \downarrow \smile \downarrow \smile |$, we may have
$\smile \downarrow \smile \downarrow | \smile \downarrow \smile \downarrow |$; or instead of $\downarrow \smile \smile | \downarrow \smile \smile |$ we often have
$\smile \downarrow \smile | \smile \downarrow \smile |$, or even $\smile \smile \downarrow | \smile \smile \downarrow |$.

This device seems either to dull our rhythmic sense by confusing us as to where the strong pulse actually should come and thus gives a certain flagging or rhythmically dulled character to what we hear; or, by strongly stimulating our curiosity as to where the beat will fall, it heightens effect and makes the music that much more interesting. (*Vide* the feet of those listening to popular music, which contains so many interesting syncopated effects.) In passing it should be noted that, despite the belief generally held that syncopation is peculiar to contemporary popular music, it has been in wide use by composers since the time of the Renaissance. For a good illustration of this listen to the first movement of Beethoven's *Eroica Symphony*, measures 250 *et seq.*

Another device employed by composers, especially the more modern ones, to avoid monotony is that of inserting a measure or two of different metrical pattern into the regular flow of pulsation — of putting, for instance, a three-beat pattern into music that is regularly in two-beat measure. Tchaikovsky does this most effectively in the principal tune in his *Andante cantabile* from the *String Quartet*, Op. 11. (See page 229.) Composers from Debussy on have not hesitated to mix more or less indiscriminately the metrical pattern of their measures; in Debussy's *Afternoon of a Faun,* as we shall see, the meter fluctuates between 9/8, 6/8, 12/8, 3/4, and 4/4, and in Stravinsky's *Sacre du printemps* one page may contain as many as four metric patterns.

A new rhythm is sometimes superimposed over the regular one, a device often used by Brahms, in this fashion: $\frac{1\ 2\ 3 | 1\ 2\ 3}{1\ 2\ \ |\ 1\ 2}$.

Sometimes in these superimposed rhythms the first beats of the succeeding measures do not coincide; then we have an even more striking polyrhythmic effect, thus:

$$\left|\begin{array}{ccc} 1 & 2 & 3 \quad\quad 1 & 2 & 3 \\ \hline 1 & 2 \mid 1 & 2 \mid 1 & 2 \end{array}\right|.$$

This can be heard in good jazz music; over a fundamental, unchanging bass rhythm, the popular composer places freer rhythms, which often seem to play havoc with the underlying pulse of the piece. Again this is nothing new, for the same device was used, and very cleverly, too, by the scores of madrigal composers who flourished all over Europe before the time of Shakespeare; some of these madrigals contain most ingenious conflicts of meter between the various parts of which they are made up.

PRACTICE IN METER

The metrical pattern of a piece of music is comparatively easy to recognize, since this sort of rhythmic pulse is so largely physical and our response to it is almost a reflex action. Everyone can be taught to "keep time" to a metrical beat, even if some of the other fundamentals of music persist in escaping him. Here are some suggested examples for practice in determining the difference between duple, triple, quadruple, and sextuple meters. Hum or whistle the tunes, tapping out the heavy beats with a pencil or with your foot on the floor:

Old Black Joe
America (God Save the King)
Humoresque
Long, Long Ago
Abide With Me
Onward, Christian Soldiers
Sur le pont d'Avignon (On the Bridge at Avignon)
The Last Rose of Summer
Annie Laurie
O Tannenbaum (Maryland, My Maryland)
Ach! du lieber Augustin
Minuet in G by Paderewski

OTHER ASPECTS OF RHYTHM

It should not take much listening practice to make one realize that there are rhythmic schemes in music other than purely metrical ones. In other words, the recurrence of some readily recognized metrical pattern is not the only way by which the features of a musical conception may be organized so as to "produce a harmonious whole through the correlation and interdependence of its parts." (See the definition of *rhythm* at the bottom of the picture on this page.) There is, for example, the rhythm of note duration, which music imposes upon the underlying metrical scheme of

A Magnificent Example of Rhythm in Architecture

Rhythm is a characteristic common to all the fine arts. It may be defined as the regular recurrence of like features in an artistic composition, producing a harmonious whole through the correlation and interdependence of parts.

This is the south door of twelfth-century Kilpeck Church in Herefordshire, England.

a composition. We do not necessarily have a note for each beat of the meter; some notes are held for one or two beats, while often a beat is divided among several notes.[2]

In the familiar tune "Old Folks at Home," we can easily establish the underlying metrical pattern as being 4/4; but if we tap this out rhythmically while singing the melody, we shall find that the note values of the melody are in the following proportions:

The nature of these note values contributes another rhythmic scheme to the whole effect which we gain from listening to music and has a great deal to do with the impressions we receive.

Then there are other rhythmical designs in music, many of them intricate and difficult to hear, for they are made up of melodic and chordal features; these we may leave to the carefully trained expert to recognize and enjoy. The idea that several kinds of rhythmic schemes exist side by side in an art work may be difficult for the listener to grasp at first; but if we compare music with literature, which likewise has various types of rhythmic organization,[3] the realization may be made easier.

If we recite Housman's lines from "A Shropshire Lad," stressing the regular beats of the metrical scheme, we get the following:

With rue my heart is laden

For golden friends I had,

[2] Silence regarded as the mere absence of sound is an important factor in music; its length of duration is indicated by rests, which have values corresponding to the notes.

[3] In order to avoid confusion we should apply the term *rhythm* in general to the organizational schemes by which the various features of a piece of music or poetry are formed into an integral whole — the organization of tones of differing lengths, the subtleties of placing measure against measure, phrase against phrase, sentence against sentence. Meter should be used to describe that type of rhythm which is measured by dividing the flow of music or poetry into units made up of definite arrangements of pulses or beats.

For many a rose-lipt maiden

And many a light-foot lad.

Notice (1) that there is a certain rhythm in the line lengths —
lines 1 and 3 have four metrical units in them, but lines 2 and 4 only
three; (2) that in order to get the real sense of this verse we must
continue without pause (we must "phrase," as the technical term
has it) from line 1 into line 2 and from line 3 into line 4. Full comprehension of these lovely lines comes only when we combine,
when reading them, all the rhythmic elements they possess.

So, too, with music; it is made up of many subtle interactions of
the various rhythmic elements. This is easy enough to prove; listen
to these examples of 2/2 meter, all of them chosen from Beethoven's
scores. Notice how all the elements which go to make up the
rhythmic impression are responsible for the total effect you receive
from the music:

(1) *Eroica Symphony,* Second Movement (at the beginning). Here
the slow tempo (pace of the music) and the way the notes are grouped
in the measure give a solemn-heavy, funeral-march effect.

(2) *Seventh Symphony,* Second Movement. Here a quicker tempo
and a broad arrangement of the notes give an effect that is not so
overpowering and oppressive.

(3) *Fifth Symphony,* Fourth Movement. The dignified tempo and
the exultant melody combine to give a joyous, buoyant effect.

It is the same with 3/4 measure:

(1) Johann Strauss's waltz, "Tales from the Vienna Woods," or
any other good waltz, such as Tchaikovsky's from *The Nutcracker*
suite. The lively tempo and the enticing melodic patterns make us
want to dance.

(2) *Largo* by Handel. Here the slow tempo and the dignified arrangement of the notes give a sort of religious effect. If you look at the
melody carefully, you will find that only two measures of those which
contain more than one sound have the same rhythmic pattern. This
theme *grows.* In the hands of an ordinary patterer, measures 5–8
would probably have reproduced the lengths of measures 1–4. But

Handel was after real rhythm, and so he subtly varied his scheme. This subtlety is an essential part of musical form.

If further time allows, you will be interested in determining the metrical schemes of such examples as these:

March from *Tannhäuser*   Wagner
Mazurka in C Sharp Minor, Op. 63, No. 3   Chopin
Polonaise in B Flat Major, Op. 40, No. 1   Chopin
Minuet from *G Minor Symphony*   Mozart
Bolero   Ravel
Pavane pour une infante défunte
  (Pavan for a Dead Princess)   Ravel
Tango in A Minor   Albeniz

Enough suggestions have been given here to enable the hearer to realize how some recognition of the rhythmic structure of a piece of music will help his enjoyment. The important thing to remember is that in learning to listen, not everything can be grasped at once; a general conception of the rhythmic flow is all that is necessary for the amateur.

TOPICS FOR FURTHER DISCUSSION

Lovers of modern dance music often speak of it as "rhythmic music" as if to distinguish it from "classical" or "serious" music. But the first complaint of musicians against jazz is that it lacks rhythmic life. What do the musicians mean?

Is rhythm an end, or a means?

What is meant by "cross rhythms"? Find and discuss the use of cross rhythms in such composers as Brahms and Beethoven.

EIGHT

MEANS BY WHICH MATERIALS

ARE MADE INTO MUSIC (*continued*)

MELODY

If, as we have said, "in the beginning of music there was rhythm," the element of melody could not have been far behind; it is impossible to discuss one of these primary factors of present-day music without considering the other. Melody, which can be defined as a successive sounding of tones that are related to each other in such a way as to make musical sense and coherent expression, has an emotional significance in music, just as rhythm has a physical significance. Neither can be thought of as separate, disembodied entities, except in the most primitive music (such as the exciting examples brought to us from Africa by the recording companies); whenever we think of rhythm we think also of the shadow of the melody associated with it. You can easily prove this for your own satisfaction: try to think of the rhythm of even such a simple piece as "Old Folks at Home" or "Tales from the Vienna Woods," and you will find yourself humming the melody in order to do so. These two elements may be called the inseparable Siamese twins of music.

All compositions are made up of some sort of melodic and rhythmic patterns, repeated and varied in different ways throughout the course of the music. And so if we are to gain an adequate knowledge of the music we hear, it will be necessary for us to train ears and minds so that we become conscious of these musical *themes* and remember them. Such simple tunes as we have mentioned above are recognizable to us readily enough because we have heard them from our earliest days. But what about those others with which we are not familiar — those hundreds of themes or motives, sometimes only a few notes in length, sometimes several measures long, which occur in the compositions that are unknown to us — how are we to learn and remember these?

MEMORY HINTS

Here are some hints for assisting your memory in this respect:

(1) Notice the peculiarities of the melodic flow, whether, for instance, it is limited, as is the case of this theme from the slow movement of Beethoven's *Seventh Symphony* (the interest here is almost entirely rhythmic):

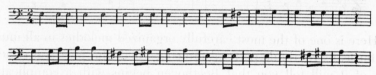

Or whether it skips about more or less adroitly, as in these two examples from Mozart's *G Minor Symphony,* first movement:

(2) See whether the quality of the melody is essentially vocal or instrumental — whether it was meant to be sung or played.

Such a theme as this, from Beethoven's *Ninth Symphony,* first movement, is obviously instrumental in style, its wide range and great leaps making it almost impossible to be sung:

The following theme, from Verdi's *Rigoletto,* was, on the other hand, meant for singing:

Such themes as that from Handel's opera *Xerxes,* quoted on page 91, or from Schubert's *Unfinished Symphony,* first movement (page 99), or Dvořák's *New World Symphony,* second movement (page 218) are suitable for either playing or singing. They are naturals in this respect, a fact which accounts for their unusual popularity.

(3) Observe the characteristic rhythmic patterns of the themes.

The theme from Beethoven's *Seventh Symphony,* quoted on page 93, has a rather monotonous rhythm — probably Beethoven intended this in order to emphasize its quality. But notice the rhythmic vitality of this melody from Mozart's *G Minor Symphony:*

Here is one of the most carefully organized melodies in all music, so far as its rhythmic patterns are concerned. But even a first hearing of it will tell you that Beethoven begins with a complicated, "dotted" rhythm and then follows with a broad, simple one:

(4) Take notice of the *scale* or *scales* used by the composer in forming his melody. As suggested by the meaning of the Italian *scala* (a staircase), a scale may be said to be the pattern according to which the octave is divided into a specific succession of tonal steps. There can be a wide diversity in these scale patterns; a famous theoretician has said that it it possible to construct a hundred scales within the tonal space of an octave. Fortunately for the listener, only a few of these are in practical use, evolved out of grouping together certain formulas common to melodies through the ages; but it is important for everyone who listens to music to

know something about these scales, for on their structure depend the character, expressive quality, and style of the melodies and harmonies he hears.

According to our Western music system, the smallest interval used in its scales is the half tone or semitone — the tonal distance between B and C, or E and F on the piano, for example. Twice this tonal distance we call a whole tone — the interval between C and D, or F and G are good examples. Most of present-day scales consist of these intervals arranged in varying combinations. The much-used major scale consists of the following series, making up the octave: tone, tone, half tone, tone, tone, tone, half tone. If we go to the piano and, starting from C, use this formula, we will hear what we call the major scale of C: (C), D, E, F, G, A, B, C. Starting from any key, the same order of sequence may be used. It will be found necessary to use the black keys occasionally, in order to keep the proper sequence of tones and half tones. Thus we have the major scales of D, E, F, G, etc. Much of the music we know well is written in one of these major scales; the use of this pattern gives a bright, rather full and cheerful character to the music, as is evident from this major tune, taken from Haydn's *Surprise Symphony*, second movement:

Further along in the same movement, Haydn uses the tune in this fashion:

Here he uses a minor scale, based on the following tonal pattern: tone, half tone, tone, tone, half tone, tone and a half, half tone. Thus, starting from C, we get this progression: (C), D, E flat, F, G, A flat, B, C, which is called the *harmonic minor* scale, largely used in instrumental music, in distinction to another (called the *melodic minor*) devised in order to avoid the interval of a tone and a half, which is difficult to sing. The melodic minor has a different arrangement ascending and descending, in order to give a smooth progression.

Ascending:

	TONE	HALF TONE	TONE	TONE	TONE	TONE	HALF TONE
(C)	D	E flat	F	G	A	B	C

Descending:

	TONE	TONE	HALF TONE	TONE	TONE	HALF TONE	TONE
(C)	B flat	A flat	G	F	E flat	D	C

To most ears, the use of the minor scale gives a somber or melancholy tinge to the music, although this distinction is by no means universal, for many lively tunes have been written in minor in some countries. Here is a further example of a minor melody:

The major and minor scales determined much of the dance and song type of music of the seventeenth, eighteenth, and nineteenth centuries. Later on came the wide use of the *chromatic* (highly colored) scale, which comprises in succession all the twelve available semitones into which the octave is divided. This gives to music a peculiarly agitated, gliding, questioning, sensuous character, well suited to the needs of the Romantic period.

A good example of the use of the chromatic scale is:

Rimsky-Korsakoff
Sadko

The *pentatonic* scale, with its familiar gaps and jumps, makes use of only five tones (instead of seven) in the octave. There are many patterns of this, the easiest to find on the keyboard being that of the five black keys, starting from the lowest of the three-group. This gives F sharp, G sharp, A sharp, C sharp, D sharp, (F sharp). If we transfer this pattern to the white keys, starting on C, we have C, D, E, G, A, (C). This scale seems to satisfy the needs of simple as well as sophisticated peoples, for it is known to all music systems, both Eastern and Western, and it is responsible for much of the charm and exotic character which we associate with the music of distant lands. Chinese, Indonese, Javanese, Scottish, Russian melodies all use it. Here are two simple examples:

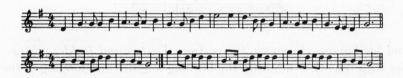

Out of the Oriental music which he heard, Debussy devised a six-tone scale comprising six whole tones in the octave, thus: C, D, E, F sharp, G sharp, A sharp, C. This scale, which has a peculiarly exotic character, gives much of the color to such things as *L'Après-midi d'un faune* and other works of Debussy's. It is found, however, in a rudimentary form in Liszt and other nineteenth-century composers. Example:

This is a good place to note the fact that Indian and other Asiatic music makes use of scales that are composed of intervals smaller than the semitone: quarter tones, eighth tones, etc. These have no place in European music and cannot be reproduced on many of our instruments or indicated by our ordinary system of notation.

If a melody stays for most of its existence in the chromatic scale, we call it a *chromatic* melody; on the other hand, if it does not stray from its major or minor outlines, we speak of it as being *diatonic*. There is almost as much difference between music that is based largely on chromatic melodies and that which is diatonic in character as there is between major and minor melodies. Chromatic tunes are bland and lush; in comparison, diatonic ones seem severe and plain. Compare, for example, Rimsky-Korsakoff's well-known "Song of India" with the melody quoted on page 95 from Haydn's *Surprise*

Symphony, and you will quickly hear this difference. Or notice the difference in effect (carefully calculated by the composer) between such diatonic themes of Wagner's as that of "The Sword" from *The Ring of the Nibelung*

and his famous chromatic theme from *Tristan und Isolde,* portraying with relentless intensity the burning anguish and longing of the two famous lovers:

Here is one of the most famous short themes in all music, and no better or more appealing example of how melodies are wrought into larger wholes could be found. This gives us a definite illustration of the fact that one of the best means for getting an "ear-hold" upon music is through learning to recognize good melodies, and then listening to hear how the composer builds his musical fabric out of them. This little germ is at the basis of nearly all the Prelude to Wagner's opera *Tristan und Isolde.*

(5) Finally, listen carefully to the characteristic tone quality of the instrument or instruments producing the melody. Try to memorize themes *in their instrumental timbres;* an oboe theme, for example, stays in the memory longer if we can remember it as being played on the oboe and not just as a succession of notes.

We have already discussed this matter of *timbre* at some length; here we simply remind the listener that the ability to distinguish "tone color" (this phrase is used because no better one is available) or quality of the various instruments and voices singly and in combination is one of the most obvious pleasures to be derived from listening.

PRACTICE IN MELODY

Here are some fine melodies on which to practice. Get them firmly fixed in your mind and then notice the way they are used by the composer in building up a larger organized piece; you will realize the necessity of holding fast to melodic units when listening to music:

Although consisting of but two different notes, this motive can be easily remembered because of its strong rhythmic pattern; it is the first theme (or melody) of the opening part of Beethoven's *Fifth Symphony* and might be in either major or minor mode, according to the harmonies that are used with it. Beethoven uses it here as a minor melody.

This beautiful, longer melody in the major mode is the second theme of the same movement of the *Fifth Symphony:*

Listen to the whole movement and you will hear how it is built up largely of manipulations of these two germ themes.

Here is a still longer melody, but one that is easily remembered, nevertheless. It is a theme from the first movement of Schubert's *Unfinished Symphony* and is in the minor; notice that the third and fourth measures are exactly the same as the first two measures:

The next theme of the same movement is one of the best-known melodies in existence:

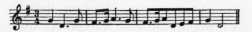

Listen to the movement as a whole, and you will hear these two tunes used constantly throughout.

In this famous tune from the first section of Grieg's first *Peer Gynt* suite there is so much repetition that it stays easily in the mind:

The whole piece will give you a fine idea of how music can logically grow out of a short, simple melody.

HARMONY

It is a common practice to use the word *harmony* to mean a pleasing concord or a musical consonance; so it will be necessary at the beginning of our discussion of this, the most sophisticated of the elements of music, to say that the musician uses the word in a different way. We may define *harmony* as the simultaneous sounding of tones as opposed to their successive sounding in melody. Both melody and harmony use the same materials: melody gives contour and color to the structure, and harmony provides it with body and substance. Although we must here treat these factors individually, melody, harmony, and rhythm are interdependent in actual practice. The detailed consideration of harmony is hardly a matter for the amateur listener, although he can readily enough realize that most of the music he hears is dependent upon harmony for its effect. Harmonic support is given melody through the forming and connecting of simultaneous clusters of tone that we call *chords,* and the science of harmony consists of a study of the ways in which these chords are built and related to one another. There are many tonal combinations that can be formed by putting together clusters of three, four, five, sometimes even as many as six and seven notes; these progress and come to rest according to certain grammatical laws common to the language of music.

If you listen to the overture to Wagner's *Tannhäuser,* you will quickly realize that the effect of the opening strains is due as much to the chords that Wagner uses as to the suitable rhythm and the impressive melody. When the change of mood comes in the middle of the overture, you will notice that the type of harmony changes as well. How much of the broad effect that we receive from Handel's *Largo* is due to the fine, straightforward, majestic chords employed! A review of the excerpts already quoted as illustrations of melodies and rhythms will show how much the chords employed in each example contribute to our interest in the music. Perhaps the most striking example of this is the Schubert melody, quoted on page 99. Hearing it alone gives us a great deal of pleasure, but when we put chords beneath it, it seems almost like another thing in the fullness of its beauty.

In general when the chords used in a composition conform to the major or the minor scale, we say that the piece is "in the major" or "in the minor." When the chords used are built out of the tones of the chromatic scale, the harmonization is said to be *chromatic;* or if the notes used keep in the diatonic scale, we speak of the chords as being *diatonic.* In the *Tannhäuser* overture the opening measures are in diatonic harmony; the middle section is decidedly chromatic in its harmonization.

Certain harmonic units, such as the chord usually found at the very end of a composition, are static and reposeful; we call these chords *consonances.* Others, used to provide impetus and zest to music, are not static, but restless and unfinished, and require some other chord to follow them and complete them. These we call *dissonances;* and the process of finishing a dissonant chord by a consonant one is called *resolution.* As music has advanced through the centuries, composers have turned more and more to the dissonant type of harmony. The music of a composer of as late a period as the eighteenth century consists largely of consonant harmonies, with occasional dissonances used to spice it up and heighten its interest. The process is almost exactly reversed in the music of almost all of the twentieth-century composers.

TONALITY

Even the briefest consideration of music from the viewpoint of its harmonic context must include a mention of *tonality,* one of the most subtle and yet powerful assets of the art. Practically all the music we hear (except that of some contemporary composers) is in one "key" or another; by this we mean that the notes which comprise our tonal system are grouped in specific sets of relationships to a tone which serves them as a sort of axis — a tone from which the movement within each of these sets of relationships (called *keys*) starts and to which it returns as a final resting place. This tone is the keynote or tonic. Since any one of the twelve tones within the octave can serve as a tonic, the composer has at his disposal twelve different tonal planes in which to write his music. Suppose he chooses one — that of the key of C, for example; he may decide to write music composed of melodies and chords that use the major scale which begins on that tonic, as Beethoven did in his *First Symphony,* or he may write music using the minor scale starting on that tonic, as Beethoven did in his *Fifth Symphony.*[1]

[1] In the case of large works such as symphonies, sonatas, and quartets, the tonality is determined by the prevailing key of the first movement — thus we have Beethoven's symphonies in C major and C minor, in E-flat major, in B-flat major, and so on.

And so with all the other tones within the octave — C sharp, D, D sharp, and the rest: each can serve as a tonic for either a major or a minor scale and, since each of these scales has its own set of tonal relationships and its own groups of chords, composers have twenty-four tonal levels on which to erect their music — twenty-four keys, twelve major and twelve minor. When we speak of the tonality or the key of a piece, then, we describe (1) its specific tonal level; that is, the tonic around which its tonal structure is centered; and (2) the set of tonal relationships (the scale or the mode) which generally prevails. The title of Bach's *Suite No. 1 in C Major* means simply that its prevailing tonality centers around C as a tonic and that the scales, chords, melodies, and so on which go to make up its fabric are in the major mode. His second suite, on the other hand, centers about B as a tonic (its pitch level is thus half a tone lower than that of the first suite), and it is written in the minor mode. When Bach wrote the two great collections of clavier music which comprise his *Well-Tempered Clavier,* he deliberately used each of the twelve major and twelve minor keys as tonics for the pieces, thus making a total of twenty-four in each collection.

This may seem intricate enough to the amateur listener, but it is not all that he should learn about the subject of tonality. For pieces have tonality not only as wholes but also in parts; in other words, a composer does not keep to the same tonality (or, putting it into other words, does not keep in the same key) throughout the course of a piece. He purposely uses changes of key (called *modulations*) to hold and increase the interest as the music progresses; a simple song usually contains several of these key changes, and a great work, such as a Beethoven or a Brahms symphony, contains scores of them. The constant shifting of tonal levels, now lower, now higher, intrigues our interest as we listen to a long work much the same way that a hiker's progress up and down a mountain affects his appreciation of the view that greets his eye as he walks. In each case the general impression received is not altered, but the continual change of points of view gives renewed interest and freshened enthusiasm.

In the case of the composer, these modulations must be skillfully and effectively wrought; any violent or awkward change from one key to another is liable to destroy rather than create interest. And it is a tribute to the technical skill of the great composers that most of us, in listening to their music, are quite unaware that such changes are taking place until they are pointed out to us. We have been affected by them unconsciously; they have increased our enjoyment of the music and heightened our imaginative realization of its content; and yet they have been so unobtrusively accomplished that we probably never knew they existed. Any attempt which the listener may make to realize the manner in which a composer takes him on these tonal adventures cannot but increase his enjoyment of the music he hears. It may be difficult to follow all the devious paths and windings; that is hardly necessary. Just to realize what is happening adds zest to listening.

TOPICS FOR FURTHER DISCUSSION

It is charged against some modern works that they lack melody. Their defenders reply that melody formerly meant simply a familiar succession of sounds and that, as modern music presents unfamiliar successions, the old definition will not do. Is there a better one?

How did our present-day conceptions of harmony originate? Do you think that these are final, or will they eventually change?

What are some of the values in the ability to follow changes of tonality in a piece of music? Name any particular instances of changing tonality which give you special pleasure.

HOW DOES THE COMPOSER WORK?

Everyone who has come under the spell of a great picture, a powerful novel, or a moving piece of music has wondered at some time or other what it was that impelled the painter or the writer or the composer to create — what there was about an artist that made him so different from his fellow men that he could paint as El Greco did, or compose as did Bach and Beethoven. Granting that such creative artists are endowed by nature with certain abilities which, when trained, enable them to excel their fellows in the technical procedures of putting ideas into paint or onto music paper, does this fact in any real way explain the qualities of such a picture as *The Penitent St. Peter,* painted by El Greco, or the glories of Bach's *B Minor Mass* and Beethoven's *Eroica Symphony?* What constrained the artist to bring such things into being; how was he able to give his work the meaning it has for us; what were the processes of his creation? These are the sorts of questions the amateur is likely to ask as he becomes more and more familiar with art.

THE CREATOR A UNIQUE FIGURE

Such questions are not easy to answer. The first thing we must realize, in trying to arrive at some explanation of the way in which a creative artist "out of nothing brings a world into being," is how far apart such an individual is from those about him. He is no ordinary man, merely interested in the world as it appears to his senses; rather is he one who searches for significance in the scheme of life. He gathers the subject matter for his painting or his music partly from his own experience as a sensitive member of human society, partly through his sympathetic observation of the actions and reactions of such a society. His greatest endowment — outside that of technical aptitude — is his imaginational ability to extend and develop his own experiences, which necessarily are limited and fragmentary. Such a power, in itself, gives the creator an insight into human experience that is far superior to any participation he may have had at first hand. It explains El Greco's ability to project so vividly St. Peter's suppliant hope of forgiveness, or Beethoven's powerful concept of man the hero, bestriding the narrow world like a colossus.

Courtesy of The Fine Arts Society of San Diego

EL GRECO: *The Penitent St. Peter*

The penitence of the Apostle who denied his Lord was a favorite subject of the great Greek painter. This picture shows St. Peter awakening, as from a dream of despair. Hope for his forgiveness fills him with ecstasy, and reaches him, in the form of spiritual light, even after he had denied his Master, who had presented him with the keys of Heaven.

Most of us are too closely concerned with life and its difficulties and joys to see things in perspective: we lack imagination to link what we experience today with what we have experienced in the past or what will follow after. Such specialists as the scientist and the historian are too far removed from realities to sense, or even comprehend, the quality and purport of life. The artist is the only one who seems able to see life steadily and as a whole, who is able to look at it as a "human being and yet not merely as a single individual, with passionate intensity, yet with dispassionate lucidity." This is what we mean when we say that men such as El Greco and Beethoven were inspired when they painted or composed; there is something in their best work — something put there by their very attributes as artists — that far transcends technical achievements or artistic proficiencies. And it is this that distinguished them from their less fortunately endowed fellows.

Most professional artists would probably deny that they have any such spiritual bases for creation. A contemporary American musician [1] has put himself on record as saying that to a composer composing is like fulfilling any other natural function such as eating or sleeping: he composes because he feels that he has been born for the job — because he can't help it. Of course, he adds, after the thing is done, everyone, especially the composer, hopes that it will turn out to have been "inspired." But that is really an idea that is tacked on at the end.

This is true enough, so far as generalities go, as everyone who has had any experience with creative workers must acknowledge. As a rule, artists do not sit around waiting for the divine afflatus; they turn to their creative tasks, whatever they may be, day after day, simply doing the best job of which they are capable. The difference between the great and the minor painter or composer is that the great artist, once the creative process is started, is likely to produce something of real significance to the world because of his greater sympathy with its experiences and his keener imaginative ability to extend and develop these sympathies — in a word, because of his ability to "apprehend the man in men." In so far as the actual physical processes of creation are concerned, the great men do not differ from those who merely produce competent work. A casual

---

[1] Aaron Copland in his book *What to Listen for in Music* (New York: McGraw-Hill).

examination of such physical processes can give the listener a great deal of information that will be of value to him in criticizing the music he hears.

VARIOUS COMPOSER TYPES

We have to face the fact, at the beginning of such an examination, that there can be no such being as a typical composer and no such thing as a regularly followed method of composing. There have been some composers — only a few — who have written music as if they had been possessed of some Apollonic daemon. Music simply welled out of their consciousness as water from a spring; their greatest difficulty seems to have been that of finding time enough to put it on paper. For them there were few problems of choice or arrangement of materials; whole works seem to have been spontaneously created in their minds with little or no conscious effort on their part. We have evidence of such prolific spontaneity on the part of two of the greatest of all composers, Mozart and Schubert, who must always remain as the outstanding examples of the inspired composer, writing music because nothing else in life seemed important or necessary.

Then there are those who have labored carefully and long over their works, starting with a few germinal ideas and painstakingly weaving them into an imposing and closely designed musical fabric. Beethoven may be cited as the characteristic example of this type; most of the outstanding men since his time — such composers as Brahms, Wagner, Strauss, for instance — have followed his example in this respect. The record shows that Beethoven was busy with his *C Minor Symphony* for a period of over five years, and that it took Brahms over twenty to write his great symphony in the same key [2]; naturally both men were busy with other things at the same time.

Some composers have given very little thought to any sort of constructive process: they simply took traditional patterns which had become well established by the time they arrived on the musical scene and used them to suit their own purpose. The composers of the Renaissance — such men as Byrd, Di Lasso, and Palestrina — used only the patterns and formal molds of their time, the motet,

[2] An early draft of Brahms's *C Minor Symphony* dates from 1850; the work was finished in 1876.

The Way from the Imagination of the Painter to the Image

These sketches are excellent examples of the manner in which Michelangelo evolved the various sections of his great mural painting on the ceiling of the Sistine Chapel in Rome. Compare these sketches for the figure of the Libyan Sibyl with the finished painting. Then contrast this method of painting with that of Winslow Homer, the American artist, who, in painting his water color of a West Indian scene, obviously did so without any hesitation, putting his idea on paper as quickly as possible.

mass, madrigal. And Bach, when he started on the tremendous project of writing the forty-eight preludes and fugues in his *Well-Tempered Clavier,* or the Brandenburg concertos, did not depart from the accepted models of his time.

However, there have been other pioneering spirits who, dissatisfied with things as they found them and with the musical styles in which they had been reared, revolted, often at the expense of the quality of their music. In different centuries, Monteverdi, Berlioz, Debussy, and Schönberg are examples of this type of composer who has opposed conventional ways of doing things and who has sought, through experimenting with new resources, to develop a different, nonconformist type of writing. Naturally such a man's method of working would differ greatly from that of the traditionalists.

The Libyan Sybil

FIRST, THE IDEA

But there are certain fundamental practices common to all composers; the first of these is getting started. How is the creative process actually begun? A famous old recipe for rabbit pie, written in the days when meat was not so plentiful as it is today, starts with the admonition: first, you must catch your rabbit. Similar advice must be followed by every composer who would set about concocting tonal delicacies. All compositions, whether they are short or long, whether they are traditional or experimental, start with a musical idea [3]; perhaps it first occurs to the composer in the shape of a melody that he can hum to himself, or a rhythmic pattern, sometimes merely as a suggestion for an accompaniment. Whatever it is, or however it may come, this theme (the name we give to such a musical idea) is the real *germ* out of which the composer later

[3] Sometimes these ideas come to the composer in the most incongruous circumstances. It was the Austrian composer, Bruckner, who, pointing out the theme of a movement in one of his symphonies, is said to have remarked that it had come to him on a picnic, just as he was unwrapping the sandwiches.

fashions his whole piece. It is, as Copland rightly says, a "gift from Heaven which comes almost like automatic writing"; the composer has no control over it except to write it down as quickly and as accurately as he can, adding it to his collection of similar items.

Obviously an important part of the composer's creation of such a musical theme is his evaluation of it in what might be called both its emotional and its musical terms. He is aware of its emotional value instinctively, realizing whether or not it provides the starting point for, or helps to develop, the type of human expression with which he is concerned at the moment. He examines it as music, noting its outline, its possibility for later "development," perhaps altering it here and there so that it may better fulfill his musical requirements. It may be that he is quite unconscious of the process, but the composer, once his thematic material has been revealed to him, immediately sets out to determine its nature and then to see what can be done with it.

Courtesy of The Metropolitan Museum of Art

WINSLOW HOMER: *"Tornado" — Water Color*

It may be that a theme carries with it some emotional suggestion which the composer feels called upon to develop; it may well be the other way about, that some sort of emotional background was realized first, and that out of it there came the musical idea; or it may be that the whole creative process took place on a largely formal plane, the composer thinking of his music as music, without paying much attention to its expressive values. There are examples of all three of these different processes of composing. The sketches left by Beethoven may be interpreted to show that many of his themes came to him in a purely musical form, and that such expressive ideas as those dealing with the "awful powers of Fate and ending with a triumph song of the human will" were evolved afterwards, during his long struggle with his material. We know, on the other hand, that in such works as Richard Strauss's *Don Juan* and *Don Quixote* the whole of the extramusical program was achieved first, and that out of it came the musical material. And it is difficult to believe that Bach had anything in mind other than the formal manipulation of his material when composing some of his great works.

It is impossible to know whether the composer decides as to the medium that he will employ — whether he will write a string quartet, a symphony, an opera, or a piano sonata — before or after the time he catches his musical rabbit; that is, conceives his thematic material. Here again we have conflicting evidence. Instead of pondering as to whether his theme belongs in a symphony or in a string quartet, many a composer has evolved his themes directly for some work he had in mind. No other medium than the opera could ever have been intended for the delineative themes that Wagner created; he evolved them for particular dramatic purposes. Schubert's lyric melodies were, for the most part, conceived as songs, with no thought of their being used in any other medium. On the other hand, we have Brahms hesitating whether to use the thematic materials which finally went into his first piano concerto, in a sonata for two pianos, a symphony, or a concerto. Some of the most effective thematic material in Bach's great choral work, the *B Minor Mass,* had been used by him in earlier works, sometimes in quite a different medium [4]; his contemporary, Handel, did not hesitate to lift themes from his own works — and sometimes from those of another composer — whenever they seemed to fill some particular need of the moment.

Generally speaking, however, the composer has little trouble in satisfying himself as to either the inherent value or the essential

[4] The theme of the *Osanna,* for instance, was originally used in a composition written as a welcome song to Bach's monarch, the King of Saxony.

quality of the ideas he has conceived. Once he has decided what he is going to write, his immediate problem is what to do with his thematic material, for, significant and suggestive as it may seem, it is far from being a piece of music. How is he going to spin it out into a composition that will last anywhere from several minutes (in the case of a song) to an hour (in the case of a symphony) or to several hours (in the case of an opera)?

PRINCIPLES OF DESIGN

In following the conventional ways of accomplishing this, the composer instinctively uses certain principles of design which are the foundation of all good art. If we examine any outstanding art work — a finely designed building, a beautifully executed painting, a good piece of sculpture, a poem or a drama that has survived through the centuries — we shall find certain general principles of design that control the use of its structural elements. The creator may have followed these principles of design consciously or intuitively: the one thing for us to realize is that he did follow them. The most important of these principles are:

1. *Repetition,* usually according to some rhythmic scheme
2. The dominance of some particular feature of design and the subordination of others, so as to secure *Unity in Variety*
3. *Balance* or *Symmetry,* by means of which the various elements are held together and yet synthesized and organized into a harmonious whole

No definite rule or formula can be given for the use of these, or any other, artistic principles. But there exists within us a certain innate sense for good design, which, if we cultivate it, will grow into a power of discrimination of which we can be strongly conscious. We all react, for example, to these structural principles as they have been exemplified in the Parthenon, a religious temple built on the Acropolis at Athens, after plans by Ictinus and Callicrates: we instinctively know that this must have been a *good* building. Even today, some twenty-four hundred years after it was built, this magnificent structure still holds our attention and arouses our enthusiasm.

Notice the rhythm of the repeated vertical columns; the builders definitely established this sense of verticality as the dominant feature of their building; but see how carefully they used it in contrast to the horizontal lines above and below the repeated upright columns. The manner in which the various structural details are balanced and symmetrized, each having its part in the harmony of the whole, shows how keenly sensitive to beauty the Greeks were, and how highly developed were their tastes.

Courtesy of The Metropolitan Museum of Art

The Ruined Parthenon

The composer, if he wishes to create a musical work of lasting value, pays careful attention to the same schemes of design. The principle of repetition is essential to any real intelligibility in music: in such a transitory art, the listeners must have certain features that can be grasped easily and recognized pleasurably. If you are inclined to doubt this, listen to some easily followed popular song, or to such a composition as Gershwin's *Rhapsody in Blue,* and see how many times certain themes and phrases [5] are repeated. This device of repetition is not confined to simple or popular music, however; composers of all sorts and in all periods have woven their musical fabrics out of a repetition and diversification of some melodic,

[5] By *phrase* in music we mean certain melodic "sentences" which belong together and which come to a natural pause at their end; they are usually discernible by such exterior means as the number of measures they contain and the symmetry of their harmonic background.

harmonic, or rhythmic pattern.[6] While not many of them have gone to the lengths of Bruckner, who, in the scherzo of his *Eighth Symphony*, repeats the same pattern dozens of times, this device of repetition must always remain one of the composer's most useful assets. In the case of music, as has been well said, variety may be the spice of its life, but repetition is its bread and butter.

Every intelligent listener to good music has realized that there are certain dominant elements that stand out clearly in the musical fabric, that certain themes are emphasized and others added to complement or supplement them. These secondary themes may contrast strongly with the original ideas, or they may carry them along to final completion. Since the composer cannot jump abruptly from one theme to another, he has learned to make use of certain subordinate passages which he calls "bridge passages" — carefully designed links which carry the listener almost imperceptibly from one main idea to another. The beautifully constructed bridge material linking the first and second themes in the first movement of Beethoven's *Fifth Symphony* is a case in point.

Still another device at the disposal of the composer for this purpose is what we call *development*, something that is difficult to describe in words, although it can be recognized readily enough when heard. Listen to the middle section (that immediately following the double bar) of the Beethoven first movement just mentioned, and you will find that the composer views his original theme in a number of different aspects and puts it through a number of metamorphoses; this is the development, a logical and almost inevitable process that, when well used, adds greatly to our listening enjoyment. We shall have more to say about this later on.

There are a number of different ways by which the composer may obtain balance and symmetry of design in his music. In fact, the musical *forms* — such as the fugue, the sonata form, the theme and variations — about which we have so much to tell later, are simply convenient and well-tried devices for achieving this end. They have changed throughout the centuries and are still in process of evolution; they have been variously used by different composers,

[6] Here are some striking and easily recognized instances of musical repetition of one kind or another:
Drink to Me Only with Thine Eyes
Preludes in A Major, C Minor, and E Minor, Op. 28, by Chopin
Opening movement, *Appassionata Sonata*, by Beethoven

but they all help to solve the same problem, that of attaining good balance and effective symmetry.

All these devices must be used by the composer in such a way as to secure an intelligent and pleasurable whole. This is where the skill of the composer comes in, in this welding together of disparate elements according to the structural principles of good design. He does not necessarily follow any rules, but he must so order his music that the listener can find his way around in it, can realize at any given moment what is going on. The piece, no matter how long it may be, should proceed logically from its beginning to its end; there should be a sense of relation of parts that leaves no room for confusion in the hearer's mind; and the music should be so cunningly put together as to show none of the seams by which its parts are joined, to use Tchaikovsky's picturesque phrase. Above all else there must be, in Mahler's words, "abundance and continuous *flow* if the music is to be any good." This all sounds easy enough in the telling; as a matter of fact, it is tremendously difficult of achievement, and upon it depends to a large degree the real quality and staying powers of a composer's output.

TOPICS FOR FURTHER DISCUSSION

Novelists have described their various methods of composition; for example, some think first of a plot, some of the idiosyncrasies of character in their figures; others build around a dramatic situation or a single scene. Are these processes paralleled in music?

Discuss the possible influence of *place* on composition.

Find elements of unity and variety in any simple compositions you may study.

Compare development in a symphonic movement with that in a novel or a play, either generally or with specific instances in mind.

Compare unity-plus-variety in a musical work with the same elements in a familiar picture or piece of sculpture.

NINE

OUR WAY OF APPROACH

ART AND LANGUAGE

A poetic critic, Romain Rolland, has said that music can be all things to all men: tonal architecture in certain centuries and among certain peoples; design, line, and plastic beauty to such nations as have cultivated a sense of form — to painters and sculptors like the Italians; an intimate poetry, a lyric efflux, a philosophical meditation to a poetic and philosophical nation such as the Germans; an *art de cœur,* gallant and graceful to Francis I or Charles IX; a weapon of faith and combat to reformers such as Martin Luther; a matter of princely pride and royal pomp to kings such as Louis XIV; an art of the salon during the eighteenth century; a lyric expression of tremendous personalities during the nineteenth. It is obviously not only an art but a language, capable of expressing widely divergent ideas and conceptions, including those generally regarded as belonging to the spheres of the other arts.

MUSIC'S WORLD OF THE SPIRIT

A moment's reflection, however, will show us that music has its own distinct province and that while it perhaps can go as far as embodying moral ideas, it expresses some things much better than others. Its great strength lies in depicting emotions rather than thoughts, in realizing intangible moods rather than concrete forms, in depicting ideality rather than reality, and, most of all, in appealing to the spirit rather than to the senses.

We readily follow a great man like Beethoven when his music stirs our emotions as it does in the *Fifth Symphony.* But we are not so sure of him, or of ourselves, when he places mottoes like *Tantôt libre, tantôt recherché,* or *Muss es sein? — es muss sein* at the beginning of certain movements in his last quartets as if he would convey some metaphysical concept in his music. We quickly respond to the melancholy brooding of Tchaikovsky in his *Symphonie pathétique,* or to the alluring Eastern colors of Rimsky-Korsakoff's *Scheherazade,* or to the healthy vigor of Brahms's *First Symphony;* but it is more difficult for us to realize the comparatively simple structural design of these compositions, and thus to appreciate their architectural proportions. We seem ready to follow Schubert as he describes for us *The Wanderer's* search for a home, but we are more reluctant to trail Honegger's locomotive, *Pacific 231,* as it snorts and groans in its attempts at realism. Wagner, who wrote that great series of operas, *The Ring of the Nibelung,* and Debussy in his tone poem *L'Après-midi d'un faune* appeal mightily to our spirits, but it will seem difficult for many of us to get "sense" from these works.

Furthermore, music possesses a distinction from its associated arts in that it is so largely independent of exterior associations, this very fact constituting one of its chief glories, or its most confusing difficulties, according to our point of view. By comparison the static arts are easier of comprehension. No matter how imaginative the treatment, in order to convey his meaning the painter, architect, or sculptor commonly uses means that are closely associated with the consciously experienced world. Even literature, which comes closest to music as a means for emotional and imaginative suggestiveness, must use a medium closely associated with everyday life — that of language.

Everyone knows the familiar story of Turner, the English artist, and the woman who told him that she had never seen such sunsets as he painted. "No, but don't you wish you could?" was certainly the right answer to such a statement. Music does not even need to try to explain the lack of such relationships. Although it works with two familiar yet intangible factors, rhythm and sound, it uses them for the most part in ways entirely different from those in which they occur in nature. The combination of these elements in music affects our senses in ways different from those of the other arts, ways which we hardly understand and which have no counterparts in our other emotional experiences. And they make of music a peculiarly dynamic art; instead of allowing it to be examined at any length, they cause it to rush precipitately at us, sometimes with the passionate eloquence of a great orator, sometimes with almost intangible persuasiveness. But in any case it is gone beyond recall almost before we are conscious of its having existed, and must be re-created before we can again be aware of its qualities.

PROGRAM MUSIC

Various types of music differ in their extra-musical associations. All of us can remember music which definitely imitates sounds such as bird-calls, storms, and so on, and many an older musician has in his listening career suffered under the "storms" of the sensational organ player's making. That such definite imitations of nature are not necessarily the resort of cheap musicians only is shown by the fact that no less a composer than Beethoven makes use of these very devices; in his *Pastoral Symphony* we find the mood of the music heightened by a musical suggestion of a peaceful brook rippling over the stones, the calls of various birds, the growling of the thunderstorm. We all know that certain sounds definitely suggest certain states of mind to us; in fact, these sounds may induce these states of mind. The hunt is suggested, for example, by the sound of the horn as it is heard at the beginning of the second act of Wagner's *Tristan und Isolde*. In the last section of Liszt's rather oversensational *Les Préludes*, the blare of brass, delivered in all the enthusiasm of this composer's style, excites us to martial ardor. The plaintive longing of the English horn, wonderfully expressed in the shepherd's tune at the beginning of the last act of *Tristan und Isolde*, awakens our consciousness to an answering mood of brooding melancholy. Many other similar examples could easily be cited. And so a composer, using these means and coupling them with the various devices of composition, may easily give music an extraneous implication, may make it set forth a sequence of pictures, tell a story, or what you will. This kind of music having connection with something outside itself we know as *program music*.

Here comes in again the consideration as to the composer's working within the natural limitations of his material, a matter discussed earlier; for program music does require an intellectual approach. Since tone, the natural sensuous element of music, does have duration in time, it would seem aesthetically justifiable to relate, by means of a "program," what is happening at any particular moment in the music to what has already happened and to that which is going to happen in the future. Provided — and this is the crux of the whole matter — the composer can convey the objective quality demanded by the program of the music itself. In other words, in works inspired by a literary association, if the music as music (and not because of its intellectual program) communicates to us a conception of inherent beauty and organic unity, our enjoyment of it cannot be questioned, even on the strictest aesthetic grounds. For this reason, Beethoven's *Eroica Symphony* in memory of a great man is an outstanding musical triumph, for the music is essentially heroic in itself; Strauss's *Till Eulenspiegel* and *Don Juan,* Wagner's "Siegfried's Funeral March" or "Isolde's Love Death," all of them frankly programmatic to the utmost degree, can nevertheless be ranked as among our greatest masterpieces. In all of them one can sense the spirit of their program *in the music itself,* and one does not have to depend upon an intellectual reading to give them meaning.

In order to clarify the issue, it may be well to define here just what is usually meant by the term "program music." Ever since the time of Berlioz and Liszt at the beginning of the nineteenth century, it has been applied to instrumental music that not only is intended to express ideas outside the realm of the art but also is conditioned and shaped by extra-musical ideas rather than by primary considerations of proportion and form. Although it covers a wide range of styles and schools from Berlioz to Richard Strauss, the term is never applied to *opera* or *song,* forms which associate music directly with words.

ABSOLUTE MUSIC

In direct contrast is the pure or absolute type of music. This music is based upon definite laws of structure and development rather than depending upon an appeal through associations with literary or illustrative ideas. In this music the tone must be good, the proportions well-balanced, the harmonies clear and understandable. But it is difficult to draw a line of demarcation between these types and say that on one side is program music, on the other absolute. Such a thing as a Bach fugue (the organ *Fugue in G Minor* is a good example), in which the structure of the music is a matter of paramount importance, the whole thing growing to a tremendous climax under the structural genius of its composer; or a Haydn quartet (the one in F major, Op. 3, No. 5, for instance) with its detached, impersonal attitude to everything except the weaving together of tonal patterns — these are as near to absolute music as we can get. The materials in these compositions are arranged in certain sequences, and their significance is of aesthetic beauty rather than of emotional content. But music which seems to have been written with the idea of pure tonal concepts may contain dramatic and impressionistic material, and vice versa, so that definite boundaries between these types are not easy to establish.

The subject of program *vs.* absolute music has given rise to many vigorous debates. One of the best discussions of it will be found in Ernest Newman's *Musical Studies.* We need not even attempt to summarize further the arguments here; the topic would make an excellent one for debate among music lovers. It will suffice to suggest that, as program music has always existed (there are naïve examples in the earliest art music), it evidently springs from a deep natural desire to relate music to life. Obviously, such music is likely to appeal in its own terms. If we are really musical, we work through the more simple forms of program music pretty quickly, but he would surely be a sadly pedantic person who would refuse to open his heart to *Till Eulenspiegel* because of cast-iron convictions about the inferiority of program to absolute music! The main thing is to consider all music on its merits. A good program should not allow poor music to scrape through; on the other hand, we must not expect a program piece either to declare its program without the use of words or to be as impressive without its program as with it. In the best program music, the composition so richly interprets or suggests the verbal ideas that the two are inseparable. There are many examples of this: for instance, Vincent d'Indy's *Istar,* wherein the music suggests by its essential structure the story of the goddess, who, to free her lover, must pass through seven doors, at each of which a demon robs her of adornment.

It is well to remember that the novelty of an exciting program may attract for a while, and that then the music may become stale with familiarity. Hence, we should give program pieces a good many hearings before deciding whether they wear as well as non-program favorites.

In listening to program music we have a double task, because we have to take in the program plus the music, and be deciding all along how the music carries out the literary idea. There must be *form* in both, and the comparison of the two provides an enjoyable task.

HERE WE TAKE THE ROMANTIC ROAD

We have now arrived at a point from which it is possible to see the best road to use in approaching this difficult problem of learning how to listen. It lies naturally through that kind of music which recognizably maintains a connection with things outside itself, with things which can be definitely recognized and easily understood. Most of the works known and loved by the intelligent amateur in music belong in this category. This is a realm of beauty and interest, "a land bounded on one side by the austere peaks of the classics and on the other by the broad plains of conscientious mediocrity. It is an irresistibly lovely tract, its valleys and mountains perpetually varied by the wandering clouds of romanticism, its streams darkened by winds blowing from the other world of mysticism; a land where sensuous beauty, the immediate delight of the ear, is of primary importance and logic a reluctant necessity" (Hubbard Hutchinson in *The New York Times*). Using this kind of music first of all to establish a delight in listening and then as a means for acquiring familiarity with the problems of technical structure, details of melody, harmony, rhythm, orchestration, and so on, the would-be listener can soon journey into the more abstract difficulties as well as the greater beauties of absolute music. Using his days in the delectable land of romantic beauty as a preparation, he should gradually gird his loins and quicken his spirit for the journey to the rarer heights and wider visions of the "austere peaks of the classics."

Throughout his whole journey the musical wayfarer must keep in mind his ultimate goal — the acquiring of the ability to listen to music in its own terms, without the outside props that have helped him to get started. Thus only can he do full justice to its glories by giving it a fair opportunity of working in its own particular field. It is in its very being-itself-ness that music becomes most difficult — so that when it is most necessary to understand it (that is, when it is "purest"), it is most difficult to grasp. This applies, of course, to the more complex works; but we must point out, at the same time, that there is ample music that is only slightly complex and at the same time as absolute as can be; and that the complexity of the music is a real necessity, not a thing put in by the composer "to make it more difficult," like a mis-lead in a crossword puzzle. A student starting to learn to listen to a piece of absolute music that is fairly complex is apt to think that the composer has made it as difficult as possible, whereas all good composers strive to make their utterances as clear to the hearer as they can, consistent with the magnitude of the ideas they are expressing. Complexity in music is more obvious than in the other arts, and more difficult to grasp, because of music's fleeting character and its appeal to the least trained of our senses.

But we have already warned the student that he has not set forth on an easy journey, even though it is a very delightful one, and that too rapid progress cannot be expected at first. The listener can gradually learn to get from the music the sense that the composer would convey, once his attitude towards the art is an active rather than a passive one. By developing an ability to remember musical phrases and patterns, by trying to train his powers of discrimination, and by keeping an open mind and a sympathetic attitude towards all kinds of music, he will greatly forward his own progress. By confining the music he hears to that which, because of its content, can justify its existence as a means of "enriching and sanctifying life," he will educate himself in the real sense of the term. In a valuable essay on *Music and the Cultivated Man*, Gilman quotes William Orton's definition of education as an initiation of the mind to ever new and finer types of experiences. And it is these new and finer types of experience which music will give us if we learn to choose it carefully and to listen to it properly.

LIST OF SUGGESTED MUSIC

Symphonie pathétique   Tchaikovsky

The last movement especially should be heard, since it is illustrative of "melancholy brooding."

Scheherazade Suite   Rimsky-Korsakoff

The third movement has "alluring Eastern colors."

First Symphony   Brahms

The last movement is full of "healthy vigor."

Der Wanderer   Schubert

The following translation of the German will help you follow the varied beauties of this mastersong:

Ich komme vom Gebirge her,   From mountain summits I come,
Es dampft das Thal, es braust   Through foggy vales and ocean's
das Meer.   foam.

Ich wandle still, bin wenig froh,	I wander on, am full of care,
Und immer fragt der Seufzer wo,	And always ask in sorrow, Where,
immer wo?	where, where?
Die Sonne dünkt mich hier so	The sun shines here so wan and
kalt,	cold,
Die Blüthe welk, das Leben	The flowers are dead, and life is
alt,	old,
Und was sie reden, leerer	And what they tell me, empty
Schall.	sound.
Ich bin ein Fremdling überall.	I am a stranger no one knows.
Wo bist du, wo bist du, mein	Where art thou, my beloved land?
geliebtes Land,	
Gesucht, geahnt, und nie gekannt!	I've sought, I've dreamed, yet
	never known.
Das Land, das Land so hoffnungs-	That land where all my hopes are
grün,	green,
Das Land wo meine Rosen	That land where all my roses
blühn,	bloom,
Wo meine Freunde wandelnd	Where live the friends I dearly
gehn,	prize,
Wo meine Todten aufer-	Where all my dead will one day
stehn,	rise,
Das Land, das meine Sprache	The land that knows the tongue I
spricht,	speak,
O Land, wo bist du?	O land, where art thou?
Ich wandle still, bin wenig froh,	I wander on, am full of care,
Und immer fragt der Seufzer wo,	And always ask in sorrow, Where,
immer wo?	where, where?
Im Geisterhauch tönts mir zuruck:	In spirit tones there comes reply:
"Dort, wo du nicht bist, dort ist	"There, where thou art not,
das Glück."	there joy is found."

TOPICS FOR FURTHER DISCUSSION

Has music any emotions of its own which have no connection with any other kind of emotion? Or are the feelings that music arouses all derived from our experience of life and literature?

Do you think that program music is in itself a lower type than absolute music?

Is Honegger's *Pacific 231* (a railway engine) a legitimate subject for a tone poem, or not? And why?

Discuss Charles Morgan's dictum that "Art is news of reality not to be expressed in other terms." And this artist's recipe, from Bourget: *Sois belle, et tais-toi!* "Be beautiful, and let it go at that."

TEN

STRAUSS'S *Till Eulenspiegel's Merry Pranks*

A GAY BEGINNING FOR OUR JOURNEY

Our musical journey may well begin with one of the most significant pieces of program music ever written, *Till Eulenspiegel's Merry Pranks* by Richard Strauss. Upon hearing this, even for the first time, we can hardly fail to be impressed with its greatness. It is very evident that the orchestra is telling us a story in which something is happening every minute. What is perhaps not so immediately evident is that the composer's ability in construction is on a par with his imaginative facility. Here is music inspired by the liveliest of imaginations and created by the most consummate skill imaginable.

Strauss, who wrote this music in 1895, tells us that his original intention was to let the music speak for itself, giving the hearer the title, and letting him guess the details and enjoy the music for its own sake. But this was said with his tongue in cheek, for no one knew better than did Strauss that if the hearers are to share a composer's enjoyment in the treatment of a programmatic subject, it is necessary that they know something of the story unfolding in his mind as he writes the music. So he later gave us his program. "Till Owlglass," to use an English translation of the fanciful name, is a character not very well known in this country; in Germany every schoolboy could tell the adventures of this medieval character who is the hero of a fifteenth-century book which relates his journeys through life and tells of how he managed to live by his wits. He is supposed to have lived in Brunswick, and to have died in 1350 at Mölln, near Lübeck in the north of Germany. He came to be recognized during the Middle Ages as a sort of personification of the triumph of nimble wit over bourgeois dullness and vanity. He was an amusing rogue, as amoral as Punch, jack-of-all-trades, a universal swindler, yet ingratiating himself with everybody by his hail-fellow-well-met gusto; something of a poet, with a streak of childish heedlessness; ramshackle, a danger to the community, yet with a likable turn to his folly; likable, perhaps, mostly in the retrospect; not so

Richard Strauss at the Time of Writing Till

much when his insolent pranks drove nearly frantic the honest dullards on whom he delighted to exercise his wits. "When he was grabbed by the collar and hauled along to the gallows, he went as a matter of course, without knowing why. He took life after the manner of a poet, just as he took the goods of others" (Eugene Bacha).

AN IDEAL PROGRAM

What a program for a creative musician of Strauss's imaginative power and technical resource! And in working it out, the composer makes his music not only an apotheosis of this medieval character, but, as we have said, a running commentary on life in general and the individual who dares to stand out against generally accepted opinions. Coming as he did after Liszt and Wagner, Strauss was able to base his developments upon the foundations laid by these great giants. Possessed of a most unusual talent in writing for the orchestra, he was able to make this huge instrument subject to every dictate of his thought. Even a casual hearing of this music will prove that its pictures are very clearly drawn, the instruments saying exactly what the composer wants them to say. There is a strong sense of folk-feeling pervading this work; in the first bars we hear two themes which seem to suggest to us that "once upon a time there lived a wag named Till Eulenspiegel." And Strauss carries these themes throughout his whole work, weaving them in the most manifold guises, moods, and situations, right up to the catastrophe where Till, after he has been condemned to death, is strung up to the gibbet. We can learn a great deal as we enjoy this vivid, vigorous score. The chief thing to observe is how the composer builds his music out of the manipulations of the two main themes, following, in as much detail as possible, the various phases in the process.

The two themes are strikingly characteristic; they are both heard at the very beginning of the composition. The first four notes from the orchestra (measures 1–2) vividly suggest the rogue-hero, the quirk of the notes describing him as exactly as music can describe anybody or anything. Almost immediately after the first little theme, we hear a rising, quickly repeated, humorous theme played on the horns (5–12). The ability to recognize such tone color in the orchestra will give added pleasure to our listening! *Keep these two Till themes in mind,* for out of them is fashioned the fabric of the whole piece.[1]

[1] BY WAY OF PRACTICAL SUGGESTION: There is much to be said in favor of the listener following this and other music which will be suggested later in this

TILL IN THE MARKET PLACE

As the music gets under way, notice how the second theme (the rising, repeated horn theme) gradually becomes more lively (25–35); it is taken up by the various instruments in turn and finally proclaimed in a *fortissimo* passage by the whole orchestra (35–40). "The *milieu* is thus given by which we are enabled to recognize the pranks and droll tricks which the crafty schemer is about to bring before our ears." (This and following quotations are from the analysis of the score by Klatte, approved by the composer.) A clearly marked drop of an octave (44) suggests that the rogue is really off on his adventures. Till is suddenly before us; the clarinets sound his theme and there follow a few sharp chords for the wind instruments (49–50). It is not difficult to recognize the outlines of the story which Strauss tells us were in his mind; Till, his clothes tattered and torn, puts on his best manners, slyly passes through the gate of a city and enters the market place. "It is market day; the women sit at their stalls and prattle. Hop! Eulenspiegel springs on his horse, gives a smack of the whip, and rides into the midst of the crowd. Clink, clash, clatter! A confused sound of broken pots and pans, and the market women are put to flight. In haste the rascal rides away, an incident which is suggested by the trombones in a loud phrase,

book with the printed score before him — provided that he is able to read musical notation. Picking a detailed structure apart is as good a way to find out how it is put together as can be found, if the observer has technical knowledge to appreciate his analysis. The logical build-up and "feel" of the music can be obtained better in this way than in any other. If the hearer can even find the places in the score where the principal themes occur, he will gradually learn to read the printed page more eloquently. In order to help him in this process, figures are inserted in the text in this and following chapters, these figures referring to the numbers of the measures in which the feature under discussion occurs. The piano score is best for the amateur reader, for it is a condensed version of what the whole orchestra is doing; later on he may learn to use the orchestral score, where all the parts for the various instruments are laid out before him. In each chapter reference will be made to the publishers of both orchestral and piano scores. Reference will not always be given to the various phonograph recordings, but no music is used for illustration that is not immediately available in one or more recordings and which is not likely to remain permanently in the lists.

If the listener does not read music, he need pay no attention to the figures. In numbering the measures, passages that are repeated have not been counted twice.

The piano score of *Till Eulenspiegel* is available in the following: Universal Edition No. 1106; Breitkopf Edition No. 2752.

The orchestral score (miniature size) is available in the Kalmus Edition, an American reprint, excellent and reasonable in price.

and secures a safe retreat." The jogging market tune (51–54) heard in this incident is obviously a variant of the second theme, using many of its very notes. As Strauss works up this scene to a climax, notice how he plays with the first theme, making it serve in different ways, breaking it up into little two-note groups (110–120), and expanding it to fit the situation exactly (135–150).

TILL THE PRIEST

The first prank is followed immediately by a second. A straightforward tune is suddenly heard in the midst of the whirling music (179–182), strongly resembling a German folk tune. Thus it is that the scene changes for us. It shows Till disguised as a priest, dripping with unction and morals, Strauss tells us. Note the sudden interpolation of the quirky Till theme on the clarinet (191) in the midst of the bourgeois folk tune; it is as if the preacher's mask has slipped and suddenly Till's mocking, grinning face is revealed beneath. But he begins to get qualms at having mocked religion, and fears for the success of his scheme. A veiled proclamation of the horn theme sug-

"The Professors," Costume Sketch for the Ballet Till Eulenspiegel

In 1916 Diaghilev commissioned a ballet on this medieval subject, using the Strauss music. The American scene designer Robert Edmond Jones made the settings and designed the costumes. The choreography was by Nijinsky.

gests that perhaps he does not feel any too comfortable in his borrowed glory. He makes up his mind — away with all scruples, he is himself again.

TILL IN LOVE

A sort of shuddering phrase for a solo violin (207) marks the beginning of a new adventure, and the music which immediately follows shows its character. The principal theme is brought forward in lively time, but subtly metamorphosed and chivalrously colored (209). There is no doubt about it — Till is in love. "He has become a Don Juan and one pretty girl has made quite an impression." Hear how now, glowing with zest, the violins, clarinets, and flutes sing! (229) But all this ardor is in vain; Till's advances are received with derision and he goes away in a rage, swearing vengeance on all mankind. A tremendously loud passage on the brass (267) developed out of the first short theme, with change of rhythm, and several times repeated, leaves us in little doubt about this.

TILL AND THE PHILISTINES

Then after a short pause another adventure starts. The violoncellos announce, with a peculiar hopping insistence (293), the arrival of some strange personages, who turn out to be honest, worthy doctors and professors. In an instant Till's anger is forgotten in his joy at the opportunity offered of making fun of these solemn old self-important dry-as-dusts. The second theme suits itself to the new rhythm (303–305), as if to suggest how easily Till falls in with the ways of living and thinking of his new companions. He begins to propound a few amazing theses to them, as is apparent from the way fragments of the theme come from various parts of the orchestra. There follows a rhythmic phrase (344) representing the dull stodginess of the Philistines and the rapid quirks of the Till motive, as if he were propounding one amazing idea after another in such quick succession as to leave his hearers open-mouthed in astonishment. He works himself up into a perfect frenzy of excitement, but after he has had his joke, he loses interest in the whole thing and drops it, leaving the professors and doctors behind in amazed stupefaction.

TO BE OR NOT TO BE HIMSELF

Now comes material more suited to the real domain of music than these pictorial elements with which we have been concerned up to now. A happy *gassenhauer* (a street song) is heard (375), its short staccato phrases emphasizing Till's essential naïveté. Then follows a sort of psychological struggle in the hero's mind, between the various elements in his character. The different themes are taken up and bandied about in various rhythms as if Till thought sometimes he ought to reform his ways and settle down, and then again he decided against it. But the arch villain "gets the upper hand and the merry jester, the born liar goes wherever he can succeed with a hoax. His insolence knows no bounds; the Till themes fairly dance in unholy glee (555). Finally the coarse street tune is heard again, sung by the whole orchestra as if in jubilation at the hero's final determination to be himself again."

TILL'S SAD END

Suddenly comes the denouement. "The drum rolls a hollow roll (575); the jailer drags the rascally prisoner into the court room." This is one of Strauss's happiest characterizations, this Court of Justice theme — heavy, pedantic, threatening chords on the wood winds and lower strings (577–580). The impudent Till theme (582) replies brazenly to these somber thunderings of the court; it sounds as if the prisoner were thumbing his nose at the solemn-faced jury. Finally he realizes that the jig is up and his pranks are over. Fear seizes him as he is marched to the gallows. There he swings as the trap is sprung, this rather gruesome incident being marked by a peculiar drop in the pitch of the orchestra. A last, piteous struggle suggested principally by the clarinet and the flute (615), and his soul takes flight. The mortal Till is no more.

After a sad *pizzicato* passage for the strings (625), the composer adds a delightful epilogue, a sort of improvisation on the opening measures. It is as if he would say, "Till thus becomes a legendary character; after all, there was a lovable side to his ramshackleness, and the people will always tell tales about him — 'Once upon a time,' etc." But in all the retrospective affection with which Strauss clothes Till, he does not let us forget the fact that he was a devil and an immortal rogue. To this appraisal of his character the final measures, sounded by the full orchestra, testify most eloquently.

FEELING BEFORE ANALYSIS

No matter whether he can read the score or not, the listener should always keep clearly before him the necessity of cultivating an eloquence of heart if he is to come to a real understanding of this magnificent music. He must realize the necessity of getting back of the music, of sensing its spiritual communication, of letting himself be "reminded by the instruments," as Walt Whitman has put it. This does not mean that he should give himself over merely to the summoning of vague, shifting, sentimental images when he listens to the music. This sort of thing is ridiculed by the purists in art, and with good reason. But the more one hears, sees, and reads, the more one must be convinced of the necessary and salutary relationship between art and life. All art must spring from nature; art for art's sake is nonexistent, nor can it be produced. If art is to maintain itself and is to assure its own existence, some kind of moral and spiritual stimulus must be given to the people. It is the sharpening of his faculties of apperception, so that he can realize this relationship, that is necessary for the listener as he hears this music. He must learn to respond to the emotion in such music as this, to feel its beauty, before he attempts to explain it. He should sense its connection with life in general, its "ulterior and philosophic meaning"; in this particular case he must realize, as we have said, that this music is jubilantly conscious of that which "soars high above and beyond prison bars or scaffolds, or even the excellent rulings of worthy people." [2] Then can he proceed to analysis and appraisement, a mental process which will no longer hinder his progress by assuming undue importance. Rather will it increase his enjoyment by rendering his possession of the music more sure. This process of developing from a purely sensual and subjective state of hearing into a more objective and analytical type of listening is a glorious experience.

Till Eulenspiegel should awaken within us a new understanding of life and the universe; in realizing the humor as well as the tenderness, the eloquence as well as the joy of life that is in this music, in signalizing its triumph of the spirit over material obstacles, we open

[2] Olin Downes, *Symphonic Broadcasts* (New York: Dial Press).

our hearts to new powers of feeling and understanding. And, having cultivated this power of understanding, we can learn to appreciate the effective arrangement of idea and event within this music, its masterful descriptive ability, and its outstanding scheme of construction. Only then can we really say that we have made it our own.

ADDITIONAL EXAMPLES OF PROGRAM MUSIC

L'Apprenti sorcier   Dukas

Danse macabre   Saint-Saëns

The first is a humorous translation into music of a ballad by Goethe about a magician's lazy apprentice who, while his master is away, uses the incantations he has learned for bringing to life brooms and buckets. These he succeeds in making work for him, but they get out of control, for the apprentice forgets the spell which will make them stop. Frightened, he chops the broom in two; but then the halves begin sweeping. The floor is deluged with water from the buckets. Finally his master returns and solemnly utters the spell which puts things right.

Saint-Saëns's symphonic poem (written in 1874) was based upon a French poem describing how at midnight Death summons the skeletons in the graveyards to revels. We hear him tuning his fiddle; then midnight strikes and the specters arise. They dance to waltz themes, and on the xylophone we hear the clanking of their bones. When the cock crows at break of dawn, they speed back to the shades.

TOPICS FOR FURTHER DISCUSSION

What in your mind makes *Till* so perfect a work of art? What else has Strauss done in the field of program music? Do these works equal *Till* in vividness, truth, and the balancing of description and imagination?

Do any of the episodes seem to you less completely successful than others? If so, which, and why?

DEFINITE SUGGESTIONS FOR READING

The Stream of Music by Richard A. Leonard (New York: Doubleday), Article on Richard Strauss.

In order fully to appreciate the music of the great composers, it is necessary to know something of their lives and times. Hence references will be given from time to time to help the listener acquire this important information. These articles are short and very much to the point.

Music in History: Richard Strauss

The authors of this book have elaborated the subject of many of these discussions in their companion volume, *Music in History* (New York: American Book Company), to which references are made from time to time.

ELEVEN

ROMANTICISM:

LISZT'S *Les Préludes*

A NEW SPIRIT DEVELOPS IN MUSIC

Having enjoyed a piece of program music such as *Till Eulenspiegel,* in which the composer carefully elaborates a detailed program, the listener may well turn to music which extends into a wider imaginative realm and does not of necessity follow an exterior programistic outline. Liszt's *Les Préludes* will do well for an example, although it can hardly be ranked with the Strauss work as a musical masterpiece. Play through a good interpretation of this music of Liszt's. You will find it introspective and contemplative as well as external and pictorial; the composer is dealing with emotional states as well as with events — more so, in fact. In this sense this music belongs to the real realm of art, since it presents us with images rather than ideas, and these images produce in us definite states of feeling. It was written at a time when men were not ashamed to feel deeply and express themselves luxuriantly. Full of color, possessing dramatic force, with melodies of frank and robust sentiment, *Les Préludes* is characteristic of the Romantic Movement which gave it birth, and in which its composer played so prominent a role.

A revolt against the more formal and severe elements of the classic ideals of the seventeenth and early eighteenth centuries, the Romantic Movement in art came into existence during the late eighteenth and early nineteenth centuries. Its tendencies were marked by such writers as E. T. A. Hoffmann and Jean Paul Richter in Germany, Stendhal in France, and Wordsworth, Byron, Coleridge, and Shelley in England. Through the aspirations which developed from experience in the new political ideals of the time, aspirations which insisted upon more freedom for the individual, the Romantics came to look upon the world not so much as it affected the past, but in the light of its effect upon the individual. "I am different from all men I have seen; if I am not better, I at least am different," said Rousseau, one of the leaders of the movement in France. And it was this self-conscious attempt to give expression to the qualities which determine the characteristics of personality that typifies the art of the time and gives this music its peculiar quality.

AN ART OF REVOLT

It will be worth our while to turn briefly aside and try to realize the true character of this Romantic spirit, the better to sense it when we come across it in music. Artists of the time were so preoccupied with self, so lacking in surety of proportion and balance, that they plunged wildly into a passionate, surging conflict with life, to come out of the struggle, not with balance regained, but with a sense of dissatisfaction, a resolve to flee the world and retreat into the solitude of self. A quotation from Shelley's "Ode to the West Wind" will give us as good an example of Romantic characteristics as could be found:

If I were a dead leaf thou mightest bear;
If I were a swift cloud to fly with thee;
A wave to pant beneath thy power, and share

The impulse of thy strength, only less free
Than thou, O uncontrollable! If even
I were as in my boyhood, and could be

The comrade of thy wanderings over heaven,
As then, when to outstrip thy skiey speed
Scarce seemed a vision; I would ne'er have striven

As thus with thee in prayer in my sore need.
O! lift me as a wave, a leaf, a cloud!
I fall upon the thorns of life! I bleed!

A heavy weight of hours has chained and bowed
One too like thee — tameless, and swift, and proud.

It is all here: the apotheosis of self, the pessimism, the sense of passionate struggle, the poignant dissatisfaction with life, the nostalgic longing for the past, the struggle against destiny and the final resignation. We could well choose a motto for Romantic art from the above lines: "I fall upon the thorns of life! I bleed!" It is this exaggeration, this insistence upon the picturesque and extravagant, that has brought the whole Romantic Movement into disrepute in more recent years; our present-day attitude of realism rather mercilessly exposes these very evident weaknesses.

ROMANTICISM IN PAINTING: *Liberty Leading the People* by Eugène Delacroix

Here the spirit of Romantic revolt is portrayed in a setting dramatizing the French uprising of 1830 which deposed the Bourbon king. Note the bold, personalized treatment characteristic of Romanticism.

And yet Romanticism has been one of the most stimulating influences in the whole development of music. Before the Romanticists, the basis of music's life was a sort of disciplined intellectualism, with its beauty largely of the abstract, impersonal sort.

There was a classic reticence, a carefully maintained balance in this earlier music that subordinated, while of course by no means rejecting, personal feeling. Beethoven marked a transition; after him came the Romantic deluge. Schubert, Schumann, Liszt, Chopin, Wagner, Strauss, Brahms, even men of our own time like Delius and Schönberg (at least in the latter's earlier works), all have been possessed of the Romantic spirit and have written music which is not content only to shine, but which must also sparkle. These qualities, because of their very nature, were destined to make Music a more human goddess, and one much more immediately appealing.

ROMANTIC DRAMA IN SONG

A good idea of the stimulation given the artists of the time by the spirit of Romanticism may be gained from observing their treatment of such a subject as the Erlking. Legend has always been a fruitful source of artistic inspiration, and the Romantics found it especially congenial. One of the most famous treatments given a legendary subject is the ballad which Goethe (1749–1832) made out of the German folk-specter inhabiting the dark forests and luring people, especially children, to their destruction.

This poem so impressed the young eighteen-year-old Schubert that he made out of it one of his, and the world's, greatest songs. His wonderfully imaginative setting depicts in turn the wild ride of the father through the night with his sick child in his arms, suggested by the pounding rhythm of the accompaniment throughout the whole song; the voices of the *dramatis personae* of the poem, each with his own characteristic tone: the terror-stricken boy, the beguiling Erlking, the reassuring father, and the dramatic poet describing the scene; the final heartbreaking climax as the father, exhausted and trembling, reaches home only to find that the child in his arms is dead.

One of Schubert's closest friends and confidants in his life as a young musician in Vienna was the painter Moritz von Schwind; he too was struck by the dramatic possibilities of this story and made a Romantic painting out of it. If we compare the three versions — poem, song, and painting — we get an excellent suggestion of what is meant by the Romantic spirit in art. The poem and the painting are given on the following pages.

Der Erlkönig (The Erlking)
Words by JOHANN WOLFGANG VON GOETHE (1749–1832)
Music by FRANZ SCHUBERT (1797–1828)

Wer reitet so spät durch Nacht und Wind? Es ist der Vater mit seinem Kind;

Who rides there so late, through night and wind? It is a father with his small son;

Er hat den Knaben wohl in dem Arm, Er fasst ihn sicher, er hält ihn warm.

He has the boy safe in his arm, He holds him tightly, he holds him warm.

Mein Sohn, was birgst du so bang dein Gesicht? Siehst, Vater, du den Erlkönig nicht?

My boy, why in terror do you hide your face? Father, can't you see the Erlking?

Den Erlenkönig mit Kron und Schweif? Mein Sohn, es ist ein Nebelstreif.

The Erlking with crown and robe? My son, it is only a streak of mist.

"Du liebes Kind, komm', geh' mit mir! Gar schöne Spiele spiel' ich mit dir;

"Pretty boy, won't you come with me? Such merry games I'll play with you;

Manch' bunte Blumen sind an dem Strand, Meine Mutter hat manch' gülden Gewand."

Many gay flowers are blooming there, And my mother has golden robes for you."

Mein Vater, mein Vater, und hörest du nicht, Was Erlenkönig mir leise verspricht?

Oh, Father, my father, cannot you hear what the Erlking is saying to me?

Sei ruhig, bleibe ruhig, mein Kind, In dürren Blättern säuselt der Wind.

Don't talk so, my boy. It's only the wind in the dry leaves.

"Willst, feiner Knabe, du mit mir gehn? Meine Töchter sollen dich warten schön;

"Come, pretty one, and fairy princesses shall wait upon you,

Meine Töchter führen den nächtlichen Reihn Und wiegen und tanzen und singen dich ein."

They'll play with you, dance with you, sing to you."

Mein Vater, mein Vater, und siehst du nicht dort Erlkönigs Töchter am düster'n Ort?

Father, Father, don't you see the Erlking's daughters there?

Mein Sohn, mein Sohn, ich seh' es genau, Es scheinen die alten Weiden so grau.

My boy, there is nothing there but the old gray willows.

"Ich liebe dich, mich reizt deine schöne Gestalt, Und bist du nicht willig, so brauch ich Gewalt."

"I want you, pretty one; if you're not willing, I shall use force."

Mein Vater, mein Vater, jetzt fasst er mich an! Erlkönig hat mir ein Leids gethan!	Father, Father, he is seizing me! Save me, save me!
Dem Vater grauset's, er reitet geschwind, Er hält in den Armen das ächzende Kind,	The father shudders. He rides like the wind, the pale, sobbing child close in his arms.
Er reicht den Hof mit Müh' und Noth; In seinen Armen das Kind war todt.	Gasping and sweating, he pulls up at the gate of home. But the child in his arms is dead.

Painting by Moritz von Schwind (1804–1871)

Les Préludes — TYPICAL ROMANTIC ART

Another outstanding example of Romanticism in music is Liszt's tone poem *Les Préludes;* [1] it suggests both the strength and the weakness of this type of art. Its very program is somewhat extravagant, its melodies overluxuriant and nostalgic to a generation so thoroughly removed from the vapors of Romanticism as to incline to the other extreme, that of demanding art without expression. But Liszt was no precious *poseur;* he knew how to make his music telling, and he had a thorough command of the technic of musical

[1] The piano score of *Les Préludes* is available in the Breitkopf Edition No. 2443. The orchestral score (miniature size) is available in the Kalmus Edition No. 29.

construction. He may have been exotic and picturesque, but he was never disorderly or flabby. We may well examine this tone poem, not so much as an example of great music as of consistent, well-ordered construction in the Romantic vein. A realization of its fervor and exuberances should not deter us from gaining a helpful insight into the processes of its musical composition.

Liszt chose a quotation from Lamartine as his program: "Is our life anything but a series of Preludes to that unknown song of which death sounds the first and solemn note? Love is the glowing dawn of all existence, but in whose destiny are not the first delights of happiness interrupted by some storm whose blast dissipates its fine illusions? And where is the cruelly wounded soul, which on issuing from one of these tempests, does not endeavor to find solace in the calm serenity of country life? Nevertheless man can hardly give himself up for long to the simple beneficence which he at first finds in nature, and he hastens to the dangerous post wherever war calls him to its ranks, in order to recover at last in the combat full consciousness and entire possession of his energy."

This obvious program gives us life as material for the composer to work upon, viewed first from the aspect of Love, its greatest fulfillment; second, as a struggle for an Ideal, and the inevitable disillusionment that follows; third, as an opportunity for regaining spiritual equilibrium in the solitude of Nature; and finally, as a glorious re-entry into Conflict. Liszt made his tone poem conform to these four varying moods of the program, and to give unity to his work, he used only two short themes (47–50 and 70–73)

as a basis for the whole structure, changing and coloring these to suit the needs of the various parts of the orchestral poem. Thus the hearer is given the necessary contrast without which any music becomes unbearably tiresome (witness the modern jazz piece), as well as coherence, without which it would be meaningless. Notice that the first four notes of the first theme constitute a germinal unit out of which Liszt makes a great deal, particularly in the long introduction which precedes the sounding of the first theme, and the effective concluding measures which give a sort of post-oration effect. The little three-note germ is sounded by the whole orchestra at the very beginning (1–3):

The music that follows is obviously developed out of this idea and is self-propellent, moving towards a definite goal. This goal we find to be the expressive first theme, broadly sung by all the strings; as though to make sure we shall not forget it, the composer repeats it almost immediately, this time with some of the brass instruments added. Then comes the second theme, a quiet but intense tune, softly intoned by the brass and then repeated on the wood winds (oboe, clarinet, and bassoon). There is no doubt that Liszt, *l'homme d'amour,* as Pourtalès calls him, is here discoursing at some length upon a subject dear to his heart!

The cellos and clarinets (110) unite to give us the first inklings of the coming storm which occupies the second section of the musical form. A series of chromatic rumblings, based again upon our little three-note theme, presages the storm. When it finally arrives, the keen observer will note that the material from which these storm passages is built (131–160) is a shortened, intensified version of the principal theme:

Allegro tempestuoso

This works up to a climax in which the second theme is brilliantly used (161). But unfortunately this Lisztian storm is more objective than subjective; we are reminded of the rushing roar and muttering outbursts of a storm in nature rather than of the tempestuous, spiritual struggle that is suggested by the program. And it does not help the general effect that these chord progressions used nearly a century ago by Liszt have come into the current repertoire of the movie-mongers, so that the whole episode today has a melodramatic, cheapened aspect undreamed of when it was written.

The next section (201–344) contains some of the most colorful music in the whole tone poem; here the oboe gives out the first theme in languorous, pastoral eloquence:

Moderato

Here is really

> Beauty clear and fair
> Where the air
> Rather like a perfume dwells.

Liszt sings his charming *bergerette* with great skill and here colors his themes with unfailing good taste.

Once again the mood changes, and we hear the two themes (346 and 370) in a quick martial rhythm,

Allegro marziale animato

and delivered with so much pompous grandeur as to make them sound like different tunes from those heard in the first episode. All is bustle and stir; the struggle and glory are, however, again purely objective. It is in the pomp and circumstance of war that Liszt's hero recovers his individuality and regains possession of his energy. A vigorous coda (405 to end), already mentioned as suggestive of the introductory measures, brings the work to a close; in it notice how the reference to the thematic material with which the piece began rounds out the whole, and gives the effect of unity.

A DOUBLE PERSONALITY

Liszt once jokingly referred to himself as a musician-philosopher, born on Parnassus, coming from the Land of Doubt, and journeying towards the Land of Truth — a description of himself that is more accurate than his sometimes rather tawdry music would lead us to believe. Ernest Newman in one of his articles in the London *Sunday Times* wonders "how there came to be so much originality, so much distinction, so much downright commonness united in Liszt. . . . Somewhere or other in the course of even his best and most sincere thinking the old *cabotin* will rise up in him again and he becomes, once more, the flashy, flowery, too-effusive Liszt of the

Franz Liszt

This portrait of the young composer has a Romantic quality about it in its powerful, aggressive confidence and self-assurance.

Paris salon. Here in *Les Préludes,* for instance, we can see, again and again, the self-conscious and self-approving air with which, in the days of his handsome and seductive youth, he was wont to throw back his mane, put his whole romantic soul into his fingers and his eyes, and slay a gushing countess with a glance."

ADDITIONAL EXAMPLES ILLUSTRATING THIS CHAPTER

Vltava (The Moldau)   Smetana

Smetana, the Czech composer (1824–1884), who was the most notable nationalistic musician in that country before Dvořák, told in his score how in the deep Bohemian forest two streams arise, one warm and swift, the other cold and quiet. Rushing down from the rocks, they unite and flow happily in the rays of the morning sun. In time the swift brook becomes a river, the Vltava. It flows through dark, mighty forests, where the huntsman's horn is heard; it streams through rich pastures in the plains and hears the songs of peasants at a village wedding. By moonlight water nymphs play in its waters. Upon its bosom are mirrored the towers of castles that in past days resounded with the clash of arms and the great deeds of warriors. In the gorge of St. John rocks seek to oppose it, but it bursts through in foaming torrents. Then, broadening out into full majesty, it sweeps nobly past Prague, greeted by the ancient fortress of Vysehrad, and then in all its power and splendor it is lost to the poet's vision.

The Fountains of Rome   Respighi

Though Italy has not so far, like some of the Middle European nations, new and old, developed a strongly self-conscious school of composition based upon folk music, those of its writers who have turned rather to orchestral than to operatic expression have upheld the country's reputation for brilliant, colorful, dynamic depiction. Among them one of the most notable is Ottorino Respighi (1879–1936). Though he wrote for the theater, much of his best-known work is in the form of tone poems, a series of which is devoted to the glories of Rome. Typical of a certain pictorial luxuriousness which is widely enjoyed, and may well be compared with Liszt's, is his *Fountains of Rome*. It may be suggested that there is some special consonance between this type of program music, with its flowery, literal, prose style (as distinguished from Liszt's poetical searchings) and some aspects of modern life and thought.

In his clever depictions, which date from 1916, the composer (in his own words) "endeavored to give effect to the sentiment and vision suggested by four of Rome's fountains, contemplated at the hour at which their character is most in harmony with the surrounding landscape, and in which their beauty appears most impressive to the observer."

1. The Fountain at Valle Giulia at Dawn. "A pastoral landscape. Droves of cattle pass and disappear in the mists of a Roman dawn." Muted violins suggest the fountain, wood winds the pastoral scene.

2. The Fountain of the Tritons, in the Morning. "A sudden loud and insistent blast of horns . . . is like a joyous call, summoning troops of Tritons and Naiads, who . . . pursue each other and mingle in the dance between the jets of water."

3. The Fountain of Trevi, at Noon. "A solemn theme from the

wood and brass assumes a triumphal character. Trumpets peal across the radiant surface of the water. Neptune's chariot passes, drawn by sea-horses and followed by Sirens and Tritons. The procession vanishes. . . . " The magnificence of the fountain, with its waterfall, its statues of Neptune and those illustrating the legend of the discovery of the Virgin's Spring, gives the composer fine scope for elaborate, gorgeous writing.

4. The Fountain of the Villa Medici, at Dusk. "A sad theme rises above a subdued warbling. The air is full of tolling bells and birds twittering; then all dies peacefully in the silence of the night." The music suggests the chaste dignity of the fountain in its oak-guarded seclusion — a scene meet for half-sweet, half-melancholy meditations as the day is dying.

Carnival of the Animals Saint-Saëns

A bulwark of conservatism and a believer in the value of absolute music, Saint-Saëns (who died in 1921 at the age of 86) did not allow this "grand zoological fantasy" to be published or performed during his lifetime. One hearing will show why; for it is a most unconventional piece (it was originally written as a sort of musical joke), and its realism has become famous. In the various sketches the composer not only reproduces the sounds made by the various animals but also delights in satirizing the music of his own day. The orchestration includes a two-piano part and a well-known solo for cello. The sections are labeled:

Introduction and Royal March of the Lion

Hens and Cocks

Wild Asses

Tortoises (The composer here mocks an Offenbach cancan by playing it very slowly.)

The Elephant (The tune to which the elephant lumbers is Berlioz's *Waltz of the Sylphs!*)

Kangaroos

Aquarium

Personages with Long Ears

Cuckoo in the Woods

Birds

Fossils (Saint-Saëns does not hesitate to ridicule himself, for he includes a theme here from his *Danse macabre.*)

The Swan (This is the most famous of all sketches, and includes the famous cello solo, "The Swan.")

Pianists (Concert players, with their phenomenal runs and crashing chords, are here put in their place. Without interruption, the music goes into a brilliant Finale, in which all the animals are passed in review.)

The whole thing is not much more than a well-done pre-Disney "Silly Symphony"; but it is clever and witty music and has found a place on concert programs.

TOPICS FOR FURTHER DISCUSSION

Is *Les Préludes* as fine a work as *Till?* If not, where is it weaker? What do you like most, and least, in *Les Préludes?* Do you find any of its qualities prominent in any other music by Liszt that you have heard?

Could you summarize, in a single phrase, Liszt's besetting sin? In so far as music history is concerned, what is his outstanding contribution to the development of the art? What do you know of his qualities as a man, not as an artist?

Do you think any rivival of the *Les Préludes* type of Romanticism is possible in the near future? Would such a revival attract you personally?

Discuss the theory that history moves in cycles, and that the same "movements" return at intervals (this with reference to Romanticism).

What is the present tendency in art, and what seems likely to follow it?

DEFINITE SUGGESTIONS FOR READING

Music in History: The Romantic Ideal in Art
Liszt: A Soul Divided Against Itself

TWELVE

THE QUESTION OF FORM

Form in art means exactly what it means in life in general — the successful co-ordination of elements so as to produce the most effective results possible. When we speak of the form of an athlete, we have reference to the intangible something that has enabled him to bring all his powers into proper relationship and co-ordination so as to attain the greatest possible effectiveness. Form in art means the organizing process — in plain terms, the plan — by which all the fundamental elements which go to make up that art are arranged so as to secure the maximum impression upon the consciousness of him who perceives. A piece of music, for example, may have good melody, with well-arranged rhythmic patterns, may be well harmonized, with effective combinations of timbre; but unless it has, in addition, a good plan of organization by which its materials are significantly ordered, it fails of full effect. This ability effectively to organize his materials is the most intellectual part of a composer's equipment; it may to a certain degree be acquired, but it must be present if a man is to write good music. The greatest composers have been those who have had consummate skill in creating great ideas and an organizing ability to present them well.

We have already suggested the need for design and form in all art; that need is even more necessary in the immaterial and transient art of music, which goes as quickly as it comes, than it is in the material arts of painting, sculpture, and architecture. A composer must know how to present his ideas so as to arrest our attention and so as to hold it. The various elements that make up his whole composition must be contrasted in a way that will give effective balance, without being so diffuse as to make them difficult to remember. A composer must have some design or formal scheme in his mind when he writes, else his music will be simply a hodgepodge of ideas, unintelligible to other minds.

FORM IN PROGRAM MUSIC

We have just studied some representative examples of program music; the composers of these works were not greatly concerned with the problem of "how to make their music last." They simply took a suitable story or a philosophical concept and, using a few themes as generative material, let the music they wrote follow the necessities of the program. We can be sure, however, that when composers such as Liszt and Strauss chose programs, they kept a weather eye out for genetic possibilities: they made sure that the program in itself was constructed so as to provide elements of contrast, balance, and unity (review briefly the programs of *Till Eulenspiegel* and *Les Préludes* and see how true this is), that it made an effective start, and that it led through a number of contrasting episodes to a convincing finish. Hence the music with which they clothed the program possesses the quality of good formal design.

These compositions are called *symphonic* (or *tone*) *poems,* a term invented by Liszt, who wrote thirteen works of this kind. The listener should be able to realize that in them the formal structural plan follows the program, without having any set outline. A work of this kind having several movements, such as Rimsky-Korsakoff's *Scheherazade* suite (to be studied soon), is called a *symphonic suite*. There is usually little thematic development in these works, its place being taken by alterations and paraphrases of the themes to fit the program.

FORM IN ABSOLUTE MUSIC

An even greater concern with the principles of good construction is necessary in writing absolute music, for in it there is nothing in the way of an underlying poetic program to carry us along. The best way to sense this is to listen carefully to a well-constructed piece of absolute music where the formal patterns are comparatively easy to follow — again the first movement of Beethoven's *Fifth Symphony* is an ideal example. Upon hearing music such as this, even for the first time, you will observe that there are several well-defined themes, such as were found in the program pieces, that occur and recur frequently. But in the absolute music these themes are presented in a logically and carefully ordered manner so that they may be readily grasped; they have, of course, no connection with any story. It is not difficult to see, then, that some

Photograph by Muller

Capital from the Church of St. Michel-de-Cuxa, Roussillon, France

Showing a twelfth-century sculptor's understanding of *form.* Abstracting the shapes of well-known animals and birds, this unknown artist made them into a beautifully shaped capital, or head of a pillar designed to support an archway. Here, indeed, "all the fundamental elements are arranged so as to secure the maximum impression upon the consciousness of him who perceives" and incidentally to make a most functional architectural design.

understanding of this controlled imaginative thinking, as form has been defined, is necessary if we are to increase our enjoyment of music through comprehending it.

Before we try to explain the rather intricate details of musical design, it will be well to clear up one prevalent misunderstanding as to the general nature of form. In discussing the problems of the composer we have said that he has at his disposal a number of structural plans or molds, evolved by his predecessors through the centuries, which aid in the coherent organization of his material. We are apt to think that a composer chooses one of these formal molds that seems best suited to his purpose and then designs the substance of his music to fit its requirements. It is customary to suggest in this respect that in art there are *form* and *substance* — the vessel and that which the vessel contains. This is not true; an examination of any great masterpiece of music, painting, or architecture will show that it seldom fits neatly into a prearranged scheme of formal design such as is laid down by textbooks. In art, form and substance are one, inseparable, born together in the mind of the creator and growing together as do the veins and arteries in our bodies and the blood they contain. Rightly considered, any study of the formal element in music or in any other art is made in order better to understand the living thing, a process similar to that undertaken by the medical student in order that he may thoroughly understand the living organisms with which he must deal. We must realize that a composer can, at the same time, work within a formal mold and yet be independent of it. Almost every great symphony written is a good example of this: while keeping to the general formal outlines laid down by his predecessors, Beethoven did not hesitate to depart from them whenever he felt that such a procedure would make his music more effective. It may truly be said that the "form of any genuine piece of art is unique."

It would seem foolish for any composer to discard the well-tried and proved formulas that had been developed through the combined effort of generations preceding him. These predetermined formulas are in the back of his mind as he writes, acting as guides and incentives. But it would be even more foolish for him to attempt anything in the way of absolute fidelity to such formulas; this could only result in what the Germans realistically call *Kapellmeistermusik* — music that is correctly written but which possesses no spark of life. The character of the composer's thought, the exigencies that develop as he proceeds in his work, make it necessary that he use any formal scheme that he may choose only as a prop, discarding it whenever it does not seem to suit his particular and personal need. In this sense we can see that each masterpiece makes its own rules.

All this does not mean, however, that the listener cannot profit greatly from an understanding of these design patterns that have been used by the composers. There are a number of ways in which we may classify these forms, the better to realize their full significance. Perhaps the most useful of these distinctions is that between

(1) forms used in vocal music,
(2) forms that may be either vocal or instrumental, and
(3) forms peculiar to instrumental music

There are a number of these various types of forms, and they are discussed in some detail in various sections of this book. We are giving here a complete table of them, arranged so that you may see their relationships and significance:

Vocal Forms

IN SECULAR MUSIC:
1. The song
2. The opera
3. The madrigal
4. The cantata

IN SACRED MUSIC:
1. The song
2. The chant
3. The hymn (chorale)
4. The motet (anthem)
5. The mass (communion service)
6. The oratorio (passion — cantata)

Forms That Are Both Vocal and Instrumental

1. Contrapuntal forms based on a *cantus firmus*
2. The fugue

Instrumental Forms

SECTIONAL FORMS (Forms in relation to separate, short divisions of a work)
1. Unitary form (One-part form)
2. Variation form
3. Rondo form
4. Binary form (Two-part form)
5. Ternary form (Three-part form)
   a. In songs
   b. In short instrumental pieces — the minuet, and so on

     c. In small piano pieces — nocturne, waltz, impromptu, and so forth

     d. In slow movements of sonatas and symphonies

     e. In first movements of sonatas and symphonies (sonata form)

  6. Free forms: overture, fantasia, prelude

CONJOINT FORMS (Form in relation to the piece as a whole)

  1. The march

  2. The waltz

  3. Small instrumental pieces (nocturne, étude, and so on)

  4. The suite

  5. The sonata

  6. The symphony

  7. The concerto

  8. Chamber music: trio, quartet, quintet, and so forth

  9. The symphonic poem (program-music form)

VOCAL FORMS

It is difficult for most listeners to realize that vocal music reached a height of perfection long before instrumental music did, for our attention is largely centered on the latter type, almost to the exclusion of interest in the former. Naturally form in vocal music follows the words; the composer of vocal music takes a series of words — a poem, a liturgical text, or a dramatic libretto — and "sets" them to music. The result depends so largely upon the character of the text that the first requisite in following the vocal forms is a complete understanding of the words used. We come here upon a difficult and vexatious problem, one that is of great importance for the English-speaking listener who would familiarize himself with vocal music: the outstanding examples of the various types of vocal form — song, oratorio, opera, mass — have foreign texts. And, strange as it may seem, fashion and usage have decreed that nations such as the United States and England, where the people generally have little experience with any language other than their own, must listen to their songs, operas, and oratorios in Italian, German, French, and Latin, but have difficulty in hearing them in English. Little wonder that opera in both these English-speaking countries is almost a dead issue, precariously supported by all sorts of social snobberies and extra-musical resuscitators; or that the song literature, one of the finest in all music, is so little known!

There is no need to attempt a definition of a *song;* every individual, whether or not he is really musical, has experienced the satisfaction of expressing his feelings through bursting into song: it is the most immediate and intimate musical manifestation that man knows. We shall have a great deal to say later about the various types of songs. Here we can distinguish between the simple *folk song* and the consciously composed *art song;* both have their own form, and there can be no prescribed patterns. We should also mention here the difference between the semi-spoken portions of opera, called *recitative,* and the songlike *arias,* so often used apart from their context; and the *madrigal,* a song for several voices, set to secular words, with or without instrumental accompaniment, so popular in the sixteenth and seventeenth centuries.

There are a number of forms in sacred music. The simplest of these is the *hymn,* a stanzaic religious song composed in a style that is effective for massed singing. Hymns have been used by all civilizations and have become an integral part of the Christian liturgy; the type introduced by Luther into the Protestant Church at the time of the Reformation — the *chorale* — avoids the unfortunate sentimentality found in so many English hymns and constitutes one of music's greatest treasures, especially as elaborated and harmonized by J. S. Bach.

A *motet* may be defined as the sacred counterpart of the madrigal; a sacred song for a number of voices, it has no definitely fixed place in the liturgy of the Church. Its English counterpart is the *anthem.*

The *Mass,* speaking musically, is the setting given to those fixed portions of the Eucharistic rite of the Roman and Greek churches that are appointed to be sung by the choir. Some of the world's finest music has gone into these settings, most of them unheard today because of their specific ritualistic character. Beginning with those unknown composers who wrote Gregorian chant settings of the Mass away back in the early centuries of the Church's existence, almost every composer up through the seventeenth century has given attention to this form. Even such outstanding men as Bach and Beethoven wrote Masses, compositions which, considered as music, rank high among the works of these composers, although they are not suitable for liturgical use in church. The *Requiem Mass* is a special type sung for the repose of the souls of the dead. The *Communion Service* consists of the translated parts of the Catholic Mass that have been retained in the ritual of the Anglican churches.

An *oratorio* can be described as a sort of non-acting version of opera, having a dramatic text or libretto (which may be either sacred or secular in character), recitative, arias, and choruses, with orchestral accompaniment, but no stage action, scenery, or costumes. The *Passion* is a special form of oratorio developed in the German Lutheran Church, with the text, drawn from the gospel narratives, descriptive of the sufferings of Christ between the night of the Last Supper and his death. Literally a *cantata* refers to any composition that is to be sung; specifically it means a small-dimensioned oratorio; historically it may be either sacred or secular in character, for either a solo voice or the usual performing apparatus of the oratorio — solos, chorus, and so on.

The Columbia University Professor of Philosophy, Irwin Edman, wrote some verses for *The New Yorker* magazine which he called "Varieties of Musical Experience"; these contain such good, humorous descriptions of some of the most used forms that we are quoting them in this and following chapters with his and *The New Yorker's* permission. Regarding the cantata he says:

No person's more *persona grata*
Than he who's penned a sound cantata;
Would there were lots of him! But ach,
There are but few, and none like Bach!

FORMS THAT ARE BOTH VOCAL AND INSTRUMENTAL

It does not take a great deal of musical experience to realize that most of the forms employed by composers through the ages have been either vocal or instrumental; but a few forms were developed at the time when vocal music, which, as we have said, reached a high point of development long before the appearance of a distinctive instrumental style, was gradually being supplanted by instrumental. Early instrumental music was merely the playing on instruments of that which had been written originally for voices; through a method of trial-and-error experimentation, there gradually developed a style that was characteristically suited to instruments. At first this imitated vocal music, and so the earliest instrumental forms that we find in the developing history of music are those that could be used for either singing or playing. An examination of these identical forms will show that they are all *contrapuntal* in character.

TEXTURES IN MUSIC

The term *contrapuntal* is one which needs special description; this seems as appropriate a place to attempt it as any other, even though such a description risks a diversion from the main points at issue. In general, the texture of music (its peculiar structural quality resulting from the blend of its elements) may be said to be of three different kinds: *monophonic, homophonic,* and *polyphonic.* Derivatively, the first two of these words mean the same thing: sounding alike, of the the same pitch; technically, they have two quite different meanings. The third word means, literally, "many-voiced" and in general is used as synonymous with *contrapuntal.*

Monophonic music is the simplest we know — a one-voiced, unaccompanied line such as is found in Chinese, ancient Greek, or Hindu music; or, in our Western system, in the Gregorian chant of the early Church.

Homophonic texture in music can easily be recognized in such selections as Handel's *Ombra mai fu* (Largo) from *Xerxes,* the second movement of Dvořák's *Symphony No. 5,* or, in fact, in most of the music written from the end of the sixteenth century to the present day. Its distinguishing characteristic is that it consists of a principal melodic line supported by a *chordal* accompaniment, the sort of thing we discussed in our earlier remarks about harmony. This accompaniment may consist of simple successions of blocks of chords, as in the Handel excerpt, or these chords may be broken up, their tones sounded not simultaneously but one after the other, in some sort of *arpeggio* formation, like this:

There is a third kind of texture, one that is much more difficult to recognize and hear than the two we have just described, largely because it is not used in the music making of today as it was in earlier times, and therefore our ears have to become accustomed to its peculiar characteristics. This kind of musical texture was employed by composers before they adopted the general ideals of the homophonic style somewhere around the beginning of the seventeenth century. We call it *polyphonic* or *contrapuntal* because it is made up of a number of separate and independent melodic strands, each with its own rhythmic values, which, taken together, form harmonies. This is the way all part music before 1600, and a considerable amount of it for some time afterwards, was written; and it is necessary to learn to listen to this type of music in a different way from that which is used for the works of later composers. In polyphonic music we should try to hear separately the various strands that are sung or played by the different parts, instead of being content to hear the customary main melody, supported from moment to moment by chords in vertical fashion.

Even for those who do not read music, the following selections will help to clarify the differences between these three textures: the very look of the notes on the paper shows the essential characteristics of the music.

(A) *Monophonic Music*

A - gnus De - i, ✳ qui tol - lis pec - ca - ta

mun - di: do - na no - bis pa - cem.

(B) *Homophonic Music*

Symphony No. 5, in E Minor
Second Movement

Dvořák

Largo

(C) *Polyphonic (Contrapuntal) Music*

Mass, "Assumpta Est Maria"
Christe Eleison

Palestrina

HOMOPHONIC AND POLYPHONIC MUSIC

A piece of music does not necessarily keep strictly to any one of these textures. Generally speaking, the earlier it comes in the line of historical development, the greater the probability that it will be written with only one kind of textural fabric. We have already said that the earliest European music we know consists of a single unaccompanied melodic line, and that up to the beginning of the seventeenth century music was almost entirely polyphonic. After that there was a graceful blending of the homophonic and the polyphonic manners of writing until the nineteenth century, when composers began to emphasize the basic homophonic style. Of late, because of a neoclassic reaction against the romantic excesses of the nineteenth century, there has been a revival of interest in counterpoint (a term synonymous with polyphony).

A good example of distinction between homophonic and polyphonic styles is in the chorus "Glory to God" from Handel's *Messiah;* this is written at first in harmonic blocks, and then, at the words "good will towards men," it changes to polyphony. This is easy both to hear with the ear and to see with the eye, in the score. Another outstanding example of the practical use of these various textural styles is the slow movement of Beethoven's *Seventh Symphony:* the earlier part is almost entirely homophonic — all chords, with hardly a suggestion of melody. Then comes a middle part that is partly contrapuntal, partly homophonic, because of a new, fully expressed melody that is woven against the chordal background. Later on, there are several short, purely contrapuntal sections where the violins weave a distinctive counterpoint against the melody that was heard in the opening measures.

This distinction between the polyphonic and homophonic styles of writing is a vital one, and it is necessary to understand it thoroughly if we are to realize the fundamental qualities of music written in different historical periods. The polyphonic style, with its intricate weavings of parts, was a natural one for composers to use in writing for voices. When the instrumentalists began to develop an independent style that would realize the possibilities of their instruments, they started with some of these vocal contrapuntal forms, and so it came about that certain forms were used both vocally and instrumentally.

These were all based on some clearly defined theme that could easily be recognized and followed throughout the course of the music; they consisted of ingenious contrapuntal manipulations of this fundamental generative idea, which was called the *cantus firmus* (literally, "fixed song"). Composers of the great polyphonic period (the fifteenth, sixteenth, and seventeenth centuries) did not consider themselves so much inventors as builders; sometimes they did not even use their own themes for the foundations of the imposing tonal structures they reared. Many of the countless Masses and other church compositions written during this time were based on themes taken from Gregorian chants or from the works of other composers, or, strange as it may seem to us today, on the often incongruous tune of a popular song of the day. Later, in the Lutheran Church, the same practice was followed, except that the *cantus firmus* was usually a chorale tune well known to the congregation for which the music was written. Many of Bach's church cantatas contain elaborate contrapuntal numbers for voices and orchestra consisting entirely of the treatment of some chorale *cantus firmus*. Likewise Bach and his predecessors and followers wrote a large number of *chorale preludes*, service pieces for the organ with a chorale as *cantus firmus*; and these little works, many of them programmatic in character, since they often depict some idea suggested by the words of the hymn, show Bach's genius at its zenith.

The *fugue* was one of the most popular of these overlapping vocal-instrumental styles; it may be said to have been the outstanding one for both vocal and instrumental music during the seventeenth century. Technically it consists of an elaborate polyphonic texture — it can hardly be called a set "form" — that was evolved during the fifteenth and sixteenth centuries from the simple principle of imitative writing.

Everyone knows the *round*, or *canon* as it is more formally called, a sequential presentation of one musical phrase by a number of different voices, the phrase being so devised as always to serve as its own polyphonic accompaniment. It is this fundamental idea that underlies the construction of the fugue. But in its more elaborated presentation, the texture is so woven as to allow each of the two, three, four, or more voices in which the fugue is written equal participation in the general effect. Starting with a single part, unaccompanied, the fugue, in its contrapuntal weaving course, builds up irresistibly and inexorably to an architectural sort of climax at the very end. Between the presentations of the main *theme*, or *subject*, episodes, mostly made out of the same materials, are introduced. Thus there are high unity and wide variety in the fugue, and the composer's skill must provide cumulative interest; as Edman puts it in his little verses:

> In fugues the listener rejoices
> To follow keenly several voices
> And at the close greet with a shout
> The way they neatly all work out.

It might be thought that such a complex musical pattern, more or less strict in its fashioning, variable only through the amount of musical invention the composer puts into it, would be stiff and academic. But Bach was able to make this complicated process of weaving tonal lines yield some of his most imaginative and surprisingly beautiful music. It has appeared, usually written in a rather free style, occasionally since.

LIST OF SUGGESTED MUSIC

Songs

FOLK: Early American Ballads

These comprise a number of American mountaineer ballads whicn can be traced to English, Scottish, Irish, and Welsh sources, sung in traditional manner by John Niles: *The Gypsy Laddie; My Little Mohee; I Wonder as I Wander Out Under the Sky; Lulle Lullay; The Seven Joys of Mary; Barberry Ellen.*

ART: *Der Erlkönig*   Schubert

Der Wanderer   Schubert

Other Forms

ARIA: *Cielo e mar!* from the opera *La Gioconda*   Ponchielli

MADRIGAL: Sweet Honey-Sucking Bees   Wilbye

HYMN: Onward, Christian Soldiers   Sullivan

CHORALE: *Ein' feste Burg*   Luther

MOTET: *O Bone Jesu*   Palestrina

ANTHEM: The Bell Anthem   Purcell

MASS: *Assumpta est Maria*   Palestrina

The Requiem Mass (K. 626)   Mozart

ORATORIO: *Messiah*   Handel

St. Matthew Passion   Bach

CANTATA: (Sacred) *Christ lag in Todesbanden*   Bach
(Secular) *Nell' dolce dell' oblio*   Handel
MONOPHONIC MUSIC: Any part of the Gregorian setting
to the Mass *Lux et origo*
HOMOPHONIC MUSIC: *Ombra mai fu*
from the opera *Xerxes*   Handel
POLYPHONIC MUSIC: Any part of the setting
of the *Missa Papae Marcelli*   Palestrina
MIXED STYLES (both homophonic and polyphonic)
Seventh Symphony, Second Movement   Beethoven
INSTRUMENTAL TREATMENT OF A *Cantus Firmus:*
Chorale Prelude: *Das alte Jahr vergangen ist*   Bach
Chorale Prelude: *Liebster Jesu*   Bach
Fugue in G Minor (Lesser)   Bach

TOPICS FOR FURTHER DISCUSSION

Can Form and Substance ever be separated in a work of art?

Discuss the peculiar suitability of early forms to the use of either voices or instruments.

Consider the importance of Key in form, taking as an example any simple two-part or three-part form and noting how key changes afford variety.

Is Polyphony as valid for our pleasure and for the creation of masterpieces today as it was three hundred years ago? If not, account for its decline.

Can you think of any new musical form that the future is likely to produce, or any return to an old one?

[THIRTEEN]

INSTRUMENTAL FORMS

When we listen to music that has no associa-
tion with words, it is often difficult to recognize the various units
which go to make up its formal architecture, for we do not have the
structural outline of the poetry to help us. Just as in writing this
book words are put together to form phrases, phrases are joined into
sentences, sentences grouped so as to make paragraphs, paragraphs
are molded into chapters, and chapters added together to form the
whole work, composers deal with similar structural units in building their music. The smallest is a little melodic or rhythmic group,
sometimes containing only a few notes, such as the famous so-called
Fate *motive* in the first movement of Beethoven's *Fifth Symphony*. These motives are usually combined into larger units, forming a more complete melody of several measures, called a *theme*.
These themes can, in turn, be extended and enlarged with congruous material into *sections*. And sections can be gathered together
to form what is called a *movement*, the very meaning of which suggests that it is a structural division of an even more extended composition such as a *symphony*.

A description such as this cannot be exact, and you will find in
reading about musical form that there is by no means any uniform
agreement about these terms. In studying form as a help in listening
we should be content with finding out generalities and approximations, and "look for exactness only so far as the nature of the subject permits," to borrow an Aristotelian phrase. General methods of
procedure can be deduced from observing individual works of art;
but no genuine art work can be formulated according to exact
prescription. If it were, it would certainly cease to be art. Although
there are general formal principles that underlie the construction of
all instrumental music, each composition, large or small, elaborate
or simple, must in reality make its own rules.

VARIOUS TYPES

The easiest musical forms for listeners to recognize are those which are put together sectionally, each section being made up of material that hangs together naturally.

1. The simplest of these sectional forms is that which consists of a single division — a short composition that was conceived all of a piece, without break from beginning to end. This type of form is not very usual and when employed is limited to small pieces in which there is no need for contrast. The first prelude in Bach's *Well-Tempered Clavier* and Chopin's Prelude Number One in his Opus 28 can be cited as effective examples of this "unitary" form.

2. It would be perfectly possible to make an extended piece of music out of an indefinite repetition of one of these single-division forms; but the result would hardly be interesting. Basically, as the early composers of instrumental music quickly found out, either one of two things can be done to a tune to stretch it into an extended composition: repeat it or vary it. And, since literal repetition is dull, they soon found out how to repeat it with diversity. Edman puts it neatly:

It's fun to watch while a musician
Dotes on a theme by repetition.
There is no other art I know of
Where anyone can make a go of
Saying once, then ten times more,
The same thing one has said before.

So we find the *theme and variations* (which may be represented to the literal-minded by the formula: $A - A^1 - A^2 - A^3$, and so forth) used by many of the earliest instrumental composers. Some of the first examples of this form are not very exciting to modern ears: such things as Byrd's "The Bells" and Morley's "Goe from My Window" are variations done according to formula and tend to become tiresome. The seventeenth-century and eighteenth-century *air with doubles* (so-called because each successive variation was written with faster notes), although not profound, contains some interesting technical devices. The most famous example of this type of variation is the one that has been called "The Harmonious Blacksmith," from Handel's *Suite in E Major*. Other early variation forms were two varieties of the *basso ostinato* (literally, obstinate bass, since a short phrase is repeated over and over in the bass), the *chaconne* and the *passacaglia,* forms which consist of a series of variations built around the reiteration of a melody or a set of chords. All these were widely used by the "pre-classic" composers: Frescobaldi and Purcell wrote some of the best we know.

With the advent of the classic composers, Haydn, Mozart, and Beethoven, the theme and variations became a more interesting form. The theme was usually straightforward, and the variations followed it closely as to melodic outline, dimensions, and structural relationships. Haydn's well-known set in the second movement of his *Surprise Symphony,* the first movement of Mozart's *A Major Piano Sonata,* the slow movement of Beethoven's *Kreutzer Sonata,* Op. 47, should be listened to carefully as excellent examples. Even the nineteenth-century composers found this form exceedingly useful although they did not follow it closely: their compositions might better be called "meditations" or "divagations" than "variations." Schumann's *Études Symphoniques,* Brahms's *Variations on a Theme by Haydn,* César Franck's *Symphonic Variations,* and, above all others, Elgar's *Enigma Variations* are works of considerable length and great interest. Such modern writers as Stravinsky (in his *Octet for Wind Instruments*), Roy Harris (in a string quartet), and Hindemith (in his *Schwanendreher*) have used this oldest of all instrumental forms for shaping their contemporary musical thoughts.

3. The *rondo* form is another way of organizing an extended piece out of a single-sectioned form. Here we have a scheme in which a section is literally repeated a number of times, with extraneous material in well-varied keys (which play a considerable part in the interest of the work) inserted between each repetition, thus: A–B–A–C–A–D, and so on. There are different kinds of rondos, but they are all symmetrical in construction; their derivation was probably from the literary *rondel,* invented in the fourteenth century and largely used by medieval French poets. There was a certain rhyme scheme in its fourteen lines; here is a nineteenth-century example, by Dobson:

A
Love comes back to his vacant dwelling
The old, old Love that we knew of yore!

B
We see him stand by the open door,
With his great eyes sad, and his bosom swelling
He makes as though in our arms repelling
He fain would lie as he lay before:

A Love comes back to his vacant dwelling
   The old, old Love that we knew of yore!

C Ah, who shall keep us from over-spelling
   That sweet, forgotten, forbidden Love?
   E'en as we doubt, in our hearts once more,
   With a rush of tears to our eyelids welling

A Love comes back to his vacant dwelling
   The old, old Love that we knew of yore!

It is not difficult to see how the composers adapted this repetitive scheme for their purposes; and so we have the rondo, with its sections contrasted in key and character.

BINARY FORM

4. A sectional form that has been widely employed, especially by composers of an earlier time, is the *binary* or *two-part* form (represented symbolically by the formula A–B), consisting of two consecutive divisions [1]; sometimes the second is entirely different from the first, sometimes it is simply a new aspect or rearrangement of it. The A section usually ends in the key of the dominant; B leads back to the tonic. The tune "America" is an illustration of simple binary form; the musical phrases to which the first three lines of the text are sung comprise the first section; those set to the last four lines make up the second division. Many of the Schubert and Brahms piano waltzes are written in this form.

Binary form was extremely popular in the seventeenth and eighteenth centuries and was often used by such composers as François Couperin and Domenico Scarlatti in the pieces they wrote for the harpsichord. Listen to some of Couperin's fancifully titled clavecin pieces or to one of Scarlatti's brilliant sonatas, and you will have heard this form in its best estate.

TERNARY FORM

5. Still another easily recognized scheme is that of *three-part* or

---

[1] Either or both of these divisions may be repeated, but it is customary in analyzing forms not to take these literal repetitions into account.

ternary form (A–B–A), perhaps the most universally used of them all. Listen to this French folk song:

The two sections marked A are exactly alike, excepting at their end; the second has a more final air about it than had the first at this point. This is likewise true of this German folk tune:

But if you follow these tunes through, you will find that their composers were not satisfied with just this simple repetition of ideas. In the French song, a new contrasting idea is inserted, consisting of two short phrases, the second an exact duplicate of the first; and after this the first section, A, returns again:

So with the German song:

This gives us a basic picture of the pattern which is used continuously throughout music, in all kinds of simple and complex ways:

1. The statement of an idea or a section
2. The placing in contrast of a new idea or section
3. The restatement of the first idea so as to give unity and finality

We find examples of this form in music of many styles and periods:

A. It has been employed by the composers of many simple songs. Hum or whistle through the following tunes, and you will find that they are all built according to this three-part form:

Ye Banks and Braes, Scots folk tune
The Flight of the Earls, Irish folk tune
All Through the Night, Welsh folk tune
Drink to Me Only With Thine Eyes, English folk tune
Turkey in the Straw, American folk tune
O Tannenbaum, German folk tune
Humoresque, Dvořák

B. It was used by composers of the classic period for certain of their short instrumental pieces, particularly the minuet. Of all the dances developed during the course of European history, this seems to have had the greatest effect upon music; starting as a French peasant dance, it was adopted by the aristocratic court circles and then taken over by the writers of instrumental music. Almost from its earliest existence it has been written in ternary form — a first stanza, followed by a second, and then the first again. In Bach's time the two contrasting sections of a minuet were thought of as separate pieces and so labeled: Minuets I and II. These were played successively, after which Minuet I was repeated (see Bach's *B Minor Orchestral Suite*). In order to provide better contrast, the second minuet was written for three instruments or in three-part harmony, and so came to be known as the *trio*. This name stuck, even after the reasons for it had been lost. So the plan came to be:

(*a*) Minuet
(*b*) Another minuet called a *trio*
(*c*) The original minuet repeated intact

When Beethoven supplanted the minuet by the *scherzo* in his piano and orchestral pieces, he kept the same general form, merely changing its mood and speed; some of this composer's most characteristic contributions to symphonic literature took the form of *scherzo* and *trio:* for example, the third movement of the *Eroica* and the *Seventh Symphony*. Many composers since his time have followed his example in using the scherzo in their symphonies.

C. The three-part form, with slight adaptations, was used for many of the small pieces which were popular with the nineteenth-century piano composers, such things as the nocturne, the waltz, the prelude, the impromptu, and so on. It makes an ideal form for this purpose, for in a limited scope it offers plenty of opportunity for ingenious architecture and strong emotional contrasts. Here are some characteristic examples from Chopin:

Nocturne in F Major, Op. 15, No. 1.

A beautiful slow melody (marked *adagio cantabile*) is the feature of the opening section (1–24); the middle section (25–48) is marked by a fiery series of broken chords and brilliant runs for the left hand; and then the quiet, peaceful melody returns in its original mood.

Nocturne in F Sharp Major, Op. 15, No. 2.

Here again the A section (1–24) is marked by one of those slow, rather melancholy melodies that Chopin knew so well how to write. The middle section (25–48) has in contrast a series of interlocking chords supporting a melody that moves twice as fast as did the original one. Then the first section is again heard almost exactly as before.

Prelude in D Flat Major, Op. 28, No. 15.

Here the contrasting section (28–75) is carried over logically from the first (1–27) by a clever device: the almost maddening repetition of a note that has been very prominent in the melody and harmony of the first section. Upon its return A is somewhat shortened.

Étude in F Major, Op. 10, No. 8.

The different sections are not always clearly defined. Here the middle section (41–60) is marked out, not by the introduction of new material, but by the reshaping of the ideas of the first part. A (1–40) is distinguished by a running figure in quick time in which the accent is heavily marked out at the beginning of every second measure. In B we seem to sink to a new tone level, and the rhythmic pattern is obscured by the bright chromatic harmonies, making a blaze of color which quickly subsides when A (61–86) is reintroduced. There is a distinct coda (87), a prolongation of the section, due to the natural tendency of an artist to end whatever he attempts in as impressive and complete a way as possible.

D. An extended ternary form is sometimes used for the slow movements of sonatas and symphonies; when this is the case, the result is simply a lengthened song form such as that employed by the unknown composers of *Sur le pont d'Avignon* and *Ach! du lieber Augustin.* Grieg used this extended three-part song form most effectively in the second movement of his *Sonata in C Minor* for violin and piano, Op. 45. In this the first division of 44 measures is played by the piano alone, and then repeated by the piano and the violin together; the B section offers new material in decided contrast to the A; and then A returns, this time with the violin part an octave higher than before.[2]

[2] Wagner, the great opera composer, had a peculiar name for this form: he called it

E. The most complex and, at the same time, most widely used of the tripartite forms is the *sonata form*, generally used in the first movements of sonatas, symphonies, and quartets. Musical nomenclature is here sadly at fault, for it gives plenty of opportunity for confusion in the use of this term, which is used for two different things: we use it when we speak of the form of the sonata as an entire work, consisting of three or four movements; we use it also when referring specifically to the structural plan that is generally used in the first (and sometimes in the last) of these movements.

AN IMPORTANT DISTINCTION

The listener must keep the distinction clearly in mind between (1) a type of composition — the sonata as a whole — and (2) a movement form — *sonata form*, sometimes termed *first-movement form* or *sonata-allegro form*. This form was first developed by the generation of composers following Sebastian Bach, especially by one of his sons, Carl Philipp Emmanuel, and his contemporaries. It reached full maturity at the hands of still another generation centering around Haydn and Mozart; from their time on it became the usual form for the first, quick movement of sonatas, symphonies, quartets, and other instrumental music. Followed in general by Beethoven, it was sometimes sorely strained by his innovations; and later on, as Romanticism developed, it became somewhat modified by such composers as Schumann and Liszt. But in general it can be said to be one of the soundest structural schemes used by composers, satisfying the needs of men as widely different as Haydn, Beethoven, and Brahms. Some of the greatest music has been composed in this form, and it has proved to be a stimulant for important composers to do their best work.

The cardinal principle of this sonata form is that of the manipulation of two main thematic groups of contrasting character, the one

---

a *bogen*, and used it frequently during the course of the musical development of his great works. A slightly different three-part form was also used frequently by him, a form consisting of two identical or similar parts (each of which he called a *stollen*), completed by a third part, known as the *abgesang* — A–A–B instead of A–B–A. This unit Wagner called a *bar*, taking the name from the old nomenclature of the medieval guild of the Mastersingers. Indeed, his whole opera *Die Meistersinger* is filled with *bars*, varying in length from phrases a few measures in length to others occupying many pages of score. Notable among these is the music which fills the Prize Song section in the last act and which accompanies Walther's *Am stillen Herd* in the first act.

vigorous (masculine, it is sometimes designated), the other (feminine) gentler and more lyrical. These groups are usually, but not very accurately, described by the terms *first theme* or *subject* and *second theme* or *subject*. The first group centers about the home or tonic key, the other about a contrasting, related key — almost always the dominant in a major-key movement, and the relative major in a minor-key movement. Each of these thematic groups has room for connecting and subsidiary themes.

The general scheme of procedure in the sonata form is as follows: There is a first thematic group in the tonic, followed by a transitional or bridge passage to another key, when there appears a second or subsidiary group which comes to an end in a definite, final manner. This part thus far is what is called the *Exposition* or *Statement* of the theme and is often repeated, especially in classic symphonies and sonatas. Then follows a section called the *Working-out* or *Development*, in which the previous materials are shown in new ways and there are some new groupings of parts of the themes, with a number of changes of key; and sometimes new material is introduced. Eventually this leads back skillfully (if the composer knows his business) to the tonic key and the *Recapitulation*. This section restates the Exposition but puts it this time all in one key. The Development and the Recapitulation often are followed by a *Coda*, to bring the whole movement to a fitting conclusion.

For handy reference, the basic construction of this form may be diagrammed in this fashion:

AN INTRODUCTION (Not an essential part of the scheme, and not found in many instances after Haydn)

A: THE STATEMENT OF THE THEMES (Exposition)

Tonic key	(1) First theme group connected by means of a bridge passage to
Dominant key (*Relative major, if first theme is in minor*)	(2) Second theme (or group of themes), complementary in character, sometimes (as in the developed Beethoven style) closely connected with a
	(3) Closing passage. This may consist of a new theme (which would then be called the third theme) or of a modification of the other themes. This part brings the whole section to a definite close.

B: THE DEVELOPMENT OF THE THEMES

Many keys	Here the composer re-creates his themes in new ways, often pulling them apart and re-combining them in new patterns, letting his skill and imagination deal with them in various ways. This section is marked by many changes of key, thus providing constant new interest.

A: THE RESTATEMENT OF THE THEMES (Recapitulation)

Tonic key	(1) Restated as before, and connected with
	(2) Restated, and in turn often connected with
	(3) Restated, after which the movement is brought to a close.

The coda, or post-oration, often follows, thus providing a final climax.

This, it must always be remembered, is a simplified, skeletonized plan of sonata form, and many deviations from it are possible and have been made by various composers. Actual listening practice [3] will show that the sonata form is not so simple as the above outline might lead us to believe. For instance, what we have called the first and second *themes* are often not so much clear-cut themes as series of compacted fragments of themes. The important thing to realize is that this section which we have labeled "The Statement of the Themes" contains one group of themes that are similar in character, in juxtaposition with another group of themes that are like in character; the strong contrast between these two groups provides dramatic interest and the material for this section of the movement. The first group is usually powerful and aggressive, vital; and it stands in strong key contrast to the second group, which is exactly opposite in mood — relaxed, lyric. The last theme or themes may be of almost any nature, so long as the material is sufficiently conclusive to indicate the end of this whole "statement" section, and suggest that the "development" is about to begin. In passing, we may note that this A or exposition section is sometimes repeated (as was the

---

[3] No better example of this form can be found than the first movement of Beethoven's *Fifth Symphony:* here everything is as clear and forthright as it possibly can be. See Chapter Twenty-nine.

custom in earlier times), or the interpreter may go on directly to the development. The bridge passages may be short or long, but they should always be consistent, really leading out of one set of thematic ideas into another. The tendency with some composers has been to use rather meaningless musical figuration in such passages — what Wagner (in speaking of Haydn's symphonies) rather pointedly described as "the clatter of the dishes between the courses at a royal feast." Most of Beethoven's bridge passages are striking examples of what can be accomplished.

The great second or B section of the sonata form, instead of consisting of new material such as we found to be the case in the other tripartite forms, features the development of materials already presented. This feature of evolving new musical substance out of old ones challenges the skill of every composer, for it requires not only technical resources but outstanding imagination. All sorts of expedients are available: fragments of the themes with which the listener has become familiar are tossed about, pulled apart, recombined in different ways, put into new key relationships. Sometimes all the themes are treated, sometimes only one or two. There are no fixed rules nor set patterns other than the fact that the section usually opens with at least a suggestion of the first theme in order to orient the listener, and, after modulating through a varied series of keys, finally arrives at the end back in the original key level of the first theme, so as to be ready to start the recapitulation. Almost anything may happen in between; even new themes are sometimes introduced. In the hands of a skilled composer such as Beethoven, whose architectural sense was matched by his imaginative phantasy, this development section can be the source of the greatest possible pleasure and excitement for the listener.

The restatement or recapitulation follows the development section without pause; in the classic sonata form it is almost exactly like the statement, except for the fact that all the themes are now in the same key, in order to give a sense of unified finality. The bridge passages have to be altered somewhat, since it is no longer necessary to lead from one key level to another, and the tendency of modern composers has been to shorten this section. Even those who do so, however, take care that the recapitulation ends with a definite culminative impact, sometimes in the shape of a forceful coda, sometimes without it. Beethoven, especially, wrote mighty codas, containing sometimes almost a new development. A well-constructed first movement should leave us with a satisfied sense of arrival home after a series of colorful and exciting adventures.

Composers, ever seeking freer forms, devised the so-called *sonata-rondo*, a combination that is much more fluid than the rather square, older, simple rondo type, since it contains elements of both sonata and rondo forms. The usual plan for this sonata-rondo is as follows: A–B–A–C (a third section in place of the development) –A–B–A. It was this type of rondo (with slight variants) that was often used by Mozart and Beethoven; examples may be found in the latter's piano *Sonata in B Flat*, Op. 22; the piano *Rondo in G*, Op. 51, No. 2; and the piano-and-violin *Sonata*, Op. 12, No. 2.

FREE FORMS

Strictly speaking, there is no such thing as "free" form, for no matter how free a piece of music is, it must always have form; that is, it must have some basic structural plan if it is to make any sense for the listener. But there are certain kinds of musical writing that do not fall naturally into the basic formal types that we have just been considering. These, for lack of a better term, we call *free forms*.

One of the most important of these is the *overture*, literally an opening piece. In its essence it is closely connected with the theater: it may be the opening selection before a play, provided to heighten emotional mood; more likely it is the introduction to an opera, with themes taken from the score. Sometimes it merely sets the mood — suggests whether the work to follow is a light comedy (*vide* Mozart's inimitable overture to *The Marriage of Figaro*, which is in modified first-movement form, without development [4]), or a deep tragedy (such as the music provided by Wagner for playing before his *Tristan und Isolde*). Or it may foreshadow the events to come, as Beethoven did in the overtures which he wrote for his one opera, *Fidelio*,[5] thereby, as someone has sagely remarked, making the opera itself unnecessary. Composers have also applied this term to independent concert pieces composed in the style of an operatic

---

[4] Mention should be made here (this is as good a place as any to introduce such an irregularity) of this sort of first movement that has no real inner structure, the sort of thing that is used in many *sonatinas* (sonatas of less serious, or less developed, character) and opera overtures. Other examples may be found in Mozart's *Piano Sonata* in F (K. 280) and Schubert's *Rosamunde Overture*.

[5] The composer made four attempts at writing an overture for this work.

overture, as Brahms did in his "Academic Festival" and "Tragic" overtures.

Originally overtures were written without any great concern for form: they just "grew." In the seventeenth century they crystallized into two general types, the Italian and the French overtures; both were in more than one movement. The Italian type (popularized by A. Scarlatti, 1659–1725) was made up of

A quick movement
A slower movement
A quick movement

The French overture (most effectively used by the composer Lully, 1632–1687), on the other hand, had

A slow movement (played twice)
A quick movement
A slow movement, usually part of the first, sometimes a new, slow dance form

These types, especially the latter, were in use for a long time (the overture to Handel's *Messiah* is a good example) but were gradually pushed aside by the development of the sonata form, which became the accepted type of overture form during the nineteenth century. Later composers freed themselves again from formal considerations in writing overtures, as, for example, Wagner did in the overtures to his operas *Lohengrin* and *Parsifal*.

As a matter of fact, Wagner called the overtures we have just mentioned "Preludes" — the word in this sense meaning the same thing — an introductory piece played before an opera. The term is likewise applied to small, independent orchestral or piano pieces and to introductory pieces placed before a fugue; in both cases the free form of the prelude is a distinguishing feature.[6]

A *fantasia* may be defined as a composition in which the formal demands are subordinated to those of imagination or perhaps pure willfulness; one dictionary definition goes so far as to say that a composer uses the term *fantasia* when no other name happens to occur to him. But there is always a suggestion of the imagination in this term. Rousseau, in the great dictionary of music he published in

[6] Some Preludes, as we have seen, are in strict three-part form.

the eighteenth century, defines *fantasia* as "a piece of instrumental music that one performs as one composes it" and adds that a *fantaisie* can "never be written, because as soon as it is written or repeated it ceases to be a *fantaisie* and becomes an ordinary piece." This is not strictly true, because Beethoven, Chopin, Brahms, all left us fantasias, some of them quite informal in character, others rather strict as to form. As always, Edman is to the point here:

Yes, the sonata form is neat,
But on occasion it is sweet
To wander freely here and yon
As melodies meander on.

For this fantasias are the stuff;
They wander artlessly enough,
Relaxed and tender, casual, human,
Most notably when they're by Schumann.

Classic examples of the fantasia are two which Bach wrote as introductory movements to organ fugues, one in G minor, the other in C minor. (The complete titles are *Fantasia and Fugue in G Minor; Fantasia and Fugue in C Minor.*) Mozart wrote three fine piano fantasias, two in C minor (K. 396 and 475), and one in D minor (K. 397); the first of these is strangely prophetic of Beethoven's style. Unfortunately, the term has had rather too many meanings, good and bad, over a long period of years; in its tawdry sense, this form can descend to a very low level, for example, when applied to strings of tunes from an opera or a musical comedy, hashed together and served up in unappetizing fashion; for example the *Fantasia on William Tell.*

THE VALUE OF RECOGNIZING FORM

If he has followed this chapter thus far, the musical neophyte is probably thoroughly confused by this time in his attempt to grasp the underlying principles of so many different kinds of form. He is, in fact, probably tempted to turn his back on the whole matter and ask, "After all, what is the use? Can I honestly expect to enjoy music any more by trying to follow these architectural plans and understand all these technical terms, many of them so confused and inexact in meaning?"

The only answer that we can give is that even a slight acquaintanceship with the way music is put together will help to remove this sense of bewilderment and futility from which so many suffer when listening to great music. In its place there will come — gradually, to be sure, but none the less surely — the pleasure of observing a composer's designs and of realizing how they are (or are not) being fulfilled. This sense of the design and plan back of the music becomes an almost intuitive part of the listener's equipment, and, when added to the sensuous pleasure he gets from what he hears, helps his experience and cultivates his taste. Form is by no manner of means all there is to music; it is not even the most important aspect of it. But the more one understands it, the surer he is of his musical judgment.

LIST OF SUGGESTED MUSIC

One-Part Instrumental Form

   Prelude in C Major, Op. 28, No. 1   Chopin

Theme with Variations

   The Bells   Byrd
   Suite for Harpsichord, No. 5 in E Major   Handel
   Passacaglia: Last Movement, *Fourth Symphony*   Brahms
   Chaconne in D Minor from *Partita No. 2*
      (violin, unaccompanied)   Bach
   Surprise Symphony, Second Movement   Haydn
   Kreutzer Sonata, Op. 47, Second Movement   Beethoven
   Variations on a Theme by Haydn   Brahms
   Symphonic Variations   César Franck
   The Enigma Variations   Elgar
   Octet for Wind Instruments   Stravinsky
   Der Schwanendreher   Hindemith
   Under the Spreading Chestnut Tree   Weinberger

Rondo

   Rondeau   Chambonnières
   Surprise Symphony, Last Movement   Mozart
   Piano Concerto in D Minor, Last Movement   Mozart
   Suite for Orchestra, Op. 19, Last Movement   Dohnányi

Two-Part Instrumental Form

   Twelve Ländler, Op. 171   Schubert

Waltzes, Op. 39   Brahms
Sonatina in D Major (Longo No. 262)   D. Scarlatti

Three-Part Instrumental Form

Humoresque   Dvořák
Nocturne in F Major, Op. 15, No. 1   Chopin
Nocturne in F Sharp Major, Op. 15, No. 2   Chopin
Étude in F Major, Op. 10, No. 8   Chopin
Sonata in C Minor (violin and piano),
    Op. 45, Second Movement   Grieg

MINUET

From *Suite in B Minor* (orchestra)   Bach
Symphony in G Minor, Third Movement   Mozart

SCHERZO

Symphony No. 7 in A Major, Third Movement   Beethoven
Symphony No. 4 in F Minor, Third Movement   Tchaikovsky

SONATA FORM

Symphony No. 5 in C Minor, First Movement   Beethoven
Symphony in G Minor, First Movement   Mozart

Sonata-Rondo Form

Rondo in G Major, Op. 51   Beethoven
Piano Sonata in B Flat, Op. 22, Last Movement   Beethoven

Free Forms

OVERTURE

Overture to *The Marriage of Figaro*   Mozart
Overture to *Fidelio*   Beethoven
Academic Festival Overture   Brahms
Overture to *Semiramide*   Rossini
Sonata for Flute and Strings, First Movement   A. Scarlatti
Overture to *Thésée*   Lully
Overture to *Messiah*   Handel
Prelude to *Tristan und Isolde*   Wagner
When Johnny Comes Marching Home   Harris

FANTASIA

Fantasia in G Minor (organ)   Bach
Fantasia in C Minor (organ)   Bach
Fantasia in C Minor, K. 396 (piano)   Mozart

TOPICS FOR FURTHER DISCUSSION

Find and briefly analyze other good examples of simple binary and ternary forms.

Compare the older (for example, up to the time of Mozart) variations with the more modern ones (those of Franck and Elgar). What seem to be the chief differences?

If you can, hear some of the late Beethoven works in the variation form (for example, Op. 109 and the string quartets, Op. 127 and 131) and consider whither Beethoven's variations were tending, and what spiritual qualities they seem to express.

Why did composers of operas prefer an overture that had no real development?

To your mind, has the sonata-rondo form any great advantage over the simple rondo form?

[FOURTEEN]

INSTRUMENTAL FORMS (*continued*)

CONJOINT FORMS

H aving obtained an idea of the sectional forms that have been used through the centuries by composers, the listener should investigate some of the larger aspects of form — how it shapes the constitution of a piece as a whole. For he will find that a great deal of the instrumental music he hears at concerts and over the radio consists of compositions of extended length — sometimes lasting well over an hour — that are made up of a number of separate elements or "movements," as the musician calls them. When these are grouped together under a single title, they may be called one of several names, depending on the general character of the composition and the instrument for which the music was written.

Among the simplest of these conjoint forms is the *march*, a piece of strongly rhythmical music designed or fitted to accompany marching and used from early times to "enliven the spirits and minimize fatigue." As used today, it consists of a sort of rondo, with a principal, strongly melodic section that comes round again and again, separated by intervening tunes, some of which are called, with as little reason as in the minuet, *trios*.

Another simple conjoint form is the *waltz*, which, while designed for dancing, is often played in concerts. It consists of a string of seven or eight different short waltz themes, the whole being prefaced with a suitable *introduction* and often followed by a *coda* recapitulating some of the tunes used in the body of the work. See Johann Strauss's *Wiener Blut* and *Geschichten aus dem Wiener Wald*, two of the finest waltzes ever written.

Still another of these simple conjoint forms is the *suite;* the literal meaning of this word gives us its musical definition: a series or group of things belonging together and forming a unit. Just as we have suites of rooms or of furniture in everyday life, so in music we have suites of compositions, each of them complete in itself. These separate units may be written in any form — binary, ternary, rondo, theme with variations, sonata form — that the composer may choose, and can be played and enjoyed as entities, without relationship to any other music. But they were intended by the composer to be played in sequence, and they give their full effect only when so used.

In the early days of instrumental music, suites were invariably made up of dance tunes which were all in the same key. The usual convention was that there should be four of these — the allemande, the courante, the saraband, and the gigue; between these, the composer was at liberty to insert as many other types of dances as suited his fancy — gavottes, minuets, polonaises, rigadoons, bourrées, and so on. Usually a prelude or an overture was added and the whole work was arranged so as to secure the maximum effects of contrast in tempo and style. The form was thus quite free, and may best be studied in the suites of Purcell, Bach, Handel, and Corelli. Other names were often given to the suite by some older composers: *serenade, partita, divertimento,* and *cassation.* All these have the same general structure and were written for a wide variety of instruments, singly and in combination.

Suites are, of course, often written today on the same free lines as in the eighteenth century, although the classic dance forms are no longer used. Sometimes composers try to evoke the spirit of former times, as in Ravel's lovely suite, *Le Tombeau de Couperin;* sometimes they simply string together materials from theatrical or ballet music, as Grieg did in his much-played *Peer Gynt* suites, or Tchaikovsky in his *The Nutcracker* suite; sometimes they simply try to provide a series of entertaining and contrasting movements such as there are in Dohnányi's fine *Suite for Orchestra,* Op. 19.

THE SONATA FAMILY

A whole group of compositions, numbering among them some of the greatest things ever written, may be classified under one generic category. These works are of an extended type and are made up of a number of separate divisions or movements (usually four, quite frequently three), each of which, while maintaining its individual identity, is an inherent part of the whole. These compositions have been given different names, according to the usage for which they were designed:

1. A *sonata* (literally a composition that is sounded or played, in contradistinction to one that is sung) is a work of the type described above, written for one or two solo instruments.
2. A *trio* is a sonata for three instruments.
3. *Quartet* means a sonata for four instruments, usually first and second violins, viola, and cello; or piano, violin, viola, and cello.
4. *Quintet* means a sonata for five instruments.
5. *Sextet* means a sonata for six instruments.
6. A *symphony* is a sonata for orchestra.
7. A *concerto* is a sonata for solo instrument (or instruments) with orchestra.

Here again, although there are no fixed rules, tradition has dictated that each movement of these works should be written according to a different form. The usual procedure has been as follows:

The First Movement (of a vigorous, quick, *allegro* character) is written in sonata form (perhaps better termed "first-movement form").

The Second Movement (usually *andante* or *adagio*) is, in contrast, slow and lyric in character. It may be in sonata form, a theme with variations, or in ternary (song) form.

The Third Movement is strongly rhythmic in character and provides relaxation for the listener. In reality it is a dance movement: with the composers Haydn and Mozart it took the form of a minuet and trio; Beethoven substituted a scherzo, in which the tempo of the minuet was speeded up and the general mood of the movement lightened. Later composers have in general followed Beethoven's example.

The Fourth Movement is again rapid and complex, something like the first but with more of an air of finality, leading to either a triumphant or an irresistible close. It is usually in rondo or sonata form.

What a common-sense procedure this is! The first movement is designed to arrest our attention; the second to set us dreaming, or at least contemplating; the third gives us a chance to relax; and the fourth puts us in a cheerful or exalted frame of mind. All composers, from Haydn to Shostakovich, have realized the effectiveness of this traditional scheme and have followed it more or less closely, for to date it has been impossible to think up a better one. The greatest composers have excelled in maintaining the essential character of each of these movements, at the same time weaving them into a congruous and climactic whole. They have been, as Lawrence Abbott has said, master architects and dramatists in the opening movement; imaginative poets and tender lyricists in the second; rhythmic dance musicians in the third, with plenty of boisterous rhythms up their sleeve; and eloquent prophets and effective spellbinders in the fourth. Study such works as Beethoven's *Fifth Symphony* or Brahms's *Second Symphony,* and you will hear how effectively these plans have been used by the great men.

There are some changes from this general procedure that have become familiar with certain composers: the order of the second and third movements is sometimes reversed, the scherzo coming second and the slow movement third (as in Beethoven's *Ninth Symphony*); there is often, especially in sonatas, only one middle movement; usually it is the scherzo that is omitted, or the slow movement and the scherzo may be telescoped into one whole.

It should not be thought that, because their general formal patterns are the same, there is no difference in the style of these big extended compositions. The very meaning of the word *symphony* (sounding together) suggests the seriousness of purpose and high ideals associated with this form of writing. Generally speaking, although there are varying qualities of mood and purpose in the symphonies of the different periods, this form represents the best in musical thought throughout the years. In a quartet, more attention is paid, naturally, to perfection of part-writing and delicacies of rhythm and nuance: it is meant for the delectation of a few listeners rather than of the many. Throughout the quartet (and its closely allied forms the trio and the quintet) there must be a constant interchange of ideas between the various instruments; if one is exalted too greatly at the expense of the others, the essential quality of the work is sure to be lost. In the concerto [1] the listener must realize that there are two masterful forces in action throughout, the solo instrument or instruments and the full orchestra. Care must be taken by the composer that he does not slight one or the other, and that there are plenty of opportunities for drama in the interaction of the dominant powers. Since the same opportunities for dramatic

---

[1] We refer here to the three- or four-movement concerto; *concerti grossi,* an earlier type, are really suites for solo instruments and orchestra.

contrast exist between the two themes of the concerto, this form may be said to be a sort of heightened or intensified symphony, with two important kinds of dramatic interactions being developed. So, too, in a sonata for violin and piano: the two instruments are on an equal footing and are supposed to share the honors evenly. The best way to familiarize oneself with the characteristics of these compositions is to listen to a number of representative examples of each and compare them carefully. A list from which to choose is given at the end of this chapter.

For completeness of the record, we add here Professor Edman's verses on the *tone poem,* the form which program music takes, as we have already shown in an earlier chapter:

The Tone Poem

This is the music that demands
Always a program in your hands,
So that on hearing Section VIII
You know if it is Love or Fate
You're hearing, and if Section VII
Speaks of the sea, or war, or Heaven.
The program helps you to enthuse
With learnèd — and surprising — clues:
The muted trumpets, these are death;
The treble flutes, Spring's earliest breath!
I am among the louts, I fear,
Who do their listening by ear,
And, leaving program notes unread,
Don't care much *what* the music's said.

LIST OF SUGGESTED MUSIC

March

Semper Fidelis; The Stars and Stripes Forever   Sousa
The Washington Post; El Capitán   Sousa

Waltz

Wiener Blut   Johann Strauss
Tales from the Vienna Woods   Johann Strauss

Be sure to obtain authentic Viennese interpretations of these, not modern, streamline versions; there is all the difference in the world.

Suite

EARLY

Suite No. 1 in G Major   Purcell
Sonata for Flute and Strings   A. Scarlatti
Suite No. 2 in B Minor   Bach
Suite for Strings   Corelli

LATER

Holberg Suite, Op. 40   Grieg
Le Tombeau de Couperin   Ravel
Suite, Op. 19   Dohnányi
Caucasian Sketches   Ippolitov-Ivanov

The first three of these attempt to catch the spirit of the old suites, but employ more modern idioms; the last is a descriptive program suite.

Peer Gynt (Suite No. 1)   Grieg
L'Arlésienne (Suite No. 1)   Bizet
The Nutcracker (Suite)   Tchaikovsky
Daphnis and Chloe (Suite No. 2)   Ravel
Pulcinella (Ballet Suite)   Stravinsky
Lieut. Kiji Suite, Op. 60   Prokofieff
The Incredible Flutist (Ballet Suite)   Piston

These are all based on concert treatment of theater music.

Sonata

Sonata pathétique, Op. 13 (piano)   Beethoven
Sonata in A Major, Op. 47 (violin and piano)   Beethoven

Trio

Trio for Piano and Strings, Op. 99   Schubert
Trio for French Horn, Violin, and Piano, Op. 40   Brahms

Quartet

Quartet in F Major, Op. 18, No. 1 (strings)   Beethoven
Quartet No. 1 in G Minor, Op. 25 (strings and piano)   Brahms

Quintet

Quintet in A Major (Trout)   Schubert

Sextet

Sextet in B Flat Major for Strings, Op. 18   Brahms

Septet

Septet in E Flat Major, Op. 20   Beethoven

Octet

Octet in F Major, Op. 166   Schubert

Symphony

Symphony No. 5 in C Minor, Op. 67   Beethoven

Concerto

Concerto in D Minor (piano and orchestra)   Mozart
Concerto No. 4 in G Major, Op. 58
  (piano and orchestra)   Beethoven
Concerto in D Major, Op. 35
  (violin and orchestra)   Tchaikovsky

TOPICS FOR FURTHER DISCUSSION

What is the function of the cadenza in a concerto? Discuss its value.

What advantages has the symphonic poem over the symphony as regards (a) freedom of form, and (b) interpretative power? Are there any drawbacks or dangers to be considered along with the advantages?

Have any composers been equally remarkable in writing both symphonic poems and symphonies?

Do you think that ability in writing one of these forms tends to cramp it in another?

Do you know of any symphonies that have more than four movements? If so, where are the extra movements added?

[FIFTEEN]

RUSSIAN NATIONALISM

THE FORCES IN NATIONALISM

We have seen how Romanticism meant a revolt against the accepted traditions of the past, an intensification of the qualities that determine the characteristics of the individual, and a revolution which changed the intellect of Europe from a monarchical into a popular state. Among the Romantic artist's greatest sources of material in his struggle against heritage and convention were the half-forgotten folk tales and colorful legends of the various countries; the search for these really represented a movement towards national freedom, a movement that was greatly aided by the series of European wars stirred up by Napoleonic ambitions. These nineteenth-century wars aroused feelings of national consciousness and roused hopes of revolt in all the countries, hopes and feelings which were, after all, but magnifications of the consciousness of the individual. These essentially Romantic ideals, once aroused and abetted by the political situation of the times, developed into an artistic chauvinism, from the effects of which we still suffer today.

In the latter part of the nineteenth century we thus find the peoples of the different countries turning their attention more and more inwards, striving in every possible way, practical as well as spiritual, to foster their own national resources. It was but natural for the artists of each country to fall in with such a movement, and so we find them at this time struggling to free themselves from the bondage of the foreigner, using every means they could devise to stimulate their own national expression. The unique environment of each land, its physical and climatic conditions, its historical vicissitudes, its future possibilities — all were excellent grist for the nationalistic mill.

In so far as the production of music was concerned, Italy, France, and Germany had had the field pretty much to themselves up to the beginning of the nineteenth century. In 1843 Robert Schumann, an outstanding musical *littérateur* as well as composer, realizing that the nations bordering upon Germany were desirous of freeing themselves from the influences of German composers, had perspicacity enough to advise the musicians in these countries to develop the qualities to be found in their own native music. And composers in countries (such as Spain and England) which had formerly been very prolific musically but which had dropped behind in the race with Central Europe turned their attention to the development of their native resources in the hope of attracting more attention. Thus there developed a new and important phase of Romanticism, a phase that we call Nationalism, the manifestation of a people's characteristics through their art.

The great ideal of this new development in music and art was the presentation to Europe in general of national characteristics — such as melodies, rhythms, etc. — that were part and parcel of the individual life and living of each country. This had a sensational effect: exoticism, the admiration for everything introduced from a foreign country, became the fashion. This tendency was especially true regarding the literature and music of Russia, a country which had been so completely isolated from the rest of Europe as never to have been affected by the Reformation, the Renaissance, or the French Revolution; a country which, on the other hand, because of its long Asiatic land frontier and its close contacts with the Turks, Persians, and Chinese, had strongly been. influenced by Oriental ideals. No wonder that the exotic and unfamiliar rhythms, the unusual and different harmonies of this non-European music made such an effect upon European listeners; the lethargy of generations is to be heard in its strains, and its spell transports us as upon a magic carpet to lands that are far beyond our ken; just as the intense introspection, the penetrating portrayals of strange life, and the skillfully drawn character sketches found in the novels and plays of such Russian nationalists as Dostoevski (1821–1881), Tolstoy (1828–1910), and Chekhov (1860–1904) seem somehow to give us a refuge from the commonplaces of our everyday lives.

The less spectacular nationalism of Bohemia, a country (now known to us as Czechoslovakia) which in the middle of the nineteenth centry was struggling to throw off the oppressive power of a neighboring state, likewise had its appeal. The triumph of such men as Smetana and Dvořák was achieved not only through the innate vigor and charm and color of their music, but also because they represented a conscious struggle on the part of a suppressed people to assert national ideals. During the Renaissance, Spain and England had been among the most brilliant musical nations of Europe; for one reason or another, their creative musical power declined during the centuries which followed. And it was not until the nationalistic strivings of the nineteenth century that creations of world significance again were manifest in these countries: Albeniz and Granados in Spain and Vaughan Williams and his successors in England.

THE REVELATION OF RUSSIA

The effects of musical nationalism may best be observed among the Russians, where it worked most strongly. The sources of Russian music are obvious: an irregularly rhythmed, deeply melancholy folk music, suggestive of the limitless plains, the great rivers, and the impenetrable forests of this vast land; and a religious vocal music based on the Byzantine chant, related to pre-Christian, Asiatic melodies and developed in opposition to European ideals. Up until the seventeenth century the church represented the chief cultural force in Russia and regulated every national development; popular amusements, including singing and dancing, were frowned upon. It was not until the time of Peter the Great, eighteenth-century czar, that the power of the church was broken; since then until today, music, like all the other arts, has been subjected to the political orientation of the Russian court.

At first this orientation was strongly slanted toward European influences: Italian and French painters, architects, and musicians were the favorites. Every attempt to foster national music, contemptuously referred to as "coachmen's music," was strongly discouraged. It was not until Glinka (1804–1857), a friend of the first great nationalistic author, Pushkin, animated by a desire to "write something Russian, comprehensible to every Russian," composed his opera A Life for the Tsar in 1836 that the Russian musical awakening came.

Following in Glinka's footsteps and emulating his desires there arose a group of composers called at first derisively the Kutchka (a

little heap — handful), usually translated in French and English as
The Five: Balakirev, Cui, Borodin, Rimsky-Korsakoff, and Moussorgsky. None of this gifted group had originally intended to become a
musician; the training of all of them, with the exception of Rimsky-
Korsakoff, was somewhat desultory and sketchy. But under the
leadership of Balakirev they became united by a strong patriotic
wish to create a real Russian art; and the geniuses among them succeeded in doing so: Moussorgsky, one of the most wayward but interesting personalities in musical history, in his opera *Boris
Godunov*, his program cycle *Pictures at an Exhibition*, and his
wonderful songs; Rimsky-Korsakoff in his symphonic suite *Scheherazade*, in which all the fairy tales from *The Arabian Nights* seem
somehow to come to life.

Scheherazade.

There is excellent reason for the popularity of this music of
Rimsky-Korsakoff's, for aside from the appealing nature of the subject, he has written music that has hardly been surpassed in genuine
poetic quality and descriptive power. Much might be said here
regarding the program of this music; but we shall be wise if we
follow the composer's wishes in this respect and listen to the music
as a piece woven out of a number of themes chosen for their musical
rather than for their descriptive qualities. We have here a kaleido-
scope of fairy-tale image and design, chosen at random from that
classic folk-tale collection, the *Arabian Nights' Entertainments*.
With its rich interpretative fantasy and its unusual sense of color,
this score of Rimsky-Korsakoff's is a masterpiece among works of
its kind.

The composer has given us the following preface to his music, all
the program that we really need: "The Sultan Schahriar, convinced
of the faithlessness of women, had sworn to put to death each of his
wives after the wedding night. But the Sultana Scheherazade saved
her life by diverting him with stories which she told him during a
thousand and one nights. The Sultan, conquered by his curiosity,
put off from day to day the execution of his wife, and at last re-
nounced his bloody vow. Many wonders were narrated to Schahriar
by the Sultana Scheherazade; for her stories the Sultana borrowed
the verses of poets and the words of folk songs and fitted together
tales and adventures."

The composer's additional information is helpful, however, information that was given to the public at the time this music was first performed. He suggested the following titles for the four movements of his suite:

I. The Sea and Sinbad's Ship
II. The Story of the Kalendar Prince
III. The Young Prince and the Young Princess
IV. Festival at Bagdad — The Ship goes to pieces on a Rock surmounted by the bronze figure of a Warrior — Conclusion

There is no logical sequence to such a program. Rather, we have a series of incidents which stimulated the composer's imagination as he planned the various musical sections of his work. There is no difficulty in following the poetic suggestiveness of his music, however; its direct appeal and beautiful orchestral speech guarantee it immediate popularity everywhere. It will be of interest for us to examine this music in detail in order that we may observe the manner in which a composer builds his fabric out of simple materials. Rimsky-Korsakoff uses several principal themes in his composition, but they are not employed as we found them in the Liszt or the Strauss tone poems, that is, directly linked with the fixed poetic ideas of the program. Here they are "purely musical material, themes for musical development," to use the composer's own words. And we find that sometimes the same theme is used to suggest quite different incidents in the program.

First of all there are two themes [1]

[1] The piano score of Rimsky-Korsakoff's *Scheherazade* is available in the Schirmer Edition, New York. The orchestral score (miniature size) is available in the Kalmus Edition No. 82.

that occur throughout the whole suite, serving to provide a sort of unifying thread to connect the different sections: (1) a harsh, threatening phrase (I, 1–4), heard at the very beginning — Rimsky-Korsakoff tells us that it is meant to suggest the stern Sultan, always ready to listen to the fair Scheherazade's stories, but just as ready to cut off her head should she fail to interest him; (2) the theme of the Sultana herself (I, 14–17), graceful, lithe, given to the violin with accompanying chords on the harp. These two themes are repeated again and again in the course of the music, as if they would keep us properly oriented. Then there are other motives which thread through the various sections, alternating and twining each with the other, appearing in different contexts and different moods. In the first section, after the introduction of the Sultan and the Scheherazade themes, we hear an undulating arpeggio figure (I, 18–23), suggestive of the roll of the sea. Listen to what the composer does with it after first bringing it to our attention: first heard low in the orchestra, it mounts steadily, growing more and more intense, to a loud climax; after this quite another development of it is heard, with a different instrumentation. The climax this time leads to a new theme (I, 70–75), a series of detached chords on the wood-wind instruments. Then follow fragments of the sea theme, to which is later added the violin figure of the Sultana motive (I, 94), and finally the Sultan motive comes thundering in the bass (I, 110). A vigorous development follows: the different themes are tossed about in various parts of the orchestra, they are heard in varying keys and in different orchestral combinations, sometimes loud, sometimes very soft. The whole section gives a fine idea of the manner in which a skilled composer can treat germane material. This corresponds in manner of treatment, of course, to the development section of the sonata form. Listen to this part several times, trying to fix in your mind the intricate weavings and manipulations of the melodies, and you will secure ideal practice in listening. Naturally, as we learn more of these methods of how music is put together, our admiration of the composer's craftsmanship will add another factor to our capacity for enjoyment.

The second movement, after a brief reminder that the Sultana is still busy at her life-preserving task (II, 1–4), launches into a story told by a wandering Oriental beggar. The bassoon takes the center of the orchestral stage and sings us a theme (II, 5–25) suggestive of the burlesque, sometimes of an almost pathetic mock heroism. The oboe takes up this theme (II, 26), followed in turn by the violins

(II, 48), and then the brass and wood winds (II, 71); the pace quickens and there are furtive suggestions of the Sultan and Sultana themes. Suddenly a brilliant fanfare of the brass (II, 105) announces a new twist to the story; Rimsky-Korsakoff has wisely left us in the dark as to what particular incidents figure in it. The trombones give us a new theme of brilliant character (II, 108), and it is answered as if in echo by muted trumpets (109). A lively development follows, interrupted by two graceful arabesque-like reminiscences of the Sultana theme, the first of them given to the clarinets (II, 161), and the second, following duly after (II, 421), to the bassoon. The section between is given over to a rapidly moving development of the brilliant trombone theme heard shortly before. Fragments of these various tunes follow thick and fast, and the whole section ends with a solemn pronouncement of the Sultan theme.

The third movement is a romantic love idyl. Like all ardent lovers, the Prince speaks first, his theme being a light folklike passage for the strings (III, 1–8). There is a rushing oriental-like passage for the clarinet (III, 21), and then the Prince theme is repeated with an oboe added to the strings and in a lower, darker register of the orchestra (III, 25). When the rushing theme comes again, it is given to the flutes (III, 46). These two themes are now alternated, one answering the other until, with a sudden change in color, the Princess is heard, her theme being given to the clarinet with an accompaniment of snare drum, tambourine, and triangle (III, 70–78). The two principal themes are as much alike as lovers' themes should be; their distinguishing characteristics are their rhythms. They are now heard intermingled in lovers' discourse, only to be suddenly interrupted (III, 142) by the Sultana theme, as if to remind us that, after all, this idyllic story is a product of the Sultana's lively imagination.

The motives of the Sultan (IV, 1–4) and the Sultana (IV, 8–9) are heard at the beginning of the last movement. Then we are suddenly in the midst of a colorful festival at Bagdad in the days of the mighty Caliph, when the city was at the height of its gorgeous splendor (IV, 30 ff.). The metropolis of a huge empire, Bagdad was a city of pleasure, the Paris of the ninth century, and Rimsky-Korsakoff gives us a colorful picture of its busy streets. A riot of milling crowds, shrill Oriental instruments, the music is ablaze with the color and radiance of Asiatic cities. Suddenly, as in a sort of unbelievable dream, we are no longer on the hot Bagdad streets, but aboard Sinbad's ship, headed for the fateful rock upon which it is doomed to crash (IV, 595). The undulating sea theme and the giant Sultan theme have joined forces, and we get a vivid picture of the menacing storm, the winds whistling through chromatic passages for clarinet and flute (IV, 605–610 and 615). The waves seem to have risen with increasing force, and the vivid description of the incident as given by Henley is recalled to our minds:

> Tearing their beards
> The sailors wept and prayed; but the grave ship,
> Deep laden with spiceries and pearls, went mad,
> Wrenched the long tiller out of the steerman's hand,
> And, turning broadside on,
> As the most iron would, was haled and sucked
> Nearer and nearer yet:
> And, all awash, with horrible lurching leaps
> Rushed at that Portent, casting a shadow now
> That swallowed sea and sky; and then,
> Anchors and nails and bolts
> Flew screaming out of her . . . and she lay
> A broken bundle of firewood, strown piecemeal
> About the waters.

The whistle of the wind in the storm, the shattering of the ship, the following peaceful calm, all are clearly delineated in Rimsky-Korsakoff's music. And then in the silence, Scheherazade's "appeasing fiddle" is once more heard as she comes to the end of her tale.

"And the Sultan of the Indies could not but admire the prodigious and inexhaustible memory of the Sultaness, his wife, who had entertained him for a thousand and one nights with such a variety of interesting stories.

"His temper was softened and his prejudices removed. He was not only convinced of the merit and great wisdom of the Sultaness Scheherazade, but he remembered with what courage she had suffered to be his wife, without fearing the death to which she had exposed herself, and which so many Sultanesses had suffered within her knowledge.

"These considerations, and the many other good qualities he knew her to possess, induced him at last to forgive her. And so they lived in all pleasurance and solace of life and its delights, till there took them the Destroyer of delights and the Severer of societies, the Desolator of dwelling places and the Garnerer of graveyards, and they were translated to the ruth of the Almighty Allah."

SIXTEEN

RUSSIAN NATIONALISM *(continued)*

MOUSSORGSKY'S MASTERPIECE

The greatest genius of the Russian nationalists was Modeste Moussorgsky (1839–1881). Working largely in dramatic and program styles, and in spite of a weakness of character which strewed his life with the "ruins of large enterprises abandoned at various stages of completion," he left behind one of the most vital and truly revolutionary compositions in the whole history of music in his opera, *Boris Godunov*. And this in spite of the fact that many of the most individual and expressive aspects of the original have undoubtedly been smoothed over and ironed out in the version most commonly used in the opera houses of the world — that revised and reorchestrated by his friend Rimsky-Korsakoff.

Moussorgsky wrote his own libretto, basing it on a drama by Pushkin relating the most important episodes in the life of Boris Godunov, the regent who ruled Russia in the days immediately following the reign of Ivan the Terrible. Whether or not this sixteenth-century tyrant murdered the six-year-old czarevitch in order to gain the throne seems a debatable historical point; but Pushkin's treatment of the story and Moussorgsky's opera revolve around this incident and are filled with the remorse of the czar at the thoughts of his crime. A pretender appears in the form of a dissolute monk, Gregory, who claims to be the czarevitch grown to manhood; the Poles and the Cossacks follow him, and the Russian peasants revolt because of their sufferings under Boris; no longer able to face his adversaries, Boris is driven almost insane with remorse. Not a pretty story, one filled with gloom and anguish and somehow strangely prophetic of the peculiar fate of the tortured Russian people. Out of it Moussorgsky wove a tremendous score in which the true hero is the chorus, representing the people in their struggle for freedom. In the beginning of the opera the people cry to Boris for help:

To whom dost thou abandon us, Father,
Unto whom dost thou leave thy people, O Provider?
We are all thy poor orphans,
Poor and defenseless!
Yes, we entreat thee,
Implore thee with tears,
With hot, burning tears:
Pity us, pity us, pity us!
Master and Father!

And later, at the coronation in the Red Square in Moscow, after one of the boyars shouts: "Long life to Czar Boris Feodorovitch!" they sing:

As the sun is resplendent in heaven with glory,
Glory! Just so is Czar Boris in Russia.
Glory! Glory!
Long life and good health,
Our Czar and Master,
Sing, rejoice, ye people,
Sing, rejoice, ye true believers!
Let us extol our Czar Boris,
Hail our Czar Boris Feodorovitch,
Glory, Glory, Glory!

At the end of the story, Boris, full of remorse, dies, giving opera one of its greatest scenes:

Farewell, my son, I am dying,
Forthwith thou wilt begin thy reign;
Seek not to know the path I took to become Czar,
For thee it matters not.
Thou wilt be czar by thy own rights,
My lawful heir, my first-begotten son.
My son! Child of my flesh and blood,
Do not trust the slanders of the seditious boyars,
Watch with a hawk's eye
Their secret intrigues with Lithuania,
All treason wipe out mercilessly, without clemency!
Strictly examine the people's justice,

Judge without prejudice.
Stand on guard as Defender of the Faith,
Honor all the saints of God with devotion!

. . . . .

God, dispense from Thy unapproachable heights
Thy blessed heavenly light
Upon my innocent offspring,
Gentle and pure;
O guardian angels, shield with your luminous wings
My own, my dear son
From suffering, from evil and temptation.

(The sound of bells and choristers is heard.)

Hark, 'tis the funeral knell,
The funeral dirge!

(FEODORE: Sovereign, be calm, God will help!)

No! No, my son, my hour is come —
O God! Woe is me,
Vainly cannot I expiate a sin?
O evil Death! What torment is thy cruelty,
Wait for a little . . . I am still Czar,
I am still Czar!
God! Death! (*spoken*) Forgive me,
Here is your Czar,
Forgive me, forgive me. . . .

(Translated by Alice Berezowsky)

THE AGE OF TCHAIKOVSKY

Tchaikovsky, one of whose symphonies we shall study later, was
not considered a real nationalist by the Kutchka because of his
European training and background; with Anton Rubinstein and
other followers in St. Petersburg, Tchaikovsky always remained
outside the influence of the Moscow Kutchka group, although much
of his music sounds very "Russian" to most ears. Following directly
in his eclectic tradition of superimposing European training and
influences upon good Russian foundations were Arensky (1861–
1906); Glazounoff (1865–1936); Gretchaninoff (b. 1864), known
for some of the finest Russian church music; Rachmaninoff (1873–
1943), whose Romantic symphonies and piano concertos made
him extremely popular and very widely copied; Scriabin (1872–

1915), whose harmonic innovations, which attracted considerable attention around the turn of the century, no longer seem very important; Stravinsky (b. 1882), one of the leading spirits in modernism, a real cosmopolite whom we shall study at greater length; Medtner (b. 1879), who has written a number of large-scale works somewhat with the flavor of Brahms mixed with his Russianism; Glière (b. 1875), who, although he composed a glittering program symphony on the life and adventures of the folk hero, *Ilya Mourometz*, quite in the Wagnerian manner, became an important member of the Organizing Committee of the Soviet Composers in 1939; and Prokofieff (b. 1891), who lived long and wrote many important works outside Russia but returned there in 1934, simplifying and popularizing his style to be in fashion with the prevailing ideology of the Soviet authorities.

Continuing more in the Kutchka traditions were Liadoff (1855–1914), who wrote orchestral music based on Russian legends; Taneieff (1850–1915), who composed mostly chamber music; Ippolitov-Ivanov (1859–1935), whose researches at Tiflis, studying the native music, produced such picturesque scores as his *Caucasian Sketches*; Kalinnikoff (1866–1901); and the present-day Soviet composers, among the most prominent of whom are Shostakovich (b. 1906), Khachaturian (b. 1903), and Kabalevsky (b. 1904).

Certainly the best known of these modern Russians is Shostakovich, who at one time seemed fair to rank as a significant composer; unfortunately his work has deteriorated until he seems to have lost his early inspiration, and is of importance largely to the Soviet authorities because of his propagandistic value. He made quite a stir with his First Symphony in 1925 and with his opera *Lady Macbeth of Mzensk*, which touched low life in pre-Soviet Russia with a fiery finger. He, like others (among them Prokofieff, Khachaturian, Shebalov, and Miaskovsky), has written some music which was felt by high authorities who control art affairs in the U.S.S.R. to fall short of their ideals; for, according to the modern Soviet conception, "the *avant garde* can express progressive ideas only when it talks to the people in a new, powerful, and intelligible language. The demands of the wide masses of the people, their artistic tastes, grow from day to day. The 'advanced' composer is therefore one who plunges into the social currents around him and, with his creative work, serves the progress of mankind." [1]

[1] Grigori Schneerson; reprinted by permission of the quarterly review *Modern Music*, March–April, 1938.

When music is associated with words, films, or drama, a propaganda end is, of course, readily attainable. When, however, music is not concerned with any avowed program — that is, in "absolute" works — it is difficult for us to see how it can carry propaganda. In this case it would appear that the Soviet authorities imaginatively read into absolute music ideas derived from similar types of program music.

Composers like Shostakovich and Prokofieff have managed to interest the world at large by their individual modes of expression. Prokofieff appears, in a suite of program music like *Peter and the Wolf*, to make the best of both worlds, pleasing his fellow Russians, both official and lay, as well as attracting the attention of a large outside audience. His resort in some works to older symphonic fashions (*e.g.*, the *Classical Symphony*), his amusing key-twists and avoidance of extreme dissonance, his rhythmic vim and tuneful style, with the dramatic zest of music like that which he wrote for the film *Alexander Nevsky*, make him a popular composer in a wide sense.

Aram Khachaturian is an Armenian. The local color he early injected into his chamber pieces and his orchestral writings held yet another kind of attraction for the West, always pleased with something virile, exotic, and engagingly wild. Unfortunately, his work does not hold up under repeated hearing, when the garish banality of some of it becomes only too evident.

Even a brief listing of composers such as we have given here shows how important a contribution Russian nationalism has made to the development of our present-day repertoire.

A REPRESENTATIVE LIST OF RUSSIAN MUSIC

Kamarinskaya   Glinka

This shows what the earliest exponent of Russian nationalism could do in the way of manipulating folk songs.

Islamey, Oriental Fantasy for Piano   Balakirev

A terrifically difficult piece, after Liszt, showing the Oriental side of the Russian imagination.

Polovtsian Dances from *Prince Igor*   Borodin

Russian color and rhythmic effects have made this music popular everywhere.

Symphony No. 2 in B Minor   Borodin

Shows what this chemist-composer could do in the way of an extended piece of music.

Caucasian Sketches, Op. 10   Ippolitov-Ivanov

Easily assimilated program music, descriptive of Georgian life:

In a Mountain Pass
In the Village
In the Mosque
Procession of the Sardar

Scheherazade   Rimsky-Korsakoff
Russian Easter Overture, Op. 36

The first is discussed in the text; the second is hardly more than a splotch of Russian color, but what a gorgeous splotch it is!

Symphony No. 6 in B Minor (Pathétique)   Tchaikovsky

This is the most popular of all Russian compositions, although it is scarcely "nationalistic."

Pictures at an Exhibition   Moussorgsky

It is rather difficult to remember that this was originally a piano piece, for it has achieved popularity largely through the orchestration which Ravel made of it. It is pure program music, descriptive of various pictures painted by an artist friend of the composer. Especially effective are No. 5, *Bydlo,* a description of an old Polish oxcart; No. 7, *Two Polish Jews,* one rich, one poor; and No. 11, *The Great Gate at Kiev.*

Boris Godunov   Moussorgsky

The excerpts from this greatest of all Russian operas discussed in the text are enough to show the essential character of this music; but one should hear the whole in order to realize its cumulative power and unusual appeal.

Concerto for Piano and Orchestra   Scriabin

A *fin de siècle* type of lush romanticism on an original harmonic basis.

Symphony No. 4 in G Minor   Rachmaninoff

Here is real Russian nostalgia, deeply felt and wonderfully expressed; whether one likes it or not is a matter of taste. To have heard this work played by the composer was a great musical experience. Fortunately the symphony and some of Rachmaninoff's other works have been preserved in fine recordings which are readily available.

Symphony No. 3 in B Minor (*Ilya Mourometz*)   Glière

This is something else again; while based on the adventures of a Russian folk hero, it is largely Germanic in treatment, with resultant gorgeousness of tone and lushness of sentiment which marked the post-Wagnerian style. A rather queer mixture.

The Fire Bird   Stravinsky
Petrouchka
The Rite of Spring (*Le Sacre du printemps*)

These orchestral suites are all drawn from music originally written for the Russian Ballet, in itself a forceful and moving manifestation of the nationalist spirit. For many listeners these suites must always remain the most characteristic and significant of the great modernist's works. *Petrouchka* is discussed at some length in a later chapter. It contains a wealth of musical ideas, in strange contrast to the spareness of his later works, and a warmth that he later lost completely.

The Symphony of Psalms   Stravinsky
Symphony in Three Movements

Representative post-Rite of Spring works, in which the composer strives to reconstruct older styles as well as to indulge his late philosophy of composing music "without feeling." In listening to these it may pay to remember the admonition of another famous contemporary: "Artists who want to go back to a period, who try to obey the laws of an obsolete aesthetic or of a novel one, who enjoy themselves in eclecticism or in the imitation of a style, alienate themselves from nature. The product shows it — no such product survives its time." (Schönberg in *Style and Idea*. New York: Philosophical Library.)

Peter and the Wolf   Prokofieff

Childish (in either the real or the sophisticated sense), entertaining, and educational. What more could one ask?

Scythian Suite   Prokofieff

Russian barbarism in the raw; wonderfully effective thriller of about the vintage of Stravinsky's *Le Sacre du printemps* (see above), which latter must always remain the classic portrayal of pagan Russia.

Alexander Nevsky   Prokofieff

An example of what film music can be like if the composer really believes in what he writes; composed for Eisenstein's historical film dealing with the thirteenth-century defeat of the Teutonic Knights in their attempt to invade Russia, the descriptive power of this music is enormous. Especially effective are the *Battle on the Ice* and *The Field of the Dead,* a vocal lament for those fallen in battle.

Symphony No. 5   Prokofieff

One of the greatest achievements of Russian nationalism, although much more in the spirit of Western tradition than the Soviet authorities are considered to like. Difficult listening but worth all the time and effort it takes, which can hardly be said for most of its contemporaries. Written in 1944.

Symphony No. 5   Shostakovich

Discussed later in Chapter Thirty-one.

Symphony No. 9   Shostakovich

One has only to hear this light-weight work to prove the statement made in this chapter as to the composer's deterioration.

Concerto for Piano and Orchestra (1936)   Khachaturian

Ingenious combinations of Armenian local color and rhythms with a Tchaikovsky-like European base. In spite of clever tricks and banalities, this is a most effective piece, well calculated to appeal in rather obvious ways.

DEFINITE SUGGESTIONS FOR READING

Music in History: Nationalism — The Movement in General Russian Nationalism

SEVENTEEN

WAGNER'S *Siegfried Idyll*

A MASTERPIECE OF FORM AND FEELING

We have already remarked that the *Scheherazade* suite is a fine example of the type of program music in which the composer is more interested in developing his musical structure than in carefully following the details of an elaborate program. We are now to consider a piece of program music which concerns itself entirely with musical development. Those who are familiar with the great operas of Wagner — music dramas such as *Die Walküre, Siegfried, Götterdämmerung* — will perhaps be surprised to see the *Siegfried Idyll*, the piece which we have under present consideration, cited as an example of German nationalistic music. Most of Wagner's works, though imaginatively sprung from Germanic sources, have transcended the narrow borders of nationalism because of their tremendous scope and the universality of their appeal. Wagner based the stories of his operas on material gathered from the great medieval poems which were the heritage of the Scandinavian and the Germanic peoples. His treatment was such, however, that these operas appeal not alone to the Germans; or to other nations because of their peculiarly Teutonic qualities. They belong rather to the whole human race; the music of these works is understood as well in New York and London as it is in Munich or Berlin; their emotions are those of humanity in general, glorified and epitomized. Men of all kinds know this music to be of themselves, and warm to it because they can sense in it their own personal characteristics.

This little instrumental piece we are about to study, the *Siegfried Idyll*, is full of a quiet German beauty that is quite outside the general run of Wagner's other works. Built on themes associated with the greatest of the German folk heroes, it suggests to us the cool depths of the dense, dragon-haunted forests. Overflowing with the happiness of domestic felicity, it celebrates the family ideals of the typical German bourgeois; the intensity of feeling, the acute sensitiveness, the fundamental reflective character of this nation is felt throughout this music. If we stop to inquire into the history of its writing, we shall find the reason for its unique position among Wagner's works.

SOME WAGNER HISTORY

Wagner's career, overwhelmingly successful as it seems to us today, was an intermittent series of struggles, disappointments, triumphs. His works were written over a long period of strife, sometimes with little hope that they would ever be actually performed. Their tremendous scope, their unusual technical requirements, the difference of their constructive principles from those to which the public was accustomed, did not make for their immediate popularity with a people steeped in the traditions of the Italian opera. Wagner's personal idiosyncrasies did not help in establishing his work in public favor. Possessing luxurious habits and expensive personal tastes, he constantly involved himself in financial difficulties; of choleric, irascible temperament, he needlessly made many public and private enemies, and resentment against him rose on various occasions to such a pitch as to make it necessary for him to leave his native land. His personal affairs, even when viewed from the vantage point of distant years, seem inexplicably confused. For years he lived a troubled existence with his first wife, Minna, whom he married in 1836, and who died in 1866. Coming under the spell of one woman after another, he lived with Cosima von Bülow, wife of one of his most ardent disciples and eloquent interpreters, in a villa just outside Lucerne, Switzerland, during the years 1866–1870. At the end of this period, Cosima having been able to obtain a divorce, Wagner was able to establish her as his wife in the eyes of the law, and they were married on August 25, 1870. His happiness at this time knew no bounds. He had finished five of his great works, *Tristan und Isolde, Die Meistersinger von Nürnberg, Das Rheingold, Die Walküre,* and *Siegfried,* works which he knew would go down to posterity even though he could not secure production of them immediately in the German theaters. No one knew better than

Wagner himself that it was the loyalty, devotion, and sympathetic understanding of the amazing Cosima that enabled him to go ahead with the enormous tasks and face the terrific difficulties of his later years.

A CHRISTMAS BIRTHDAY GIFT

The birth of his son Siegfried in 1869 was a significant event for Wagner. (It is rather remarkable that both Cosima and Siegfried died within a year of each other, the one in 1929, the other in 1930, after devoting their lives to carrying on the traditions of the theater established by Wagner at Bayreuth.) Richard resolved to write a piece of music in commemoration of the birth of his son and as a

Richard and Cosima Wagner

At about the time of the writing of the *Siegfried Idyll*

graceful tribute to his wife. He prefaced it with verses which gave
his reasons for writing this music:

Thine was the loving, sacrificing thought
That gave a habitation to my art,
And through all the conflicts that I fought
Gave refuge that was constant and apart.
As we dreamed, our Teuton heroes came to us
Out of country's past reviewed in mind and heart,
Till in my life there rang in glad acclaim:
"We have a son — and Siegfried is his name."

This music now gives thanks for him and thee —
What greater prize could Love have hoped or had,
Within our souls what joy could greater be
Than now is voiced within this music glad?
For I within this offering hold united
Thou and Siegfried — wife and lad.
In all its harmonies stand revealed
Our own sweet thoughts, till now concealed.

Could any music have a more general, and yet a more personal,
program? No wonder Wagner was able to write a composition
which is a wondrous outburst of joy, celebrating the termination
of his bitter struggles, full of tender thankfulness for the haven of
Cosima's love and understanding. Taking his themes from his just-
finished opera, *Siegfried*, themes which suggest the love of the hero
of that work for Brünnhilde, the composer produced a musical
work of unusual beauty and quiet loveliness. That he was writing
program music is certain; we have it on the evidence of the music
itself, as well as on testimony of Glasenapp, one of the composer's
"official" biographers. We do not know anything of the details of the
program which stimulated Wagner's imagination (a fact which one
critic thinks may be the reason why several transitions in the music
seem rather abrupt), nor do we need to know. Wagner's imagination
caught fire at the idea of picturing his great love for his wife and
newborn son, and there "was no staying it until the fire had burned
itself out."

The *Idyll* was composed during the autumn of 1870, in preparation
for Christmas Day, which happened to be Cosima's birthday. Local
musicians from Lucerne were gathered together for the first performance. The score called for a small orchestra: two first violins,

two seconds, two violas, one cello, one double bass, one flute, one oboe, two clarinets, one bassoon, two horns, and one trumpet (played by Hans Richter, who was later to become the outstanding Wagner interpreter of Germany). This small band was secretly rehearsed, and early on Christmas morning its members came out to the Wagner villa, set up their music desks on its broad stairs, and after quietly tuning their instruments in the kitchen, took their places. Wagner, standing at the top of the stairs, conducted; then came the violins, violas, wood winds, horns, and at the bottom, out of sight of the conductor, the cello and bass. Everything went well, and Cosima tells us in her diary that the performance was a complete success. She was awakened by the music; at first she thought herself dreaming, but, as consciousness gradually returned, she realized the graceful tribute that was being paid her. When the music died away, Richard came to her room, and offered her the score of the symphonic poem. "I was in tears," she writes, "but so was all the rest of the household."

PECULIARITIES OF STRUCTURE [1]

It will not take a great deal of listening to realize that the methods of construction in this piece are different from the others we have heard so far. Wagner's unending melody, the peculiar method by which he built his musical structures by means of repetition and elaborations of the same themes, gives a cohesion and homogeneity that is found in few other musical works. Once started, it seems as if this music must run on to its inexorable conclusion. By means of themes that are in themselves marvels of beauty and suggestiveness, Wagner weaves a seamless web of music, always suited to the constantly changing words of his dreams. But though there is repetition, there is no monotony, for the composer is constantly giving us the same material in new guises. By shifting the harmonies that accompany his themes, by changing the keys, by alternating the rhythmic design, or by combining a theme with others so that they form a complex whole, there is attained a marvelous variety and yet a complete unity.

[1] Arrangements of the *Siegfried Idyll* for the piano are available in the following editions: Schott (arranged by Rubinstein) No. 329; Universal (arranged by Wöss) No. 5113; Breitkopf No. 4724. An orchestral score (miniature size) is available in the Kalmus Edition No. 52.

One of the great joys in listening to this music of Wagner's is that of being able to recognize not only the themes as they are used, but also the manner in which each is treated and woven into the fabric of his enormous tapestries. Those who are at all familiar with the opera *Siegfried* will recognize most of the themes in the *Idyll;* but, as that great Wagnerite Mr. Ernest Newman has shown, some of them were originally conceived for a string quartet that Wagner meant to write for Cosima, and were later transferred to the opera. Mr. Newman thinks that "much of the substance of the quartet has been taken over bodily into the *Idyll*"; this makes it a lovely example of the composer's power of symphonic structure — a type of writing which, had he lived longer, it seems reasonable to suppose that he would have developed.

The opening of the *Idyll* is a fine little study in free counterpoint, just the thing for anyone to ponder who doubts the value of studying this important element in composition. Notice what Wagner makes of the theme

first heard in completeness in measures 29 and 30, how he repeats it and what he develops out of it. Shortly after, we hear the slumber motive (37), and then the cradle song (91),

the only theme that is not the composer's own, at first sung by the oboe and then quickly joined with the theme heard at the beginning. These original themes are joined later (148 ff.) by new motives which we find in the closing scene of *Siegfried* (259 ff.).

From internal evidence Newman believes that the theme of measure 148 was also originally part of the never-completed quartet and adapted, rather awkwardly, to the opera. But the 259 theme "was certainly written first for the opera." As you listen, notice the manner in which Wagner manipulates these various motives; they are the roots from which the music beautifully grows. Near the end we hear added the "slumber motive" of Brünnhilde (287),

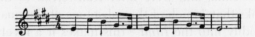

given to the oboe, and the call of Siegfried's forest bird (303 ff.). But through all the music the love themes form a dominating influence, weaving, in their varied forms, a background for the whole piece.

Then, after you have heard the different sections several times and have a knowledge of the music's imaginative and constructive background, forget this side of it entirely and put yourself into the mood for Christmas morning, 1870, and hear the whole thing again, thinking of the intimate, affectionate meaning the music would have for Cosima — music that was not intended for publication but as a private gift in celebration of the baby's birth. You will then appreciate to the full the clarity and eloquence of the music, from the pastoral-like beginning to the sighs of peace at the very end. The *Siegfried Idyll*, one of the world's masterpieces of loveliness, is the sort of music to which we can surrender ourselves unhesitatingly, confident that it will never disappoint.

SCENES FROM OPERAS

This little masterpiece of Wagner's happens not to be in the main stream of his life's work, which, as we have intimated, was the splendid flood of a new style of opera which he called "music drama." The specific nature and style of these Wagnerian operas are discussed later, in the interchapters on opera. It remains necessary to remind the reader who has just enjoyed the *Siegfried Idyll* that its small orchestra and intimate manner are not characteristic of the Wagnerian music dramas, although its method of building up its musical fabric is similar.

To prove this we are citing a few examples from the mature works of this great Romantic to show how he achieved his effects. Like all other composers who grew and developed throughout their careers, Wagner did not achieve his full effects in his earlier operas (up through *Lohengrin*). But the works beginning with the Ring cycle (including its four operas), *Tristan und Isolde, Die Meistersinger,* and *Parsifal* are all built upon the principle of "leading themes" or *leitmotives.* (Again see the opera chapter for details.) And these closely wrought works may truly be said to represent Wagner at his best.

Prelude to Tristan und Isolde
Finale (Liebestod: Love Death) from Tristan und Isolde

As these portions of the greatest of all love dramas, its opening and its close, are often played together in the concert hall as one piece, they may well be briefly described together here. The tragedy of Tristan's passion for the Princess Isolde, whom he escorts over the sea to be another man's bride, has been called one long love duet. Its theme, epitomized in this *Prelude,* as Wagner stated it, is the unappeasable longing for love and death.

The prelude is woven from several of the chief themes: first there is the one given out by the cellos, which, although it seems to sound like one theme, is in reality two, the one melting into the other — "Love's Longing" and "Desire." Another impassioned cello theme heard later is that of the "Love Glance," heard in the opera itself when a potion makes the two aware of their love. It should be interpolated here that careful annotators have given names to all these themes, relating them to the ideas, actions, persons, or things in the opera with which they are associated; it is perfectly possible, however, to enjoy Wagner without having any but a general idea of what these themes represent. The "Deliverance by Death" theme is the climactic point of the prelude; after it, the music droops in weariness.

The concert performance usually joins this without interruption to the *Liebestod,* Isolde's farewell to the dead Tristan at the very end of the opera. It is poignant with memories of their duet in the second act and ends with the motive of "Desire."

Forest Murmurs from Siegfried
Siegfried's Journey to the Rhine and Immolation scene from Götterdämmerung

Siegfried is the third, and *Götterdämmerung* (Dusk of the Gods) is the final of the series of four operas called *The Nibelungen Ring,* which Wagner built out of old Scandinavian and Teutonic legends.

This cycle centers around the story of the magic ring made out of gold, stolen from the depths of the Rhine, and the curse it brought upon all who owned it. The first opera in the series (which Wagner originally intended should be given on four successive days), *Rheingold*, tells the story of the theft of the gold; the making of the ring by Alberich, chief of the Nibelungen dwarfs; and its theft by two of the gods, upon whom the curse immediately begins its work. *Die Walküre* (The Valkyries), the second in the cycle, traces the ancestry of Siegfried, the hero of the whole saga, and tells the story of his parents, Siegmund and Sieglinde, the children of Wotan. In *Siegfried*, the hero, after slaying the dragon Fafner, guardian of the hoard of gold including the ring, secures this magic circlet and goes forth to conquer the world through love. In the excerpt quoted here, Siegfried rests in the woods just before his encounter with Fafner, musing on the fact that he does not know who his parents were and his hope of somewhere finding a mate. As background to these emotions, Wagner sketched in a lovely woodland scene: the rustle of the leaves in the tree overhead, the song of a bird, the murmur of a stream. The whole thing is as naturalistic a description in sound as music is able to give us. At the end of this opera Siegfried, in true fairy-tale fashion, finds his princess, Brünnhilde, rescues her, and makes her his bride.

In the final Ring drama, Siegfried's last adventures and his death are depicted. In the first selection from *Götterdämmerung* chosen here, Siegfried starts forth at daybreak seeking further adventure, leaving the magic ring with his bride. We hear his horn call as he leaves Brünnhilde and journeys down to the Rhine, the bold, striding, pealing theme which follows, "Love's Resolution," suggesting his hopes as he goes forth into the world. A rolling theme represents the mighty Rhine; we hear the song of the maidens who dwell in its depths and who once guarded the gold from which was forged the ring, source of so much woe. The ring theme, and others reminding us of earlier parts of the story, are introduced; there is, at the end of this orchestral interlude, a hint of the tragedy to come.

Through a magic potion (a device much employed in these old legends) given him by his enemies, Siegfried forgets Brünnhilde, who denounces him and enters into schemes of revenge. The great hero is killed at a hunting feast; his body is brought to the banks of the Rhine and placed upon a mighty funeral pyre. As the flames mount heavenwards, Brünnhilde, before sacrificing herself and her beloved steed in them, delivers an impassioned sacrificial ode (the *immolation*) telling the whole, long story of her love for the dead hero. This is a magnificent example of Wagner's use of the solo voice in these later operas not in the Italianate manner of the aria but as a sort of *recitative* without measured melody, which reinforces the dramatic communication given by the orchestra. We must always remember that it is the orchestra in these mature Wagner works that is the real medium for the conveyance of the dramatic ideas. In reality, here it tells us the story of Siegfried's long career, bringing in, one after another, the leit-motives representing the various events associated with him, weaving them all into a gorgeous, glowing musical fabric without any seams at all. Many of the references in the text are obscure to those who have not followed the whole development of the Ring story. But no better method of understanding Wagner's characteristic style of combining voice and orchestra, using the leitmotive as the basis of construction, can be found than through this thrilling *Immolation*. Here is the text to which Wagner composed the music:

Starke Scheite schichtet mir dort	[She commands that the pyre be
am Rande des Rhein's zu Hauf!	raised, that the flames consume the
Hoch und hell lod're die Glut,	corpse of the mighty hero, and that
die den edlen Leib	his steed be brought to her.]
des hehresten Helden verzehrt.	
Sein Ross führet daher,	
dass mit mir dem Recken es folge:	
denn des Helden heiligste Ehre zu	
teilen	
verlangt mein eigener Leib.	
Vollbringt Brünnhildes Wort!	

(During the Interlude, while Brünnhilde watches silently, the young vassals start to erect the funeral pyre, and women deck it with flowers.)

Wie Sonne lauter strahlt mir sein	[She reflects upon Siegfried's char-
Licht:	acter and his betrayal of her, his
der Reinste war er, der mich ver-	bride. She appeals to the gods to
riet!	hear her grief as all things become
Die Gattin trügend — treu dem	clear to her.]
Freunde —	
von der eig'nen Trauten	
— einzig ihm teuer —	
schied er sich durch sein Schwert.	
Ächter als er schwur Keiner Eide;	
treuer als er hielt Keiner Verträge:	
lautrer als er liebte kein And'rer:	
Und doch alle Eide, alle Verträge,	
die treueste Liebe — trog Keiner	
wie er! —	

Wiss't ihr, wie das ward?
O ihr, der Eide ewige Hüter!
Lenkt euren Blick auf mein blü-
    hendes Leid;
erschaut eure ewige Schuld!
Meine Klage hör', du hehrster Gott!
Durch seine tapferste Tat,
dir so tauglich erwünscht,
weihtest du den, der sie gewirkt,
dem Fluche dem du verfielest.
Mich musste der Reinste verraten,
dass wissend würde ein Weib!
Weiss ich nun was dir frommt?
Alles, Alles, Alles weiss ich,
Alles ward mir nun frei.
Auch deine Raben hör' ich rau-
    schen;
mit bang' ersehnter Botschaft
send' ich die beiden nun heim.
Ruhe! Ruhe, du Gott!

(She motions to the vassals to place Siegfried's body on the pyre, and she takes the ring from his finger.)

Mein' Erbe nun nehm' ich zu   [She contemplates the ring and ad-
    eigen.   dresses the Rhine Maidens, deter-
Verfluchter Reif! Furchtbarer Ring! mined to return it to them.]
Dein Gold fass' ich, und geb' es
    nun fort.
Der Wassertiefe weise Schwe-
    stern,
des Rheines schwimmende Töchter,
euch dank' ich redlichen Rat:
was ihr begehrt, ich geb' es euch:
aus meiner Asche nehmt es zu
    eigen!
Das Feuer, das mich verbrennt,
rein'ge vom Fluche den Ring!
Ihr in der Flut löset ihn auf,
und lauter bewahrt das lichte Gold,
das euch zum Unheil geraubt.

(She takes a firebrand from the pyre.)

Fliegt heim, ihr Raben!   [She bids the ravens fly home to
Raun't es eurem Herren,   Valhalla with tidings of the end of
was hier am Rhein ihr gehört!   Siegfried's godhead.]

An Brünnhildes Felsen fahrt vorbei!
Der dort noch lodert,
weiset Loge nach Walhall!
Denn der Götter Ende dämmert
    nun auf.
So — werf' ich den Brand
in Walhalls prangende Burg.

(She fires the funeral pyre. Two ravens fly away. Two young men bring in Grane, Siegfried's horse, which Brünnhilde addresses.)

Grane, mein Ross!	Grane, my steed,
Sei mir gegrüsst!	I greet thee again.
Weisst du auch, mein Freund,	Knowest thou, friend,
wohin ich dich führe?	Whither we journey?
Im Feuer leuchtend,	Surrounded by fire
liegt dort dein Herr,	Lies there thy lord,
Siegfried, mein seliger Held.	Siegfried, my soul's hero!
Dem Freunde zu folgen wieherst	. . . . .
du freudig?	
Lockt dich zu ihm die lachende	
Lohe? —	
Fühl' meine Brust auch, wie sie	
entbrennt,	
helles Feuer das Herz mir erfasst,	
ihn zu umschlingen,	
umschlossen von ihm,	
in mächtigster Minne,	
vermählt ihm zu sein!	Heiayaho! Grane!
Heiajaho! Grane!	Give him thy greeting.
Grüss' deinen Herren!	Siegfried! Siegfried! See!
Siegfried! Siegfried! Sieh!	Brünnhilde, thy wife, greets thee
Selig grüsst dich dein Weib!	in bliss!

(She leaps on the horse and with it plunges into the heart of the flaming pyre, which blazes up and envelops the stage. The fire dies down; the Rhine rises up, overwhelming the scene. On its surface are seen the Rhine Maidens, joyously displaying the Ring. A red glow appears on the horizon and mounts in intensity until the burning Valhalla, with its gods and goddesses, is seen as the curtain falls.)

DEFINITE SUGGESTION FOR READING

Music in History: Richard Wagner and the Music Drama

EIGHTEEN

D V O Ř Á K ' S *New World Symphony*

A SYMPHONIC NATIONALIST

Composers who have been interested in the various nationalistic movements have turned naturally to the writing of program music as the style best fitted to the carrying out of their ideas. So, to a small extent, did Anton Dvořák, the Bohemian nationalist, but most of his compositions, although they are full of the color, rhythm, and melody of the Czech folk music, are cast in the forms used by the composers of the earlier Classic school. He started his career in the traditions of the German Romantic school of Beethoven and Schubert, and this fact greatly influenced his choice of forms; but the first years of his artistic development coincided with a determined effort on the part of a group of older Czech composers to develop a school of nationalistic writing. The young Dvořák found this idea congenial, and from 1874 he threw himself body and soul into the new movement, filling his music with the spirit of his country.

Like Schubert, Dvořák was a man who lived only in the world of music, a fact that gives spontaneity and freshness to everything he wrote and that makes it very easy to enjoy. His genius was most at home in the writing of melodies and rhythms that have a folk flavor, and he was able to weave these into a fabric of real musical worth through his mastery of the older forms. In other words, he was at his best when writing absolute music, music that was unhindered by programs of any sort. He had a flair for striking and effective instrumentation, and his best music proceeded out of his ability to use resources in the most natural manner possible.

Without any doubt, his greatest work is his last (Fifth) symphony, the one in E minor generally called the *New World Sym-*

phony. It was written during the composer's short stay in the city of
New York as the head of the National Conservatory of Music (1892–
1894) and was undertaken in an attempt to show American composers what might be done in the way of writing music in the larger

Courtesy of Czechoslovak Consulate General

In Memory of Dvořák

The bronze plaque can be seen on the house in which Dvořák lived while
in New York.

forms, using folk-style themes as material. There has been a great
deal of discussion as to whether Dvořák employed melodies in this
work suggestive of the American Indians and Negroes; it is known
that one of his talented pupils, the Negro singer and composer
Henry T. Burleigh, introduced Dvořák to the beauties of the Negro
spirituals, and it seems probable that the second theme of the first
movement may have been suggested in this way. But, according to
Dvořák's friend, Josef Kovarik, who made the first copy of the
score of this famous symphony, every note and theme is Dvořák's,
and no one else's. All of the themes seem curiously like others
Dvořák wrote before going to America; and, in any case, they lose
any peculiarly New World characteristics they may have possessed

in their development at the hands of this gifted composer from Bohemia.

THE FIRST MOVEMENT [1]

The first movement of this symphony *From the New World* is as strict in its form as if it had been penned by some classic writer — Haydn, or perhaps Mozart. The sonata form can again be seen here as a logical, clear-cut, and very effective means for the expression of a composer's ideas and the ordering of his material. After a rather long introduction, Dvořák plunges immediately into the leaping rhythms of his first theme, given to the horns:

There are a number of interesting things to observe about this theme: first, that it is written in the pentatonic scale, which uses only the first, second, third, fifth, and sixth tones of our usual scale; second, that it employs the folk-song "snap," a short, snappy note placed before a long one (see the second measure of this theme); third, that there are two distinct parts to the tune, the up-and-down arpeggio of the horns, and the answering bit given to the wood winds (much use is made of both these parts in the building up of the movement).

The connecting passages leading up to the second main theme are obviously drawn from the first; they are most suggestive of the lilt and gaiety of folk music. Before we reach the second theme, however, we suddenly come upon an ingratiating little subsidiary theme,

quickly repeated while the cellos thrum a bagpipe-like bass. This is simple writing with a local (Czech) flavor and personal color that are Dvořák's signature and belong to no one else. A characteristic feature of this little tune is its lowered seventh scale step (notice the accidental to the penultimate note), a peculiarity of Negro

---

[1] The piano score of Dvořák's *New World Symphony* is available in the following editions: Simrock (arranged by Juon); Ditson (edited by Goetschius). The orchestral score (miniature size) is available: Eulenburg Edition No. 433; Kalmus Edition No. 18.

slave songs well known to Dvořák. The second theme when it arrives is somewhat like the famous spiritual *Swing Low, Sweet Chariot:*

Like most of Dvořák's themes, it is short, which makes it easy to remember and its development easy to spot.

There are just short of a hundred measures in the development section; the first and second themes are both used, although the little subsidiary theme gets no look-in, save possibly in the rhythmic pattern now and then. It may be felt that we get rather a lot of the opening measures of the first theme — that aspiring arpeggio — and that the devices are just a little overworked. Dvořák is not afraid to drive home a rhythmic pattern by repetition, a touch, perhaps, of the peasant. Compare the sometimes almost maddening repetitions of Russian composers. Color interests this writer more than debate; on the whole, the development does not lead us far down the garden, and we spend most of our time admiring the flowers.

In the recapitulation (restatement) section, Dvořák wisely makes less use of the first theme than he did in the exposition (statement); this is what we want, for we have enjoyed its company but have had enough of it for this time. The subsidiary theme comes back again, this time in a different form, which fact adds interest to our listening, even though we may not realize the reason for it. The second theme is of course again stated, and shortly after there begins a fine little coda, based largely upon the first theme.

THE SECOND MOVEMENT

The second movement is one of the most famous in all symphonic literature, for its principal theme is known to everyone in some arrangement or other. There have been many suggestions as to its inspiration: one writer thinks that this haunting song of the English horn could have been a Negro spiritual, for it is in that vein and has a typical melancholy and pathos; another says that everybody knows that it took shape "after Dvořák had been thinking of the story of Hiawatha's betrothal to Minnehaha." Dvořák's sons are authority for the statement that this tune was suggestive of their father's homesickness for his native land, a homesickness expressed while he was in the midst of a strange and unappealing environment. It seems as if this explanation is as good as any other that might be offered, if we must have reasons for the writing of beautiful music. It is not difficult to feel the nostalgia and longing that pervade this music, and for this reason it will always appeal. The movement is of particular interest to us, however, because it is a beautiful example of the form which has so often been employed by composers for the second movements of their symphonies — what has come to be known as "song form."

An expressive movement such as this does not need very detailed analysis: if we listen carefully to it as a whole, we notice that it divides into three sections, and that the first section is repeated once the second has been finished. The first section is distinguished by the well-known tune given to the English horn (*cor anglais*):

The middle section is marked by a quicker tempo and a beautiful wood-wind and string scoring, with a plucked bass a great deal of the time:

Then after a curious and unexpected interpolation with a light-hearted, open-air flavor, the slow, expressive *largo* tune enters again, this time with some effective hesitations which have the artistic effect of making us wish that it would continue just a little longer. The section closes with the same beautiful chords that we heard at the beginning. The scoring throughout is a triumph of aptness, and the formal design is handled with masterly skill.

THE THIRD MOVEMENT, A TYPICAL SCHERZO

It is hardly necessary to remark that the various movements of a symphony are purposely varied in character in order to provide new interest and hold the attention of the listener from the beginning to the end of the work. After a vigorous opening movement, the second (almost always called the *slow* movement), comes as a refreshing contrast. It is in this second movement that the composer usually displays his emotional powers; lyric in character (hence the name *song form*), the slow movement has a depth of feeling from which we in turn need relief. So the third movement is always brisk, more or less cheerful, and decidedly rhythmic. The older writers (Haydn and Mozart) employed a classic dance — the minuet — as a pattern for their third movements; Beethoven introduced a freer feeling and a livelier pace in his third movements and called them *scherzos* — literally "jests." Most symphony writers since his time have followed his example and have used the same form for their third movements. Dvořák is no exception; his scherzo here is a humorous, lively movement, again in three large sections with the same general idea predominant — restatement after contrast. Each of the sections has two main themes, and keen listening will show that the formal scheme is this:

A: First part, principally employing theme 1:

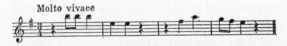

Second part, principally employing theme 2:

First part again
B: First part, principally employing theme 3:

Second part, principally employing theme 4:

First part again
A: An almost literal repetition of the whole first section.

The middle, or contrasting section (B) of the scherzo (as well as of the minuet) is called the *trio,* because in early days it was usually played by three instruments. The different sections in this Dvořák scherzo are easily recognized. Just before A is reintroduced after we have heard B, there is a sudden interpolation from the first movement, as if Dvořák would bind together his whole work by such means.

THE LAST MOVEMENT

The last movement of a symphony is very often again in sonata form, although other types of construction are sometimes used — the rondo, or the variation form, for example. Here in the *New World Symphony* we have a fairly strict use of the sonata form, with constant interpolations of themes from earlier movements; the composer seems to want us to renew our acquaintance with these older friends as the work comes to an end.

The listener may have noted that many of the themes so far used in this work have been in the minor key; but by the way he has used them, Dvořák has proved very clearly that the minor need not necessarily express a sad or doleful sentiment. The first theme of the last movement, again in minor, shows that peculiar thrusting, nervous energy and directness that is characteristic of this composer.

There are two parts, the second almost jiglike in character, giving us a hint of the rhythm that is strongly felt throughout the movement. The second theme is played by a clarinet over a delicate string tremolo:

Then follows a third theme (here is the end of it):

the last measure of which plainly says "Three Blind Mice"; just what the connection is, no one knows — perhaps just a bit of Dvořákian foolery. In the development section not only the two main themes of this movement are treated, but some from the other three are also heard. The restatement follows in due course, and the final coda brings other suggestions of earlier themes.

Perhaps the middle movements stand on their own feet best; the Largo in unequaled in its quiet beauty. Although the ideas throughout the whole work are not broadly or philosophically worked out (as we find them in the Beethoven and Brahms symphonies), and the tune material is brief, there are many ingratiating features in this symphony, and we cannot imagine that it will ever pass out of the concert repertoire. No more engaging introduction to the literature of the symphony could be found.

ADDITIONAL EXAMPLES OF DVOŘÁK'S MUSIC

In addition to Dvořák's fine string quartet, discussed in a later chapter, the listener might well observe his sixteen *Slavonic Dances* in order to get a complete picture of the musical soul of the Czechs, a soul so sorely tried during many oppressive years of the country's long history. Colorful and rhythmic, alternating gay and sad melodies, these short works are a monument to what the Czechs can produce; they are especially stirring if heard in the recording by the Czech Philharmonic Orchestra under Talish.

TOPICS FOR FURTHER DISCUSSION

Do you think that Dvořák's stay in America and his attempts to show the way to American composers have had any important effect upon American music?

Are the so-called "Negro" influences in the *New World Symphony* (as well as in the other works Dvořák wrote while in America) really Negro or not?

What are the qualities that endear Dvořák to us? And what are his weaknesses? Does he share these with any other important composer?

DEFINITE SUGGESTION FOR READING

An article in *The New York Times*, Sunday, June 25, 1950: "Dvořák's Friend, Kovarik" by Olin Downes.

NINETEEN

CHAMBER MUSIC,

"THE MUSIC OF FRIENDS"

CHAMBER MUSIC IN THE HISTORICAL SENSE

One of the most pleasurable and thoroughly satisfying forms of music which European civilization has produced, chamber music, has often been referred to as "the music of friends," that is, music produced for a small group of real music lovers, whether in the princely courts of England, Spain, or Italy during the Renaissance, the great houses of the eighteenth-century gentry, or the informal chamber-music parties of present-day amateurs. In 1622 Henry Peacham wrote in his *The Compleat Gentleman,* at a time when all instrumental music was what we today call chamber music: "There is no one Science in the world that so affecteth the free and generous spirit with a more delightful and inoffensive recreation."

Yet this friendly music is not too well known today, even by rather accomplished listeners, and certainly is not understood by the general public. Witness such slips as those that have appeared in reviews in provincial newspapers when reference was made to "chamber of commerce music"; or the regret expressed by a back-woods critic that a certain piece of Beethoven's written for a string quartet — the most usual of all chamber-music organizations — had not been "played by a larger band." The expression *chamber music* (literally "room music") originally signified the kind of music that was written to be played in the salon of a prince, in distinction to that which was written for performance in the church or theater. Let us see something of its history.

A Typical Eighteenth-Century Court Orchestra

The Hofkapelle of Herzog Friedrichs des Frommen, Ludwigslust, painted by Georg David Matthieu

Up to the time of the Renaissance the growth of music had taken place almost entirely under the protecting care of the Church; from 1600 on, it developed largely under the patronage of princes and royalty. The earlier church music was vocal in style, with little attention paid to any instrumental accompaniment. In the seventeenth century, as instrumental music came more and more into vogue, each prince gathered around him his own musical establishment for the pleasure and edification of his court as well as for the increasing of its reputation for brilliance and splendor. Just as in more recent years the great manufacturing barons often placed an organ (the more expensive, the better) in their show houses, so in the late seventeenth and eighteenth centuries most of the European princes and princelings had chamber-music organizations for the delectation of their guests.

Some of these musical establishments were of considerable size and importance; a typical and probably average one, with the exception of its leader, was that of Prince Leopold of Anhalt-Cöthen, which Johann Sebastian Bach directed from 1717 to 1723. This organization comprised some eighteen players: violinists, violists, cellists, a bassist, an oboist, a flautist, bassoonists, trumpeters, an organist, a drummer, and a copyist to prepare the music. The prince played the clavier himself, and Bach wrote much music for the various combinations possible within this group of players. This, chamber music in the real sense of the term, was played in the great room of the castle on certain days each week after dinner before invited guests and some of the prince's subjects who were known to be lovers of music. Frederick the Great, grim master of the art of music as well as of war, head of the more elaborate Prussian court at Potsdam, had his own chamber-music organization, with which he played the flute in the music room of his palace every evening that he was in residence.

IN THE MODERN SENSE

The modern meaning of the term has changed somewhat: princes no longer have a monopoly on music of this sort. It is now played almost entirely at public concerts, but its range is still limited to music suitable for rooms of moderate size, and *it is usually played by not more than one instrument to a part.* Modern chamber music may be said to date from the middle of the eighteenth century, when composers began to write for various instrumental combinations without including the clavier to hold the music together, as had been common practice up to this time. Even though we do not know much of this earlier type of chamber music in which the harpsichord or the clavichord (called the *continuo*) played an important role, we do know that its quantity was enormous. In fact, much more of this earlier kind of chamber music was written than has been produced since Haydn (1732–1809) laid the foundations for our modern style.

Not content with having a miscellaneous grouping of varied instruments held together by a harpsichord, Haydn definitely selected the string quartet as the norm and worked out for it certain principles which have since proved their validity for all other chamber-music organizations. First of all, he developed a form, using in general the same scheme that he had worked out for the symphony: four movements, each of them contrasting in mood and structure. Then he felt that the instruments in a small combination must be of equivalent musical capacity and on equal tonal terms. It would be useless, for instance, to match a slow-speaking, relatively awkward instrument with others more agile and facile — a double bass with a violin, for instance. Or it would be poor taste to introduce any instrument such as the trumpet into a group so as to shatter the tonal ensemble. Furthermore, and this was of great importance for future developments, the individual parts were written for each player, and every note written for the various instruments was intended to be heard as written. There was to be no filling-in by an instrument such as the piano, which was liable to smear the general effect while binding it together. In the style of chamber music as initiated by Haydn there is no opportunity for filling-in or thickening-up, as is so often the case with orchestral writing. And this is one great reason why it is difficult to write good chamber music, as well as why this music is not the easiest to understand or, perhaps, to enjoy.

Later there came an alteration in ideals. The conception of society as held in the eighteenth century was that there were two classes: the privileged, governing class and the servile, governed class. This conception, whatever we may think of it politically or socially speaking, had great value for the development of art, for it gave to it an intelligent support that otherwise would have been lacking. This assorting of society gave way under the personal aspirations of the nineteenth century, when it began to be realized that every man has a soul and a mind of his own, a right to freedom from oppression, and that there is a moral law directly opposed to the law of force. These new ideas led to the tremendous expressions that Beethoven gave us through the medium of the string quartet, expressions which no composer of his time, and very few since, have been able to equal. Beethoven regarded the string quartet as the purest of all musical forms and remained deaf to those who appealed to him to write more oratorios and operas; instead, he applied himself with enthusiasm to this most difficult form of pure music.

Other composers have carried on the traditions of chamber music as they were started by Haydn. Schubert wrote some of his finest things as chamber-music works. Schumann, pianist and poet, likewise wrote chamber music, with somewhat indifferent success in spite of the real power of his thought. Johannes Brahms was one of the great composers who seemed to find this kind of music especially congenial, for he wrote twenty-four important works in this form, nearly all of them very fine. There is everywhere in his chamber music a noble elevation of ideals, a virile strength, and a depth of feeling that make it one of the glories of German art. Other writers of chamber-music works deserving mention, even in such a cursory survey of the field, are César Franck, Dvořák, Debussy, Ravel, and Schönberg, the last carrying his radical tendencies into this classic field.

What is it that makes chamber music particularly appealing to some musicians who have had a great deal of practice in listening and equally baffling to others who have not versed themselves in the niceties of listening? There is no doubt that chamber music has gained a supreme place in the affections of many music lovers; nor is there doubt that the average listener is left cold by the lack of dramatic appeal in this music and is puzzled by its intricacies.

Sir Henry Hadow [1] has a good word to say on this subject; he is a writer well known for his musicianship as well as for his understanding of the average listener's position:

> Among all forms of composition, chamber music is that which to my taste is the most complete and satisfying. Its transparent texture makes it easy to hear and understand; one is never distracted or bewildered by overcharged sound or overemphasized emotion. And this very transparence renders it necessary that the composer's drawing should be perfect and his design sure. With a very wide range of emotion, it is vowed, in the first instance, to the sense of pure beauty — to beauty of melody, of harmonization, of structure, in which every point tells and every phrase is significant. Heine speaks of Goethe's prose as a pellucid ocean through which one can see his golden thoughts: that simile seems to me wholly suitable to the great classics of chamber-music composition.

TYPES OF CHAMBER MUSIC

Before we take up the study of some representative works written in this medium, it will be well for us to acquaint ourselves briefly with the general characteristics of this kind of writing. In passing, a word about the development of the stringed family of instruments will be helpful. The medieval "fiddles," variants of the bowed-string principle, all led to the viols, which, from the fifteenth century until the coming into power of the new violin tribe in the middle sixteenth, first held mastery, then contested it with the violins, and finally went under, as far as popular use was concerned. We can

---

[1] Reprinted, by permission of Oxford University Press, from Cobbett's *Cyclopedic Survey of Chamber Music.*

occasionally hear the old viols at their best in the hands of such players at the Dolmetsch family or the *Société des instruments anciens*. In Tudor and Stuart times viol-playing was popularly cultivated as part of the education of every gentleman. The violin family came from Cremona just at the right time. Amati, Stradivarius, Gasparo da Salo produced instruments of incomparable beauty, and for three hundred years the design of these instruments has remained virtually unchanged.

The most usual chamber-music combinations in use at the present time are the trio, the quartet, and the quintet, and some of the world's greatest music has been written for these combinations. German musicians seem to consider that it takes at least three instruments to constitute a chamber-music group, but the general consensus of opinion admits the duet to this classification. The usual duo combinations are those of violin and piano, or cello and piano; but many duets have been written for the piano and some wind instruments such as the horn or clarinet. Trios for piano, violin, and cello contain some of our loveliest chamber music, probably because this combination offers a fullness of tone that is unusual. Haydn, Mozart, Beethoven, Schubert, and Brahms all wrote fine trios. Then there are string trios for violin, viola, and cello (a difficult combination to make effective); trios for piano, violin, and horn; for piano, clarinet, and cello; both these latter combinations having been tried by Brahms with great success.

In the string quartet for two violins, viola, and cello we have, as has been said, the purest and highest form of chamber music, perhaps of all music. There are, however, other quartets for piano and strings (violin, viola, and cello), but this combination does not rank with the pure string quartet for beauty of tone, since the use of the piano necessarily confines the other players to its tempered intonation. String quintets are very little different from quartets, the extra instruments being either another viola (Mozart has given us the outstanding work for this combination) or a cello. Both Mozart and Brahms wrote quintets combining the clarinet with the string quartet; and there are popular piano quintets, notably those of Schubert (the *Forellen* quintet) and Schumann. Composers have attempted to write for groups of five wind instruments, such as flute, oboe, clarinet, horn, and bassoon. Brahms has given us two great string sextets — for two violins, two violas, and two cellos.

There are many different combinations for other instruments, most of them grouping the strings with one or more wind instruments: Schönberg's beautiful sextet *Verklärte Nacht* and his *Pierrot lunaire* (for piano, flute [piccolo], clarinet, violin, cello, and voice). Stravinsky's *Trois poésies de la lyrique Japonaise* (voice, piano, flute, clarinet, and string quartet) indicates the trend of modern ideas as to possible chamber-music combinations.

In hearing such a group play, the amateur is almost always disappointed; his natural mistake is in confusing volume with quality of tone. He is disappointed perhaps in listening to only three or four instruments instead of a hundred as in one of the great orchestral works. He misses the overpowering magnitude and splendid weight of the orchestral mass; there is no flashing contrast of colors, no surge of composite tone, no tremendous contrast in dynamics. The very picture before his eyes is disappointing; instead of a large group of instrumentalists, each of them blending his personality and activity with a hundred others under the kindling fire and burning enthusiasm of the conductor, he sees only three, four, or five players huddled in the middle of the stage, each of them engaged in reading his own music without the magnetic stimulus of a visible leader. Everything seems cool, calculated, cerebral.

But let him listen for other things! The clear sonority of the various instruments as they blend together or answer one another in dialogue or repartee; the strength of the whole, due to the equal importance of each part; the weighty matters upon which the instruments discourse — all these are worth his careful attention. We do not have to disparage the greatness of the orchestral masterpieces to realize that chamber music is like Abbé Dimnet's description of sculpture: the art of the noble or heroically minded, the passion of the severely artistic. In spite of the fact that the greatest success, and rightly so, perhaps, has always gone to the writers of orchestral music, chamber music will always afford a lasting and inexhaustible delight because of its clean sparingness, its lack of anything which approaches sentimentality, its disregard for virtuosity except as a means toward a perfect expression of great thought.

SOME EXAMPLES OF STRING-QUARTET STYLE

What is the best means for securing an introduction to this "sanctum sanctorum" of music? Opinions differ, but it would seem natural that it should be through the medium of the most popular of all chamber-music groups, the string quartet: two violins, viola, and cello. Perhaps the most popular single movement in string-quartet literature is the *Andante cantabile* (literally, "leisurely singing") from Tchaikovsky's *Quartet,* Op. 11. This slow movement is full of the tender wistfulness that is enhanced by the fact that it is played with muted strings. The main theme of the movement is taken bodily from an old Russian folk song; it has a peculiar alternation of measures and a most appealing melody:

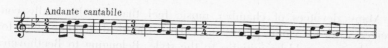

The second section is largely built over a repeated *pizzicato* figure in the cello and equals the first in beauty, while providing a fine contrast. Then the first section returns, the whole movement being a good example of the three-part song form — similar in structure to the *Largo* of the *New World Symphony.*

We have already remarked Haydn's importance in the development of the modern quartet style; one of his best-known quartets is the so-called *Emperor Quartet,* which in its slow movement makes use of the Austrian National Hymn, a tune which Haydn had written for the emperor's birthday celebration of 1797 and afterwards presented to the whole nation. This movement takes the form of theme with variations, a form that has always been popular with composers as a means for displaying skill and technic. We first hear the theme complete; some will recognize it as a tune to which a familiar hymn is sung:

After this we have a set of four variants of it followed by a short coda. In the first variation the second violin carries the tune, while the first weaves a *staccato* embroidery above it; the other instruments are silent. In the second variation the cello has the melody, while the second violin plays a counter-melody, and the first violin and viola supply an appropriate background. The viola takes the tune in the third variation, and there is some beautiful weaving of accompanimental threads by the other instruments: notice the peculiar, veiled character of the viola here. In the last variation the melody is restored to its usual position on top and is sung by the first violin while the other instruments supply a rich background. The coda is short and quiet.

A LIST OF ADDITIONAL MUSIC

Slow Movement from the *Trio in
B Flat Major (Archduke)*, Op. 97   Beethoven

Many devotees of chamber music feel that this heroically conceived work for violin, piano, and cello is the ideal stepping stone for introducing would-be initiates to the style. Belonging to Beethoven's most mature period, there is something about this music that seems to fuse its interpreters into one performing instrument, no matter how independent they may feel as virtuoso players. Two magnificent recordings of the whole trio have been made in which that rare achievement may be observed: "a virtuoso chamber-music performance in which the whole is equal to the sum of its parts." This work should be heard by everyone who has any doubts about the possibility of enjoying chamber music.

Scherzo from *Octette*, Op. 20   Mendelssohn

Written when the composer was only sixteen years old, this deft, finely finished work is conceded to be the best writing ever done for eight strings. Light, staccato, and pianissimo throughout, it is said to have been inspired by a reading of that portion of Goethe's *Faust* which describes the Walpurgis Night revels of the witches and ghosts on the Brocken in the Harz Mountains, Germany. Later on, Mendelssohn orchestrated this *Scherzo* for an orchestral concert which he was to give in London, and orchestras throughout the world have been playing it ever since. If the listener would realize the difference between orchestral style and chamber-music style, let him listen to a first-class recording of the original and contrast it with the revised form having wind and brass parts added to the strings.

TOPICS FOR FURTHER DISCUSSION

Discuss the benefits and drawbacks of the old system of princely patronage of composers. By what could we best replace it today?

A newcomer to chamber music at first disliked the tone of the string quartet, because it did not seem quite "in tune." Can you suggest the reason for his discomfort?

Name some of the outstanding chamber-music organizations of today. How many of these have you heard?

TWENTY

A ROMANTIC QUARTET —

AND A CLASSIC ONE

DVOŘÁK's *American Quartet* [1]

No better introduction to the beauties of quartet style could be found than Dvořák's *Quartet in F Major,* Op. 96, written just after the *New World Symphony* while he was a resident of the United States in 1893. Both these works, together with his *Quintet in E Flat,* Op. 97, are alike in color and style and in their attempt to use the flavor of local folk tunes. Hence they have become known as his "American" works, although they contain much that is innately Czech in flavor.

Dvořák came to teach in the United States during the seasons of 1892–3 and 1893–4; he settled down in New York, curious, excited, and yet perturbed by the swirling American life he found about him. He soon began sketches for the *New World Symphony,* and, when it came time to finish the work and write out the score, he sought a quiet place where he could feel at home among his own people and still be under the influence of the atmosphere of the New World. His friend and mentor, Josef Kovarik, a young Czech who had been born in the Bohemian settlement village of Spillville, Iowa and had gone to Prague for training in music, recommended this little town. Dvořák and Kovarik went there for the summer of 1893; the famous composer made himself completely at home, played the organ for the early morning mass in the village church, talked to the farmers about their crops, and composed furiously. When the *New World Symphony* was finished and the

[1] The score of Dvořák's *American Quartet* is available.

JACK LEVINE: *String Quartet*

score written out, Dvořák turned his attention to a quartet, writing it quickly and playing each movement over as soon as it was finished, with the help of three members of the Kovarik family; Dvořák himself played the first violin part. Thus came into being this lovely "American quartet."

Although it follows in general the forms used by the classic writers of quartets, this work of Dvořák's can hardly be said to be typical. Its first movement has two main themes, both strongly rhythmic in a purely Czech manner and quite contrasting in key and color:

There is little development of these themes according to the manner of the usual first-movement (sonata) form; they are heard, together with subordinate themes, flashing in and out of the constantly weaving fabric and reappear at the end of the movement.

Three-part song form is an ideal mold for the *Lento* movement, just as it had been for the famous *Largo* of the *New World Symphony*. It is music suggestive of the deep woods (whether they are Bohemian or American makes little difference) and the melancholy songs of an oppressed race, perhaps the Czechs themselves, or it may be the American Indians, whose native music interested Dvořák so much. The main theme around which the first part of the movement revolves is this:

The middle section grows out of a nostalgic theme:

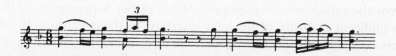

A beautiful coda for the cello brings to an end one of the most deeply expressive movements in all chamber music.

The third movement has the rather unusual form of variations on this very lively theme; the variations are mostly rhythmic in character, with some unusual twists of harmonic color that are so characteristic of this composer:

In the finale Dvořák comes as near to being natively American as he ever could; this is a gay sort of rondo, with a main theme that somewhat resembles a "break-down," but always in the background

we see the smiling face of the Czech visitor, suggested in such subsidiary themes as are used throughout the movement:

In the midst of this barn-dance jollity, there suddenly are heard
a few chorale-like measures, as though the composer were impro-
vising on the village organ. Then the dance is resumed and the
whole work concludes vigorously and happily.

HAYDN'S *Quartet in F Major*, OP. 3, NO. 5 [2]

A good contrast to the Romanticism of Dvořák's work is the classic short *Quartet* of Haydn in F major, Op. 3, No. 5. As far as we
can determine, Haydn wrote eighty-three quartets, ranging in style
from the rather tentative groping of his earlier experiments to the
magnificent maturity of his later quartets. In them all there is felt
very strongly his peculiar genial quality, using the word in its
English sense — warm and friendly — as well as in its Latin suggestiveness of the quality of genius. And this Op. 3, No. 5 is typical,
for certainly no more genial music has ever been written. The work
is very short, as quartets go, but its few pages contain some great
beauties.

The first movement is characteristic of Haydn's gusto and verve;
it is in sonata form, with the themes easily distinguishable: the first
in measures 1 to 8, and the second in measures 41 to 45. The little
development section of fifty measures contains a miniature "im-
broglio," produced from a subsidiary figure in the bridge material
connecting the two themes; yet it sounds perfectly logical and leads
beautifully back to the recapitulation.

The second movement, one of the most famous in quartet literature, is called a "serenade"; it consists of two large sections, each
of them repeated, with the melody given to the muted first violin

[2] The score of Haydn's *Quartet*, Op. 3, No. 5, is available in the Eulenburg Edition
No. 150.

and the other instruments forming a *pizzicato* background. When well played it is a particularly lovely movement, inconceivable except in terms of the string quartet. The minuet and trio run true to form, with some interesting variants of the regularity of the usual minuet rhythm. The last movement, marked *scherzando*, is surely as rapidly running sonata form as was ever written: the themes (there are three of them) are appropriately brief and snappy, and the whole thing is over almost before we know it. This is a perfect little example of Haydn's sympathetic treatment of the quartet style.

LIST OF ADDITIONAL MUSIC

Quartet in D Major (The Lark), Op. 64, No. 5   Haydn
Quartet in B Flat Major (The Sunrise), Op. 76, No. 4   Haydn

No other form of music has been better served by the long-playing type of recording than the string quartet, for the sustained and closely linked moods of this kind of composition should not be broken, as was inevitable in the older form of recording. Like so many of his other quartets, these two works of Haydn have been given nicknames not only suggestive of the composer's intimate style but also descriptive of some feature of the individual work. The lark is suggested by the birdlike main theme of the first movement of Op. 64, No. 5; and the sun rises on a lovely countryside in the B-flat-major work and later sets with peaceful quietude in its slow movement. Both these quartets have been wonderfully served by the engineers; no better value in records can be found than that LP record containing them both, played by the Budapest String Quartet, which seems to have a special feeling for the music of this composer. One critic calls this "possibly the best quartet recording ever made."

TWENTY-ONE

IMPRESSIONISM:

DEBUSSY ITS CHIEF EXPONENT

IN MUSIC

The impressionist movement in art came into being during the latter years of the nineteenth century as a protest against the exuberance and excesses of the Romantics; Claude Debussy (1862–1918) was its chief exponent in music and his masterpiece, *L'Après-midi d'un faune,* one of its greatest productions. This work, although not strictly delineative in the manner of Strauss, employs definite themes suggestive of various episodes, quite in the manner of the Strauss tone poems. Instead of giving himself over to the direct evocation of emotional states in the manner of Liszt and the other Romantic composers, we find Debussy conveying his expression through the indirect power of suggestion; he tries to suggest an emotion rather than express it directly. His music studiously avoids the dramatic and narrative aspects of his predecessors, just as they in turn avoided the formal and conventional aspect of the music of their eighteenth-century predecessors. While demonstrably an offshoot of Romanticism, *L'Après-midi d'un faune* represents a strong revolt against the overpowering and almost annihilating influences which the great giants of the Romantic period bequeathed to their successors. We have already suggested that Romanticism was one of the most stimulating and virile influences ever to affect music and have said that its ideals shaped the output of one great composer after another: Weber, Schubert, Schumann, Liszt, and finally Wagner. The cry of the closing years of the century was: "After Wagner, what?" And, as it so often has done in critical periods, history provided an ideal answer in the person of the pioneer Debussy. The peculiar characteristics of his music, those characteristics which give it "wings to send it soaring up to heights to which it could not possibly have risen otherwise," were the

Claude Debussy

results of an unusually effective blending of racial and environmental influences. Nature provided Debussy with an inquiring mind, a very sensitive musical ear, and an unbounded imagination, and in so doing formed him as the ideal leader of a new musical movement. His music, with its aristocratic bearing, its shunning of the exuberances which are commonplace, its essential restraint, its logic and balance, manifests typical Gallic qualities. And circumstances provided the ideal environment for the rapid development of Debussy's style.

SYMBOLISM — A PARALLEL MOVEMENT IN LITERATURE

Early in his creative life, Debussy found himself in the midst of movements in the other arts, especially in literature and painting, which exercised strong influences on the development of his music. It would hardly be too much to say that just as the German poets of the beginning of the century precipitated Romanticism in music, so the French poets and painters of the last of the century left the very definite impress of their ideals and methods upon the music of the next period. A grouping of poets — "symbolists" they called themselves — headed by Verlaine and Mallarmé, combined in a fight against what they considered to be the abuses of Romanticism to be found in such writers as Hugo and Lamartine. Delicate, tenuous poetry that stimulated the imagination, much of it frankly sensuous and voluptuous, expressed through extremely graceful means, was the aim of these new writers. Words were more than words — they became symbols suggesting rather than merely expressing; they were meant to evoke by means of their sounds certain subconscious sensations and ideas. The actual thought contained in a passage was of less importance than what one was led to read between the lines. Mallarmé said of these aims: "To name an object is to sacrifice three fourths of that enjoyment which comes from the pleasure of guessing bit by bit. To suggest, that is our dream." And he and his followers, Rimbaud, Maeterlinck, Swinburne, and Yeats, wrote verse that is subtly sensuous in sound and suggestive in meaning.

A translation of one of Verlaine's short poems, "Serenade," will give an idea of the spirit which lay behind the whole movement:

The shepherd's star burns dim,
Sinks in the night,
The pilot fumbles for his light.

Now is the time for him,
Dark skies above,
Whose hand seeks out for love.

Sir Atys tunes his strings, ·
His eyes to Chloris speak
Of favors he would seek

While the sad moon is up, and streams
Down on the boat which glides and gleams
Upon a sea of dreams.
— F. E. in the *London Saturday Review* [1]

A FAUN INSPIRES THREE ARTS

No better example of the poetry written by the symbolists could be given than the famous "Eclogue" of Mallarmé (1842–1898), which inspired Debussy to write the music we are about to consider in some detail. Mallarmé's poem was said to have been inspired, in turn, by a little picture of the eighteenth-century artist Boucher, now in the National Gallery, London. This shows in a highly realistic way the leering face of a satyr (the distinction between mythological fauns and satyrs is not very clear: both terms are used to describe beings with tails, horns, goat's legs and feet, and furry, pointed ears, thus possessing both animal and human characteristics) who is pursuing two girls along the reedy bank of a river. But after he had seen it, Mallarmé was moved to write some of the most impressionistically vague and obscure evocations of emotion ever conceived, all the more beautiful because of their vagueness and obscurity:

Ces nymphes, je les veux perpétuer,
*   Si clair,*
Leur incarnat léger, qu'il voltige dans l'air
Assoupi de sommeils touffus.

(I would immortalize these nymphs,
So bright their sunlit coloring, so airy light,
It floats like drowsy down.)

The poem was published in 1876; it is best known to English readers through the prose version of it made by Edmund Gosse, who has paraphrased this "miracle of unintelligibility" as well as anyone could. Even Gosse said that bit by bit, phrase by phrase, he did not understand the original; nevertheless, it gave him great pleasure and he was able to obtain from it "as solid an influence as Mallarmé desired to produce."

[1] By permission of the *London Saturday Review*.

A faun, a simple, sensuous, passionate being, wakens in the forest at daybreak and tries to recall his experience of the previous afternoon. Was he the fortunate recipient of an actual visit from nymphs, white and golden goddesses, divinely tender and indulgent? Or is the memory he seems to retain nothing but the shadows of a vision, no more substantial than the arid rain of notes from his own flute? He cannot tell. Yet surely there was, surely there is, an animal whiteness among the brown reeds of the lake that shines out yonder? Were they, are they, swans? No. But naiads plunging? Perhaps. Vaguer and vaguer grows the impression of this delicious experience. He would resign his woodland godship to retain it. A garden of lilies, golden-headed, white-stalked, behind a trellis of red roses? Ah, the effort is too great for his poor brain. Perhaps if he selects one lily from the garth of lilies, one benign and beneficent yielder of her cup to thirsty lips, the memory, the ever-receding memory, may be forced back. So when he has glutted upon a bunch of grapes he is wont to toss the empty skins into the air and blow them out in a visionary greediness. But no, the delicious hour grows vaguer; experience or dreams, he will never know which it was. The sun is warm, the grasses yielding; and he curls himself up again, after worshiping the efficacious star of wine, that he may pursue the dubious ecstasy into the more hopeful boscages of sleep.

A remarkably suggestive translation, the first lines of which we have given above, has been made of this subtle poetry by Aldous Huxley[2] and should not be missed by those who would get to the heart of Mallarmé's beauty. Poetry of this kind comes close to the qualities of music, for it attempts to express emotion without ideas; so it is little wonder that the sensitive Debussy, congenitally disposed as he was towards this kind of expression, found himself in such close agreement with the ideas of the symbolists.

IMPRESSIONISM IN PAINTING

For suggestions as to technical means for his musical expression, Debussy turned to another contemporary revolt against the traditional "high art" of the middle of the century, hedged about as it was with strict rules and limiting tradition. In reality, impressionism in painting was a new way of seeing the world, just as symbolism was another way of feeling, and musical impressionism a new way

[2] To be found in, among other anthologies, Van Doren's *Anthology of World Poetry*.

EARLY IMPRESSIONISM: *La Grenouillère* by Monet

It was at this famous bathing place that the methods of impressionism came to Monet and Renoir spontaneously, before they had evolved theories on the subject.

of hearing. It was developed by a group of young and enthusiastic painters who, around 1869, following the dynamic influence of the realistic-romantic Courbet, revolted against the academic, studio-produced art of the masters. Although he was never a full-fledged impressionist, Édouard Manet (1832–1883) may be regarded as the precursor of the movement, with his attempts to show that color and light alone have the power of providing form and composition in a picture. The real leader and the greatest figure in impressionistic painting was Claude Monet (1840–1926), who in conjunction with his friends Renoir, Sisley, and Pissarro developed its theories and invented its technical methods. Working entirely in the open air, largely at the Normandy beaches and the little bathing places and open-air restaurants along the Seine, these artists were intrigued by the vibrations of light set up by such fleeting images as the ripples seen in flowing water, the broken gleams of sunlight that played on its surface, the furtive movement of sails across the sea, the warm sun bathing the everyday objects of open-air life, the cool wind-ruffled leafage of the trees. They observed that these images changed constantly according to the varieties of light during different times of the day and conditions of the atmosphere, and their great desire was to catch at all costs the *impression* of these fleeting, "colored moments."

Courtesy of the Art Institute, Chicago

IMPRESSIONISM AT ITS BEST: *Westminster* by Monet

The peculiar quality of London's "faintly misted light" fascinated the impressionists; and this fact, together with their discovery of the English painter Turner's style, strongly influenced their work.

So they tried to analyze these vibrations of light and air and to break them up into their constituent parts, calling in new scientific theories to back up their visual observation. In order to get these sensations onto their canvases, they based their idea of divided tones and color splotches on intuitive discoveries inaugurated by

Delacroix some time before. These they juxtaposed in such a manner that they became mixed in the eye of the beholder, giving him a sense of light and air and color never before experienced in painting. The great discovery of the impressionists was thus not only a new concept of space and time but also a new rendering of light and movement. They avoided the usual subjects common to painting up to that time — dramatic sense, literary ideas, classic subjects, as well as the traditional conventions of proportion and balance and form. They tried to make out of their attempts to reproduce the quality of light on various objects a kind of "painted music." We do not get any idea of ordered structure or calculated design from these paintings — such design as we find in the Italian paintings of the Renaissance, for instance; but we do receive an impression of the scene at the moment the artist looked at it, vibrating with an effect of living light and air.

Debussy felt that this painted music could be of great service in helping him formulate new methods of expression in his own art. As a boy he had had dreams of becoming a painter, and as a mature musician in Paris he had come into direct and fruitful contact with the symbolist poets and impressionistic painters. So he was particularly qualified to adopt some of their theories to his composing. In general it may be said that Debussy's ideal was to let music convey emotion without having a definite melodic or formal structure, just as the impressionistic painters tried to convey their sensations through the eye without the use of conventional lines, patterns, and form. Just as these painters were concerned with the constituent parts of light and were able to duplicate these on their canvases, Debussy turned his attention to the elements which go to make up chords. He placed these in combinations different from those that had been customary, using plenty of dissonances and paying little attention to the grammatical relationship of one chord to another. Because of his unusually sensitive ear, he could single out the overtones that go to make up the timbre of the fundamental notes we hear, mixing and blending these so as to produce entirely new effects, much in the same way as the painters mixed their colors on the canvas to produce the effects of vibrating light. Thus he arrived at the new effects which, with other devices he used — the whole-tone scale (see Chapter Five), extreme fluidity of rhythm, and indefiniteness of melody — give his music its marked individuality.

IMPRESSIONISM IN MUSIC

These effects may be heard at their best in his masterpiece, *L'Après-midi d'un faune* (The Afternoon of a Faun),[3] written in the years 1892–4, when Debussy's genius was in full flower. There is little that will trouble us in understanding and liking this wonderful tone poem today, although for many years after its first performance it was considered extremely daring music. This is program painting that conveys the emotional suggestions of a landscape rather than attempting to re-create it in musical terms. Prunières's phrase is a happy one: this is music which in order to be sensuous, poetic, and supremely effective is developed, not according to fixed formulas but simply and logically in accordance with the poetry it seeks to express. It is a synthesis by which one is transported to another world, one which can hardly be reached through either the art of poetry or music alone. Olin Downes speaks of his vivid remembrance of his first hearing of this music, the indescribable beauty and elusiveness of its instrumentation, and the impossibility of recalling, at first, a note of the music. Probably everyone who listens to the piece for the first time has a similar experience. With the very first summons of the magic-flute passage at its beginning, Debussy's score takes us completely out of the mundane world of every day back to the sunlit slopes of Greece; this is music unlike any other in the world — pagan, full of the spirit of an ancient beauty. A dreaming faun, a child of nature in the shape of man with the horns and feet of a beast, lies slumbering in the noontime heat. The "arid" flute announces the principal theme (1–4),

full of a desire in which there is a strange tenderness and melancholy; oboes, clarinets, and French horns respond, and their chords, flooded with limpid harp tones, sustain the mood and heighten the impression of the opening measures. The rhythm fluctuates between 9/8, 6/8, 12/8, 3/4, and 4/4. The call becomes louder and more urgent, but dies away to let the flute again sing its song. A

[3] The piano score of Debussy's *L'Après-midi d'un faune* is available in the Fromont Edition (transcribed by Borwick) and in the Edward B. Marks Co. Edition. The orchestral score (miniature size) is available in the Kalmus Edition No. 17.

clarinet solo begins a new section (32), with a theme very much like the first in content, accompanied by fragmentary bits from the harp. Then we hear the oboe with a new theme (37),

again strangely like the first in outline; a lively dialogue follows (44), the music marked *toujours en animant,* leading directly to a third theme on the wood winds: flute, oboe, English horn, clarinets (55) — a theme which could be said to suggest desire satisfied.

Then the principal climax of the whole is gradually built up, and the first theme returns, more languorous than ever (79); it is flutteringly repeated by the oboe and answered by the lightest chords imaginable from the whole orchestra. New chords are heard, as harp *glissandi* suggest the fleetness of the passing vision (86). At last a solo cello joins itself with the flute (100) and then an unforgettable passage for muted horns and strings brings the whole work to a conclusion in which the music seems to vanish before our very ears. It hardly seems possible that there are only a hundred and ten measures in this score; never has such economy of means produced such wealth of beauty. Every measure is telling, with nothing wasted, the whole standing as a fitting monument to a composer who was master of a style almost too fragile and delicate for survival in this practical world.

DEBUSSY'S NOCTURNES

Aside from *L'Après-midi d'un faune* and his great opera, *Pelléas et Mélisande,* Debussy's best-known work is a set of three orchestral nocturnes: *Nuages, Fêtes,* and *Sirènes.* These, upon first hearing, may seem to lack the unity and coherence which is so striking a feature of the Faun; we hear melodies unlike any with which we are familiar, and, in addition, the various sections of these nocturnes seem to be unrelated, the instrumental combinations without apparent reason. Yet if we consider these pieces as impressionistic suggestions with a sense of beauty that is only half uttered, musical excursions into the realms of the imagination, their difficulties will quickly disappear. Of the three, the second is best known, perhaps because it is the most tangible. It is astonishingly vigorous for Debussy, for most of his music is so indefinite and intangible that it lacks force and power. But the pageants which the composer unfolds for us here are visionary ones, nevertheless; they are the imaginative and yet frightfully real spectacles such as are revealed only to the mind of the mystics. These are visions like Francis Thompson's *Hound of Heaven,* or those of which William Blake spoke: "Is it not reasonable to suppose that we can create by the working of the mind forms stronger, clearer, and more moving than anything produced by nature? If not, what is the imagination for, and what in heaven's name is the use of art?"

In notes which he supplied for the first performance of these nocturnes in Paris in 1900, Debussy said that the title is "to be understood in a wider sense than that usually given it and should be regarded as conveying a decorative meaning." In *Nuages* he had in mind "the unchanging aspect of the sky, with the slow, melancholy passage of clouds dissolving in a gray vagueness tinged with white." How marvelously the music brings the sensations of this skyscape to our minds! *Fêtes* is meant to evoke the "restless, rhythmic dancing of the atmosphere, with bursts of brusque light. There is also the episode of a procession — a dazzling and wholly idealistic vision — passing through and blended with the festival. But always the background of the festival remains: luminous dust participating in the rhythm of the universe." There is little use in trying to explain this music — it belongs to the experiences with which we are all familiar, experiences that border on the unconscious, hardly definite enough to be recognizable, yet strangely bewildering in their insistent appeal. The third nocturne, *Sirènes* (Sirens), is not often played because it requires a chorus of women's voices in addition to the orchestra. It has been the source of the mysteriously hummed backgrounds of many a moving picture; but nevertheless it is wonderful music in its own right and should always be included with the other two when the set is played.

THE LATER YEARS

Later on, Debussy's music became somewhat more tangible and realistic: *La Mer* is a powerful evocation of the spirit of the sea in a big-scaled symphonic manner, full of the drama and color and mystery of its subject and showing how well the impressionistic style can be made to serve big canvases. *Ibéria,* the middle work of his orchestral triptych called *Images,* is a dazzling summation of the spirit of Spain; although Debussy did not know this country from actual experience, his imagination was so vivid and his art so subtle that we get from the three parts of this orchestral picture, *In the Streets and Byways, The Fragrance of the Night,* and *The Morning of the Festival Day,* a vivid picture of the many aspects of this fascinating country, which seemed to be of special interest to the impressionists — its fragrant old gardens, the intoxicating spell of its nights, its riots of color, its animated rhythms, and its gorgeous national festivals.

Because the piano is an instrument peculiarly adapted to the manner of the impressionists, Debussy devoted a great deal of time and attention to the development of a characteristic piano style. He developed new sonorities and effects, quite at variance with the accepted traditions of the instrument up to that time, and many feel that the short program pieces he wrote for this instrument represent impressionism and Debussy and the piano at their very best.

It is sad to have to relate that in Debussy's later years his composing, which up to that time had seemed so fresh and spontaneous, degenerated into mannerisms and formalistic copying of earlier styles. Domestic troubles, sickness, and, above all else, World War I influenced his life and his creative powers. During the last six years of his life he turned out things in obvious haste, realizing that his days were numbered; none of these compositions compare with those written in the great days of his power. At his best, he was one of the great masters of his art, enveloping his music in a mysterious haze that is full of luminous color. He viewed the world largely from the viewpoint of the mystic, with little desire to mingle in it. There is also a peculiar sadness, a brooding for things that might have been and never will be, in so much of his work. But certainly all its seeming mistiness and haziness is attained by means of a technical structure that is taut and clear, a structure that would seem to assure this music of immortality. How this was attained was a secret that perished with Debussy, for none of his followers was ever able to equal this phantasmal, chimerical, marvelously constructed music. Perhaps it is just as well; otherwise, as someone has wisely said, we might all have become lotus-eaters!

CHARACTERISTIC WORKS OF DEBUSSY (not including the piano pieces)

Printemps (Spring), 1886

An interesting example of the beginnings of the composer's personal style, this is the first work for orchestra which he permitted to be published. Written when he was still a student in Rome, it contains a not-too-well-digested mixture of romantic style and impressionistic technic.

Prélude à l'après-midi d'un faune, 1892–4

Why Prelude? Debussy expected to follow this with other evocations based on Mallarmé's poem: *Interlude* and *Paraphrase* were never written.

Quartet in G Minor (strings), 1893

This has been called "the most distinguished piece of chamber-music writing in the French repertoire." Only faintly tinged with impressionism.

Pelléas et Mélisande, 1902

Fortunately for opera lovers, this masterpiece has been well recorded in full. For those not able to stand the expense of purchasing the whole opera, a real acquaintance with its style and manner may be obtained from the Orchestral Interludes, which are published separately.

La Mer, 1904

The titles of these three symphonic sketches are explicit enough:
1. *De l'aube à midi sur la mer* (From Dawn until Noon on the Ocean)
2. *Jeux de vagues* (Sport of the Waves)
3. *Dialogue du vent et de la mer* (Dialogue of the Wind and the Sea).
But otherwise there is not a programmatic idea in the whole work, even though a contemporary critic wisecracked that he liked particularly in the first movement the part at a quarter past eleven. A magnificent calling-up of sensations and images.

Images pour orchestre (Images), 1906–12

Gigues
Ibéria

1. *Par les rues et par les chemins* (In the Streets and Byways)
2. *Les Parfums de la nuit* (The Fragrance of the Night)
3. *Le Matin d'un jour de fête* (The Morning of the Festival Day)

Rondes de printemps (Spring Roundelays)

TOPICS FOR FURTHER DISCUSSION

Discuss the close connection between nineteenth-century French arts — music, poetry, painting, sculpture.

By what means, in *L'Après-midi d'un faune*, does Debussy convey or arouse emotions similar to those awakened in us by the poetry of Mallarmé?

DEFINITE SUGGESTIONS FOR READING

Music in History: The Modern Revolt: Realism
Impressionism in General
Debussy the High Priest of Impressionism

THE PIANO

We have said in the previous chapter that the piano is the impressionistic instrument *par excellence*. To realize this it will be necessary to give a brief résumé of the history of this most popular of all solo instruments, the one surviving representative of that type of keyboard instrument so popular throughout the development of European music. From the time of the Renaissance these instruments have always been fairly accessible and, fortunately, are fairly easy to play. The accuracy of ear that is so necessary for the players of instruments like the violin, the cello, and the trombone is not an important factor in the case of the keyboard instruments. Players of the organ, the piano, and the harpsichord find their tones already formed for them, and their ability as players depends upon their powers of co-ordination and manual dexterity.

ANCESTORS

Our present-day piano is a logical descendant of two types of earlier keyboard instruments, the clavichord and the harpsichord. These forerunners of the piano were themselves the result of the attempt, somewhere about the fifteenth century, to produce tone from the existing stringed instruments by means of a keyboard or clavier, each key of which would set in vibration one string. In the clavichord type, the tone was produced by means of metal tangents that were fixed to the end of a long lever, on the other end of which was the key. These tangents were forced up against the string when the key was depressed, making a delicate, metallic sort of tone, well suited to a small room but quite lost in a large one. Since the tone could be varied in volume (for the harder one hit the key, the firmer was the tangent forced against the string) and had a sympathetic quality, this instrument was a favorite of musicians for several centuries. The harpsichord (in its smaller forms it was called *spinet* or *virginal*) tone was louder and more definite; but it was incapable of direct control as to volume. It was produced by mechanically plucking the string by means of a plectrum made of quill or leather inserted in the action; this gave a twangy, guitar-like quality of tone that had considerable power, especially when the instrument was of concert size. But the incapability of direct variation in tonal power of this instrument led the makers to seek a new type, one that would give a brilliant tone and yet would be able to play both softly and loudly. In the early part of the eighteenth century Cristofori, an Italian clavier maker, announced that he had perfected such an instrument, a *gravicembalo col piano e forte* — a harpsichord that could play both soft and loud. But Cristofori's instrument was not a harpsichord, for the tone was produced by means of small hammers which struck the strings; it did what Cristofori claimed, however, and the name stuck. The century following the announcement of this invention was given over to improving the action of the instrument, largely by German and English makers. In the first part of the nineteenth century Broadwood, an English maker, supplied pedals which made possible the sustaining of the tones generated by the strings, as well as softening them. The problems of stringing the piano so as to produce the maximum of richness and depth of tone were among the most important that the later makers had to solve. In the early years of the nineteenth century American manufacturers invented a complete iron frame which was capable of withstanding a tension of thirty tons, and in 1853 steel wire instead of iron wire began to be used, allowing a much greater string tension and thus improving the tone immeasurably. The development of our modern Gargantuan instrument has been a gradual one, but it seems now to have reached the stage where further improvement seems improbable.

THE PIANO — BOON AND BANE

The piano — its full and formal title is the pianoforte — may rightly be called the universal musical instrument. Although, as we have already suggested, it was the typical instrument of the nineteenth century, its popularity has lasted well into our own time and programs of piano music are greeted with enthusiasm during every modern concert season. There is good reason for this popularity.

Clavichord, German, circa 1533

A direct descendant of the Monochord. Usually of four octaves, its keys were fitted with blades of brass called " tangents " to strike the string and divide it, producing at the same time tone and pitch. Clavichords had a soft, hesitating tone.

Courtesy of Steinway and Sons, New York

For not only has the piano one of the richest repertoires of any instrument, but it can on occasion assume that of other instruments, be they voice, violin, orchestra, or organ. It is one of the few instruments capable of furnishing not only a solo part but a harmonic accompaniment also, one that is sometimes of great complexity; in this way it functions as an instrument as the violin,

Spinet, Italian, Seventeenth Century

The "Plectra" or quills, fitted into the jacks, set the strings into vibration by plucking them. With one string to each note, volume was small and instruments of this type were in general incapable of dynamic modification of tone by differences in touch.

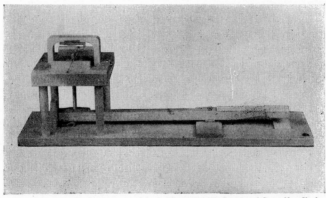

clarinet, or trombone never can. It is as well suited to the demands of the virtuoso as to those of the modest amateur — both find in it a satisfying medium for the conveyance of their ideas and the display of their abilities. It is, as Fox-Strangways has said, the boon as well as the bane of present-day music, for with all its ingratiating qualities, the piano lacks a soul of its own. And this is a fact that

Harpsichord, Italian, circa 1680

The most important keyed instrument of the eighteenth century, in form and arrangement resembling a grand piano. Usually of four to five octaves with two or three strings to each note. A jack and quill action gave individuality of tone, some power, but lacked expressive character through touch. Used more in the orchestra than as a solo instrument.

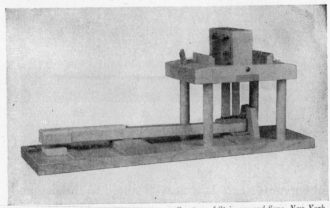

Courtesy of Steinway and Sons, New York

with instruments as with people we realize only gradually and upon long acquaintance. The piano is like a brilliant friend who seems master of every situation in which he finds himself, attractive in personality, versatile in conversation, brilliant in wit, and yet when

Cristofori's Italian "Piano e Forte"

The Dulcimer was the prototype of the Piano, and Cristofori's invention of the hammer action about 1710 gave this instrument more power and a wide dynamic range. The hammer and its escapement provided the foundation for subsequent improvements in France, Germany, and England.

Courtesy of Steinway and Sons, New York

we really get to know him, one who reveals himself as having no personality of his own. "The piano is a first-rate actor: it can assume any part and make a good thing of it — sing, dance, prattle, argue, storm, wail, and do all these things in different voices." But all the time its percussive tone is incapable of being modified or prolonged to any appreciable extent. Once the piano tone has been produced by the hammers which set its strings vibrating, there is no way of prolonging, shading, or otherwise altering the tone. The only thing that can be done is to produce another tone having the desired change. This is a serious handicap, for certainly the long-drawn melody is the soul of music. In order to have that sense of continuity — of going on — that is the very essence of its life, music must consist of more than short, choppy phrases such as are suggested by the quickly fading tones of the piano. A composer for the orchestra can make use of its power for sustaining tone, its immense range of different degrees of power, its infinite possibilities of combining different tone colors. A writer for the piano must not only recognize the incapacities of his instrument in these respects; he must find means to overcome them and to suggest to the hearer more than is actually transmitted to the ear by inferring things of which the instrument is not actually capable. In other words, the writer of music for the piano has had to evolve a style of writing which takes advantage of the instrument's peculiar characteristics — ease and facility of handling, which means that there must be plenty of fast and brilliant passages in piano writing; the attaining of great elasticity in accent through the ability of the player directly to emphasize any note or group of notes he plays, which means that piano music must have plenty of rhythmic appeal. But these are not enough in themselves. Music written to exploit these rather crude possibilities alone would make the pianoforte one of the most objectionable instruments ever invented and one of the most potent depravers of human taste imaginable. The piano, Jekyll and Hyde among instruments, can also sing angelically — fit interpreter for a Chopin or for a Franck.

Indeed, the attempt to remedy these natural handicaps of piano tone has resulted in the only individual contributions that it has made to the world's great musical literature. For in spite of the fact that since 1850, the date when the modern form of the instrument may well be said to have been perfected, piano music has been one of the most frequent forms of composition, there have been only a few great composers who have made essential contributions to piano literature — who have written music that would be unthinkable on any other instrument. And these few — Schumann, Liszt, Chopin, Debussy, and Ravel — have recognized the shortcomings of the instrument; but they have done more — they have used these shortcomings to the advantage of their own piano style. All the other great composers have, with very few exceptions, written voluminously for the piano; but in so doing they have convinced us that they could express themselves better through other instruments — the orchestra, or perhaps the string quartet.

THE RESOURCES OF THE PIANO

What are these characteristics of music peculiarly indigenous to the piano? A little practical experimenting will help to answer such a question. Go to a good piano and strike a full chord, holding down the keys after the hammers have produced the tone; the notes will

Liszt at the Piano

Cartoon of 1843

sound with gradually diminishing tone until the strings have entirely ceased to vibrate. Now strike the same chord again, at the same time holding down the damper pedal (the one to the right) and remove your fingers from the keys as soon as the hammers have struck. Exactly the same result will follow, for the pedal locks off the strings the dampers belonging to the keys that have been struck, thus allowing them to vibrate until they cease of their own inanition. The natural function of these dampers when they are not acted upon by the pedal is to clamp down on the string as soon as the player removes his finger from the key, and thus stop further vibration and consequent mixing of tones. Now, holding down the damper pedal, play the same chord in varying parts of the keyboard — low, medium, and high; or better still, break it up into an arpeggio. Notice how this sustains the tone, giving it a semblance of the same notes being prolonged; it is this plan of playing scales and arpeggios and ornamental passages so as to give the idea of sustained utterance that is one of the cardinal principles of good writing for the piano. Liszt and his followers developed this idea to such an extent and with such virtuosity of technic, massing chord upon chord in such reckless profusion and producing such climaxes of cascading tone as to make the piano seem almost like a sonant instrument.

Now try another experiment: while sounding the arpeggio of any common chord on the piano with the damper pedal down, introduce a few notes that do not belong to this chord; notice what such a procedure does to the *color* of the result, provided the added notes are not too discordant. There seems to be a new richness of *timbre;* and it is this introduction of a sort of shimmer and iridescence to piano music by the inclusion of just the right notes in his runs and arpeggios that was Chopin's great contribution to piano writing. Listening to his romantic Preludes or Nocturnes, we are almost persuaded that the piano is not a monochromatic instrument. Robert Schumann was the great Romanticist of piano music; he loved to dream "with the pedal down, and came nearer than anyone else ever has to finding a soul in the piano. He seized upon its peculiar capacities and gave it what others would have given to the orchestra, and not entirely unsuccessfully — far more successfully than when he gave to the orchestra what he should have given to the piano." His short pieces *Aufschwung* ("Soaring") and *Warum?* ("Why?"), or the *Romance,* Opus 28, No. 2, will give the hearer an idea of this composer's love for blended chords and poetic thought. The evanescent quality of the piano and its capacity for blending and mixing tone by the use of the damper pedal make it the ideal instrument for playing impressionistic music. And men like Debussy and Ravel were able to wash in their colors with broad sweeps and blur their outlines without making them so indistinct as to lose character. Debussy's *Poissons d'or,* or his *Jardins sous la pluie,* or any of his *Préludes,* as well as Ravel's *Pavane pour une infante défunte* or *Jeux d'eau*, illustrates the adaptability of the piano for this type of music. There are many who think, indeed, that this kind of writing shows the piano at its best.

A SHORT LIST OF CHARACTERISTIC PIECES FOR THE PIANO (See the *Listener's Repertoire* for a more complete listing.)

1721 *Prelude and Fugue in C Major*, No. 1
   of *The Well-Tempered Clavier*   Bach

Bach wrote these compositions so that they could be played on any keyboard instrument, although he preferred to use the clavichord. They sound well on the modern piano, if not overemotionalized with the use of the damper pedal.

1778 *Rondo alla Turca* from *Sonata in A Major*,
   K. 331   Mozart

While Mozart's piano was a less powerful instrument than our modern one, it was capable of some very characteristic effects. It will be interesting to compare a piano rendition of this lively *Rondo* in the Turkish style (an affectation of the Rococo period) with one played on the harpsichord, which was still largely used in Mozart's day. Such a comparison would show clearly the differences between the style demanded of the two instruments.

c. 1797 First Movement of *Sonata in C Major*,
   Op. 13 (*Pathétique*)   Beethoven

This strong, dramatic, sonata-form movement shows Beethoven's almost orchestral treatment of the piano. His set of thirty-two sonatas represents one of the greatest contributions to the literature of the instrument.

1837 *Aufschwung* (Soaring) from the *Fantasiestücke*   Schumann

Here is the eager Romantic poet, dreaming at the piano "with the pedal down." Very typical of this composer.

Revised 1848 *Fantasia quasi sonata — D'Après*
   une lecture de Dante (Fantasy
   Sonata — After Reading Dante)   Liszt

Franz Liszt was the first of the great modern virtuoso pianists to travel over Europe giving "recitals"; and, possessed of prodigious technical ability, he wrote a great deal of piano music to show it off. His style, like the man himself, was a peculiar combination of affecting sincerity and rhetorical bombast; but it suits the instrument well, which by Liszt's time had developed into the elephantine instrument we know today.

Polonaise No. 6 in A Flat, Op. 53   Chopin

This is one of the compositions of this master of the piano unfortunate enough to be maltreated by the abominable adaptations of adolescent arrangers. But it does show Chopin at his best and fits the style of the instrument perfectly. Note what we have said about his style above.

TWENTY–TWO

IMPRESSIONISM (*continued*)

PIANO STYLES OF DEBUSSY AND RAVEL

A good connecting link between Debussy and his greatest contemporary (although not a real disciple), Maurice Ravel (1875–1937), is the music they both wrote for the piano. Most of the nineteenth-century piano composers — Beethoven, Schumann, Liszt, and even Chopin (although he did make some wider experiments) — wrote music that, lying largely "under the fingers," came to be thought of as indigenous to the instrument. This conventional style of writing consisted largely of scale and arpeggioed passages alternating with sustained melodies and chords; it came off well, made a brave show, and thus was widely popular. Debussy and Ravel, both of them pianists of considerable ability, became impatient with this orthodox kind of writing and substituted for it ideas of their own: new and largely dissonant chords, with little attention paid to their "grammatical" progression, unusual melodies and accompaniments containing plenty of "alien" notes, the blending together of unusual and unexpected tonal and rhythmical combinations, and (like their contemporaries in painting) constant insistence upon *color* as an important constituent in expression.

Such color effects could easily be obtained on the piano through the proper use of the damper pedal, and so they came to be considered a hallmark of impressionistic pianism. New technical resources on the part of the player had to be developed in order to make it effective, and consequently we have had such impressionistic specialists as Walter Gieseking, strange to say, a German pianist.

The development of Debussy's piano style can be easily traced, beginning with the rather romantically conventional *Arabesque* and the lovely *Suite Bergamasque* (containing the popular *Clair de lune* — Moonlight), both of them quite in the salon style of the popular French composer Massenet, with but a touch of the genius that was to develop later. In 1902 he wrote a suite *Pour le piano,* which gave more of a hint, although there was nothing particularly startling except the *Sarabande* with its archaic flavor, obtained through the use of an old dance rhythm combined with seventh and ninth chordal dissonances. Not until 1903 did Debussy, in the words of one critic, catch up with himself, in so far as piano music was concerned. By this time, we must remember, he had written *L'Après-midi, Pelléas et Mélisande,* the *Nocturnes,* and was busy with *La Mer.* In that year he published *Estampes,* consisting of three numbers: *Pagodes* (Pagodas), built on a five-toned Oriental scale and wonderfully atmospheric; *Soirée dans Granade,* in which Debussy, in his attempts to capture Spanish color, comes close to imitating an early Ravel *Habanera,* later incorporated into that composer's *Rapsodie espagnole;* and *Jardins sous la pluie* (Gardens in the Rain), with its shimmering aqueous effects that were certainly adopted, to say the least, from Ravel's *Jeux d'eau,* which had been performed two years before. *Estampes* is real Debussy, the creation of a temperament of a Chopin subjected to impressionistic influences; as someone has well said, Chopin makes poetry with the piano, Debussy paints with it.

Many of the twenty-four *Préludes* (1910–1913) are hardly more than miniatures, although the two books in these collections contain some matter of considerable importance. *La Cathédrale engloutie* (The Submerged Cathedral) is based on an old Breton legend of a city submerged beneath the waves, with the myriad sounds of its daily life coming up from the bottom of the sea: bells toll, and the sound of a Gregorian Chant is heard. If one would obtain an idea of the difference between an essential piano style and an orchestral one, let him compare the orchestral arrangement which has been made of this piece with the original version; such a comparison will by no means be all in favor of the orchestral version!

Another comparison which is pertinent is that between Debussy's idea of *Ondine* (*Préludes,* Book II, No. 8) and Ravel's program piece of the same name in his *Gaspard de la nuit. Ondine* is a version of the Water Sprite legend; in Debussy's piece she is graceful, sensuous, imaginative; in Ravel's hard, glittering, and detached. The difference is characteristic.

Ravel, born thirteen years later, was as essentially French as his predecessor, who delighted to sign himself Claude Debussy, *Musicien français*. Ravel made use of many of the same devices of impressionism in his writing, but his music has sharper outlines and more developed contrasts. In some ways it is easier to get hold of, for he paid considerable attention to formal outlines, often using the conventional forms which classic composers had employed in their works. He had little of the Debussian sense of the mystery of life; rather was he a detached, cool-headed, keen-witted observer, enjoying life sensuously in much the same way as did the impressionistic painters. One feels that his aesthetic was very similar to that of Cézanne, who said that he wished to make of impressionism an art that was "solid and durable." Certain it is that Ravel's best-known orchestral works are solid and durable in a sense that Debussy's never were.

Ravel's piano piece *Jeux d'eau* (The Fountain) has just been mentioned; it is a lovely piece of program music with a program taken from a quotation descriptive of a fountain set in the midst of an old formal French garden, its figure of an ancient god happily spouting jets of water high into the air, where they are dissipated into soft rainbow clouds of vapor. Ravel has written music that carries out this poetic idea magically and yet carefully follows a set, formal scheme — that of the sonata form, if we dare to analyze it! The whole piece is largely an exploitation of one chord, the chord of the "ninth," as theorists call it. This chord may be found at the piano by starting with C and then playing in conjunction E, G, B flat, and finally D; out of it the composer weaves the loveliest of liquid sounds and color combinations. This is a dazzling little work, and it needs consummate technic on the part of the player who attempts it.

The *Pavane pour une infante défunte* (Pavan for a Dead Princess) is another example of the combining of classic form and modern expression; it is one of Ravel's earliest popular works and is an elaboration of a stately Spanish dance form current in the sixteenth and seventeenth centuries. Here again is a solidity of structure that readily allows us to understand the rather novel musical speech of the composer. The speech may be new and curiously original; but the language is the same as has served the greatest of the old masters. Ravel makes use of the rondo form here, the leading theme returning time after time like a sort of refrain.

Those who would familiarize themselves with this composer's

stylistic development will find it clearly documented in his works, beginning with the *Rapsodie espagnole* (1908). This, a four-sectioned piece of program music, shows the Spanish influence which pervades so much of Ravel's writing, an influence which was natural enough, since he was born in the Basque country, the inhabitants of which show both Spanish and French characteristics. This mysterious, rapturous music is perhaps the best atmospheric musical picture we have of that strange land.

RAVEL'S ORCHESTRAL MASTERY

Daphnis and Chloe is the title of an ancient Greek pastoral poem telling the story of these two lovers, children of a goatherd and a shepherd. It was made over, in the sixteenth century, into a more modern version which has been the inspiration for a number of works, among them the ballet for which the Russian producer Diaghilev in 1912 commissioned Ravel to write the music. This ballet was not a success, although the music shows its composer at his very best; and he was glad to salvage some of the music and make it over into two orchestral suites which, especially the second, contain a great deal of atmospheric and colorful music. The three sections of the *Second Daphnis and Chloe Suite* are: 1) *Lever du jour*, surely the most colorful sunrise ever suggested by music; in its suggestive rather than depictive powers, it can well be compared with Richard Strauss's stupendous beginning of *Also sprach Zarathustra;* 2) *Pantomime*, a necessary lessening of the tension before 3) *Danse générale*, a magnificently rhythmed, almost frenzied display of impressionistic technic. All three sections show Ravel's absolute mastery of his orchestra, an essentially aristocratic way of scoring, detached and cool, yet with the full exploitation of the possibilities of each instrument; the score glows with color and pulses with varied rhythms. In nothing else that he did was Ravel so human and warmly appealing.

La Valse, written in 1920, shortly after World War I, shows the natural disillusionment of the postwar period but is vivid with tonal hues and orchestral color. There is an inescapable feeling of bitterness and cynicism in its scraps of Viennese waltz tunes shining through an impressionistic mist which makes a striking comment on the spirit of futility and nihilism that follows great wars. The *Bolero*, in its reproduction on long-playing records, can be heard with its original intent, that of providing an unbroken, largely mechanical crescendo repetition of a rather obvious Spanish-like tune, written throughout in one key, the instrumentation piling up in intensity (an intensity completely lost when records had to be changed as in the old style of recording) and exploding, with a sudden change of key at the very end. It was written on the particular order of a rather eccentric dancer featured in Paris in the 1920's; and because of its strong rhythmic appeal, it has become popular — another example of a composer being best known by one of his weakest works.

A SYMPHONY IN THREE SPANISH GARDENS

Manuel de Falla's music is a happy combination of impressionism and nationalism. Making use of many of the technical devices of Debussy and his followers, this composer infused a peculiarly Spanish idiom into all his work. To most of us the very name Spain spells romance — the land of the fabulous adventures of Don Juan; the magic stage on which Don Quixote and his faithful Sancho played out their immortal drama; the trysting place of the gypsies of Borrow's fascinating travel tales; the home of Carmen and her castanetted rhythms, of the multicolored, cruel bullfight, of proud arrogance and fiery love. Spain arouses in our minds memories of soft music sounding through warm nights, visions of the Alhambra outlined against the radiant Andalusian sky, reminiscences of a glory that is past forever. It is this sort of thing that we listen for in Spanish music — and with good reason. One of the most important factors which influence the popular conception of a nation's characteristics is the music it has produced. Naturally the connection between the songs (together with the verses to which they are set) and the thoughts and feelings of those who sing them is very close. It was a wise rather than a boastful historian who said: "Tell me what sort of songs a nation has produced, and I can tell you what sort of nation it will become." The music which Spain has given the world is full of a soft, undulating, poetic suggestiveness quite in line with the popular conception of the country as a land of romance. And this is meant in no derogatory sense; despite the fact that she has produced no great international figures in music, Spain is a musical country. Her genius has been for glorified dance forms; descriptive music; and charming, graceful, sentimental songs. It is in her sense of rhythm that she stands supreme, and much of the attractiveness and appeal of Spanish music arises from this.

Luckily for us this popular music of Spain has not been ruined by academic influence, but has been preserved almost intact and unharmed. Before any movement for the cultivation of the music of the Classic composers of other countries could gain much headway among the Spanish, they had become aware of their own genius, and educated composers made no attempts to write after the manner of Bach and Beethoven. The music of the best modern Spaniards, men like Falla and Albeniz, although showing unmistakable influences of their neighbors the French, is peculiarly indigenous to the soil of Spain. The three numbers in Falla's suite *Nights in the Gardens of Spain* seem like a re-creation of the popular soul of the composer's native land. Based on rhythms, scraps of melody, and cadences peculiar to the folk songs of Andalusia (the southernmost part of modern Spain), this music never copies these songs exactly. If you can imagine an Andalusian trio of two mandolins and a guitar playing these folk songs in one of the old gardens of southern Spain, flooded with moonlight, you are in the proper mood for the enjoyment of this music. Although, as he himself has told us, the composer has followed a definite design as regards tonal, rhythmical, and thematic material, this design need not trouble us just now; it is sufficient for us to realize its presence, furnishing a unifying skeletal background for the whole. The end for which the music was written is that of "evoking the memory of certain places, sensations, and sentiments" — an end much more in accordance with the real province of the art than that of mere description. In the orchestration, although Falla uses no unusual instruments other than the piano, we hear many effects peculiar to the popular Andalusian mandolins and guitars.

The first number, "At Generalife," introduces us to those romantic gardens on a hillside overlooking the Alhambra — the most beautiful spot in Granada, if not in all Spain. When we first hear the music, it seems as if it had already been playing for some time, for no attempt is made at an introduction; the music simply starts. We are set down in the midst of this picturesque setting, and memories of the ancient courts of Moorish kingdoms in Spain float before us in these melodies and rhythms. Granada at the height of its glory has returned; under the long dynasty of the Nascides, greatest of the

Moorish rulers in Spain, it has become the center of Spanish culture, patron of Arabic art and learning, proud possessor of the Alhambra, its royal castle which seems like a realized vision of *The Arabian Nights*. These Oriental melodies with their tinkling, mandolin accompaniments suggest the gardens all about us with gushing fountains, dreamy patios, melancholy cypress thickets, and flowering pomegranates, much the same as they were when they belonged to the summer palace of the Moorish kings above us on the hill. All about are ghosts of the past; here under a six-centuries-old cypress was perhaps the trysting place of the Sultana and Hamet, head of the noblest family of the kingdom. A tryst which, like that of Tristan and Isolde, was destined to cost the life of the King's trusted courtier. Here —

But the music comes to a pause, and we are transported to another garden for the second part of the suite — "Dance in the Distance." About us again are the orange trees, the myrtles and the palms, the rushing and splashing of water. In the distance we hear the music which accompanies a series of dances, the mandolins sounding scraps of Oriental tunes. One dance follows another, the rhythmic figures changing in quick succession and whirling to an excited close.

Suddenly — this time without any break in the music — we are "In the Gardens of the Sierra at Cordova." The owners of the gardens are hosts to a gay party: a *zambra* of gypsy musicians plays, sings, and dances. (It is interesting to recall the fact that the gypsies came into Spain from the East at about the time the Catholic sovereigns were trying to force out the Moors — the fifteenth century.) Happy shadows flit about under the trees; the wines, set out on the long tables, flow freely. There are wild rhythms, rude songs; a dancer steps out, her stamping feet and alluring gestures flash in the moonlight. Although very few of us have experienced a night like this, we are like the sleeper awakened in *The Arabian Nights*, for we are caught up to hear things and see things with other senses than our own, and yet with senses which we realize all the time to be our own.

It is a dream, and yet we know it to be real, brought to us by the magic of this composer who has made his music able to circumvent the barriers of time and space and has brought us directly into touch with the beauty of his own people, a beauty which will last as long as romance holds its spell.

ADDITIONAL EXAMPLES OF RAVEL'S AND FALLA'S STYLE

Gaspard de la nuit   Ravel

We have already mentioned the first number, *Ondine,* of this fiendishly difficult pianistic excursion into the realm of the fantastic. Based on poems by Aloysius Bertrand, these pieces require not only an interpreter capable of conquering brilliantly Ravel's peculiar technical demands but also an imagination that gives them their proper eerie quality. In the second, *Le Gibet* (The Gallows), a mournful one-toned bell sounds throughout, forming a central pivot point for Ravel's astonishing macabre fantasy. *Scarbo,* the third, is a grimacing will-o'-the-wisp, who is finally blown out like the flame of a wax taper.

L'Enfant et les sortilèges (The Child and the Sorcerers)   Ravel

This peculiarly French ballet-opera telling the story of an evil-minded youngster, who delighted in torturing the animate and inanimate objects of the nonhuman world about him until they, in desperation, turn on him and force him to repent the evil of his ways, is characteristic Ravel. Never entirely human, delighting in all sorts of depiction of mechanical details, cynical, fanciful, and witty by turn, this music is typical of Parisian artistic attitudes of the early decades of this century. Its most famous section is the fanciful love duet between two cats; its most imaginative the section descriptive of the sounds of the tiny night animals. It needs a good imagination on the part of both the interpreters and the hearers. The former has been wonderfully provided in the complete recording released on LP.

Three Dances from *Le Tricorne*   Falla

Like most composers of ballet music, Falla has made use of the lively, exuberant music from his rather bawdy ballet, *The Three-Cornered Hat,* for a concert suite. The three dances usually heard are: 1) *The Neighbors,* 2) *The Miller's Dance,* and 3) *Final Dance.* All are authentically Spanish in quality.

Ritual Fire Dance from the Ballet *El Amor Brujo* (Love, the Magician)   Falla

Another example of a composer's being known by a work of comparatively inferior quality; this, originally for orchestra, makes a fiery virtuoso piece for the piano, with plenty of percussive noise and strong rhythmic verve. Hence it is popular.

TOPICS FOR FURTHER DISCUSSION

Compare, according to your knowledge of their works, the aims, styles, and values of the music of Debussy and Ravel. *Which do you think most representative of French culture and of the French mind?* Does one look forward and the other backward? Has either ceased, wholly or partially, to represent the artistic "movement" of his period?

What are the special attractions of the art of Falla? Are there, in your opinion, any weaknesses in his and other composers' cult of Spanish nationalism? And are these inherent in that country's folk music, or in the composers' treatment of it?

Why did Spanish music linger so long in semi-obscurity, after the great days of Victoria, of the Palestrinian age?

An English critic has said: "It matters not that we can transpose the titles of *Nuages* and *Fêtes* (two of the orchestral nocturnes), call each by the other's name and see in the magical fanfares of the second the pageant of cloud and sky or hear the echoes of rejoicing in the first." Discuss, in this connection, the value and meaning of attaching definite titles to such movements.

DEFINITE SUGGESTIONS FOR READING

Music in History: Ravel

TWENTY-THREE

BRITISH NATIONALISM

BRITISH MUSIC IN THE PAST

If this were a history of music, it would have much to say about the days when British musicians led the world: when William Byrd was admired all over Europe, and the great Dr. John Bull carried abroad the fame of English virtuosity in keyboard playing. The great Tudor school of madrigalists and church composers — Tye, Tallis, Gibbons, Morley, Weelkes, and the rest — paralleled the movement in the Netherlands (where it began) and in Italy; but about the time the Puritans landed in New England, the impetus was disappearing, partly in the face of the new solo-song movement, partly because every great "school" gives way, in time, to the next stage — though nobody, at the time of change, may know what is happening or where things are going.

Then there was a dull time, comparatively, with graceful masque music by the Lawes brothers, some writing for strings, and the like; in Purcell (1659 to, alas, only 1695) we have pure genius again, in opera, in church and chamber music, powerful, forward-looking songs (for example, the lovely "Lament of Dido"), and dance music. Then Handel overshaded all, and not in England alone; and though Arne (of "Rule, Britannia" fame) held the fort pluckily in the first half of the eighteenth century, the great foreigners — first Handel, then Spohr, Mendelssohn, Gounod, and all sorts — were cultivated to the neglect of such mild masters as England could show. In the later nineteenth century, English composers began to be more conscious of their great heritage. Sir Alexander Mackenzie, Sir Charles Stanford, Sir Hubert Parry, and Sir Arthur Sullivan stood for classic values in Victorian England, while attempting to seek out something of a national spirit. They prepared the way for Sir Edward Elgar.

DEFINE BRITISH MUSIC!

If one asks, "What is *British* music?" the experienced critic in England replies, "Why, that of Elgar and Vaughan Williams — and Delius — and Holst — and of course, on the Irish side, Bax —" And one has to cry, "Stop! What on earth have all these men in common? Surely they are all antipodal?" So they are, largely; but so are the elements of British character. And that is the first step towards understanding the British, if anyone wants to try that not-easy exercise!

All these composers have *some* English traits strongly developed, and all differ widely. No British musician could mistake one for the other, or fail to "place" a piece by any of them. There is an essence of each, and few foreigners can distill it. Newman, in commenting on a performance by the famous Toscanini of the *Enigma Variations* by Elgar, said: "We were left with the puzzled feeling that in some curious unanalyzable way this was not Elgar, that something in the blood of the music had been left out of it." And again, writing of Menuhin's playing of the Elgar violin concerto, Newman said: "I feel that now and then the thing was not English, and therefore not ideal Elgar."

SOME SAMPLES: ELGAR'S *Enigma Variations*

Of the group named above, Elgar, whom the British deem their greatest composer, is the easiest to understand as far as the style of his writing goes. He was a classical-romantic builder, a good link with Brahms, for instance, though his building material was often much more extensive than any former composer's, and he carried the use of leading themes further than anyone except Wagner. Elgar (1857–1934) stands as by far the greatest English composer since Purcell — the first real world figure. In many ways he was the typical nineteenth-century Englishman; in others he transcended typical British traits as far as Shakespeare did (and when we think of "typical" Englishmen, we have to remember Shakespeare as well as the florid John Bull of the cartoons, who really never did represent England particularly well). Elgar was the consummate craftsman, the reserved, proud, thorough gentleman. Underneath his reserve, however, there was a vein of deep and often noble sentiment — when he allows us to see it. To a listener of another nation, this characteristic reserve and careful husbanding of emotional resources are among the most puzzling attributes in Elgar's music. The emotional motivation is so clearly present in all the best things he wrote; and a foreigner cannot but wish that he had sometimes infused a greater warmth and poignancy into his writing. It is worth

Sir Edward Elgar

emphasizing that he was (like more Englishmen than you might imagine) a character full of contradictions.

But in hearing such a work as his *Enigma Variations* we are convinced that, taking the personal and nationalistic traits for what they are worth, it is great music. Elgar's pride of workmanship stood him in good stead here, for he was largely concerned in a specifically musical problem — the writing of a number of variants of a single theme. The theme-and-variation form became unfortunately hackneyed and stylized during the eighteenth century. Elgar, writing in the latter part of the nineteenth century, did not hesitate to employ this old form, and he handled it with such consummate mastery as to produce an outstanding masterpiece. The interesting thing about his treatment of it is that although the different variations present in some detail (as we know from Elgar's own program notes) musical portraits of various friends, the whole work is wonderfully effective as music *per se*. In writing this work Elgar achieved a fine combination of one of the most formal devices of absolute music and a detailed programmatic manner of treatment.

The theme which we hear at the beginning, with its slightly melancholy, serious, reserved character, is real Elgar; it was invented, in the words of the composer, to fit another and greater theme, the latter always remaining unheard — hence the title, *Enigma*. The variations are as different in substance as the idiosyncrasies of the friends they portray; but in all of them we can recognize the contour of the main theme shaping and molding the music, though at times its influence is felt rather than heard.

Here is an outline of the meaning of the variations as given by Elgar some time after the work was published:

1. C.A.E. (the composer's wife). Really a prolongation of the theme, with romantic and delicate additions.
2. H.D.S.-P. A friend who was an amateur pianist and player of chamber music; his characteristic run over the keys before beginning to play is here humorously travestied.
3. R.B.T. A friend who loved to take the part of an old man in amateur theatricals; note the low voice flying off occasionally into falsetto timbre.
4. W.M.B. Portrait of a very forceful squire, gentleman, and scholar.
5. R.P.A. Dedicated to Richard P. Arnold, son of the famous poet Matthew Arnold. "His serious conversation was continually broken up by whimsical and witty remarks."
6. Ysobel. To a feminine friend, an amateur viola player. Out of the opening phrase, difficult for one beginning string playing, is built a pensive, romantic movement.
7. Troyte. Suggests the maladroit attempts of this friend to play the piano and the efforts of the instructor (Elgar himself) to make some order out of chaos. The final section records the efforts to have been in vain.
8. W.N. The characteristic laugh of a gracious friend, whose personality and beautiful old English home are here suggested.

9. Nimrod. The record of a long summer-evening talk when a friend (A. J. Jaeger) discoursed eloquently on the beauty of Beethoven's music. The opening suggests the slow movement of the *Pathétique* sonata.

10. Dorabella. An intermezzo of dance-like lightness.

11. G.R.S. To an organist friend: descriptive of his dog's falling down a steep bank into the river (measure 1), his paddling to find a landing place (2–3), and his rejoicing bark on landing (5). "G.R.S. said, 'Set that to music!' I did; here it is," wrote Elgar.

12. B.G.N. To a serious and devoted friend, a cello player of distinction.

13. Romanza, dedicated to a friend who, at the time it was written, was on a sea voyage. The clarinet quotes a theme from Mendelssohn's overture, *Calm Sea and Prosperous Voyage*.

14. E.D.U. ("Edu," a nickname of the composer). Written at a time when friends were dubious and generally discouraging as to the composer's future. We must remember that he was then about forty; this expresses his determination to win through somehow. References to variations 1 and 9 are heard.

Elgar's other outstanding works are two magnificent symphonies, concertos for violin and cello, and one of the finest, most complex of tone poems, *Falstaff*. These are among the greatest musical glories of modern Britain.

DELIUS THE RHAPSODIST

Nothing could be further removed from the martial side of Elgar's spirit, with which the *Enigma* takes its leave, than the fragrant, delicate beauty of such a work as Delius's *On Hearing the First Cuckoo in Spring*, or *The Walk to the Paradise Garden*, an extract from an opera. Here we are in the midst of natural loveliness, distilled into music. English people find that this composer and Vaughan Williams reflect aspects of their own countryside; but the charm of Delius is universal. His music is emotionally reflective, suggestive of the poetic retrospection that is inherent in every sensitive person, of spiritual self-communion. As Heseltine, Delius's understanding biographer, put it, "One feels that all his music is evolved out of the emotions of a past that was never fully realized when it was present, emotions which only become real after they have ceased to be experienced. The message of his music is one of ultimate assurance and peace. It is full of a great kindliness which makes us feel akin to all things living, and gives us an almost conscious sense of our part in the great rhythm of the universe."

The beautiful rhapsody *On Hearing the First Cuckoo in Spring* is one of Delius's finest achievements. The musician-poet needs only the title to suggest to us what evoked this mood in his creative consciousness, and we need no further program in order to respond immediately and fully to his haunting suggestions. There is no concern here over particularized events, details of thematic structure, or other exterior considerations; we are within the true domains of music. How marvelously its magic images are communicated! With the opening measures Delius evokes immediately the mood of early spring and, by the folkish character of the tune he sings, suggests a northern spring, loveliest of all seasons. The hedgerows are wet with early morning dew, glittering in the warm sunlight; we are greeted with the sweet smell of awakening earth, and from far off in the distance comes the sound of the first cuckoo. By means of the constantly shifting harmonies which he supplies to the folk tune Delius works his spell, and we listen entranced, forgetting to be concerned with the minutiae of musical structure. A note of homesickness creeps into the music; these seem to be "home thoughts, from abroad," to use Browning's phrase. There is a suggestion of melancholy, too, as if the composer would hint, with a subtlety beyond the power of words, at that *memento mori* so peculiar to spring — the reminder, in the midst of all the growing strength, of the transitoriness of life. It is the melancholy reflected by Housman:

Loveliest of trees, the cherry now
Is hung with bloom along the bough,
And stands about the woodland ride
Wearing white for Eastertide.

Now, of my threescore years and ten
Twenty will not come again,
And take from seventy springs a score,
It only leaves me fifty more.

And since to look at things in bloom
Fifty springs are little room,
About the woodlands I will go
To see the cherry hung with snow.

This is simple, haunting melody which within its particular milieu is unequaled; when we tire of the soul-stirring struggles and seek relief from the majestic utterances of the Titans of music, it is refreshing to walk for a while the quiet, dreamy ways with Delius and delight our souls in his fragile, tender beauty. Perhaps the only detail necessary to note is the surety of this composer's expression. Delius does not give the slightest feeling of hesitancy either in the way he repeats his charming melody or in the way he makes it sing from the orchestra. All is carefully and competently ordered, though there is not the least sign of preoccupation with intellectual manipulation; here we have a happy blending of *sensibilité* and intelligence — a perfect interpretation of the idyllic in terms of music.

CONTRASTED TYPES

Vaughan Williams (born in Gloucestershire in 1872) has been compared to Wordsworth but might almost be likened to any poet of nature and philosophic leanings; in his music for the masque of *Job* there is something of Miltonic power. A *London Symphony* has been well recorded; but the *Sea Symphony*, a choral and instrumental evocation of Whitman, and the *Pastoral Symphony*, consistently cast in reflective mood and therefore of delight to lovers of nature and of the kind of music that poses no problems, are not so often heard. The composer has not hesitated to carry over into the field of opera his love for folk idioms and has achieved considerable success with his interesting and bustling *Hugh the Drover*.

A friend of Vaughan Williams's once said that the very pains this composer took to shed convention and express his innermost feelings tend to limit the appeal of his music to people of like feelings with his own. This may be true of his work up to 1934; then there came a radical change in the *Fourth Symphony*, in F minor. This is a work of violence — harsh, bitter, with tremendous drive, as if the composer would repudiate everything he had written up to that period. Certainly the temper of the times had a great deal to do with its style; its fighting challenge seems part and parcel of the epoch which foisted Fascism and Nazism upon an unwitting world.

After this ferocious piece he returned, in his *Fifth Symphony*, written during World War II, to his more peaceful, heart-easing style. Dedicated "without permission" to Sibelius, this work contains a number of high spots: the exquisite slow movement, the rather delicate scherzo, and a finale in good Purcellian manner — a series of variations on a ground bass. The *Sixth Symphony*, written in 1947, although it has no program attached, seems definitely to have come out of the composer's war experiences. It has a rather unusual order of movements: a fast, violently agitated first, followed by a peaceful resolution in the second; another fast scherzo (altered after the symphony's publication), and then a slow final movement, which in its imaginative conception, its deep emotion, and its strong restraint of expression is certainly one of the most beautiful episodes in present-day music. Here is a splendid example of what a well-equipped composer can do in the blending of old and new technics to form a really personal means of expression.

Gustav Holst (1874–1934), British in spite of his name, is considered by a few enthusiasts the peer of Vaughan Williams, Bax, and Delius. His music is often austere, sometimes astringent, though at his broadest he sounds a strongly tuneful British note. He was a lover of the Elizabethans, modeled his music on no very obvious plans of the past, and at his best combined austerity with wonderful spiritual insight, as in his choral work *Hymn of Jesus*. *The Planets*, a large-scale suite for orchestra, brought him fame. In his late years Holst wrote little, and his austerity grew; so, in the eyes of some, did beauty; but there have been many doubters as to the permanence of this music. But no one could ever doubt the sincerity and high artistic integrity of the man.

A CELTIC TONE POET

His contemporary Arnold Bax (b. 1883) represents the Celtic side of the biggest modern British music. There is in him a certain expansiveness, an efflorescence of, at its best, subtly expressive ornamentation, a length of wind that sometimes seems excessive, and an informing richness of spirit. He has composed much chamber music and several symphonies. Every now and then Bax can be gay, as the jig finale of his oboe quartet and two of the movements in the *G Major Quartet* (to name only a couple of examples) readily prove.

A good idea of his style may be gained from the *Nonet* for flute, bass clarinet, oboe, harp, and string quartet with bass, one of the loveliest works in all chamber-music literature; this has had an authoritative interpretation and a beautiful recording.

OTHER COMPOSERS

Mention should also be made of Frank Bridge (1879–1941), a prolific writer of chamber music, and the later Arthur Bliss (b. 1891), the latter a composer with ideas of his own. He was one of the first English composers to write good music for the films, and his suite from the music for H. G. Wells's famous film *Things to Come* is typical of his vigorous style.

William Walton (b. 1902) holds a firm place as a leader among those now becoming middle-aged (though commonly spoken of as the "younger") composers. A somewhat skittish, parodic earlier style, of which *Façade* (1923) is typical, gave place to the deeper power of large-scale works such as the *Viola Concerto* (1929), the *First Symphony* (1932), and the *Violin Concerto* (1939). There is also the choral work *Belshazzar's Feast,* a brilliant, even gaudy evocation a good deal in the spirit of modern ballet. His talent is sharp-edged and pungent.

Ernest Moeran (1894–1950) combines a love for folk song with an Irish background; his strong chamber music, direct and stylish, is paralleled by part songs owning affectionate allegiance to Elizabethan feeling. His *Symphony* has a striking wintry slow movement. Edmund Rubbra (b. 1901) has written symphonies and choral works having something of the weight of Brahms, though he is apt to drop into dourness: an earnest thinker rather than easy charmer. The music of Michael Tippett (b. 1905) is of harder texture. He (head of the music at Morley College) wrote a striking oratorio on a modern theme, *A Child of Our Time,* a double concerto for strings, some quartets, etc. His style is strongly polyphonic.

Elizabeth Maconchy (b. 1907) is one of very few women composers to make a name after the pioneer feminist Ethel Smyth (1858–1944). She handles cleverly a consistent multi-key style, reminding one, in part, of Hindemith. Most of the younger generation fail to integrate all the elements; their harmonic usage rarely finds a perfectly fitting melodic manner. In quartets this composer is forcible, concise, and sometimes dramatic.

Alan Bush (b. 1900) and Lennox Berkeley (b. 1903) have also

written in the more strongly dissonant fashions, the latter reminding us of Stravinsky in his Parisian period. Gerald Finzi (b. 1901) and Howard Ferguson (b. 1908) find, on the whole, smoother paths to the listener's interest. The former at times reflects Elgarian trends, as in his *Dies Natalis* for soloist and orchestra (to Traherne's poems). Alan Rawsthorne (b. 1905) became known somewhat later. He has adopted livelier ways in such works as *Symphonic Variations,* wherein keys are adroitly scattered or blended.

Benjamin Britten (b. 1913), one of the youngest moderns, has had the greatest success in getting his operas produced: *Peter Grimes,* his first big-scale work, is based on a poem by the English poet George Crabbe (1754–1832) and reflects something of the latter's dark, tragic feeling. *The Rape of Lucretia,* based on the classic Roman legend so often treated by various authors, remains a rather pallid crossing of the oratorio and operatic styles. *Albert Herring,* a "lyrical comedy" of small-town County society in England, is naturally limited in its appeal. If there are brittle parts in Britten's make-up, there are also indubitable invention and skill in swift evocation with small means — if also, as one may feel so often in modern music, with small ideas. Britten's greatest weakness seems to be his inability to come to grips with stirring emotions, a fatal shortcoming in an opera composer.

There seems to be no striking "English" quality in this art of the mid-twentieth century. Of the older founts of inspiration, folk song and Tudor music, the former has trickled into the sands and the latter has now much less force than the polyphony of the eighteenth century. The trend appears to be toward the fashions set by Stravinsky, Hindemith, Schönberg, and Bartók.

A REPRESENTATIVE LIST OF ENGLISH MUSIC GENERALLY AVAILABLE IN RECORDINGS

Enigma Variations   Elgar
Violin Concerto in B Minor, Op. 61   Elgar

Contains the ultimate expression of Elgar's nobility of thought and vitality of imagination, as well as his tendency to sentimentalize.

Introduction and Allegro for Strings   Elgar
Since Elgar was a string player, this piece shows deft manipulation of the strings, culminating in a brilliant fugue.

A London Symphony   Vaughan Williams
Symphony No. 4 in F Minor   Vaughan Williams
Symphony No. 5 in D Major   Vaughan Williams
Symphony No. 6 in F Minor   Vaughan Williams
Song Cycle with String Quartet:
  On Wenlock Edge   Vaughan Williams

This song cycle is beautifully set to poems of A. E. Housman.

On Hearing the First Cuckoo in Spring   Delius
Brigg Fair   Delius

A rhapsodic series of variations on an old English folk song.

In a Summer Garden   Delius

As near an evocation of pure emotion as music can ever achieve.

Appalachia   Delius

A long set of variations on an old slave song heard by Delius in Florida.

Sea Drift   Delius

Based on a poem by Walt Whitman, the last lines of which seem to summarize Delius's aesthetic philosophy:

Oh troubled reflection in the sea!
Oh throat, oh throbbing heart!
And I singing uselessly, uselessly all the night.
Oh past! Oh happy life! Oh songs of joy!
In the air, in the woods, over fields!

The Village Romeo and Juliet   Delius

The opera complete in a magnificent recording.

Song of the High Hills   Delius

Moody, wonderfully realized music.

Piano Concerto   Delius

More of a prolonged rhapsody than a concerto in any real sense; this shows Delius at his weakest. Perhaps it was this nonstructural aspect of the composer that inspired the famous *Punch* verses:

They shouldn't play Delius in the evening,
  it is too sad to be borne;
those lonely notes on the clarinet,
  those sultry hums on the horn,
the sweet rush up of the violins
  as they leave the bass bassoon
twiddle me round like a baby
  in a treacle molasses cocoon.
                    — V. G.

The Planets (Suite)   Holst

Recording of the four best numbers from the rather fulsome complete set of seven: Mars, Venus, Mercury, and Jupiter. The three omitted are in the same vein.

Third Symphony   Bax
Nonet   Bax
Quartet No. 1 in G   Bax
The Garden at Fand   Bax
Concerto for Piano and Orchestra   Bliss
Music for Strings   Bliss
Clarinet Quintet   Bliss
Façade   Walton

A good example of the rather skittish art of the 1920's; these settings of Edith Sitwell's expressionistic poems are not very important but are very amusing.

Belshazzar's Feast   Walton
Violin Concerto   Walton
Film Music for Henry V   Walton

An illustration of what a first-class composer can do in this difficult medium. See a later chapter on films, radio, and television music.

Symphony No. 1 in G Minor   Moeran

Fantasy Sonata for Pianoforte   Tippett
Concerto for Double String Orchestra   Tippett

Street Corner Overture   Rawsthorne
Theme and Variations for Two Violins   Rawsthorne

Orchestral Excerpts from *Peter Grimes*   Britten
  (Dawn, Sunday Morning, Moonlight,
  Storm)

These contain the four Sea Interludes from this operatic story of a fishing-village tragedy. Good examples of the composer's power to evoke a mood.

Serenade for Tenor, Horn, and Strings   Britten

The sophistication of this work is characteristic; it comprises settings of such English poets as Tennyson and Wordsworth, but hardly in the Romantic manner!

Ceremony of Carols   Britten

Written for boys' voices with harp accompaniment on the themes of old Christmas carols, this suite has an antique patina which suits it, and Britten, well.

Octet (for string quartet, double bass,   Ferguson
clarinet, bassoon, horn)

One critic has called Ferguson a "conservative-modern with romantic overtones, soundly rooted in classical constructive principles."

Sonata No. 2 for Violin and Pianoforte (1932)   Rubbra

TOPICS FOR FURTHER DISCUSSION

Do you find much, or little, correspondence between your impressions of British national character and British musical character? What strikes you most about British music in general?

Sometimes the charge of "vulgarity" is brought against such works of Elgar's as *Salut d'amour,* and the set of *Pomp and Circumstance Marches.* Do you think there is basis for the charge?

Dr. A. Einstein, a distinguished German critic, says that the characteristics of the older type of British music appear to the continental observer "to consist in the subdued rendering of rich and powerful sentiments — the open exhibition of sentiment is not permitted in England." Discuss this in the light of any knowledge you may have of English national types.

[INTERCHAPTER]

BEAUTY

WHAT IS BEAUTY?

Before we begin the study of some of the more "modern" pieces of music, it will be well to ask ourselves why this kind of music, beginning at the start of the century with the works of Stravinsky and coming down to most of the works of contemporary composers, sounds so strange to us. First of all we have to realize that the conceptions of melody, harmony, and rhythm which we hold today have changed throughout the course of the development of the art, and that those used by the more recent writers are entirely different from those with which we are generally familiar. We do not have to listen very long to a piece like the one we are about to consider — Stravinsky's *Petrouchka* — to realize how true this is. There may be formal order and reason here, but it is of a sort difficult for us to find. There is certainly harmony, but how different it is from that to which we are accustomed; there is melody of an unusual kind, and a peculiar, explosive, complicated set of rhythms. It seems somehow difficult to feel sure that these combine to make music that is worthy of our attention. Is this music anything more than an intellectual exercise done for the gratification of some esoteric individual's sense of pride in his skill? Has it, after everything is said and done, real beauty?

This question, like that famous one propounded by Pilate nineteen hundred years ago as to the nature of truth, is one that has troubled man ever since he has been aware that "beauty" exists. "What is truth?" and "What is beauty?" are questions that have held a strange fascination for men throughout the centuries. From Aristotle, who died in 322 B.C., to Croce, the present-day Italian philosopher, these perplexing questions have intrigued the minds of men,

[283]

perhaps the more so since no real answer is possible. Only the Italians have been wise enough to realize that "truth is a mirage, while beauty, however subjective, is a possession and a reality." Schiller said that truth exists for the wise and beauty for the feeling heart, and Oliver Wendell Holmes said that "beauty is an index of a larger fact than wisdom."

How may we recognize beauty when we experience it in art? How can it be measured, since it is difficult to find anything which some persons will not declare beautiful, and some — now more, now fewer — ugly? How can there be any hope in trying to ascertain whether or not there is beauty in the music we hear, when one of the greatest artists who ever lived, Anatole France, admits in his book, *On Life and Letters:* "I believe that we shall never know exactly why a thing is beautiful"? Such questions the bewildered amateur listener has every right to ask. As sensitive and thoroughly equipped a critic as Lawrence Gilman told us that there is no touchstone that will enable us to detect the presence or absence of beauty in a piece of music. No wonder, then, that it is difficult for less experienced individuals to know what attitude to take towards music that they are disinclined to like! A short résumé of the general conception of the philosophers on the whole subject may help to clarify this problem.

TWO INTERPRETATIONS: DESIGN OR ETHICS?

Roughly speaking, there have been two general schools of thought throughout the years as to the nature of beauty: First, that which holds that the intangible quality of beauty in an object lies in the skillful arrangement of its parts in terms of order and symmetry, in repetition of design — in a word, in its form. Kant (1724–1804) in his *Critique of Judgment* correlates design and beauty; the beautiful, he says, is that which shows symmetry and unity of structure "as if it had been designed by intelligence." Beethoven's *Fifth Symphony* to such a thinker would be a work of beauty because of its strongly knit design, its progressive and continuous development from its beginning to its inevitable conclusion, its manifest signs of having been wrought by a great "intelligence." The other great school of thought upon the subject maintains that the beauty of a thing resides in the reactions which it arouses in the mind of the beholder. Beauty is not intrinsic in the object itself, but has rather an aesthetic existence in the observer's perception. Spinoza (1632–1677) considers "ugly" and "beautiful" to be two subjective terms: "Only in relation to our imagination can things be called beautiful or ugly, well-ordered or confused." And Professor E. F. Carritt of University College, Oxford, whose book *What Is Beauty?* contains a good summary of thought upon this whole subject, holds as his own belief that beauty is to be found in what is "expressive of feeling . . . when an arrangement of sound, shape, or color seems the natural and not artificial embodiment of an experience." To thinkers of this school, Beethoven's *Fifth Symphony* would be beautiful because of its ability to suggest naturally to the hearer concepts of an experience which he can recognize in it — Fate challenging Man to come out and do battle with his destiny, or whatever else it may be.

There have been other teachings as to the nature of beauty. The Greeks identified it with what is good and often with what is useful. Some of the more poetic thinkers have asserted that beauty and truth are synonymous. Ruskin thought beauty to be a reflection or emanation of divine perfection and so insisted that it is correlated with goodness, a point of view hardly tenable today! Anatole France says that our feeling for the beautiful is our only guide in trying to determine what is or is not beautiful; but this is not very helpful, unfortunately, since there are not many men so sensitively equipped as he was. Professor Langfeld in his *The Aesthetic Attitude* tells us that beauty is a relationship between two variables: the human organism and the object. And this is the conception which Gilman advises us to hold regarding beauty in music; he thinks that we should not try to speak of it as if it were an absolute, detectable quality, "as positively present or absent as the property of roundness in a ball or sharpness in a needle." It can be neither subjective nor objective, neither the result of intellectual and emotional activity nor a value inherent in the object, neither dependent entirely upon the person who experiences it, nor upon the thing experienced.

WHAT IS THE MUSICIAN'S SOLUTION?

Although it negates the validity of the contentions of both great groups of thought, this practical way seems to be the only one for the music lover to follow. We do not have to hear a great deal of music in order to realize that our ideas of beauty can never coincide with those of others, nor should we expect that they would. To some, Schubert's music is supremely satisfying in its natural beauty; others are not so enthusiastic about it. There is beauty in Tchaikovsky for some, in Stravinsky for others. There can be no real reason why we should affirm or deny any of these "beauties"; only by adopting the point of view that whatever beauty there is in music is a relationship between us as human individuals and the music which the composer has left us can we proceed to discuss what we hear intelligently and reasonably. Such a viewpoint clears up the seemingly inexplicable differences of opinion that are constantly arising among music lovers and critics. A person may be sincerely convinced, for instance, that Debussy's *L'Après-midi d'un faune* is one of the world's great masterpieces, full of a strange beauty, belonging to a world entirely outside our ordinary existence. Another person may strongly deny this and feel that the texture of the music is thin, vapid, that its peculiar method of construction does not lead us anywhere, even that its elusiveness and vagueness are pretenses for hiding its essential poverty of ideas. At first we are inclined to say, of course, that either the first man is right and that the other is so obtuse that he cannot recognize beauty when it does not conform to the usual models of Brahms, Beethoven, and Company; or that the second is right and that the first cannot recognize poor music when he hears it. It is, of course, difficult to put aside these absolute ideas of music's being either beautiful or not beautiful, for there are so many times when we feel sure, as in the case of the music of Bach and Wagner. Yet the wise listener knows that it must be done; he has learned from experience that often beauty for him fades out of music which he once thought would hold it to the end of his days, and that it can come into music which he was sure could never possess it. The more experienced the music lover, the less dogmatic are his opinions as to whether or not music is beautiful.

Yet there are guides which will help a musical pilgrim through the confusing thought of conflicting opinions, pillars of cloud and fire that he can trustingly follow in his long journey. For it would be ridiculous to suppose that a person's opinions on the beauty of music are merely a matter of taste, like that in soups, dress, or other matters of individual opinion. There is, however, one test that we may well apply to the music we hear: is it alive — does it communicate to us a vividness of life, does it seem as if the creator had been "alive with it at the moment of creation"? As we become more and more familiar with music, we realize the value of such a test: for all the works that have survived the period that produced them certainly do possess this sense of freshness, vividness of life, feeling of creative vigor. This creative breath exists, of course, in varying degrees; it must have blown with tremendous force when Bach wrote his *B Minor Mass*, or Beethoven his *Eroica Symphony*, or Wagner his *Tristan und Isolde*. It came more slowly and calmly to Brahms as he set down for us the majestic measures of his *First Symphony*, or to César Franck, lovable mystic in his organ loft, as he composed his mighty *Chorals*. We may think it to have become almost somnolent in Debussy as he depicts the pagan pleasures of *L'Après-midi d'un faune*, or tells us the sad story of those shadowy, symbolic figures, Pelléas and Mélisande, in one of the loveliest operas ever written. But it breathes through all these works, as it does through the other great masterpieces of music.

MUSIC IN ITS OWN TERMS

There is another reasonable test the listener might make: Does it keep within the limits of its own element, tone? Does it degenerate into noise, or, on the other hand, appeal largely through the intellect? In either case, it is not great music. Applying this to *Le Sacre du printemps*: Does the composer descend to the level of mere noisemaking in his attempts to describe musically the rites of primitive man, or has he overstepped the natural boundaries of tonal possibilities and written music that is largely an intellectual *tour de force*? In either case, he would exceed the natural limitations of his material, and the result could not reasonably be called great art.

LIST OF SUGGESTED MUSIC

Le Sacre du printemps   Stravinsky

A good problem in musical aesthetics is presented: Is it, or is it not, beautiful? If so, or if not, why?

Prelude and Love Death, *Tristan und Isolde*   Wagner

This is music that possesses the "sense of freshness, vividness of life, feeling of creative vigor."

TOPICS FOR FURTHER DISCUSSION

Where do you conceive beauty to exist in the mind and intentions of the type of serious composer or artist broadly described as "extremist"?

Is there any parallel between the qualities of extremist music and those of modern sculpture or painting?

How is it that lovers of classical or romantic music can definitely describe and account for the beauty they find in that music, while lovers of extremist music seem unable to do so? Is this ability a legitimate standard of beauty?

Can there be a type of beauty which only the producer of the work can see or hear?

TWENTY-FOUR

STRAVINSKY'S *Petrouchka*

STRAVINSKY, A BORN BALLET COMPOSER

Musicians, as well as poets and novelists, have looked at life and wrought their philosophy of it into their art. In Beethoven's *Coriolanus Overture* or Brahms's *Tragic Overture* we feel, avowed or tacit, the drama of conflict. In Liszt's *Les Préludes* we have another view of life. It remained for some of the Russian composers in the last century to escape, in their music, into the puppet world of the folk tale and to draw after them the child that is in all of us, as the Pied Piper drew the children of Hamelin. Perhaps, in our Western sophistication, we soon tire of some of this gaily colored music; but whilst its spell works, how delightful to forgo the realities of life and follow the Russian piper!

The music now to be considered, Stravinsky's *Petrouchka,* is a gorgeous specimen of this type of art, showing the composer at his best. It might be said of him, as Newman said of Strauss, that he is a clever man who was once a genius. Those who may have disliked his later works, but missed *Petrouchka* and *The Fire Bird,* will have an altogether different idea of him after listening to these two works, masterpieces in their curious way. In *Petrouchka* the composer identifies himself with the inventor of the folk tale in looking at life with the detached observation of the cynic, amusedly watching the futile, puppetlike activities of the human race. The composer, who wrote this music in 1912, is a typical artist of his time, as all great artists must be. Anti-romantic, realistic, his music is a product of the Machine Age in revolt against the emotional softness and intellectual haziness of its predecessors. Stravinsky, like the contemporary painters, sculptors, and writers, tried to produce an art as free as possible from emotion, an art concerned chiefly with the delivery of its message in the most lucid way possible, adapting its style to the necessities of the occasion and paying little attention to older methods of expression.

This vignette from the hand of a master is a striking commentary on man, the machine, as viewed from the vantage point of the twentieth century; no other time could possibly have produced it. It is engraved with real understanding of the human's essential futility, full of laughter at his unconscious comedy and tinged with pity at his inevitable fate. As we might expect, the music is as different in its sound from anything we have heard up to this point as the idea back of its conception was different from anything felt or expressed by the romanticists or the impressionists. The older ideas of harmonic and orchestral combination are entirely cast aside; new types of dissonant chords, often frantically and forcefully emphasized, scrappy melodies that are terribly banal in their awkward simplicity (melodies that are in character in *Petrouchka*, but which are Stravinsky's outstanding weakness in his other large works), both melodies and chords in different keys at the same time, pungent rhythms which, like the chords and melodies, are repeated and repeated — all these are characteristic of Stravinsky's style and are used to suit his particular purpose here. There is seemingly no sense of continuity throughout the whole work — everything is reduced to the idea of the moment, without relation to what has preceded or what is to follow.

MUSIC FOR THE RUSSIAN BALLET

Like so many of this composer's early works, *Petrouchka* was designed originally as music to accompany one of the colorful Russian ballets. But the music is so picturesque and self-sufficient that only a general idea of the ballet scenario is necessary for completely enjoying the work. Alexandre Benois, who was responsible for the development of the story, tells us [1] that some of the music (the *Russian Dance* and *Petrouchka's Cry*) was written before any of the detailed action had been decided upon, and the program of the ballet was actually developed around this music.

The story was conceived to represent the old Butter Week carnival held in St. Petersburg and to include a performance of

[1] In his fascinating book *Reminiscences of the Russian Ballet* (London: Putnam). The motivation of the story as given here is taken from Benois, the original author.

The Blackamoor, Columbine, and Petrouchka

Petrouchka, the Russian Punch and Judy show. It was fitted into four fairly short acts, without any intermissions; the first and last take place at the Carnival Fair, the two middle ones show the interior of the Showman's theater. There are three principals — the puppets commonly found in a Russian Punch and Judy performance: Petrouchka (or Punch), a sort of personification of the spiritual and suffering side of humanity; his lovely Columbine, the incarnation of the eternal feminine; and the gaudy and brilliant Blackamoor, the embodiment of everything senselessly attractive, powerfully masculine, and undeservingly triumphant. These puppets are brought to life at the command of the Showman, and the scenes which tell of their living, working, and dying are interspersed with those which give the atmosphere of the Fair in which their little tragi-comedy is played out.

Such a background was ideal for Stravinsky's particular type of genius, and it inspired him to one of his best efforts. His music tells the story vividly, realistically, with no superfluous touches, no unnecessary details. It has little grace or charm; all its hard, brittle details stand off sharply from one another, but they are nevertheless wonderfully effective. The whole makes a complete picture for those who are able to see the man-machine in all his comedy: the music, written to depict the scenes of an old Russian fair of some hundred years ago, fits just as well the scene of a contemporary amusement park. The essential crudeness of this music, a feeling of "servant-girl grace and coachman ardor," a spirit of humanity unloosed from its fetters, make it timeless.

THE VARIOUS EPISODES OF *Petrouchka* [2]

It begins with a realistic suggestion of the bustle and confusion attendant on the Fair. A constantly repeated figure suggests the pathetic tawdriness of it all; from this undulating tonal background there stand out little whiffs of flute melody and a counter-tune on the cellos, the whole finally crystallizing into a real march tune. Presently, in the midst of the excitement, there sound the first wheezes of an organ-grinder's tune (played by four clarinets), and soon we hear the whole tune, with the piccolo and the flute adding appropriate gasps. A danseuse comes tripping up, marking the rhythm of the organ-grinder's tune with a triangle. Soon another tune from the opposite side of the stage is heard on a music box, all three tunes joining in intermingling counterpoint. But in spite of all this excitement, what a world of pathos there is in these cheap organ tunes!

The uproar recommences and continues until a drum roll introduces us to the Showman. Grunts from the bassoons and contrabassoons, followed by some excruciating chords on the clarinets, horns, celesta, harp, and strings, place him on the scene. He stands in front of his little booth and plays some charming and quite ineffectual arpeggios on his flute. The harsh chords are again heard as he pulls up the curtain and reveals the inanimate forms of his three puppets. Three quirks on his flute summon them to life, and they immediately start off in a terrific swirling dance that is full of all sorts of ingenious rhythms. How mechanized the whole dance, the same little tune appearing over and over again, hard and percussive through all its brilliance! The pages of the score here are black with notes: two piccolos, two flutes, three oboes, *cor anglais,* three clarinets, three bassoons, four horns, two trumpets, two trombones, xylophone, bells, two harps, piano, in addition to the usual strings, are all kept busy in the mad whirls of this dance. Little scraps of a

[2] The orchestral score (miniature edition) of Stravinsky's *Petrouchka* is available in the Kalmus Edition No. 79.

new tune are heard and reheard, the piano taking up the rhythm alone, and the whole thing suddenly ending in three outlandish chords.

The next scene represents the black room where the Showman imprisons his puppet, Petrouchka, now alive and fully conscious of his surroundings. Its opens with a terribly dissonant melody (the original Petrouchka's cry) which characterizes the grief, rage, and love as well as the helpless despair of the poor chucklehead. A portrait of the Showman on the wall reminds him that he is in his master's power and arouses Petrouchka's indignation, when he finds himself in solitary confinement; he shakes his fist at the picture and pours out his maledictions and curses.

The dainty Columbine minces in to the sort of inane melody so often associated with ballerinas; Petrouchka makes timid advances and is, of course, repulsed — to the accompaniment of a clarinet cadenza. Then follows a section marked in the score *Petrouchka's Despair*, amazingly effective and full of real feeling. The hopeless love of the imaginative poet is clearly suggested, with perfect understanding but no wasted sympathy.

This scene is followed by a third one entitled *Chez le Maure* (At the Moor's), showing the passion awakened in the ballerina (Columbine) by the foolish Blackamoor. Benois invented a consciously absurd pantomime to start this scene: to a characteristic Oriental-like dance tune, the Moor idles away the time of his confinement within the blank walls of the theater by playing with a coconut. The Ballerina appears (to a little trumpet melody with drum accompaniment) at the moment of the Moor's wildest ecstasy before the coconut. She flirts with him, and at the climax of their love-making Petrouchka, mad with jealousy, rushes in but is pushed aside by the imperious Moor, as the curtain falls.

The last scene contains the final *dénouement* of this story of passion and jealousy within the walls of the little theater. We are again in the midst of the Fair. The familiar din has recommenced and grows even louder as the excitement reaches its height in a merry dance of the Nursemaids. The oboe, followed by a horn and then by the strings, plays the infectious tune; a trumpet is heard in another typical Stravinskian melody. At the climax of the merriment a performing bear comes on (this incident omitted in some versions) with a high tune for the clarinets answered by growls from the tuba. The festivities are resumed after this momentary interruption: there are other square-cut tunes and heavy peasant rhythms, cheap and tawdry as the rabble they delineate. The Grooms and the Coachmen dance a stolid rhythm, to which is later added the bright tune of the Nursemaids as they join in the fun. The mirth grows more and more frenzied as a troupe of mummers joins the mad circle. Wild, whirling wood-wind and string figures suggest the antics of these new arrivals, and the concert version of the suite ends on this note. In the complete version, Stravinsky does not have to maintain the fetish of the happy ending and proves himself a greater artist. He uses this frenzy of excitement as the prelude to the final tragedy; a sudden cry from a muted trumpet stops all the excitement. Petrouchka dashes out of the little theater followed by the angry Moor; there is a brief, terrible struggle, and the Blackamoor kills him with a blow from his sword. The final measures, in which Stravinsky expresses Petrouchka's agony and his piteous good-by to life, are among the composer's finest inspirations. We hear a kind of broken sob — produced by throwing a tambourine on the floor — as Petrouchka's soul departs to a better world. But in the end he proves to be immortal, for as the old Showman drags the broken doll through the snow, the spirit of Petrouchka suddenly appears above the little theater (to a piercing trumpet melody), and the terrified old man throws down the doll and rushes off. The curtain falls to a suggestion by three horns of the repeated figure heard at the beginning.

Martin Johnson, in his penetrating series of historical studies, *Art and Scientific Thought*, defines the central philosophy underlying this gay and tragic fantasy: "There are few modern people who do not occasionally suffer from the disease which Petrouchka symbolizes, the disease of possessing an oversensitive consciousness of ugliness and deficiency without the strength or the wit necessary for escape."

STRAVINSKY'S CAREER AND INFLUENCE

Something needs to be added as to Stravinsky's tremendous influence as a composer: in this respect he stands directly in the great line of innovators that starts with Wagner and carries on with Debussy. No other twentieth-century composer has exercised anything like the continuing hold he has had on music during the first half of the twentieth century, and it may truly be said that he has changed, for better or worse, the whole course of its development through his influence upon composers of recent times. His work divides itself into three periods naturally and chronologically.

The first begins with *Fireworks* (1908) and ends with *Le Sacre du printemps* and *Les Noces*. It contains works of tremendous originality and power, written, as one admirer has said, when

From a charcoal drawing by S. J. Woolf

Stravinsky Conducting an Orchestral Rehearsal

Stravinsky was still more of a musician than a theorist, with a richness of musical ideas that he did not permit himself later on, with a human warmth that he later lost, and a variety of styles that hold together because they are suggested by life itself and not by speculations about aesthetics. Six of the most important works of this period were ballets — pure program music, of course. Strikingly original were the polytonal dissonances (see Chapter Twenty-six) and the strongly emphasized accents displaced from their usual place in the music's rhythmical structure. Few composers of this period, and for a number of years afterwards, escaped their influences.

Then came a complete about-face: Stravinsky forsook entirely the program, descriptive style and entered a neo-classic period, followed by most of his disciples and imitators. All sorts of experiments with dry, dissonant tonalities, "homages" to the styles of composers of other periods, simplification of means, attempts at making music "more purely musical," reactions against mass effects, have not endeared the music of this period to the average listener. He feels that Stravinsky's genius no longer has the dazzling glow of his earlier period. But there are those who claim that once again Stravinsky is in the van and that the reasons for not understanding this new style of the 1940 *Symphony in C* are exactly the same as for not understanding *Le Sacre* — "the public is too lazy to accept immediately new ways of enjoying art, it is not ready to increase its own capacity to enjoy or understand."

Looking ahead, his admirers see still a third period of Stravinskian influence, that based upon certain new structural procedures with which he has been experimenting since 1945. According to them, "the organization of musical materials in the first movement of his *Symphony in Three Movements* opens new paths into the little-explored region of musical coherence." (Aaron Copland)

In the face of so much difference of professional opinion, the musical amateur must attempt to formulate his own opinion on this nonacademic, unforeseeable, unmistakably original composer. Here is a representative list of recorded music to help him do so. The important thing to realize is that, claiming he is no longer interested in "decadent music" (meaning the music of his earlier periods), Stravinsky is still writing problem music.

A REPRESENTATIVE LIST OF STRAVINSKY'S
RECORDED WORKS

First Period

  L'Oiseau de feu (The Fire Bird) 1910
  Petrouchka 1912
  Le Sacre du printemps (The Rite of Spring) 1913

Le Rossignol (The Nightingale) 1914
L'Histoire du soldat (The Soldier's Tale) 1917
Les Noces (The Wedding) 1917

Second Period

Octet for Wind Instruments 1923
Capriccio for Piano and Orchestra 1929
Symphonie des psaumes (Symphony of Psalms) 1930
Concerto for Violin and Orchestra 1931
Dumbarton Oaks Concerto (for 16 instruments) 1938

Third Period

Scènes de ballet 1945
Ebony Concerto (for Woody Herman's Orchestra) 1945
Symphony in Three Movements 1945
Concerto in D for String Orchestra
Danses concertantes
Orpheus Ballet 1948

TOPICS FOR FURTHER DISCUSSION

What are the differences between the Russian mind of *Petrouchka* and that of Rimsky-Korsakoff's *Scheherazade?*

Do you think that Stravinsky represents more than a mere national spirit of his age? Will this endure, and do you think that it ought to?

If you have heard other music by Stravinsky, discuss the statement by an English critic that his nickname might well be "What-shall-I-do-to-be-saved?"

What is Stravinsky's philosophy about emotion in music? Discuss his mastery of the technic of composition.

DEFINITE SUGGESTIONS FOR READING

Music in History: The Impact of Stravinsky
Excerpts from *Stravinsky: An Autobiography* in *Stravinsky in the Theater, A Dance Index Symposium prepared by Minna Lederman* (1947)

THE BALLET

This will be an appropriate place to interrupt our discussion of purely musical topics in order to consider briefly one of those fascinating combinations [1] that music has made during the course of its development with a sister art — in this case the art of dancing. We have just finished a description of what may be called a perfect dance drama, the most Russian of all Russian ballets, *Petrouchka*, for which Stravinsky composed his music in 1912. But this comes very late in the history of the ballet, and the inquiring listener will want to know something of its antecedents and how they have affected the history and development of music.

Dancing may be said to be the most universal of all the arts, for at some time and in some phase of his activities everyone has participated in it. We can define it very simply as *movement that is guided by music;* and a study of the life of any primitive human society shows clearly that these two arts, music and dancing, have been associated since their very beginnings. In its primitive form, dancing was connected with the tribe and the temple — with social ceremonial and religious ritual. In addition, in the more "civilized" societies it has been indulged in to express the personal pleasure of the performers or because the performer has wished somehow to entertain a public. It is in this last sense of a highly complex activity, confined to specialists for the pleasure of an audience, that we are interested; for this is in reality what the ballet is.

EARLY HISTORY

Dancing of this kind existed, of course, in a highly developed state among the Greeks and Romans; during the seventeenth and

---

[1] The other is, of course, *opera*, made up of a combination of music and drama; this is described in another chapter.

eighteenth centuries the scene of its activity was transferred from Italy to France, where it was further developed, and settled down into the form we know today; it was exported into Russia, and from there scattered abroad throughout the European world as "Russian Ballet"; and today it enjoys a greater and more widespread popularity than ever before in history. There are as many balletomanes (a word used first in Russia to describe ballet fans) in New York as

Louvre, Paris

DEGAS: *Ballerina on Stage*

there are in London, Paris, or even Moscow; and the influence which this combined art has had and is having upon the development of music is considerable.

One man, the eighteenth-century *maître de ballet*, M. Noverre, may be said to have been largely responsible for influencing the development of modern ballet, for he changed the elegant pastimes of the French court of that time, imported from Italy for the delectation and flattery of the king, into the sensitive art we know today. It was Noverre who, in his teaching and in the writings he left, insisted that the ballet should not be used merely as an excuse for putting on a huge spectacle containing dance movements, but that it must be a *means for expressing a dramatic idea*. Arnold Haskell, in his admirable little book,[2] thus sums up Noverre's aesthetic principles, upon which all our modern concepts of ballet are based: the well-composed ballet must be a living painting of the drama, character, and customs of mankind; it must be acted, as moving in its effect as a declamation, so that it can speak through the eyes to the soul, just as music speaks through the ears. And, Haskell adds, ballet has flourished as an art when these precepts of Noverre's have been followed, has declined when they were forgotten.

Louvre, Paris

DEGAS: *Ballerina with Bouquet*

Music, as well as the scenic background (technically called the *décor*) against which the ballet's action develops, is an important part of the concept of the founder of the modern ballet. For it must guide the spirit and suggest the tempo for the interpretative dancing that develops the ballet's theme or tells its story; just as the *choreography* (the arrangement of the movements of the dancers) and the *décor* suggest its atmosphere. It may be laid down as a fundamental precept that in good ballet, music, movement, and decoration are of equal importance and parallel in idea.

Naturally it is the personality and technical ability of the dancers (particularly the feminine ones) which have interested the public

2 *Ballet:* Penguin Books (London).

most in ballet; the careful planning of the choreographer who arranges their movements, or the inspiration of the composer who gives them rhythms to interpret, are much less evident and much less personal factors in the final result evidenced on the stage. Many a great dancer has arisen, flourished, and passed from the scene since Louis xiv started the modern ballet on its course with the founding in 1661 of *L'Académie Nationale de Musique et de la Danse.* Especially was this true during the time of the early nineteenth-century Romantics, when ballet was used to exploit the new enthusiasm for the individual. Such great ballerinas as Taglioni, Elssler, Grisi were among the most popular figures of the day in Paris and London, and there was great rivalry among them, much as there is today among baseball stars or professional pugilists. Two of the ballets still in the repertoire of today, *Les Sylphides* and *Giselle,* have come to us, either directly or by implication, from the rivalries of this active nineteenth-century scene.

With the decline of these great figures and the substitution, towards the latter part of the century, of the ideals of realism, the art of the ballet in France waned and finally became entirely bankrupt. The principles of Noverre were forgotten, and ballet was no longer looked upon as an art but as a spectacle for the eye of the tired businessman, who evolved in Paris and London as a by-product of the Industrial Revolution. It became a popular feature of music-hall programs, such as those given in the Radio City Music Hall in New York. It was rescued from this sad state by the invasion of the Russians (1909 in Paris and 1911 in London) under the leadership and direction of one of the most dynamic personalities in the whole history of the art — Serge Diaghilev.

THE RUSSIAN REIGN

This is not meant to be even an outline of the history of ballet; and so we make no attempt to explain why the Russians, following the example of the court of Peter the Great (1672–1725), became so enamored of the ballet during the eighteenth and nineteenth centuries. It will be sufficient to state that, under the direction of foreign masters, the Russians did develop their ballet to such a high state of interpretative perfection that when Diaghilev, after reforming some of its artificialities and impressing his own artistic personality upon it, took a company to Paris, the whole course of the

The Museum of Modern Art, New York

Costume Sketches for the Ballet The Firebird
  By Marc Chagall

art was changed. Nothing like it had been seen there before; and it was Diaghilev, an impresario who had good sense and taste enough to employ anyone who could carry out his ideas, who was personally responsible for this triumph of the Russian Ballet style as we know it today.

This is particularly true of the music; before his time, ballet music had been either adapted from other sources or had been composed by men of inferior ability. Diaghilev commissioned Stravinsky to write the music for a whole series of ballets which he produced: *The Fire Bird* in 1909–10; *Petrouchka* in 1910–11; *The Rite of Spring* in 1912–13; *Renard* in 1916–17; *Pulcinella* in 1919; *Les Noces* in 1917–23. It was these works that made Stravinsky's name as a composer and that interested other serious musicians in the ballet. Among these was Ravel, who wrote *Daphnis and Chloe* for Diaghilev; Richard Strauss, who was commissioned for *Joseph's Legend;* and Falla, who did *The Three-Cornered Hat.* In addition, Diaghilev presented a number of ballets to music written by other composers for other purposes: *Les Sylphides* to music by Chopin; *Carnaval* to an orchestration of Schumann's famous piano piece; *Scheherazade* to Rimsky-Korsakoff's tone poem; *Prince Igor,* an adaptation of the Polovtsian Dances from Borodin's opera; *La Boutique fantasque* with music by Rossini adapted by Respighi; and *Le Spectre de la rose*, with music by Weber. Diaghilev also revived, re-created, and repopularized some of the ballets from an earlier day: *Giselle*, the famous Romantic ballet with music by Adolphe Adam; *Swan Lake* and an abbreviation of *The Sleeping Princess*, two of Tchaikovsky's original ballet scores, containing some of his finest music. Most of these Diaghilev productions and revivals are, in one form or another, in every ballet repertoire today. No wonder audiences called him *ce prodigieux animateur* — that prodigious animator!

PERSONALITIES

There have been, of course, others who have aided the present popularity of ballet in Europe and America: De Basil, under whom for the first time ballet became self-supporting through barnstorming tours all over Europe and in many parts of the American continent; Massine, a choreographer of unusual ability originally discovered by Diaghilev in 1914 and the inventor of the choreography of many popular works; Ninette de Valois, the "animator, organizer, and teacher" of the excellent English Sadler's Wells Company, which has shown what can be accomplished in the way of national ballet; Sol Hurok, the daring impresario who risked his money to make the ballet popular in the United States; Lucia Chase, a leading spirit and financial angel of the American Ballet Theatre, a company which has greatly advanced the native technical and artistic talents among dancers, producers, and composers in the United States.

Of necessity good ballet music is program music, with a real story to unfold, a definite plot to develop, or a distinct mood to create. It should possess obvious rhythmic qualities and should also be of a nature to inspire the dancer so that he in turn can interpret it to the audience. It is, or should be, action music rather than contemplative, the controlling factor for the choreography and not simply a means for furnishing the right beat for action on the stage. Although most ballet music makes good concert music, and so the average listener hears it in this form, it must be remembered that in doing so he loses much of its significance. He is usually surprised to perceive, in seeing a ballet for the first time, how much the effectiveness of the music is increased by the simultaneous paralleling of action, *décor,* and music. Since ballet is, as Haskell says, the result of the collaboration of a musician, painter, and choreographer in interpreting a common subject, each one in his own medium, the closer the collaboration, the better the result. Remember this in listening to ballet music on the radio, in concert, or on records.

A REPRESENTATIVE LIST OF RECORDED BALLET MUSIC

Excerpts from *Giselle*   Adam

Famous excerpts from this Romantic ballet of the middle of the nineteenth century. Rather tinkly and not very exciting musically apart from the ballet, yet interesting as characteristic of that period.

Les Sylphides   Chopin

Based on a re-creation of the spirit of Taglioni's famous work, this "white ballet" (a term which suggests that it is largely for the *corps de ballet* with their lovely white costumes) was set to Chopin's music by Fokine, a choreographer who, according to Haskell, is beyond all question the father of contemporary ballet. A variety of instrumentation has been made of this music, although the piano pieces chosen remain the same. After listening to some of this, we cannot but appreciate how effective Chopin's music is on the piano!

Swan Lake   Tchaikovsky

First produced in 1877, this music was then considered too symphonic in style for good ballet; we have changed our minds about this and realize that this score contains some of this composer's finest dance music.

Le Beau Danube   Johann Strauss the Younger

Delightful Strauss waltz melodies woven into a charming ballet; a refreshing reminder of the real musical quality of the Strauss waltzes.

The Fire Bird   Stravinsky
Petrouchka
The Rite of Spring

The latter two are discussed in other places. *The Fire Bird,* written in 1910, is a magnificent composite of iridescent Rimsky-Korsakoff, Debussian impressionism, and neo-primitive Stravinsky. A wonderful score!

L'Histoire du soldat (The Soldier's Tale)   Stravinsky

Calling for actors and a reader in addition to the dancers and a small orchestra, this is an interesting experiment in "chamber ballet" that could easily be produced with minimum stage equipment. Lively dance tunes, tango-waltz-ragtime, some marches, and a chorale indicate the scrappy, rather flip nature of this ballet score, imitating the French mannerisms of the time.

Les Noces   Stravinsky

Angular, percussive, dissonant, this is written for soprano, contralto, tenor, baritone, four pianists, and a percussion ensemble. The last of Stravinsky's Russian ballets, it is suggestive of the informality and ruggedness of folk music.

La Création du monde   Milhaud

A ballet depicting the African Negro's concept of the creation of the world; interesting as showing the composer's use of the jazz idiom in serious music. Someone has well said that the music sounds like a combination of Duke Ellington and Bach, with an occasional polytonal procedure enlivening the whole.

Job   Vaughan Williams

Not ballet music in the usual sense, the seven numbers of this "masque for dancing" tell the story of Job in the spirit of the celebrated paintings of William Blake, thereby greatly increasing the difficulties of the choreographer and the composer. The latter, at least, brings it off wonderfully, for this restrained style of writing is what he does best. Some idea of the character of the music can be gained from the sections *Sarabande of the Sons of God, Vision of Satan,* and *Pavane of the Sons of the Morning.*

Miracle in the Gorbals   Bliss

Melodrama in the underworld effectively told in modern musical writing.

Ballet Music from *Faust*   Gounod

This Walpurgis Night music is entirely different from the nature of Goethe's original conception and is characteristic of the French passion for interpolating ballet in any operatic scene.

Cinderella   Prokofieff

One of this composer's best recent scores; the music is interesting in itself quite aside from its connection with the old fairy story of the ballet.

The Good-Humored Ladies   Scarlatti

A charming evocation of the rococo style of this eighteenth-century composer, whose music has been skillfully woven into a modern ballet score by Vincenzo Tommasini (b. 1880).

Fancy Free   Leonard Bernstein

A lively, typically brash American score dealing with the story of three sailors on shore leave. Excellent music, rather on the popular side.

Billy the Kid   Copland

The earliest ballet score of this outstanding American composer, this music is as fresh as its name would indicate; far from the classic or modern Russian ballet idiom.

Appalachian Spring   Copland

A lovely ballet based on a very simple theme: a newly-wed couple build their home in the Pennsylvania hills in the early part of the last century and settle down to their pioneer life of hardship, love, joy, and prayer. Full of folksy feeling, tender passion, and rhythmic square dances. American in quite a different way from the other scores mentioned above.

TWENTY-FIVE

MODERN TRENDS IN ART

WHITHER, AND WHY?

The works of Igor Stravinsky (born in Russia in 1882) and his most important contemporary, Arnold Schönberg (Vienna, 1874; d. 1951), are for us important landmarks in music. Both these men stand at the parting of the ways. Stretching back from them on one hand we have the line of the past, a heritage that contains most of that which we consider great in music. Beginning with them, on the other hand, is the line which stretches out uncertainly into the future, tenuous and yet holding tremendous possibilities of developments as yet undreamed of. The early works of these composers — things like Stravinsky's *Fireworks* and *The Fire Bird* suite, and Schönberg's *Verklärte Nacht* and *Gurrelieder* — may be said to belong to the era of the past. In fact, in point of time, though certainly not as regards importance, these works represent the climax, the peak of the whole development of the past. Their later works (Stravinsky's *Le Sacre du printemps* and *Oedipus Rex* and Schönberg's *Pierrot lunaire*) are examples of the opening of another, newer era in music.

The listener who is trying to familiarize himself with the masterpieces of music is apt to halt abruptly and become hesitant about trying to go further when confronted with some of this newer work. He realizes that he has to grow into music and learn to appreciate its qualities and beauties gradually. But, as we have said earlier in this book, there is nothing in the music of Richard Strauss, Wagner, Beethoven, Mozart, Haydn, or Bach that will not yield to such practice and experience. Much of the music written within the first half of our own century, however, is likely to baffle the amateur listener; he senses that he is somehow at a disadvantage with it,

PICASSO: *Three Musicians*

A cubist style that became more and more overtly neo-classic

like a person lost in a fog without any tangible means of communication with familiar surroundings. And he is right! This figure of his being lost in a fog is an apt, if crude, description of most listeners' reaction to the music produced in the period beginning with the works of Schönberg and Stravinsky, the composers who broke so strongly with past tradition at the start of the century. In our attempt to find out why this is true and what the listener may do to rid himself of this sense of puzzlement, we should first of all realize that modern music has but followed the general trend of the arts during this time in turning away from things connected with the past. In experimenting with new devices, many of them so violent and radically different that they have inaugurated a revolution in artistic expression, the twentieth-century artist, like all his predecessors of the past, has shown himself an individual unusually sensitive to the times in which he lives, and often prophetic of the times to come. And since the half century has been dark and troublous, its mirror in art has been often dim and disturbed.

As a curator of the Metropolitan Museum [1] has said: "If we understand history fully we should understand the art of our times; for it is still, as it always has been, the mirror of ourselves. If our art seems violent, it is because we have perpetrated more violence than any other generation. If it deals with weird dreams, it is because we have opened up the caverns of the mind and let such phantoms loose. If it is filled with broken shapes, it is because we have watched the order of our fathers break and fall to pieces at our feet."

TWENTIETH-CENTURY CHANGES

No one can understand the fundamental reason for so much of the insecurity, the experimentation, the dehumanization, and the increasing unintelligibility which we feel in twentieth-century literature, painting, and music without realizing the great breach which the First World War (1914–1918) made in our way of thinking and responding. While we go on living in much the same exterior way, with the visible monuments of the nineteenth century still about us, all our "invisible landmarks" have been debased, distorted, or destroyed.

The nineteenth century was a period of cocky confidence that was poetically expressed by Browning's essentially Romantic outburst:

God's in His heaven —
All's right with the world.

The belief of that time was that the law of Progress (with a capital P) held everywhere. Just as the technical achievements of modern culture progressively advanced from the beginnings of the Industrial Revolution down to the development of the airplane and the radio, so its spiritual achievements — its literature and art and philosophy — were thought to be better and richer than those of times past. Degeneration of any kind was thought impossible in

[1] Robert Beverly Hale in his Introduction to *100 American Painters of the XX Century* (New York: Metropolitan Museum).

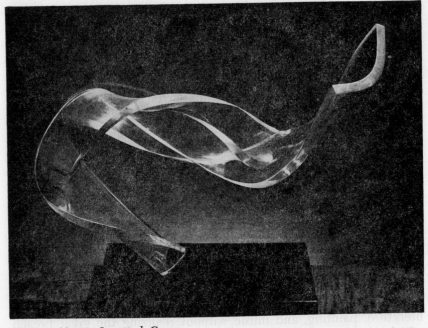

Moholy-Nagy: *Inverted Curve*

A plexiglas sculpture on black wood base (1946)

what was bravely called a Century of Progress. And so nineteenth-century artists were inclined to be buoyant, confident, secure, and more or less complacent; Utopia was just around the corner, and those who thought otherwise were looked on as neurotic prophets of degeneration. As a modern historian has put it: "Under the influence of the new ideology that had grown up with capitalism and mechanical invention, the leading minds of this period thought that mankind had found the secret of happiness by turning his attention to burying his doubts under the quantitative solution of its problems." [2]

But all this changed under the impact of thirty terrible years, years which included two World Wars and the dreadful suffering which they inflicted upon the world, the restoration of such institutions as had long been thought relegated to the Dark Ages — slavery and torture and the mass destruction of human beings. In view of what he accomplished in the twentieth century, man is no

[2] Lewis Mumford in "Mirror of a Violent Half-Century," *New York Times Book Review*, Jan. 15, 1950.

AMERICAN CUBISM: *My Egypt*

An oil painting by Charles Demuth (1833–1935)

longer sure of himself or his capabilities, or even of his ultimate destination; the revelations of Freud, in an attempt to establish a system of psychology that was not based on mere external evidence, have shown him that the world is full of "instinctual urges and explosive emotions." And he no longer is able to feel under him any base of steadiness such as the belief in progress which sustained the nineteenth century, the power of reason in which the eighteenth century so firmly believed, or the light of religious faith which illumined some of the darkest stretches of human existence during the Middle Ages. For most men today, and especially for the artists, such "buttresses of existence" simply do not exist.

Is it any wonder then that the art of the twentieth century turned experimental, objective, abstract, ugly, and often brutal in its violent revolt against the Romantic cultivation of emotion and the Impressionistic fostering of sensation for their own sakes? In addition, there was the reaction against the smug, storytelling kind of art which had developed during the nineteenth century to meet the needs of an industrialized, largely unimaginative civilization, one which cared fundamentally little about art but was sure that it knew what it liked. This spirit of modernistic revolt crystallized into certain general principles which may be said to hold for all the arts — music, literature, sculpture, as well as for painting, the art which was the battleground where most of these ideas were originally fought out.

A MODERN CREDO

First of these general principles underlying modern art is the right of the artist to express his own individualism, regardless of tradition or officialdom, or the customs of the past. This has, of course, been a fundamental belief of artists in all ages, but it has never been held more strongly or with such utter disregard for the consequences. André Malraux has put it well: "The longdrawn struggle between officialdom and the pioneers draws to a close. Everywhere, except in Soviet Russia [the moderns] are triumphant. Modern art has become a law unto itself which has replaced traditional art with a system of research and exploration. In this quest the artist (and perhaps, modern man in general) knows only his starting point, his methods and his bearings — no more than these — and follows in the steps of the great sea adventurers." [3] Whether or not the artist has ventured too far and has been stranded on the sands of his own impotence is a question that only time can answer. But there is little doubt that this struggle and determination of the artist to be himself has resulted in beneficial broadenings of the horizons of art, which, during the nineteenth century especially, had become rather painfully constricted.

A second general principle underlying modern art is that nature is not merely a subject to be imitated on canvas or in marble or clay, or which has a "meaning" to be conveyed through the use of words, but that it is rather a "jumping-off place" for whatever the artist thinks or feels. This principle is naturally a corollary of the first, and it is the basis for the reasoning in what has come to be known as abstract or nonrepresentative art. This is art that is responsive to its own laws of aesthetic and structure, an absolute in itself rather than a means for transmitting experiences or feelings, suggesting ideas, or picturing definite objects. The average person

[3] In *Psychology of Art* (New York: Pantheon Books, Inc.).

AMERICAN SURREALISM: *Interwoven Thread* by Kenneth Callahan

likes to get pleasure from what he can recognize in a picture or what he can get out of the meaning of what he reads. Modern artists are inclined to deny him this pleasure, at the same time offering him other, sometimes quite shocking, pleasures which tend to "feed the imagination with new fires of experience." These contemporary artists are asking, as Walt Whitman did: "Who are you that needs to be told what you already know?"

In this respect, as Pater has reminded us, the other arts tend toward the condition of music, the one art in which this state of abstraction is completely natural. As we have already said, "since music does not have to mean anything, it can mean everything"; and it is this happy state that the modern creators in the other arts have envied and have tried to attain.

Still a third general characteristic of modern art is the absence of what may be called rhetoric, that is, the doing of a thing supremely well for the joy and pleasure that can result from such an achievement. This is the sort of satisfaction we get from the realization of how wonderful the development of musical ideas is which takes

AMERICAN ABSTRACTION: *The Dragon* by William Baziotes

place in the symphonies of Beethoven or from the rich ornamentation in Baroque architecture or from the lifelike depiction and coloration to be seen in the works of the great Dutch genre painters. The modernists demand simplicity, terseness, sometimes even brutality of expression, such as that which is found in the drawings of Picasso.

In this again they have had a salutary influence upon artistic creation, which during the preceding century had inclined toward grandiose, rather elephantine dimensions. Milhaud's (b. 1892) *Opéras-minutes* (lasting from five to ten minutes) are in strange contrast to Wagner's great five-hour operas; whether they are as effective or not is another question. And Schönberg's little piano and orchestral pieces written in his later, more modern style stand in vivid contrariety to his romantically conceived cantata *Gurrelieder*, written under the older ideals and demanding five soloists, three separate male choirs, an eight-part mixed choir, and a larger

and more complicated orchestra than had ever been used up to
that time (1900).

In no art has this concern with essentials and this impatience
with decorative rhetoric been so effective as in the art of architecture. The present-day architect, following the lead of certain Americans of the latter part of the nineteenth century, notably Louis
Sullivan and Frank Lloyd Wright, believes strongly in the theory
that "form should follow function," thus doing away with many of
the rhetorical elements in building design, elements that are not
absolutely indispensable to the function which the building must
fulfill. Many structures that are most effective for the practical,
hustling life of today have been the result: hospitals, factories, skyscrapers, even homes as "machines for living."

But all this can be overdone; brevity and terseness and essen-
tiality can be tiresome as well as useful; and the experienced listener
or observer or reader is often inclined to miss some of the leisurely
treatment given their subjects by older artists, treatment that is an
essential part of the successful results they achieved. For, as
Voltaire has said, "The superfluous are sometimes the necessary
things."

Photo by Gottscho; Eggers and Higgins, Architects

FUNCTIONAL ARCHITECTURE: *Triboro Hospital, New York*

CONTEMPORARY PARALLELS

It is not difficult to illustrate definite ways in which creators in the modern arts have followed these artistic trends. We have already mentioned some. In literature perhaps the most distinguished examples are the works of T. S. Eliot, who seeks to probe the forces that have undermined and debased and brought us to our present

Photo by Paul Davis, Boston

A Modern Room Interior

state of affairs: such things as *The Love Song of Alfred J. Prufrock, The Waste Land,* and even the popular Broadway-hit play, *The Cocktail Party.* Or that picture of the disintegrated man of our time, abstracted and served up to us in a language that is sometimes very hard to follow, in James Joyce's *Ulysses.* Or that strange, rather macabre account of creative activity so strongly affected by its own hero's disintegration as to be almost unintelligible at times, a history of the deterioration of civilization in the last hundred years — Thomas Mann's *Doctor Faustus.*

In painting there have been a number of "ism-revolts" against the weaknesses of impressionism, whose painters thought they were opening new windows onto sunny worlds. Following the lead and embracing the ideas of three important post-impressionist painters — Cézanne, Van Gogh, and Gauguin — there developed the following: the *Fauves* (literally, the wild beasts), who believed strongly in the laying-on of color to the exclusion of almost everything in their pictures; *cubism*, which mistreated nature by reducing all objects to their geometrical forms and then did not hesitate to reassemble them into new designs which banished ideas of natural appearances and literary meanings; *expressionism*, which tried to project the artist's state of mind, his emotion, and his thoughts, without paying much attention to the technical problems of art; and *surrealism*, which was concerned only with painting what was dictated by the unconscious mind of the artist, without the control of reason or preoccupation with aesthetic or moral considerations.

In the pursuit of these and other adventures into the unknown, some startling as well as effective results have been achieved, results which certainly mirror our half-century of violence and darkness, as well as of energy, invention, and unconventionality. But how large will they loom in the future? That is the important, and at present unanswerable, question.

TWENTY-SIX

"THIS MODERN STUFF"

In the case of no other art has the epithet "This Modern Stuff" been applied so frequently and bitterly as it has been to the art of music. And, if we are honest in our reporting of the contemporary aesthetic scene, we shall have to add that this epithet is usually accompanied by expressions of distaste and even disdain. Before we discuss in any detail the reasons for this, it will be necessary to consider a matter of technical procedure which lies at the very root of the modern processes of composing and accounts for many of the difficulties of apprehending contemporary music, even more than do the aesthetic considerations we have been discussing in the previous chapter.

TONALITY AS FOUNDATION

It is because he is so largely unaware of the technical changes undergone by the art during the twentieth century that the average listener becomes confused and sometimes angrily bewildered when listening to modern music. For he has lost one of the compasses that formerly had kept him fixed in his listening course, no matter how strongly the dissonantal winds might blow or how thickly the key-changing fogs might settle down about him.

This is a matter of losing the sense of what we call *tonality*, that is, the awareness of certain foundational centers of rest and finality about which the music written from the time of Bach to that of Wagner has evolved. This earlier music had as its grammatical foundations the major and minor scales, the common chords built out of them, and the sense of key relationship which they gave. Bach established this sense of tonality very firmly in his music, and most of the composers of the music of the eighteenth and nineteenth centuries built upon the foundations which he laid. One of the most famous of his works is a collection of compositions (preludes and fugues) comprising a complete cycle in all the major and minor keys. In these, and in everything else he wrote (for there is a great deal of his music which can be thought of as "modern"), the whole composition revolves around a key center, starting from it and — no matter how far removed it may get from it — returning to it at the end. This can be heard in an example we have already quoted, the *Prelude and Fugue in C Major*, from this famous collection — *The Well-Tempered Clavier*. Throughout the whole of these two pieces the key center is firmly fixed and constantly referred back to.

Exactly the same is true in the symphonies of Mozart, Beethoven, and Brahms; take any single movement from their works, such, for instance, as the first from Beethoven's *Fifth Symphony*. It starts with a strong marking of the tonality of C minor and finishes, after wandering through other key centers, firmly in the same key. So it is with Brahms and even with Richard Strauss, who in spite of his contemporaneousness (he died in 1949) and his strong, pungent dissonances, cannot be called modern in this technical sense. We can say specifically that the proportion of music that can be referred to common chords and keys — that is, music that has this sense of fixed tonality — is proportionately little less in such a work as Strauss's *Domestic Symphony* than in Bach's *St. Matthew Passion*, works which are one hundred seventy-five years apart. In this sense the two works have a common grammatical foundation that is not modern at all.

CHROMATIC UNHINGING

It was the old magician Wagner who was responsible for this concept of unhinging the sense of fixed tonality prevalent in music up to his time. His late, mature works are characterized by an increasing use of dissonance, that is, by chords that are not immediately and pleasantly satisfying to the ear, being incomplete in themselves and not restful as tonal entities. But the trick which provided the basis for the modern idea of "atonality" was Wagner's absorption into his fundamental system of harmony of what before his time had been ornamental, incidental notes — *appoggiature* is the technical term for them. The Prelude to *Tristan und Isolde*, already quoted, shows this clearly; in fact, the whole opera is the climax of this use of the *appoggiatura* as a means for musical expression and musical continuity. Listen to the way it starts, with so much emphasis, in both melody and harmony, on those notes (marked in this excerpt with circles) which in the older system would have been incidental and which Wagner here makes fundamental. You cannot but realize immediately that in such a quotation we are already removed from the sense of tonality as expressed by Bach, each of the twelve half-steps making up the octave being of equal significance and importance:

Thus was established a new tyranny of chromatic or half-tone harmony and melody, based on all these steps and without any of the sense of finality expressed in the older system. Succeeding composers revolted in turn against this new, restless harmony; we have seen how the impressionists, led by Debussy, added their floating chords based partly on the whole-tone scale and their parallel chords made up of unusual intervals. This resulted in still vaguer and less fixed tonalities, such as those to be heard in Debussy's *Nuages* or Ravel's *Daphnis and Chloe* suite. All of these innovations made for more and more unhinging of the feeling of tonality that is present in the older style.

POLYTONALITY

Stravinsky, in such a work as his ballet *Petrouchka,* which we just studied, employed still another freeing and unhinging device, that of *polytonality* — the simultaneous use of two tonalities, one superimposed on the other, the result being a very unorthodox combination of sounds, with little sense of finality. A great deal of the puzzlement which arises in hearing this work for the first time is due to this superimposition of key planes upon one another; but the initial shock experienced by the listeners of 1911 has long since passed, and we accept polytonality without question as an integral technical device of the modern composer.

This same device is even more apparent in Stravinsky's next work, his great *Declaration of Independence of Modernism,* as it has been called: *Le Sacre du printemps* (1913). This again aroused great antagonism at its first performance in Paris, with its pitiless polytonal dissonances and its furious rhythms caused by the bold displacement of usual accents. Today it is looked on as one of the

Stravinsky Rehearsing Le Sacre du printemps
From a drawing by Cocteau

great "classics" of modernism, and no one walks out of the theater or concert hall when it is played.

Jean Cocteau, contemporary poet, playwright, and propagandist for modern art, and at that time a great friend of the composer, has thus described the simple theme of this ballet, based on the new enthusiasm of the time for the primitive in art:

First Tableau:

The prehistoric youth of Russia is reveling in the game and dances of Spring (Dance of the Youths and Maidens — Dance of Abduction — Spring Rounds — Games of the Rival Towns); they adore the earth and the Sage who reminds them of the Sacred Rite (Entrance of the Celebrant — The Kiss to the Earth — Dance to the Earth). Notice the brusque shifting of accents and the rough polytonal chords of these sections.

Between the two parts of the ballet is the Interlude of the Pagan Night, full of the strange stirrings and the mysterious questionings of a primitive world as darkness settles upon it.

Second Tableau:
    For Spring to return, these primitive and credulous people believe it necessary to sacrifice a young girl, a Chosen One. (The Mystic Circle of the Adolescents — Dance to the Glorified One). She is left alone in the forest; the ancestors come out of the shadows and form a circle (Evocation of the Ancestors). Inspired by them, the Chosen One dances in rhythms marked by long syncopations (Sacrificial Dance). When she falls dead, the ancestors approach and, picking her up, lift her toward the skies. . . .

This theme, says Cocteau, which seemed so simple and free from symbolism, revealed its symbol later. "In it, I recognize the pro-dromes of war" [1] — a war which broke out, we remember, within the next year after the first performance of this music. As we have said, the artist is often a prophet as well as a recorder of his times, and the shadows which haunt us so on his canvas or in his music can be prophetic of his awareness of the future.

ATONALITY

From this device of polytonality it was but one step further to the use of *atonality,* that is, music without any key sense at all; or, as its greatest exponent prefers to call it, the *Method of Composing with Twelve Tones* (dodecaphony), thus achieving the fullest possible freedom from every conceivable combination and progression within the chromatic, or twelve-tone, scale. This marks the full un-hinging of the older tonality concept, and it was completely achieved by the end of the second decade of our century. With this dissolution of the classical system came the need for a new one that could give some sort of order and stability to the music, and new theories to account for the materials used.

[1] Prodromes are premonitory symptoms.

This was provided in the works and theoretical treatises of Arnold Schönberg and his two pupils, Alban Berg and Anton von Webern. We have here a close parallel to developments in other fields of twentieth-century activity: like the Newtonian system in physics, the older Bach-Wagner classical system of tonality seemed perfectly satisfactory in view of the facts known and recognized at the time. But it appears inadequate in the light of recent discoveries; and so new theories have had to be evolved (which, of course, in time may again be displaced) in order to interpret for us the whole universe of musical sounds as it is now conceived, contained in the twelve notes of the chromatic scale.

Beginning in a style strongly reminiscent of Wagner and endowed with an extraordinarily facile technical equipment, Schönberg wrote such things as *Verklärte Nacht* and *Gurrelieder,* both of them pieces that are strongly communicative, highly romantic, and thoroughly enjoyable from the older viewpoint. But style in art, as Schönberg himself has said, changes approximately every ten to fifteen years; and, feeling the necessity for developing a style which would take advantage of the emancipation of the dissonance which had gradually been taking place since the time of Wagner, he began, around 1908, with his Op. 10, writing compositions which differ not only harmonically but also "melodically, thematically, and motivally" (his own words) from anything that had been done up to that time.

Pierrot lunaire

The outstanding work of this period of change is *Pierrot lunaire* (Moonstruck Pierrot), written in 1912. It is set to twenty-one poems by Albert Giraud (translated into German by Hartleben) that treat in a highly expressionistic manner the subject of this simple figure from the early pantomimes, a pathetic figure who hides his real feelings behind a mask of fantasy. The score calls for only a small complement of interpreters: a vocalist who neither sings nor declaims but "recites in song-speech"; a violin or viola, a cello, a piano, a flute or piccolo, and a clarinet or bass clarinet. Out of this rather meager combination of instruments Schönberg has wrought his expressionistic score, which stabs with color, sears with dissonance, but which lingers in our memory. We may or may not "like" it, but we have to acknowledge that it communicates something that is part and parcel of its time; and that in it Schönberg mirrors his own inner feelings about that time, quite in defiance of set theories or usual connotations.

Particularly effective, and really indicative of the character of the whole work, are the following numbers, each of them expressive in its own extraordinary way:

1. *Mondestrunken* (Moonstruck), telling of the wine that the moon pours nightly on the waves of the sea, the "wine that we drink with our eyes."
2. *Colombine*, Pierrot's beloved, like "pale blossoms of the moonlight, the white wonder roses."
8. *Nacht*, an invocation to the black night.
9. *Gebet an Pierrot*, a prayer to restore something of life's gaiety to one who has forgotten how to laugh.
13. *Enthauptung* (Decapitation). Pierrot gazes in anguish at the unsheathed Turkish sword of the crescent moon and imagines that he has been decapitated.
20. *Heimfahrt* (Journey Home), journeying homeward to Bergamo, with a moonbeam for a rudder and a water lily for a boat.
21. *O alter Duft* (Oh, Olden Fragrance) concludes the set, describing the charm of old tales which can dispel our gloomy moods.

Not very healthy art, to be sure, but suggestive of the Viennese *mal de siècle* of the first decade of this century, a sign of a culture that had grown overripe almost to the point of decadence.

In his *Third Quartet* and *Serenade for Orchestra*, Op. 24 we find Schönberg adhering largely to his twelve-tone technic; in these he makes constant and exclusive use, with musically convincing and highly original results, of a basic set of twelve different tones, which we call a *tone-row*, invented anew for each piece — no tone being repeated within the series. Here is one of these tone-rows, together with its inversion, as given by Schönberg in an explanation of his system: [2]

Basic Set

Inversion

[2] In *Style and Idea* (New York: Philosophical Library).

SCHÖNBERG AND HIS FOLLOWERS

In this he was followed by his two outstanding pupils, Berg and Webern. The *Lyric Suite* of the former is a good vehicle for securing an introduction to this style, since it is by no means entirely in the duodecimal system; its quotation from Wagner shows what we

Arnold Schönberg

have already stated, that the germs of this method of composing in tones without using the device of tonality were already present in his music. Webern's *Six Bagatelles for String Quartet,* some of them only a few seconds in duration, show the remoteness of his writing for the average listener.

In general it may be said that Schönberg and his school, whatever may be the future of their music, are no mere destroyers of the old. As has so often been pointed out, what they have tried to do is to intensify human emotion in a new, concentrated, introverted manner, with all the musical abilities at their command, which are, to say the least, considerable. In this they may be said to be simply extenders of Romantic ideals. Whether in so doing they have led music off on a tangent into a development which must of necessity come to a dead-end, remains to be seen. There are critics who feel that this is the case and that the sooner we get "back on the main highway of the evolution of music," the better for the future of the art.

After the Second World War the practice of composing in twelve tones was revived in Paris, and the young atonalists there attempted to create a nonmetrical rhythmic style that, in its asymmetry, would be comparable to the freedom of the earlier achievements in tonality. Thus they initiated, at the beginning of the second half of the century, a second period in atonal development.

OTHER PUZZLING PROBLEMS

There may be possible other systems beyond this, based on smaller divisions of the tone than that used as the basis for all European music, classic and modern — the half tone. At one time during this century there seemed to be considerable interest in such possible microtonal developments, using such divisions as 1/4, 1/8, 1/16 tones. But so many new combinations have been shown possible with the use of the present divisions of the scale — half and whole tones — that these microtonal investigations have been largely dropped. Perhaps, after all, our tonal universe will prove finite although unbounded.

Other new features tend to bother the listener to contemporary music, however. One of these is the use of asymmetrical meter — free or stretched meter, it is often called. Contemporary composers are becoming preoccupied with a rhythmical system that is much less regular than that which underlies most of the repertoire familiar to average listeners. If we care to carry the metaphor further, it is possible to say that in modern music the sense of rhythmic pulse has become unhinged as well as the sense of tonality. This makes for freedom and spontaneity unknown in the older style and resembles the free meters of the earliest music of the Christian era. Often several of these free rhythmical patterns are piled on top of each other, so that the older bonds of rhythmical patterns are still further broken.

Nor does the attempt to substitute new forms or constructional plans for those that have been used for centuries make listening any easier. The great difficulty for both listeners and composers, in a formative period such as the present, when the older bonds of key, rhythm, melody, and form are all thrown over at once, is that, however logical such processes of advance may seem on paper, the composers are unable to use all the new-shaped elements at once, and the listeners appear unable to take in more than one or two of them at a time. This appears to be the case at the halfway point of the century: the shock engendered by the new experiments is over, the shock technic that seems to be necessary in order to win the attention of the slow-moving public mind. And both composers and listeners are settling down to digest and evaluate some of the results and future possibilities. Thus it is that, although contemporary composers are thoroughly aware that they cannot return to the technic and ideals of an earlier time, they have come to realize that the break with the past has been too violent; and that any substantial and permanent change must be founded upon the best of the traditions and practices of earlier music. The revolutionary pendulum has been swayed too far on the side of shocking and needed innovation; it must now settle down, as it is doing in the work of the best composers of today, to produce a more viable and communicative music.

PAUL HINDEMITH

There are several important twentieth-century composers who, while they have been in the forefront of this revolution which looks to the future, at the same time have received their main sustenance from the past. One of the most important of these is Paul Hindemith, a German who settled in the United States when the Nazis came to power in his native country. An excellent craftsman, familiar with all styles, the early medieval as well as the latest dodecuple, he has written an enormous number of works — operas, chamber music, orchestral works, as well as piano and choral pieces.

Around 1920, following the fashion of the time, Hindemith produced *Gebrauchsmusik* (Utility Music), written in a modern, anti-Romantic style but easy enough for amateur musicians to play and sing. In this, contrary to the ideals of many modernists, he tried to make himself intelligible to the average person. Although many of his works are complex enough in texture, their tonality is clearly defined, Hindemith believing that "tonality is fundamental to music just as gravity is a fundamental force in the natural world." His tendency to look backward to the medieval style is shown in two of his best works, the *Mathis der Maler* symphony extracted from his opera on the subject of Matthias Grünewald's wonderful altar piece, painted with the intensity and angularity of the medieval style; and the wonderful ballet music, *Nobilissima Visione*, written around the life of St. Francis of Assisi.

As is the case when any composer writes a great deal, Hindemith has produced works that are interesting only from the viewpoint of technical resource and interpretative facility. But at his best, he stands as the last representative of the German line stretching clear back through Beethoven and Bach to Heinrich Schütz in the seventeenth century. In addition, Hindemith is the best all-around musician of our time, creatively active as a theorist, teacher, player, and conductor as well as composer.

BÉLA BARTÓK

A second significant composer whose works have come very much into their own since his death as an exile in New York in 1945 is Béla Bartók. He was originally a folklorist, interested chiefly in establishing the true character of the native songs of Hungary as distinct from the *ersatz* gypsy product that had been foisted off on the world by such important composers as Liszt (in his *Hungarian Rhapsodies*) and Brahms (in his *Hungarian Dances*). Using his extensive knowledge of this folk material as a basis, Bartók drew on all the new harmonic, rhythmic, microtonal resources of his time to evolve a distinctive and unusual personal expression, one which many feel to be the most significant in present-day music.

Like Dvořák, Bartók was essentially a peasant, and his music is direct and down to earth, no matter how bewildered or troubled it may seem. His was a typical artist's mind reacting to the violence and insecurity of his time; yet it never produced, as did Stravinsky's, merely witty or superficial music, nor did it lose itself in introspective lamentation, as did Schönberg's. He wrote a set of six string quartets which may turn out to be the major contribution to this medium during the twentieth century; three concertos for piano and orchestra; a violin concerto; two violin sonatas; and a set of 153 piano pieces called *Mikrokosmos,* carefully graded for educational purposes, from the simplest to the most technically advanced styles.

In many ways his crowning work is the *Concerto for Orchestra,* written in 1943, a dramatic and ingratiating composition, admired by musicians and the general public alike. His last work (left unfinished at his death and later orchestrated and prepared for performance by Tibor Serly) was a *Viola Concerto,* commissioned by William Primrose in 1945. In all these later works, Bartók seemed to have become acutely aware of the fundamental problem of the twentieth-century composer discussed later in this chapter — that of communicating new musical ideas in terms that are intelligible to the general public. He was one of the few moderns who was not afraid to face this problem squarely, and in all of the music written during the last ten years of his life he sought a progressive clarification and simplification of style. So he abandoned whatever seemed meaningless and merely fashionable in his earlier writing and developed what seems to be the most powerful and meaningful expression to be found in the music of his time.

As a final summation of the technical achievements of the modern composers, we should try to compare the older and newer systems at a point where they approach the same sort of problem. This can be done quite easily and neatly. Bach, as we have said, exploited the tonal universe as fully as the classical system of tonality would allow; while able to use every key, he had to be fundamentally diatonic in each, as is shown by the example already quoted from his *Well-Tempered Clavier,* the *Prelude and Fugue No. 1* in C major. Hindemith, over two hundred years later, approached the same problem from the modern standpoint in his *Ludus Tonalis,* a collection of interludes and fugues in all the different keys. And we shall see, or rather, hear, the difference if we compare Bach's fugue with that of Hindemith in the same key; this latter is fully chromatic and freely uses all the intervals and harmonic combinations possible in the new system. It is, therefore, simply a measure of the extension of musical materials since Bach's time, materials out of which our future music is bound to be formed.

OUR ATTITUDE

What should be our attitude toward these novel changes and experiments? Realizing that there has been and will be more "faking" by innovators who wish to attract attention to themselves by producing something "new," we must nevertheless keep an open mind on the whole question, especially since the employing of so many new and partly unproved resources makes the truth hard to get at. Dr. Buck's admonition, in his admirable little *History of Music*, needs to be kept always in mind: "We must remember that what we call 'ugliness' is merely a convenient name for things at the moment outside the cluster of the things we are accustomed to call 'beautiful,' and that the life of music depends upon our keeping that cluster elastic."

The final factor in every judgment of contemporary art is the natural unwillingness of the public mind to accept aesthetic ideas that are strongly at variance with those with which it is familiar. For those concerned with its propagandism, the cause of modern music is no longer a *cause célèbre;* it has already been won. But the average listener is still unwilling to accept it. This seems the great weakness of modern art, this inability of the artist and his public to meet on anything like a common ground — what might be called the ivory-towerism of the creative artist, who remains quite unconcerned with the opinion of his contemporary listeners or observers or readers. In fact, he is rather inclined to treat such opinion with contempt, and thus much of the music originating in this period fails to obtain a permanent hold on the affections of contemporary audiences. In spite of the fact that the average listener probably absorbs more good music in a week than his ancestors did in a year, and has a correspondingly greater acquaintance with music of all types than had his predecessors, there is no real demand for the work of contemporary composers.

Audiences will listen to modern music politely and even complacently, but without any great enthusiasm. We are speaking now of average, cross-section audiences, even those of the quality attending good symphony concerts, and not of cult-audiences. And in spite of the fact that a considerable amount of contemporary music has been recorded, it does not sell and is often cut from the catalogs. Contemporary music, to an extent that is not equaled by modern painting or literature, has become a thing apart from what the public thinks of as music — "something that aesthetes and professors discuss, that composers argue about, that foundations support with fellowships and *avant garde* societies are formed to propagate. But it still remains outside the general consciousness, despite a generation and more of feverish and enthusiastic societies, leagues, and guilds." (Winthrop Sargent)

Part of this is the fault of listeners who are not inclined to realize the significance of the inevitable changes brought about by the nature of art itself. Too many modernist composers have considered their craft as a complex problem in musical structure or as an art of arranging sounds in an intriguing, provocative manner rather than as a means of communication. No genuine, lasting art can ever be produced under these circumstances. For it is absolutely true, as the Dean of Fine Arts in a great American university has said, that to succeed, "art must be understood by the great masses of the people. If only the artist or the initiated coteries can understand and appreciate a type of art, then performance in the name of art with such limited appeal fails to meet the test of the primary definition of art and thus fails to perform its primary function."

This remains the real failure of modern music. How such a problem can be resolved remains to be seen; but somehow it must if our contemporary expression in music is to have any permanent validity.

A LIST OF RECORDED EXAMPLES OF MODERN
MUSIC (in addition to those already given elsewhere)

For Stravinsky's works see the previous chapter.

Verklärte Nacht, Op. 4   Arnold Schönberg
Gurrelieder   Arnold Schönberg
Kammersymphonie, Op. 9   Arnold Schönberg

This is the final work in Schönberg's first period; still influenced by the works of Wagner, Strauss, and Mahler.

Pierrot lunaire, Op. 21   Arnold Schönberg
Serenade for Orchestra, Op. 24 (Septet)   Arnold Schönberg
Quartet No. 3   Arnold Schönberg

Twelve-tone technic throughout.

Chamber Concerto   Alban Berg
Lyric Suite   Alban Berg
Wozzeck   Alban Berg

Surely some of the grimmest realism ever put into music; the entire opera comprises fifteen scenes and is one of the most powerful of all modern works.

Symphony, Op. 21   Anton von Webern
Five Movements for String Quartet, Op. 5   Anton von Webern
Six Bagatelles for String Quartet, Op. 9   Anton von Webern

Mathis der Maler   Paul Hindemith
Nobilissima Visione   Paul Hindemith

Both of these contain some of this composer's finest inspiration as well as emotional elements that are not too frequent in his music.

Symphonic Metamorphoses on a Theme by Weber

Light-weight, if heavily scored, Hindemith.

Viola Sonata, Op. 11, No. 4   Paul Hindemith
Viola Sonata, No. 3 (1939)   Paul Hindemith

The first early and ingratiating, the second mature and difficult, these two compositions show the development of the composer's style.

Sonata for Viola d'amore and Piano, Op. 25, No. 4   Hindemith

Neo-classic in style.

Quartets   Béla Bartók
  No. 1 in A Minor, Op. 7 (1908)
  No. 2 in A Minor, Op. 17 (1917)
  No. 5 (1934)
  No. 6 (1939)

Covering thirty years of the composer's career, these works show how completely his style changed.

Concerto for Orchestra   Béla Bartók
Concerto for Violin and Orchestra
Concerto for Piano and Orchestra, No. 3 (1945)
Sonata for Two Pianos and Percussion

Two pianos, xylophone, cymbals, bells, and a variety of drums welded into a composite percussive instrument.

Prelude à Cristobal Colon   Julian Carrillo

Not very important as music but an interesting experiment in micro-tonalities.

Lento from *Symphony for Four Pianos*   Ivan Wyschnegradsky
   in Quarter Tones: "Thus Spake
   Zarathustra"

Paris may be said to have developed its own style of modernism, a style which was largely influenced by the post-World War developments which took place there in the other arts. These centered largely upon the activities of a group of composers, young in 1917, called *Les Six*, whose ancestor was Eric Satie.

Three Pieces in the Form of a Pear   Eric Satie

Characteristic of the rather trivial note found in much of this Parisian postwar music, this is in reality a protest against the overseriousness of much of the art of the early twentieth century. This is simply Satie's way of saying that he was not overimpressed with the necessity of providing "form" in music. These three pieces are clever, sophisticated, clear-cut.

Le Bœuf sur le toit (The Bull on the Roof)   Darius Milhaud

Again typical of post-World War I smartness. It is comprised of a rondo on South American rhumba themes, interspersed with Russian gypsy tunes, jazz, and a lot of polytonality. Not very important, perhaps, but significant.

Concerto in D Minor for Two Pianos and   Francis Poulenc
   Orchestra

Another tongue-in-cheek work, suggestive of the diverse elements contained in the work of *Les Six*, ranging from Mozart to music-hall styles. Well-written.

Selections from *Le Roi David* (King David)　　Arthur Honegger
and *Jeanne d'Arc au bûcher* (Joan of
Arc at the Stake)

By far the most important of *Les Six*, Honegger was a Swiss. These
two dramatic oratorios show him at his very best, employing all the
devices of modernism in one of the oldest musical forms.

Visions de l'Amen　　Oliver Messiaen
Vingts regards sur l'enfant Jésus　　Oliver Messiaen
Te Deum　　Oliver Messiaen

Theatre Overture　　Zoltán Kodály

TOPIC FOR FURTHER DISCUSSION

Do you agree that the older means of expression have been exhausted by composers and that it is necessary for modern men to
employ different ones?

TWENTY-SEVEN

MUSIC IN THE AMERICAS,

NORTH AND SOUTH

"Culturally, it is true that America, which had begun with the inheritance of the whole European past, had never known infancy; it is equally clear that she is not decadent. Between these two extremes it is difficult to generalize."

— HENRY STEELE COMMAGER in *The American Mind.*

John Tasker Howard has written a book on American music (*Our American Music*); it is a good book and one that should be consulted by all those interested in the details of the development of music within the United States of America. In the course of its seven hundred pages Mr. Howard does not succeed in answering, however, the two questions which have always confounded writers on this subject, namely: "Who are the American composers, and why?" and "What can legitimately be called *American* music?" Probably no definite answer to these can be made, but some consideration of them is necessary if we are to come to a conclusion regarding the present status and the future hopes of music in America.

In any such consideration the word *American* will be used in its usual connotation as pertaining to the inhabitants of the United States, although such a nomenclature is obviously faulty and unfair. For there are other Americans of importance, who should be included in such a term — the peoples of Mexico and Central America and those inhabiting the South American continent. We will have something to say later about music in these lands, which had developed important musical systems long before the European

settlers arrived, and where European music was extensively cultivated even before it had secured a foothold in the northern part
of North America.

AMERICAN MUSIC HISTORY

The history of music in the United States is a comparatively brief
one, covering only three hundred years. At the time when Elizabethan England was a "nest of singing birds," when Palestrina and
Di Lasso were carrying Italian music to its greatest heights, and
when Schütz was laying the foundations for the future greatness of
German music, America had not yet even been settled. New Am-
sterdam, the Dutch colony, became New York, the English possession, at about the time two of the greatest of the German composers,
Handel and Bach, were born. The embattled farmers at Lexington
fired their famous shot at the time when Haydn and Mozart were
at the height of their brilliant careers, and when Beethoven was
just starting his stormy life. The end of the first decade of the nineteenth century witnessed the birth of the great men of the German
Romantic movement — Chopin in 1810, Liszt in 1811, Schumann in
1810, and Wagner in 1813, as well as that of the man responsible for
the establishment of the permanent American union — Abraham
Lincoln, in 1809. During the great years of the flowering of European music, the United States was largely concerned with the basic
work of pioneering and economic expansion; and it is little wonder
that music led rather a pitiful and meager existence during that time.

Howard divides musical history in the United States into the conventional three periods: (1) that from 1620 to 1800, in which
"Euterpe came to the wilderness" and made the best of a rather bad
situation; (2) from 1800 to 1860 when "Euterpe made up her mind
to stay" and the alien tides of immigration, particularly that from
Germany, gave a tremendous stimulus to the arts; (3) from 1860 to
the present day, during which time "Euterpe makes a home in
America"; native-born composers received encouragement, and an
attempt was made to determine just what the "American idiom"
should be.

SEEKING A DEFINITION

The definition of the term "American composer" is difficult. Some
writers insist that any man, whether born in the United States or

Edward MacDowell

The first American composer of note

coming from abroad, who is trying to express in his music what he feels to be the spirit of the country, and using materials that are largely indigenous, is a real American composer. Others feel that native-born composers, whether or not they pay homage to the national spirit, have sole right to this title but only as long as they follow modern tendencies. It has been maintained that the composer, whether born in the United States or elsewhere, who takes the materials he finds to hand (Indian or Negro folk music, jazz, and so on) and adapts these to suit his purpose is an American composer. The view of the conservatives is that any resident composer who writes good music may be called an American composer, though his work be based on the conventional European types without attempting to be new or startlingly national in spirit.

And what determines the characteristics of American music? Should it be based on the native folk idioms? Is it American simply because the composer has passed part of his physical existence within the country? Must it express some phase of life, some aspect of feeling that can be definitely recognized as American? Or is music American because it contains new ideas created by an American resident or peculiar to the American people? Can the men who have infused native feeling into the conservative idioms be called American composers?

Howard's definition of both American composer and music is helpful in trying to answer such perplexing questions. He says that a composer is an American if by birth or choice of residence he becomes identified with our life and institutions *before his talents have had their greatest outlet;* and the music he writes is American if it makes a genuine contribution to the country's cultural development. This will not do for Roy Harris, however, who, in an essay on "The Problems of the American Composer," insists that an American composer must be able to be recognized as belonging to that race which the peculiar climatic, social, political, and economic conditions of the United States have produced. His moods must not be the warmed-over ones of eighteenth-century and nineteenth-century European society, nor his material merely the rearranged formulas of the conventional type. Still another writer on the subject, Lazare Saminsky, says that any music that is born of, or at least with, the creator's conviction that America is his native soil is American music.

THE INDIVIDUAL AMERICAN QUALITY GROWS

It is difficult for the European to envisage Americans as being anything but transplanted Europeans of various types and differing qualities, and thus incapable of producing anything in the way of an indigenous art. It is almost impossible for anyone not on the immediate scene to realize that there is gradually coming into being in the United States a population which, because of its past and present experiences, its geographical surroundings, and its future hopes, is sharply different from that of any European country. Frank Ernest Hill in his book *What Is American?* states this clearly: "We have thought of the American quality as a modification of the European. If we are to realize it fully we shall perhaps give it as definite and separate a place as we give to 'African' or 'Oriental.'"

Courtesy of The Metropolitan Museum of Art

AUGUSTUS SAINT-GAUDENS: *The Puritan*

This being the case, why should it not lead eventually to the production of a really national art?

There are a number of factors that have contributed to forming the background of this American race. Prominent among them has been the constant absorption with the problems of the frontier, a factor which we have already mentioned. The tremendously pressing business of gaining a living left little time for any consideration of art. Thus the American has no ripened and matured civilization to serve as a ready soil from which his art can flower. As Mr. Hill puts it, the frontier has no place for a Michelangelo or a Shakespeare (or for a Bach!), although it may conceivably produce a Lincoln. And unfortunately the Puritan attitude of mind did not concentrate upon artistic life, since it viewed cultivation of the arts as a ministration to that pleasure which should not take up much of man's time. Then, too, the dominance of the Machine Age, which seems to be able so effectively to outlaw beauty and romance as well as that "priceless thing, true individuality," has had a strong influence upon the art life of America. These things, together with the generally unstable influence of American life, have been largely responsible for the fact that the Americans as a people have as yet produced no great art.

Yet there are elements in the American character at present which give promise of a richer future. The dominating moralistic influences which so long played havoc with the country's artistic possibilities have been strikingly mitigated. The American melting pot is gradually integrating bloods of a widely differing character, and the science of genetics teaches that genius is more likely to spring from a hybrid race than from a pure strain. The courage, resourcefulness, and energy of the people, features which always impress Europeans, have been healthfully tempered by a forced realization that the material aspect of life is not necessarily all-important; the very wealth and leisure which the machine has made possible have given a wider and more understanding interest in art, an interest that has dynamic possibilities for the future. When the American has learned, as Hill says, to integrate art and life, to blend practical life with imaginative creation, there are good reasons for thinking that he will be able to produce native art that can be called great.

A treatment of American music, no matter how brief, naturally involves a discussion of three of its aspects — folk music, popular (composed) music, and what, for want of a better term, may be called art music. Folk music in America means just what it means in Europe and elsewhere: traditional music of indeterminate antiquity, the origins of which are unknown and which has been handed down aurally from one generation to another, often in several different versions. Such songs and dances flourished in pioneer communities where someone of the family was singing most of the time and where this sort of music provided the only family pleasures. It is a far cry from the modern urban "civilization" of today, which depends so largely upon others for its amusement and entertainment; perhaps this is one reason why the appeal of folk music has returned so strongly to the country as a whole.

Courtesy of The Metropolitan Museum of Art

PAUL SAMPLE: *Janitor's Holiday* (1936)

In this picture Paul Sample gives an answer to "What is American?"

Popular (composed) music has an existence quite apart from both folk and art music; its more formal verses and music, although influenced by folk music, were consciously created for different purposes — patriotic, social, and entertainment — and have secured a wide recognition throughout the world as being characteristically American. Evidence is accumulating that art music, that is, music that has been written by an individual artist in order to communicate his experience and feelings, and that has therefore taken on a fixed, completed form, has entered a new and important phase in the United States within the last twenty-five years. Under the political, economic, and social conditions of the present-day world it would seem that the future of this type of music, for a great many years at least, lies largely in this country.

AMERICAN FOLK MUSIC

Anton Dvořák, who came to New York in 1892, was the first well-known composer to recognize the individual character and importance of American folk music. He believed, and there are students of the subject who agree with him, that the so-called American Negro music is in reality a representative American folk music, a mixture of the musics of the white, black, and Amerind races, something that is entirely indigenous to this continent.[1] Most authorities agree that the Negro spirituals and plantation songs as they are used today are an adaptation by the Negro of the traditional hymns and songs of the whites with which he became familiar; in adapting this music to his idiom, the melodic and rhythmic peculiarities of his race, brought with him perhaps from Africa, played an important role. The result, together with some characteristics taken from the music of the American Indian, is a folk music different from that of any other country. Whether or not it is representatively American, this folk music has become known the world over and was the prototype for the characteristic composed songs of Stephen Foster, written originally for the troupes of Negro minstrels that were popular in the second half of the nineteenth century.[2] These Foster songs have become so integral a part of American tradition that "My Old Kentucky Home" and "Old Folks at Home" are considered the world over to be American "folk" songs.

Another source of American folk music, the richness of which is only now beginning to be realized, is the music brought over by the settlers of this huge continent and preserved, with or without alteration, by them from generation to generation. Sometimes this traditional music has survived almost intact, as in the case of the Scotch-Irish settlers who, coming to the South and finding the best of the land already occupied, moved into the hills of Kentucky and Tennessee. Their descendants, isolated for more than a century from the rest of the continent, still sing the old-country songs with pris-

[1] See an article which was published by Dvořák in 1895 in *Harper's Magazine*.
[2] According to tradition, it was "Daddy Rice" who first started the minstrel vogue in Louisville, Kentucky, when he put on a "Jump Jim Crow" act there in 1830. The most famous of all the troupes was the Christy Minstrels, for whom Foster wrote his best songs. When these were first published they were attributed, with Foster's consent, to Christy. But in 1852, Foster asked the band leader that he be given proper credit in the future: "I find I cannot write at all unless I write for public approbation and get credit for what I write."

Courtesy of Associated American Artists

THOMAS HART BENTON: *Threshing Wheat*

Another well-known American artist gives his idea of " What is American? " in this lithograph.

tine purity, at a time when the original forms have vanished from the land which gave them birth.

Most of the transplanted European folk songs have been altered and fitted to suit local conditions and American customs; oftentimes their form and subject matter are so changed that it is difficult to recognize their original source.[3] Thus there has grown up a great body of ballads, pioneer songs, sea chanteys, drinking songs, and the like, songs that are American in the real sense; no matter what their origins, these folk songs have so assimilated the American spirit as to make them expressive of a whole culture, and they reflect a democratic community of thought so perfectly as to make them adaptable to every type of citizen and singable by every sort of people. In this way they are unique.

Americans have always been hard-working people and as such have always sung; each new frontier has created its own music. The

[3] John Lomax, who has collected hundreds of American folk songs and preserved them in the Library of Congress, Washington, tells of recognizing the lovely Scotch ballad, "Barbara Allen," in the Negro convict song "Bobby," the subject of which the Negro ships as a corpse out of the railway depot at Dallas, Texas, leaving her relations "squallin' an' holl'rin' with grief."

GEORGE BELLOWS: *Forty-two Kids*

Still another artist's answer to the question "What is American?"

cowboys on the prairie,[4] the roustabouts on the rivers, the workers on the canals and railroads, the soldiers fighting the country's wars, the backwoods pioneers bent on relaxation, all have made original and unique contributions to American folk song, contributions that are as native as "corn pone, chewing tobacco, or Boston baked beans." Recent research has shown that these native songs, instead of being confined to a few types such as hillbilly ballads or cowboy songs, have been produced everywhere, from Vermont to Florida, from Michigan to Texas. The Library of Congress has many thousands of recorded disks of these native songs — play, party, and

[4] Illustrating the fact that there can be a modern growth of folk song, Lomax thus describes the origin of cowboy songs:

"Not only were sharp, rhythmic yells (sometimes beaten into verse) employed to stir up lagging cattle, but also during the long watches the nightguards, as they rode round and round the herd, improvised cattle lullabies which quieted the animals and soothed them to sleep. Some of the best of the so-called 'dogie songs' seem to have been created for the purpose of preventing cattle stampedes — such songs coming straight from the heart of the cowboy, speaking familiarly to his herd in the stillness of the night."

square dances, prison wails, work songs, folk hymns, and the like. These embody the very spirit of the country, a youthfulness, gaiety, crudeness, sentimentality, cocksure braggadocio, and homespun sincerity that is far more genuine than most of the intellectual and serious music as yet produced in America.

POPULAR MUSIC

Like most music, popular music in America has had various origins. The early settlers had little time for what they called "amusements"; life with them was grim and serious, and the use of music was largely confined to occasions of religious worship or social intercourse. The first native form of amusement music to thrive in the United States was that connected with the Negro minstrel show (already mentioned in connection with Foster's songs); this was popular throughout the country for over sixty years. Then followed the more sophisticated variety and burlesque shows, patterned after continental models and flourishing in the larger seaboard towns. The Gilbert and Sullivan comic operas became almost as well liked here as they were in England, and native composers imitated them as well as their French and Viennese counterparts. Victor Herbert's graceful works in this genre, while based on European types, are definitely American in the lilt of their melodies, the verve of their rhythms, and the sparkle of their wit. Even more nationalistic are the marches of John Philip Sousa, known the world over; nothing better characterizes the "youthful spirit, optimism, and patriotic fervor" of the United States of their day.

The heyday of the Herbert operettas and the Sousa marches witnessed the development of the peculiarly American coon songs and ragtime, music marked by a strongly accented melody superimposed on a regularly accented accompaniment. This is an African characteristic, brought to America by the slaves and used by their descendants in their dance music; during the latter part of the nineteenth century it was imitated by white composers because of its happy, infectious rhythm, and developed, through the infusion of other folk elements, into jazz and then into swing.

There have been a number of contributions to this evolution. Among them may be mentioned the intensely felt, everyday, worldly, disillusioned songs of the Negro, the spiritual and the blues with

their familiar rhythmic inheritance from African dances; [5] the particular social background of the city of the birth of this music — New
Orleans — at the turn of the century; the spread of the jazz style
by its enthusiasts, both Negro and white dance musicians, up the
Mississippi Valley and into the great metropolitan centers —
Chicago, San Francisco, and finally New York; the effective attempt
to popularize it by composers steeped in these metropolitan traditions — such men as Irving Berlin [6] and George Gershwin; the
fabulously successful efforts of the "arrangers" who prepared the
jazz scores for the great bandstand gods of today and yesterday in
New York and Hollywood.[7]

It was Paul Whiteman who first tried to popularize what he called
"symphonic jazz" — music written for the theater and concert hall
rather than for the dance band. In as late an Americana item as one
published in 1926 Whiteman was given first and Beethoven second
place in a plebiscite taken of the students in an American university to determine the identity of the world's greatest musician. Such
fame came from his commissioning and playing Gershwin's famous
Rhapsody in Blue, a work which certainly owed some of its success
to its scoring by other men. In addition to this work, Gershwin
made other experiments in symphonic jazz, several of them quite
successful, especially when interpreted by such a sympathetic
exponent of the Gershwin tradition as Oscar Levant. *An American
in Paris,* the *Concerto for Piano and Orchestra in F,* and the *Second
Rhapsody,* the best of the orchestral music Gershwin left at his
death in 1937, have a rhythmic urge and a melodic freshness that

[5] The difference between the religious spirituals and the secular blues has thus been
characterized by a Negro writer: "To the spiritual writers, a great flood would have
been considered as a visitation of a wrathful God upon a sinful people; the blues
singer would simply have raised the question, 'Where can a po' girl go?'"

It was W. C. Handy who first caught the spirit of this Negro form and who made
it a vital part of American dance music with his "Memphis Blues" (1912) and the
even more famous "St. Louis Blues" (1914).

[6] An early writer on jazz called Berlin the "Bach, Haydn, Mozart, and Beethoven of
jazz — all the old masters in one."

[7] None of the authorities on the subject seem to be clear as to the exact differences
between jazz and swing; all agree, however, that swing's outstanding characteristic
is its driving rhythm over which soloists improvise as they play. The terms "straight"
(or sweet) jazz and "hot" jazz are generally used to designate the difference between jazz played as written and jazz that is largely improvised. Louis Armstrong
puts it this way: "There'll probably be new names for the same music. There have
been several names since I remember the good old days in New Orleans, when hot
music was called 'ragtime music.' So you see instead of dying out it only gets new
names."

keep them popular. Gershwin was not a great composer, as so many of his countrymen seem to think, but he was a natural one, writing fluently and spontaneously, and therefore his music appeals in a way that the more intellectual American composers never will. His slangy musical vernacular did not serve such a subject as *Porgy and*

Acme Newspictures, Inc.

George Gershwin

Bess (his popular opera) as well as it did the numerous Broadway-hit shows that he turned out. In these he was at his inimitable best.

THE SWAY OF JAZZ

Other American and European composers (for jazz is popular not only in America, it has swept the world) who have been influenced by the ragtime and jazz idiom are Debussy, Stravinsky, Hindemith, Gruenberg, Křenek, Constant Lambert, Sowerby, Carpenter, Kurt

Weill and Copland. But these composers have always seemed too hampered by such characteristics as the monotonous harmonic schemes and the necessary violent rhythmic disturbances to feel at all at home in this medium. Jazz is, as has so often been pointed out, largely a bag of tricks; and the composer who tries to develop this type of writing is on the horns of a dilemma. Ernest Newman, the well-known English critic, has shown that if the composer makes use of these tricks, he is in danger of losing his individuality; if he does not, he ceases to write jazz. Perhaps the chief contribution which this style of American writing can make to the general idiom lies in the new methods it has of exploiting musical instruments and producing tone color by employing different orchestral combinations.

The serious study of jazz as a popular development of American music has come into considerable prominence. Such a study separates the real, improvised "hot jazz," which had its beginnings with the Negro musicians of New Orleans some time around the turn of the century, from the "sweet" and "swing" versions, developed and commercialized by Tin Pan Alley and used in dance halls the world over, as well as from the still later "bebop." To the real hot-jazz enthusiast there is not only sincere artistic utterance in this music, all the more powerful for him because it is crude and unsophisticated and largely spontaneous, but it also represents a "nostalgic defiance of an oppressed minority." As such it has a special social significance for the changing world of today and deserves careful study.

MUSICAL COMEDY

Some very successful indigenous contributions have been made by American composers to the field of musical comedy. Gershwin's music in *Lady, Be Good* and *Of Thee I Sing* is some of the best he ever wrote.

Irving Berlin's infectious lyrics and music in *Annie Get Your Gun* could have come from no other country. Richard Rodgers, in conjunction with Oscar Hammerstein, Jr., has composed some of the most topical, effective works in this genre, notably *Oklahoma!*, *Carousel*, and *South Pacific*. Kurt Weill, who, before he settled in the United States in 1935, had written a number of operas and operettas in Europe, was able to adjust his brilliant dramatic talent to the American scene. His first success in combining the usages of Broadway with the traditions of opera was *Street Scene,* a wonderful handling of the tensions and melodramatic incidents of life in a New York City tenement. This was followed by *Lost in the Stars,* a sensitive portrayal of the difficult race problem posed in the novel *Cry, the Beloved Country;* and a native folk opera designed for amateur production, *Down in the Valley.* Weill's death in 1950 removed one of the most promising sources of real American opera.

TWENTY-EIGHT

MUSIC IN THE AMERICAS (*continued*)

AMERICAN ART MUSIC

The American composers able to stand on
their own feet in comparison with contemporary Europeans can
conveniently be classified into "generations." The earliest of these
centered largely in New England, and its prominent names were
those of John K. Paine, Edward MacDowell, Arthur Foote, George
W. Chadwick, and Horatio Parker. Of these only the music of Mac-
Dowell can be said to have any real vitality; it has a characteristic
refreshing quality that keeps it alive, but it can by no means be
called original or great. Nor does it echo any strikingly individual
or national idiom, what MacDowell himself suggested he would like
to feel in American music — "the youthful, optimistic vitality and
the undaunted tenacity of spirit that characterizes the American."
The other men of this period wrote good music, which was unfortunately unoriginal.

A SECOND GENERATION

Later writers in the larger forms (symphonies, operas, quartets,
etc.) who would conform to Mr. Howard's requirements but hardly
to Mr. Harris's, include Edgar Stillman Kelley, Daniel Gregory
Mason, John Alden Carpenter, and Deems Taylor, whose two operas
were the most successful of a long line of native works produced by
the Metropolitan Opera in New York. Writers who have employed
folk idioms in their compositions include Henry F. Gilbert, Harvey
W. Loomis, Charles W. Cadman, John Powell. Charles W. Griffes
was a young composer who at his death in 1920 showed unusual
promise. Whether or not Ernest Bloch can be called an American

composer is a question, but there is little doubt that he has produced the most significant music of any man who has lived and worked in America. A Swiss Jew, Bloch did not come to the United States until 1916, and some of his most important works were written previous to this. But Americans have given him a great deal

Photo by V. Hirsch-Hess

Ernest Bloch (1950)

of encouragement; he has had a number of important teaching positions and has guided the training of some of the most important American composers of our day. His later years have been spent in retirement, but he has continued to work at his very individual composition. His style has never followed the fads and fancies of the day, although he has not hesitated to use dissonance and radical harmonies when needed for his particular expressive purpose. It would seem, as one of his critics has said, that his finest works have a better chance of enduring than the music of some of the more publicized composers of the day. Another gifted, although not very original, foreign-born composer who spent his best creative years in the United States was Charles M. Loeffler.

The most individual composer of this generation is Charles Ives, who, although born in 1874 and although he has written a great deal of music, has not become widely known. His composition has been compared with the "barbaric yawp" of Whitman — a strange mixture comprised of undigested eclectic elements, pre-dated experiments in polytonal rhythms and harmonies and a sprinkling of naïve Americanisms, such as cowboy tunes, hymn melodies, and ragtime. As such it has been called the first really American music of important stature.

MEN OF THE 1920's

The next generation comprises men active in the 1920's, of more striking musical physiognomy and coming from various back-grounds and showing different tendencies. Most of them, like their confreres, the painters and writers, reflect contemporary European tendencies in art. A few were conservatives, others rebelled strongly against European backgrounds; some were romantics, others neo-classics [1] in their predilections; some were frankly nationalistic, others made no attempt to be American in content.

Without attempting anything in the way of a complete list, the following significant composers of this generation may be men-tioned: Louis Gruenberg; Edgar Varese (a naturalized American born in Paris), whose *Music for Percussion and Winds* includes such characteristic titles as *Ionization, Density, Integrade,* and *Octan-dre;* Robert Russell Bennett, largely known as a skillful arranger and orchestrator, principally of other composers' works; and Aaron Copland, whose music, in its characteristic harmonic features, the slowness of so much of its rhythmic design, and the melancholy sparseness of its melodic patterns, suggests to a foreign observer the loneliness of great American cities "merging into the vast stillness and timelessness of the prairie." Copland's earlier works show a stridency and drive characteristic of their time; in such later works as the *Lincoln Portrait, Appalachian Spring,* and his *Third Symphony* (1946) he seems to have mellowed and developed a real power of romantic communication.

[1] Roger Sessions sums up the ideals of this group as he sees them:

"Younger men are dreaming of an entirely different kind of music — a music which derives its power from forms beautiful and significant by virtue of inherent musical weight rather than intensity of utterance; a music whose impersonality and self-sufficiency preclude the exotic, which takes its impulse from the realities of a passionate logic; which in the authentic freshness of its moods, is the reverse of ironic and, in its very aloofness from the concrete preoccupations of life, strives rather to contribute form, design, a vision of order and harmony." (Reprinted by permission of the quarterly review *Modern Music,* November–December, 1927.)

Henry Cowell's innovations of tone clusters and the like have not proved very significant; Howard Hanson's symphonies show a curious predilection for overstatement and bombast, considering the rather meager quality of their northern-hued musical content; Roy Harris, who above all other American composers has had opportunity to hear his works played, does not seem in his later compositions to have been able to sustain the level of his *Third Symphony* (1933), which has justly been called the most distinguished work in this form yet produced by a native American. With its awkward angularity, its powerful rhythmic effects, its sprawling form, it curiously suggests, too, the vast and curiously empty quality of so much American life.

Roger Sessions, a composer of music that is difficult for the average listener to apprehend, is, as one of his friends has described him, a man of "profound culture and granitic intellectual powers — essentially a thinker." Unfortunately, his music often sounds that way; it thinks for measures on end, and this seems a rather questionable asset. Walter Piston's works are also rather meager in expressive content, although this composer's skill and sincerity are evident enough; he appears to have attempted to remove some of this obscurity in his *Third Symphony* (1947). Randall Thompson's music is more in the European late-nineteenth-century idiom than is that of his contemporary, Virgil Thomson. The latter's operas, *Four Saints in Three Acts* and *Mother of Us All* (1947), with librettos by Gertrude Stein, show the characteristics of the milieu from which they sprang, that of Paris in the 1920's. He has written some excellent music for the films, particularly *The Plow That Broke the Plains* and *Louisiana Story*. His orchestral *Five Portraits* is chiefly remarkable for the fact that in all its thin musical painting it is the composer's physiognomy that is mostly lacking.

MORE RECENT COMPOSERS

Still a younger generation includes Samuel Barber, whose earlier works such as an *Essay for Orchestra* and his *First Symphony* were conservative in their insistence upon architectural details and romantic powers of communication. In his later compositions he seems determined to come to grips with a more "advanced" style. Another important figure is Marc Blitzstein, whose most distinctive works, *The Cradle Will Rock* and *No for an Answer*, are theatrical hybrids, partaking of the characteristics of social drama, of revue, and opera, all with social implications; these, in the composer's phraseology, "pack a terrific wallop" and point towards a real union of American speech and American music. Paul Creston and David Diamond are other significant writers of this time. William Schuman has doubled in the fields of composer and educator; his ballet *Undertow* (1946) and his *Violin Concerto* (1949) show his rather composite style. Gian-Carlo Menotti (born in the land of opera and a naturalized American) has given the American stage some delightful and adroit modern pieces in the Italian *buffa* tradition: *Amelia Goes to the Ball, The Old Maid and the Thief,* and *The Telephone.* His attempts at verism, *The Medium* and *The Consul* (1949), are sterner stuff which, in spite of obvious theatrical mannerisms, shows Menotti to be a composer possessed of real dramatic stature.

THE YOUNGEST GENERATION

A fifth generation of promising composers writes music that is enormously skillful from the standpoint of craftsmanship but that seems to lack the distinct and often exciting characteristics of the music of the preceding generations. Among these younger men are Robert Palmer, Alexander Haieff, Harold Shapero, Lukas Foss, Leonard Bernstein, William Bergsma, Norman Dello Joio, and John Cage. With two exceptions they are all native-born and native-trained, a fact showing the tremendous advances which have been made in the field of professional musical training in the United States.

World War II peculiarly accelerated the growth of the country as a musical nation, for all of Europe's outstanding composers, performers, conductors, critics, and scholars who could get away came to the United States and became integral parts of American musical life. What will come of this new amalgamation of cultural influences only time can tell; there can be little doubt, however, that the center of the world's creative activity in music moved from Europe to the Western Hemisphere and that the future of the art will be closely identified with whatever is accomplished in the United States of America. It is this fact that makes American music of such significance today.

MUSIC IN THE AMERICAS SOUTH OF THE UNITED STATES

In pre-Columbian days there flourished in Mexico several civilizations which cultivated the arts extensively. Recent archaeological research has shown precisely the degrees of progress achieved by these Aztec cultures; and there are irrefutable proofs that music played a role of real importance in government, religion, and war and that it was the object of special study and cultivation by the state.

Basing his materials not on archaeological melodies or quotations from pre-Conquest music, for no such records exist, but on a study

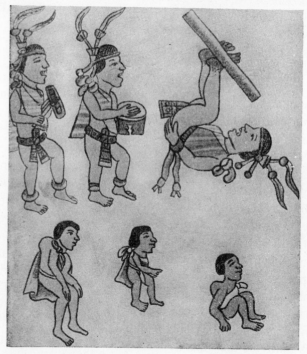

Museum of Modern Art

Ancient Aztec Musicians
From THE CODEX FLORENTINUS

of Aztec instruments and the way they must have sounded, Carlos Chávez, a modern Mexican composer, has given us an impression of how he believes this ancient Mexican music must have sounded in his *Xochipili Macuilxochitl*. In addition to the influence of these ancient American cultures, present-day Mexican and South American music has been affected by the music of Spanish and other origins that has come into the countries from the four corners of the globe, together with the influence of the peculiar native admixtures resulting from these elements. This folk music, as well as the more popular *topical* urban music of the streets, cafés, and ballrooms, and the serious art music of Central and South America, is the result of a peculiar admixture of three components:

(1) The music which survived from the original *Indian* inhabitants of the continent.

(2) That which was brought from Africa by the Negroes and developed by their peculiarly imaginative powers and strong rhythmic sense.

(3) Music imported by the European colonists, chiefly Spanish and Portuguese.

The particular social and geographic conditions of Central and South America have blended these components into a style of music that is strikingly original, rhythmically fascinating, melodically pleasing, and thoroughly alive.

Fortunately, due to the enterprise of the Folklore Section of the Library of Congress and a few of the smaller recording companies, a great deal of this ethnic folk music from Latin-American countries is readily available for study and enjoyment. These recordings, actually made in the field, are able to give the listener that fragile and intimate spirit of "unawareness in music making" that is the exact opposite of the rather glamorous sophistication induced by the radiobroadcast studio's interpretation of folk music. The backgrounds of Equatorial Africa, out of which sprang the whole of American Negro music, the Afro-Bahian religious songs of Brazil, as well as many of the other folk songs of that great country, West Indian songs and dances of all sorts, the folk music of Venezuela, Mexico, Peru — these are but some of the riches available in this great treasure chest of Latin-American folk music. As one lover of this sort of music has well said, without falling into the trap of the superficially intellectual or into one of the many cults of precious snobbism, this music should be cultivated by any listener who wishes to enlarge his taste and deepen his understanding of music in general.

There has been a wide exportation of the popular, topical music of this region in recent years. Such native songs and dances as the calypso, habanera, tango, béguine, rhumba, conga, and samba have become favorites in European and North American circles. These are only some of the more obvious of these fascinating Latin-American exportable musical products; there are many more which, in

Museum of Modern Art

Ancient Aztec Musicians
From THE CODEX FLORENTINUS

their mixing of exotic and colorful elements, are worth knowing. Unfortunately, because of the influences of popular taste and the necessity of streamlining it for commercial consumption, what we hear in North American and European performances of this music is oftentimes quite different from its original flavor and character.

IN MEXICO

The most important figure in the modern Mexican scene is the aforementioned Carlos Chávez, conductor and composer, whose music achieves a real indigenous blend of the influences that have gone into the folk music of his country. But this is likewise music that has been affected by the developments of the composer's generation, as is evident in its linear contrapuntal lines and its stark objectivity. At one moment it seems to express a primitive barbarism, in the next a machine-age spirit. The list of other Mexican composers of serious music includes Silvestre Revueltas [2] (who based his work on the popular music of his country's fairs and taverns and whose tragic death in 1940 robbed Latin-American music of one of its finest and most individual talents), Luis Sandi, Daniel Ayala, Salvador Contreras, and Blas Galindo.

SOUTH AMERICAN CREATORS

Small but active groups of composers have been functioning in the South American countries of Brazil, Chile, Argentina, and Uruguay. Here, as in Mexico, there has been a peculiar blending of many diverse elements and resources — chiefly Portuguese, Indian, and African. Of all these countries, Brazil has had the richest and most important musical development; by the middle of the nineteenth century its greatest city, Rio de Janeiro, had a cosmopolitan music culture comparable to that of the great European centers, supporting first-class operatic and concert performances and a good national conservatory. The first Brazilian composer to win universal renown was the nineteenth-century Carlos Gomes, who was the first opera composer of the Americas to win European recognition. Alberto Nepomuceno was a strong nationalist and sponsor of Brazil's greatest composer to date, Heitor Villa-Lobos. A genius with an insatiable curiosity and seemingly inexhaustible energy, Villa-Lobos is almost an entirely self-taught composer. He has written over fourteen hundred works in every musical idiom; the best of these show great ingenuity, strong individuality, and real originality. Such a thing as his major chamber-music work, the *Nonetto* for chamber orchestra and chorus, could have been written by no other composer. His great suites, the *Bachianas Brasileiras*, attempt to "transmit the spirit of Bach — a universal spirit, source, and end in itself" — into the soul of Brazil, and are worth careful study.

[2] Mayer-Serra, in his book *Panorama de la Música Mexicana — desde la Independencia hasta la Actualidad* (published by El Colegio de México in 1941) makes this distinction between the two leading Mexican composers:

"For Chávez the aboriginal musical culture is the most important in the history of Mexican music; he tries to reconstruct musically this atmosphere of primitive purity, thinking to find in it the true Mexican character; for Revueltas, on the other hand, Mexico is genuinely represented by the remains of primitive cultures as well as by the surprising results of that mixture of races and civilizations that is so characteristic of modern Mexico."

Other leading Brazilian composers who are trying to build a contemporary national school are Oscar Lorenzo Fernandez, Francisco Mignone, and M. Carmargo Guarnieri.

In the Argentine, the best-known name seems to be that of Juan José Castro, conductor of the Colón opera, Buenos Aires, a brilliant and very successful composer as well as conductor; his brother, a composer of even greater talent, José Mario Castro, is not so well known outside his native country. Juan Carlos Paz seems to have become enamored of Schönbergian twelve-tone ideals, while the young Alberto Ginastera is looked upon by the Argentine musicians as their most promising composer. Prominent progressives in Uruguay include Carlos Estrada and Vincente Ascone.

In general it must be stated that, with one or two outstanding exceptions, these South and Central American composers, like so many of their contemporary brothers to the north, have shown a tendency to ignore their own birthright and imitate European music that was modern some years ago. The resulting music is both unfertile and unrepresentative.

In most of the South American countries there are folklorists who conduct important research work along the line of native songs and dances, as well as scholars who try to piece together these valuable finds in pre-Columbian music. Chief among these are Carlos Vega of Argentina and Dr. Luiz de Azevedo of Brazil.

It seems strange that it has taken a world war to awaken the curiosity of the people of the United States to the activities of their neighbors to the south. All signs point to an increasingly active and profitable interchange of ideas between the countries of the American hemisphere in the years that lie ahead. In this, music is bound to play an important part.

A CHECK LIST OF RECORDED AMERICAN MUSIC

Like all lists of recorded music, this becomes dated as it is compiled, for new recordings are constantly being issued and old ones dropped from the catalogues. The advent of LP has made the obtaining of many important older records difficult, if not impossible. But all of the recordings named on the following pages were available at the time this list was prepared. If some numbers have been dropped, other representative recordings will be available. A star (*) indicates an album. LCR indicates Library of Congress recordings, which are standard and obtainable only from the Library of Congress, Washington, D.C.

Folk Music

AMERICAN INDIAN MUSIC:

* Indian Music of the Southwest, collected by Laura Boulton
* Sioux and Navajo Ethnic Music
* Seneca Songs from Coldspring Longhouse   LCR
* Songs from the Iroquois Longhouse   LCR

NEGRO MUSIC:

* Backgrounds of African Negro Music   LCR
* Afro-American Blues and Game Songs   LCR
* Afro-American Spirituals, Work Songs and Ballads   LCR
* Afro-Bahian Religious Songs of Brazil   LCR
* Negro Religious Songs and Services   LCR
* Negro Work Songs and Calls   LCR
* Sinful Songs by Lead Belly

FOLK SONGS:

* Anglo-American Ballads   LCR
* Anglo-American Shanties, Lyric Songs, Dance Tunes and
    White Spirituals   LCR
* Play and Dance Songs of the Appalachian Mountains   LCR
* Sacred Harp Tunes and Fuguing Songs   LCR
* From *The American Songbag* by Carl Sandburg
* Drums of Haiti
* Bahaman Songs, Spanish-French Ballads and Dance Tunes   LCR
* Cult Music of Cuba
* Folk Music of Puerto Rico   LCR
* Folk Music of Mexico   LCR
* Folk Music of Brazil   LCR
* Folk Music of Venezuela   LCR
* Folk Music of Peru   LCR
* Brazilian Folk Songs by Elsie Houston

Although these have highly sophisticated accompaniments by Villa-Lobos and others, they are wonderfully evocative of the native spirit of this vast land, due largely to the unusual skill of this much-lamented Brazilian singer.

Popular (Topical) Music

Stars and Stripes Forever March   Sousa
The Fairest of the Fair March   Sousa

Although the recordings are old, these should be heard as played by Sousa's own band; they are in the repertoire of every marching band in the world.

Show Boat Scenario for Orchestra   Jerome Kern

In his *Show Boat* Kern established something of a norm for this style of American operetta; this well-written pastiche contains all the best tunes in their characteristic, flavorful orchestrations.

Rhapsody in Blue   Gershwin

This should be heard in an authentic version with a pianist sympathetic to the Gershwin style: Oscar Levant fits the bill here. In spite of its great popularity at one time, this is not a very successful attempt at combining "proper" structure with singable tunes.

An American in Paris   Gershwin

Likewise needs an authentic interpretation; this time the best is that under the direction of a young American who knows both Paris and Gershwin — Leonard Bernstein.

Excerpts from South Pacific   Rodgers

Another in the long line of popular successes in the field of operetta by Rodgers with words by Oscar Hammerstein, Jr. Vigorous, telling music set to slangily effective lyrics.

American Jazz

NEW ORLEANS STYLE:

Sidewalk Blues   Jelly Roll Morton

An often-quoted example of the original "sweet" New Orleans style.

DIXIELAND STYLE:

At the Jazz Band Ball

Characteristic of the period when jazz moved up the Mississippi from New Orleans to Chicago and, later, New York.

LATER DEVELOPMENTS:

* Kansas City Seven Album

Largely built around the *riff*, a constantly repeated little phrase from which the various characteristic solo parts take off. Typical of Count Basie's Band of 1935.

SYMPHONIC JAZZ:

Mood Indigo   Duke Ellington

An attempt by a Negro composer with real talent to merge the African origins of jazz with European styles and traditions. Whether or not it is successful depends upon one's point of view.

USE OF JAZZ IN CONCERT MUSIC:

Aria and Toccata in Swing   McBride
Blues   William Grant Still
Ukulele Serenade   Copland

Instead of citing examples of the use of jazz in concert music by European composers (and there are plenty which could be quoted), we are giving some short examples by American composers who have been brought up with the jazz idiom and who can, therefore, use its possibilities to the best advantage.

Grand Canyon Suite   Grofé

In spite of lustrous orchestration by a master hand and a wonderful recording by Toscanini, this remains a thoroughly undistinguished attempt at program music, descriptive of one of America's seven scenic wonders.

Art Music

COLONIAL:

Fuguing Tunes   Billings

Of much greater historical than musical interest, these show the self-taught Revolutionary patriot's attempts to inject life into the contemporary church music of his time. Billings, we must remember, was a contemporary of Haydn!

Early American Psalmody
Ballads of Colonial America
Chamber Music of Colonial America
Instrumental Music of Colonial America

Likewise of more historical than musical interest, these works show that there was considerable creative activity in colonial America by transplanted European musicians.

LATER NEW ENGLAND ECLECTICISM:

Prelude to *Oedipus Tyrannus*   Paine

Jubilee from *Symphonic Sketches*   Chadwick
Suite in E for Strings   Foote
Piano Concerto in D Minor   MacDowell
Dance in the Place Congo   Gilbert

These are illustrations of works by the first generation of American composers able to stand on their own feet, strongly assisted, it is true, by European props. Fortunately, several of them are collected in one album.

THE NEXT GENERATION:

The White Peacock   Griffes

An American adaptation of impressionism; not particularly distinctive.

Quartet in G Minor on Negro Themes   D. G. Mason

The composer is a distinguished member of a well-known American musical family descending from Lowell Mason, the "Father" of School Music in the United States.

Schelomo (Hebrew Rhapsody)   Bloch

An early pre-American representation of this composer's impassioned, romantic style; really a one-movement concerto for cello and orchestra.

Second Quartet for Strings (1945)   Bloch

One of the finest of World War II works; the composer's intensity is still here, but there is a contemplative beauty and controlling power that was lacking in the earlier Bloch style.

Music for Four Stringed Instruments   Loeffler

This music sounds strangely dated and synthetic, in spite of the composer's obvious sincerity and technical ability; it is a good example of the eclectic period around the turn of the century.

Concord Sonata   Ives

(Emerson, Hawthorne, The Alcotts)

The three movements of this difficult and diffuse work are dedicated to three famous members of the New England group of Transcendentalists, who, we are told, "affirmed the importance of phenomena that transcend the experience of the senses." This is rather an apt description of the nature of this music.

Second String Quartet   Ives
Through the Looking Glass Suite   Deems Taylor

Charming music, thoroughly conventional, most effective for its purpose of catching the spirit of Lewis Carroll's famous story.

A THIRD, VERY ACTIVE GENERATION:

Concerto for Piano, Op. 36   Hanson

Very characteristic of the churned-up, neo-Sibelius style of this Scandinavian-American composer and educator.

Symphony No. 3   Harris

Suggestive of the rather Whitman-like utterance of a composer brought up under the influences of the American West. Written in 1933, it still stands as one of the most effective symphonies produced in the United States.

The Incredible Flutist   Piston
Sonata for Violin and Piano   Piston

The distinguished Harvard composer in two diverse styles, gay and grave. Neither of these pieces, however, is thoroughly representative of this composer's personality.

Music for the Theatre   Copland

Early, quite modern, with more than a hint of the jazz style.

El Salon México   Copland

Amusing Latin-American café music with modern trimmings. A North American's account of a famous tourist spot in Mexico City.

A Lincoln Portrait   Copland

See the next chapter.

Appalachian Spring   Copland

Thoroughly integrated, mature Copland, showing him at his best.

Suite for Piano (1939–41)   Copland

Copland's abstract, neo-classic style; music reduced to its absolute essentials, stripped of all nonmusical excrescences.

Music for Percussion and Winds   Varese

See text.

Symphony No. 2   Sessions

This composer's aim, one of his propagandists says, is to make "each work different from anything in that form before"; laudable ambition surely, but one that makes his music difficult to listen to.

Four Saints in Three Acts   Thomson

An opera based on the story of four sixteenth-century saints, told in typical Steinese:
"How many saints can be and land be and sand be and on a high plateau there is no sand, there is snow and there is made to be so and very much what there is to see when there is a wind to have it dry and be what they can understand to undertake to let it be to send it well as much as none to be to be behind."
Thomson has a keen ear for prosody and a keen memory for other composers' styles, as well as a keen sense of humor. The total result, provided no one takes it too seriously, is effective.

Music for the film *Louisiana Story*   Thomson

Discussed in another chapter.

Essay for Orchestra, No. 1   Barber
Symphony No. 1   Barber

Good examples of the earlier, more conservative style of this talented composer.

Capricorn Concerto (1944)   Barber

More contemporary in style but seemingly with less to say; written after the old *Concerto Grosso* form.

Airborne Symphony   Blitzstein

Characteristic of this composer's "artifaction of popular sounding materials." In order to get across his descriptive effects, Blitzstein uses two soloists, a choral group, and a narrator. More significant for its attempt to picture an industrial civilization in one of its greatest triumphs than as pure music.

Romeo and Juliet Suite   Diamond

The old motive in modern, American dress; comparison is inevitable with other music on the same theme, notably Prokofieff's.

Symphony No. 3   Wm. Schuman
Undertow   Wm. Schuman
The Telephone   Menotti
The Medium   Menotti

The first a sparkling comedy, the second a dark tragedy, these two operas are indicative of this young American's operatic abilities. Theatrically effective and very powerful when necessary, these works made a good introduction to Menotti's later masterwork, *The Consul*.

THE LATEST GROUP:

Excerpts from the ballet *On the Town*   Bernstein

The rather harsh Gershwinesque style of this composer here may be said to be decorated, as one critic has said, with sequences by Stravinsky.

Age of Anxiety   Bernstein

The musical speech of his generation as remembered and recreated by a talented, rhetorically inclined, and not very original composer.

New York Profiles   Dello Joio

Two rather gentle vistas of America's greatest city, *The Cloisters* and *Grant's Tomb,* are alternated with two lively, polytonal sections, *The Park* and *Little Italy.* Capably put together, with little to say that has not been said, and with more distinctive style, by an earlier generation.

Three Dances for Two Prepared Pianos   Cage

Prepared so as to suggest the sound of Balinese gamelon orchestras, these pianos give forth rather sterile, barren music. The real thing is more impressive.

Danza a Centeotl; Xochipili   Chávez

La Hija de Colquide Suite

Interesting examples of the manipulation of Mexican folk materials, beginning with a "reconstruction" of earliest Aztec themes, by a modern composer.

Sensemaya   Revueltas

See text.

Bachianas Brasileiras No. 1   Villa-Lobos

An attempt on the part of the most important South American composer to re-create, of all things, the spirit of Bach. Effective music written for eight celli, with little suggestiveness of the spirit of the old Cantor of Leipzig; but interesting, just the same.

Bachianas Brasileiras No. 5   Villa-Lobos
   (for soprano and eight celli)

Worth most of the other works on this list put together in so far as communicative values are concerned. Certainly one of the most consequential pieces yet produced in America, with a haunting melody above a rather modernistic accompaniment of unusual flavor and timbre.

FILM, RADIO,

AND TELEVISION MUSIC

One of the most outstanding influences that have helped shape music in recent times is that which has been exerted by the largely American-developed styles in music furnished for film, radio, and television productions. Just as the demands and fashions of former times produced such widely employed forms of music as the Passion, the opera, the string quartet, and the symphony, so today's demand for background and running-commentary music for films, radio, scripts, and television productions has influenced the style of contemporary writing. Moreover, the kind and quality of music that is composed and produced for these media depends to a surprising degree upon the intricate technical procedures involved.

EARLY FILM MUSIC

The earliest moving pictures were merely transcriptions from actual life — train rides, circuses, etc. — with little attempt at artistic arrangement. But as soon as films began to be produced for their own sake, as a form of dramatic entertainment, music (literally speaking) "entered the picture" if for no other reason than to cover up the mechanical noises incident to the showing of these images on the screen. The early silent photo-dramatizations carried their thought and developed their action largely by means of pantomime, with the aid of printed matter thrown on the screen to explain otherwise unintelligible situations. Music was expected to help overcome the limitations of these silent films by emphasizing the dramatic situations and heightening the emotional moods. It was provided at first by a pianist or organist placed in a pit in front of the screen where he could watch the picture's development and, drawing on his own "inspiration" and the memory of other people's music, piece together an improvised musical accompaniment whose quality depended entirely upon his powers of invention, the effectiveness of his memory, and the resources of his musical technic. In most cases, especially in small theaters, these were not likely to be at a very high level. Gradually these single musicians were replaced by orchestras, whose leaders arranged the music that was played as accompaniment for each picture.

To aid in this, "cue sheets" were prepared by the producers of the picture, specifying the music to be used and supplying, in addition to suggestions from the standard and popular repertoire, quantities of specially concocted mood backgrounds — hurries, agitatos, love themes, mysteriosos, and the like, for use over and over again under similiar situations. A few especially written scores were made for some of the most important films, but until the advent of the sound film this rather haphazard treatment was all that was given film music.

SOUND AND THE CINEMA

When the new era of sound film arrived in 1927, after years of experiment, an entirely new vista was opened to composers and arrangers. For now all the preparation of the music, the cutting and fitting it to meet the different dramatic needs, could be done beforehand at the studio where the picture was taken; and then it could be recorded on and reproduced from the same film as the picture itself. Thus the same musical effects were available to the small, formerly poorly equipped theater as to the grand cinema palace which before had been boastful of its symphony orchestra. And the whole structure of the motion picture was changed so as to gear speech and music to ideas and emotions, rather than having them merely suggested as before in the silent film. This resulted in all sorts of improvements, not the least being that of the type and quality of the music used. The directors of these new sound films did not hesitate to call in the aid of better composers than had before been associated with moving pictures, and some of today's best-known writers, such as Weill, Toch, Shostakovich, Prokofieff,

Walton, Vaughan Williams, Copland, and Thomson, have provided music for the movies.

Unfortunately, because of the fact that he must write for mass audiences who have little sympathy for, or experience with, good music, the movie composer is limited in what he can write. And the unique technical problems which he must solve in order that his

Paramount Pictures

On the Sound Track

Aaron Copland leads a studio orchestra through the score he composed for *The Heiress*.

music can fit the constantly changing rhythms of the story, do not help him either. Suppose, as one of them puts it, that a "composer of screen music is asked to provide 72 seconds of music for a love scene. He invents a melodic theme and sets to work on its development. Just about the time he gets into the middle of some really interesting composition, the action shifts to sea, and his tender music is rudely interrupted by a foghorn or a ship's whistle. Then he must return to the beginning and shape and trim his material according to the time pattern. He is very fortunate, indeed, if the length of the scene is not changed several times during the production, thus requiring his music to have rubber-band flexibility." In spite of the fact that Aaron Copland has said that this kind of timing does not straight-jacket his imagination, it is doubtful whether music composed under such circumstances will command any great amount of serious attention and interest when performed apart from the theater.

A factor which favors the production of movie music rather than concert works is that the former work pays the composer so very much better. It is obviously impossible to make a living from large-scale composition *per se,* and so it is inevitable that the good composer should turn to the medium in which he is well paid and can do reasonably good work. However, the artistic possibilities are necessarily limited by the time-needs of the film, and the very modest listening capacity of the audience. There is also the drawback of their divided attention, between the film and the music, resulting in neither being fully comprehended.

THE RECORDING PROCESS

The music having been finished, it is recorded, usually on a number of separate sound tracks. The dialogue of the actors is put on one; if the piece is musical, and the actors are called upon to sing, they only mouth the words, leaving them to be furnished later from another sound track, often made by entirely different artists. The orchestral background, usually well played and interpreted, is put on a different track, the sound effects on still another. These are all blended together on one master sound track in the "dubbing room" by sound engineers, who control a series of dials regulating the volume of the various components of this mixed mechanical brew. No wonder a well-known Hollywood musician has observed sarcastically that a movie composer's immortality "lasts from the recording stage to the dubbing room." Often parts of the score over which the composer has labored so carefully are entirely cut out so that these men must then feel, as one of them has put it, like nothing but a face on the cutting-room floor. Whatever effectiveness the music may have finally has to survive all these technical hurdles: the wonder is that anything worth while musically comes through at all.

In view of these trials and tribulations in producing music for actual use on the films, it is only natural that the movie composer hopes to be able to use what he has written in making a separate concert score for orchestral performance. If movie music has enough individuality to attract attention to itself to the detriment of what is projected upon the screen, it automatically destroys its own effectiveness. This fact would seem to mitigate against any great success when good movie music is made into concert music; but no hard and fast rule is possible here, and a number of very successful orchestral suites, in which the composer is no longer limited by the technical demands of his medium, have been developed from movie sources. A short list of them will be found at the end of this chapter.

THE ROLE OF RADIO

The role of radio in American life has been an extremely significant, if not very inspiring, one. Beginning some time around 1910 [1] when experiments proved that programs of speech and music could be successfully transmitted over a wireless, the radio industry as we know it today may be said to have started on November 2, 1920, when broadcasting began as a regular service to the public from Station KDKA in Pittsburgh. What potentialities in the way of dispersing music and literature and of cultivating taste the new medium possessed!

These have to a degree been realized, for certainly a fair share of the credit for increasing interest in good music must go to the activities of broadcasters. But that so many opportunities have been missed is evident from the disappointment expressed in a letter sent to the National Association of Broadcasters by Dr. Lee DeForest, the so-called "Father of the Radio" because of his inventions which made this device possible:

> What have you gentlemen done with my child? He was conceived as a potent instrumentality for culture, fine music, the uplifting of America's mass intelligence. You have debased this child, you have sent him out on the streets in rags of ragtime, tatters of jive and boogie-woogie, to collect money from all and sundry for hubba hubba and audio jitterbug.
>
> You have made him a laughing stock of intelligence, surely a stench

---

[1] Some claim that these experiments took place as early as 1906. See *History of Radio to 1926* by Gleason L. Archer (New York: The American Historical Society).

in the nostrils of the gods of the ionosphere; you have cut time into tiny cubelets, called shorts (more rightly stains), wherewith the occasional fine program is periodically smeared with impudent insistence to buy or try.

The nation may have no soap, but soap opera without end or sense floods each household daily. Murder mysteries rule the waves by night and children are rendered psychopathic by your bedtime stories.

This child of mine has been religiously kept to the average intelligence of thirteen years. Its national intelligence is maintained moronic, as though you and the sponsor believe the majority of listeners have only moron minds. The curse of his commercials has grown consistently more cursed, year by year.

RADIO MUSIC

As with the movies, music has been a concurrent part of radio production from its earliest days. Beginning with the earliest scripts prepared in 1922, when advertising began to assume the necessary role of the angel that supports the American radio show business,[2] music has been used as the "come-on" for all sorts of programs. The best talent in all fields, from crooners (who are in reality a creation of the radio), through name bands to the Metropolitan Opera and Toscanini, has been attracted to the microphone; and all sorts of new talents, policies, and production procedures have been developed in order to exploit to the full the advantage of the radio advertiser.

Today radio scripts of every kind, commercial as well as educational, are unthinkable without music. Some of them contain especially prepared scores written by highly talented and salaried composers, bringing together custom-built scraps to suit the dramatic needs of the script in a workmanlike and thoroughly competent manner. And some of them consist of entirely original music composed for the occasion, often exploiting the new effects of sonority and color made possible by the radio medium. These composers have evolved a radio style of underscoring words and situations which, when used as skillfully as in the *Lincoln Portrait* of Copland, is really effective; and when combined with the proper sound effects as in such things as Corwin's *On a Note of Triumph*, with music by

2 This is in strong contrast to the British system of broadcasting supported by license fees paid by the owners of receiving sets; thus a more independent policy is possible.

Herrmann, or the documentary *Ballad for Americans* by John La Touche, with music by Earl Robinson, can be genuinely moving.

But in the main, commercial plugs on the radio have the same importance as symphonic themes; as a matter of actual record, the plugs outnumber the themes a hundred to one. And so musicians

Ewing Galloway

Behind the Scenes in a Television Studio

are apt to bemoan the fact that so much talent and energy go into the production of programs on the radio with so little in the way of real achievement to show as the result. Radio music has been too largely associated with the tricks of the market place to have much significance as art. Like the music of the movies, the music associated with the radio is an important and significant part of the American scene. If it can be improved and if it develops better content, the taste and appreciation of the American public will likewise grow and improve. If not, any possible beneficial effect it may have will be, in the disconsolate words of a former Director of Education to a big broadcasting concern, little but a "waif in the mounting radio storm."

One thing is certain, however: with the advent of all this radionic cacophony pouring out increasingly from loud speakers and television receivers in homes, hotels, trains, busses, any real contemplative activities on the part of the individual, such as reading or listening to music or just plain thinking, becomes literally impossible. The two things above all else which seem characteristic of modern life in the United States are motion and noise. The American novelist William Faulkner thus describes the joys of a growing American town of today:

". . . But mostly and above all the radios and the automobiles, the juke boxes in the drugstore and the poolhall and the cafe and the bellowing amplifiers on the outside walls, not only of the sheet-music store but the army-and-navy supply store and both feed stores (that they might falter) somebody standing on a bench in the courthouse yard making a speech into one with a muzzle like a siege gun bolted to the top of an automobile, not to mention the ones which would be running in the apartments in the homes where the housewives and the maids made up the beds and swept and prepared to cook dinner so that nowhere inside the town's uttermost ultimate corporate rim should man, woman or child, citizen or guest or stranger be threatened with one second of silence. . . ."

We all realize the final truth of such an unattractive picture. What will come of it all, especially since television will further complicate the outlook?

SOME RECORDED MOVIE AND RADIO SCORES

The Warsaw Concerto from the film
   Suicide Squadron   Addinsell

This music by an English composer shows how widespread is the traditional style of movie music; in every respect this out-Hollywoods Hollywood. Containing little but outworn clichés and stale repetitions of ideas that have been better expressed by others, it may be cited as an unfortunate example of bad music, the sort that passes itself off as significant but really contains nothing of importance.

It may be asked in this connection just what is the difference between good and bad music. Simply this: good music has a significance that makes a deep impression on the hearer; it is original, well-wrought, shows evidence of skilled craftsmanship; it is ordered and unified so as to impress its message clearly and distinctively. Bad music, on the other hand, overstresses cheap and emotional material, often emphasizing the sex aspect; is usually inartistically put together and simply a copy of other styles and mannerisms.

Music from the film *Alexander Nevsky*   Prokofieff

This, on the other hand, is of a type that will probably remain a model of its kind for many years; excellently written in the main, it is effective and exciting, especially in conjunction with the Eisenstein historical film for which it was written.

Suite from the H. G. Wells' film *Things to Come*   Bliss

Good, straightforward cinema music of no great importance.

Music from the film *The Loves of Joanna Godden*   Vaughan Williams

The dean of English composers has written a number of scores for important films; this one is in his characteristic folk-pastoral vein, quite appropriate to the rather quiet nature of this moving picture.

Music from the film *Scott of the Antarctic*   Vaughan Williams
Music from the film *Oliver Twist*   Bax

Incidental Music from the films *Henry V* and *Hamlet*   Walton

Contains some effective reproduction of the actual style of the music of the time of the plays. Although not especially significant as music, the scores underline the texts of Shakespeare's plays in excellent fashion, no mean achievement.

Suite from the film *Our Town*   Copland

Although the recorded version is arranged for the piano alone, this simple music conveys the real naïveté of one of the finest films produced in the United States, adapted from Thornton Wilder's play.

The Plow That Broke the Plains   Thomson

An excellent opportunity for showing how music can improve even a documentary film; this has no Hollywood flavor whatever.

Louisiana Story   Thomson

Another film of American life in the bayous of the South; very simply set with real effectiveness and considerable musical skill.

A Lincoln Portrait   Copland

Fine example of what may be done in the way of underscoring words so as to increase their significance in radio scripts.

On a Note of Triumph   Corwin — Herrmann
I Can Hear It Now   Murrow — Friendly

Outstanding radiobroadcasts gathered from effective historical documents.

Genesis Suite   Shilkret — Tansman —
Castelnuovo-Tedesco —
Toch — Stravinsky —
Schönberg

Although actually not written for the radio or the movies, this is a compilation of pieces by composers who have in one way or another been associated with that center of movie-radio culture, Hollywood. It is made up of the reading of excerpts from the Book of Genesis, with a musical background underscored by an all-star cast. As one critic has well said, it seems merely another example of the grandiose bombast that is somehow closely associated with Hollywood productions and so, in spite of the character of its composers, is mostly bad music. It may be said to have the dubious distinction of containing, with one exception, what are probably "the worst compositions of the respective composers ever released!"

TWENTY-NINE

BEETHOVEN'S *Fifth Symphony*

BEETHOVEN'S EXCITING BACKGROUND

A regression from the study of modern trends to a consideration of the *Fifth Symphony* of Beethoven is not so abrupt as it first seems. We have suggested that the leaders of musical thought of the first two decades of the twentieth century have been looking for a new freedom from the older conventions. During a period marked by violent changes — physical, spiritual, and economic — these composers have demanded that music be permitted to cast off the fetters of the past and develop along the abstract lines of musical design. We have likewise suggested that the process of experimentation in these new fields, even though it has not yet produced figures which approximate the great masters of the past, deserves our attention even if we cannot give it our sympathy. But the weaknesses of the results that have followed the practice of these modern ideals show up in rather unfortunate relief against the striking work of the Titan who lived and composed in a period of upheaval almost exactly like that which has given us our present-day conditions.

Ludwig van Beethoven wrote during the period of unsettlement and doubt that followed the French Revolution; he was born in 1770 and died in 1827, and the fall of the Bastille occurred, you remember, in 1789. It was Beethoven who voiced the thoughts and emotions of that great time as did no other, raising himself and his music into the very "realms of the sunlight itself." His music is the incarnation of Taine's description of the period; it is filled with discontent with the present, a vague desire for a higher beauty and a more ideal happiness, the painful aspiration for the infinite. But it was because of the manner in which he sang of these desires and aspirations that we listen to him today; he spoke a universal language, and his message has reached the whole cultured world. He was not merely content with a garrulous protest against things as they existed. The music of the time had reached heights, under the genius of Haydn and Mozart, that seemed to make any further progress difficult, if not impossible. But, building firmly on the past, realizing that ideas are best communicated through music that follows fundamentals of design, Beethoven gathered up the surging discontents, strivings, and aspirations of his time, and voiced them through a universally understood medium, charging them with a vitality and emotional power that is as strong today as it was in the early part of the nineteenth century. And so he remains a man, not of historical yesterdays, but of today, and for all time. Shall we be able to say the same of the Stravinskys, Schönbergs, and their like a hundred years hence?

Some of the music that Beethoven wrote has become dated and old-fashioned. The quality of his work is uneven, for he had to live from the practice of his art and sometimes wrote things that were obviously designed for immediate consumption. While all of his work is filled with what one writer has called "moral intensity" — that is, with a struggle to express the infinite — this intention is not always realized, and we have music that is grandiose and impressive rather than really great. But in his best works, things like the *Eroica Symphony*, the *Fifth Symphony*, the *Ninth Symphony*, and the last string quartets, he stands unequaled both in the force of his thought and in the quality of its expression.

THE *C Minor Symphony*: A DRAMA IN PURE MUSIC

It is unfortunate, but perhaps inevitable, that the *C Minor (Fifth) Symphony* of Beethoven, one of the most epochal of his works, has suffered from overplaying almost from the day of its first performance. Sir George Grove tells us that the conductor who first introduced orchestral music into England played this symphony week after week; and it was his opinion that the tremendous hold which this work had upon audiences is due to its "prodigious originality, form, and conciseness." The very qualifications that have made its popularity are those which have given it staying power; present-day writers might well ponder these two characteristics, popularity and staying power! They might, if the task is not too obvious for them, try to realize how Beethoven achieved this popularity and staying power.

For it is this work that stands above all others as a triumphant demonstration of the eternal necessity of shaping expressive materials according to fundamental laws of design. It proves, as does no

Courtesy of Steinway and Sons, New York

N. C. WYETH: *Beethoven and Nature*

The composer's close contact with the beauties of nature was the source of some of his finest music. The painter has depicted him here in the mood of the *Pastoral (Sixth) Symphony*.

other single piece of music, that only if various elements at the disposal of the composer are combined according to organized plan will the final appeal of the whole be realized. No one knew better than did Beethoven that the formal principles of music are not arbitrary rules laid down by authoritative fiat. Rather were they the result of continued experimentation from the early unidentified writers of simple songs down to the composers of his own day. The final object of experimentation was to find the best method of composing music so that it could give the hearer a feeling of definiteness, clarity, and unity of expression.

BEETHOVEN'S SHAPING OF FORM

We have already said what the most usual forms available to the composer of Beethoven's day were; in view of what we have just stated, it will be no surprise then to find that he employed them all. As Grove says: "The *C Minor Symphony* is from the beginning to the end as strictly in accordance with the rules that govern the structure of musical composition as any symphony of Haydn." But the important thing is that while the symphonic form as he used it was rigidly definite in outline, his method permitted the widest liberties of style and idiom. While the music is conceived in the most rigorous of intellectual methods, it nevertheless is incandescent with fiery emotion. In this *Fifth Symphony* Beethoven brought the organization of form to a state of perfection, but he was "no theorist endeavoring to demonstrate the validity of his innovations. He was working in obedience to the dictates of his artistic soul" (Henderson in the *New York Sun*).

This work is a most significant example of the necessary interrelationship of form and substance. It is perfectly easy to dissect the first movement, for example, and show that it is written almost exactly according to the strictest pattern of sonata form. This is interesting — and helpful, if we are trying to arrive at an understanding of the demands that this form makes upon the composer. But what is significant is that the substance of this music grows inexorably out of the formal design — that one would be unthinkable without the other. Beethoven could have produced neither the logical coherence nor the dramatic intensity of this movement if he had not observed the necessities of formal design. On the other hand, the obedience to all the laws of structure known to artists would have been of little avail if Beethoven's thoughts had not been so original and the glow of their emotional power had not been so intense.

THE FIRST MOVEMENT [1]

The first movement, as in every great symphony, gives the clue for the whole work. It is tensely dramatic — one of the few movements in all music, as a great contemporary composer has said, that we feel to be absolutely perfect, every note of it being incapable of change. The gist of the movement, and for that matter of the whole symphony, lies in the first theme, Fate knocking at the door, hammered out on the whole orchestra.

Worth noting and delighting in is the passage which immediately grows out of this opening summons, the bridge passage leading over from the first to the second theme. This was a master stroke in 1808; and no one has yet produced a finer growth from a tiny seed. During it all, the first theme is driven home to our minds, and its rhythm and mood pushed onward for some sixty measures. Just as we are ready for the second theme, we hear the first once more on the horns (59–62). And while the second theme is being given out by the strings and the wood winds, in a sudden change of key and mood, we hear the first softly reflected by the basses (63–76).

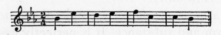

There is a short third theme,

and then Beethoven rushes onward impetuously to finish the first section (the Statement, or Exposition) of 124 measures. In the old-fashioned, leisurely eighteenth-century manner, Beethoven there draws a double bar and marks these measures for repetition. The

[1] The piano score of Beethoven's *Fifth Symphony* is available in the following editions: Universal (in a volume with other symphonies) No. 525; Breitkopf No. 36665; Schirmer (edited by Daniel Gregory Mason); Ditson (edited by Percy Goetschius) No. 3. The orchestral score (miniature size) is available in Kalmus Edition No. 5.

chief object of that procedure was to enable the hearer to get the themes well in mind. But in the hurrying tempo of modern life, this repetition is not often carried out.

The development, or "working-out," is short, only 123 measures to be exact. The perhaps overenthusiastic Berlioz suggested that in it Beethoven revealed all the secrets of his being, his private griefs, his lonely meditations, his bursts of enthusiasm, his anxious search for love. The gentle second theme has no place in this emotional display; practically all the material is drawn out of the first theme, even the dramatic series of alternating high and low chords between the strings and the wood winds. The development section ends with an insistent hammering out of the rhythm of the opening, leading directly into the Restatement, or Recapitulation, with a typically Beethovenish turn just after the first theme is heard again. At the moment we are all ready for the bridge passage that will lead us from the first to the second theme, a curious little oboe cadenza is interpolated (269), the sort of surprise that Beethoven so often uses to give added piquancy. It lasts for just a moment, and then we are off again. The Restatement is almost an exact replica of the Statement (there are 126 measures), but instead of ending it abruptly as he did the first time, Beethoven adds a long coda of 129 measures in order that he may pile up a bigger and more impressive climax. This is almost like another development; it seems here as if Beethoven felt that he had more material at hand than he could logically crowd into his development section; the motto theme is again the predominating feature, but there is also a new theme (424). The coda is as well built as the rest; indeed, we may well ask whether there is a more keenly knit half-a-thousand bars in all music. It moves as an organic whole, bound together by the masterful motto theme, and drawn to its logical end with inexorable force.

THE SECOND MOVEMENT, A THEME WITH VARIATIONS

The second movement is necessarily a relief, and through it runs a note of quiet resignation and strength. It follows the general formal scheme that we know as the Theme and Variations, but Beethoven adds some passages that are developed out of the main theme instead of being merely variants of it. This freedom displayed in the treatment of accepted and traditional formal schemes is another characteristic of Beethoven. The main theme

of this movement is gracious, leisurely, kindly; it comprises three divisions of unequal length: 1–10, 11–19, 29–31, and ends with a little coda of its own, 40–48. Thus we have the main section of forty-eight bars complete; this is followed immediately by a variation of the material, the general scheme employed being the use of an accompaniment with notes twice as quick as those in the original statement. In the second variation (commencing at 98) the motion is sustained in still shorter notes. After this second variation come several interpolated ideas that Beethoven developed out of the main theme; particularly effective are twelve humorous bars of duet by the wood winds (flute, oboe, and clarinets), interrupted by a loud insistence upon the third part of the main theme by the whole orchestra (148). And this is again interrupted by a passage where everything seems to stop, as if the composer were hesitating to decide in which direction he would go. Finally (at 185) we come to the last variation, to which is again added a coda, giving a touch of beautiful pathos. Beethoven ends the movement suddenly.

THE THIRD MOVEMENT

It is important to note that Beethoven did not label the third movement a *scherzo:* he merely marked it *allegro.* For this is not a joking movement, nor a humorous interlude; we feel rather that Fate's grim pursuit has again begun. The first whisperings of the basses,

are sinister enough; the upper strings take up the same figure and pause.

Then we are left in no doubt of the composer's intent; the

main motto theme is again heard here as the second theme,

but now in a rhythmic pattern of threes — notice the difference in effect. These two themes are alternated and somewhat developed for the remainder of the first part of the movement. The second section (usually called the Trio) is, in contrast to the first, in major, and in it we feel that Beethoven has indulged in the kind of writing more in the usual mood of his third movements. The opening section, quick and staccato, is given to the double basses,

the instruments least fitted by nature to deal with this type of music, but they manage it, and then the violas, second violins, and finally the firsts have a try at the same theme, as if they would show how easy it really is. The whole section is repeated, and the second part of the Trio appears. It is introduced by several false starts on the part of the basses; they finally dash off, inviting the rest of the orchestra to join them. Instead of going back, as was customary, to the opening section of the Trio, Beethoven repeats the second part and then leads us directly back to the beginning mood of the movement — but this time with what a difference! Now it is more eerie than ever; the wood winds alternate with plucked strings and everything is rushed along, faster and faster. Suddenly there is an interruption — everything stops, the rhythm being continued only by a kettle-drum beating against a strange low note held by the strings. Gradually this astonishing interlude gathers pace, increases in volume, and before we realize what is really happening, there come those three glorious crashes that usher in the greatest finale devised up to that time, one that has hardly been equaled since.

THE TRIUMPH OF THE LAST MOVEMENT

What strength and conviction and everlasting ardor breathe through this last movement! There is no doubt here of the composer's intent; this is triumph — "Oh, life is so beautiful, let me live, live!" If one has had many years' experience in listening, this music, if properly interpreted, never seems to lose the thrill which will lift one out of one's seat. Between the first and second themes,

(at measure 26) there is introduced a subsidiary theme,

which leads in turn to another secondary tune,

in triplets (45), before we are formally introduced to the second main theme. Both these secondary themes are used later in the development section. At measures 62–63 there is a change of key, after which the second theme is heard, and shortly after the exposition section comes to a close. Again, as in the first movement, this is marked for repetition, but is rarely so played. The development uses the subsidiary themes almost entirely, a fact which again shows Beethoven's unconventional freedom of treatment when he finds such will suit his purpose. In this last movement the orchestra has had added to it a piccolo, three trombones, and a double (bass) bassoon, and their additional weight shows. Just at the climax of the development, there comes a dramatic pause, a change of time from two's to three's, and an astonishing appearance of the ghost of the motto theme, as if the composer would suggest that even in the midst of joyful triumph the specter of man's inevitable fate lurks in the background. But this "flashback," played by strings and wood wind, is a most effective dramatic device for providing contrast before the return of the first theme in the Restatement section. It quickly fades into the background, there is a short, sharp crescendo, and we are back again at the opening theme of the movement, all the more brilliant now for it comes like the sun bursting from behind a cloud. The themes we have heard before are again presented, now in the key unity of C major. When we are more than a hundred bars from the end, the grand coda begins (318) with an exultant little fanfare. More and more intense, faster and faster, higher and higher grows the music; Beethoven working up the excitement until the final chord, which he hammers almost as if demented. But the cool head is in command of the warm heart all the way through, and this glorious rampage is carefully calculated and controlled down to the smallest detail. In the manner of a great artist, every detail is closely watched and designed, even when the music seems most free; and so the resultant effects are sure, beyond peradventure. Here, as in almost everything he did, Beethoven was absolutely individual, unlike anyone before or since. Here, indeed, "God rests in reason and moves in passion."

This symphony piles up, as all great works should. It begins with astonishing freedom of expression, achieved through strictness of structural detail, goes on to Variations, again with spacious freedom and emotion in them, something quite different from the brief, rather stilted variations written by the older composers. Then there is the third movement, with its touch of the demonic, running without interruption into the magnificent finale. Masterful construction, magnificent tunes which everyone can remember, and the authentic thrill of music that cumulates in power and repose — no wonder the *Fifth Symphony* stands, a world's masterpiece for all time!

TOPICS FOR FURTHER DISCUSSION

A recent writer, in commenting upon the remark "Thus Fate knocks at the door," which Beethoven is supposed to have made in answer to an inquiry about the meaning of the four-note motive which opens the Fifth Symphony, says, "In the philosophical sense, I submit that there is no purpose to music; that it is not 'for' anything. . . . Beethoven's *Fifth Symphony* may be Fate — or Kate — knocking at the door. That is up to you." What did he mean, and do you agree?

Is there any reason, in general, why we should look for the "meaning" of symphonies? Discuss, in this connection, Sir John McEwen's saying: "While language seeks to express a meaning, *music is itself the meaning.*"

DEFINITE SUGGESTIONS FOR READING

Music in History: Beethoven the Liberator
Beethoven, His Spiritual Development, Sullivan (New York: Knopf)

THIRTY

BRAHMS'S *First Symphony*

MAKING THE BEST OF BOTH WORLDS

Johannes Brahms (1833–1897) has of late years become popular because he made the best of both the "Classic" and the "Romantic" world. And so, when people want to go back to something satisfying, they find that Brahms enriches both the mental and the emotional life. In early days he foolishly signed a manifesto against the sort of "new music" that Wagner was supposed to have brought in. So he was thought of as a stern defender of the classics and was labeled for life. But he really was at heart a Romantic, and a pretty wild one, as his first *Piano Concerto* shows. He was a superb lyricist, as his songs prove; and he could build on the big forty-minute-symphony scale. Some think that he lacked "passion"; he had it, and sometimes it comes out, all the stronger and sweeter because it is not thrown about all over his music. There is no lack of deep feeling in Brahms's music, even if he keeps "passion" under most of the time; and music lovers cherish his pages as the purest quintessence of German Romanticism. The *First Symphony* [1] shall stand as our example of Brahms, for admiration and brief analysis. Although this was the first big work he wrote for orchestra alone, he was forty-three when it appeared, and thus finely mature.

FIRST MOVEMENT

A slow introduction sets the scene — for what? Everyone can make his own background, provided he remembers that the com-

---

[1] The piano score of Brahms's *First Symphony* is available in the following editions: Universal No. 2105; Schirmer (edited by Daniel Gregory Mason); Ditson No. 20. The orchestral score (miniature size) is available in Kalmus No. 12.

Brahms as Pianist

From a contemporary print

poser meant his work to be listened to in terms of the dramatic life of music itself, not of the other arts. If we like to think again of Life *vs.* Destiny, well and good, but it is music's life, not just man's. The bass throbs; it binds the music — perhaps to earth. The first theme

of the main movement (42, hinted at in measure 21 of the Introduction) soars in arpeggio, as do so many of Brahms's tunes. This and the second theme,

given to the oboe (121), a theme which is again evolved from the introduction, form the chief material from which the movement grows. It never loses the cast of melancholy, or pathos; indeed, that mood is never altogether absent, in some form or other, from the next two movements also. Brahms has lovely taste in allowing the varying shades of musical feeling to follow each other with the maximum of emotional effect, and in the meantime sustaining the flow of the music and its argument and interest; so that one feels each mood transition to be at once refreshing, since it comes at just the right moment, and vital to the continuity of the work — woven into its texture. Therein, of course, lies one of the greatest qualities in any composer. In this movement he may be said to attain even a tragic mood, but restrained, reflective pathos (suggested by the descending chromatic harmony he so often uses) is perhaps the emotional keynote.

SECOND MOVEMENT

The second movement is a fine example of Brahms's power of varying his emotional stresses, while maintaining something of the same atmosphere as in the first movement. Yet here we have lyrical expansion instead of the keen, close development of seminal motives. There is something of Beethoven's breadth of spirit too, in the themes, as a few notes of each will show:

Notice how the oboe (17), in replying to the strings' enunciation of the first idea, is taken up by the strings before it has had the opportunity of finishing its theme (22), as if they were eager to add sweet strength to the tranquillity of the oboe theme. After a section in which the solo parts for both oboe and clarinet predominate — very typical of Brahms's manner of writing for the orchestra — comes the repetition, freshly scored, of the original theme, followed by a leisurely, gently pathetic coda, with a final cadence. This is reminiscent of the opening of the first movement and, with its flat-

tened sixth of the scale, has become only too well known in vul-
garized forms, at the tail end of cheap ballads, since the days of its
fully expressive use by real composers.

THIRD MOVEMENT

Brahms's scherzos are much meatier and more solid in style and
a bit slower in tempo than those of the other writers of symphonies.
This one shows a feeling of German hominess most charmingly interpreted in terms of art music. The general structural scheme of the
scherzo-trio-scherzo is carried out. There are three main themes in
the scherzo section: the one on the clarinets at the very beginning,

the one heard on the combined wood winds which follows shortly
after (11),

gracefully descending its melodic way; and the clarinet tune which
comes shortly before the trio section is introduced (45):

Brahms loved the warm, rich quality of the clarinet and used it
frequently in solo parts. The trio has a 6/8 swing, is a bit faster, and
is almost entirely given over to discussions between the wood wind
and the strings. When the first section returns, the themes have a
little more elaborate accompaniment, some of them borrowed from
the trio; Brahms never wastes material, but loves to tie his whole
structure by interrelating themes in this fashion.

FOURTH MOVEMENT

Brahms followed Beethoven's example (in his *Fifth Symphony*)
in using the trombones in the last movement for the first time in this
work. Again a slow introduction, deeply dramatic. The violins and
the horn (1) hint at the great tune that is to follow; the chromatic

Brahms in Heaven

Silhouette by Otto Böhler

Haydn. Weber. Wagner. Bach. Beethoven. Mozart.

Gluck. Handel(?).

Brahms. Schumann. Bruckner. Mendelssohn. Schubert.   Liszt. Bülow. Berlioz.

element, so prominent in the first movement, is again noticed. The exciting plucked-string working up that begins at measure 5 is extremely brief; it leads to higher agitation, finally leading (29) into a magnificent horn theme,

one which Brahms tells us he heard first from the Alpine-horn players in Switzerland. In this introduction, we might figure a giant's heavy sigh as he strives to throw off a mood of depression. Then comes the horn's peaceful entry. One could not wish a more beautiful example of this composer's evoking with serene surety a new mood at a vital moment; this is a true stroke of fine art, in its swaying of the balance of emotion. We realize again, as David Stanley Smith succinctly puts it, that "technical subtlety is the prime quality of great music"; and we understand more deeply how worth while is the closest study we can make of the thousand subtleties of a great composer's technic. After the horn theme, a short hymnlike section on the brass,

one of the finest bits of the whole work (46), leads to the entrance of the *Allegro* (60), with one of the world's great tunes,

bracing the nerve and warming the heart. This, with succeeding passages that keep up the feeling of exhilaration, forms a splendid foundation for the movement, which, although fairly complex, carries us along in a tide of powerful rhythms and glorious harmony. The second subject (117)

and another theme later on (147)

build up the movement's life. Near the end, in a Beethovenish coda, the solemn brass tune of the introduction arises in the full glory of its strength (406); and so the magnificent work takes its leave.

The man who is fit for big music does not come out from hearing the best of Brahms at the same door of the spirit in which he went. Few of us win at once to the heart of this composer; we have to grow up to him, and that means work and time; but how often will equal labor give greater joy, and expense of time so great a satisfaction? The biggest, broadest art seeks for its service devotion and the refreshment of one's faculties. The man who makes music such as this symphony one of the broad bases of his experience and one of the touchstones of his taste wins something that he will never willingly let go, something that in the truest and deepest sense will gladden and enrich the rest of his life.

TOPICS FOR FURTHER DISCUSSION

What distinctions of style come to mind between Beethoven's *Fifth Symphony* and Brahms's *First*? Which makes the more immediate appeal to you, and why?

The *First Symphony* of Brahms has been referred to as the *tenth*, meaning that it is a logical successor to Beethoven's nine symphonies. Do you think this a wise statement?

DEFINITE SUGGESTIONS FOR READING

Music in History: Johannes the Great
Lives of the Great Composers, Vol. III: Brahms (New York: Pelican Books)

THIRTY-ONE

THREE LATER SYMPHONIES

After two of the great masterworks of symphonic literature have been studied, it is important to see what later composers did with the form, and to realize that, although they may have followed in general the formal schemes of Beethoven and Brahms, these men made contributions that mark their works as distinctly individual and characteristic of the periods in which they lived. We have seen that Beethoven used the fundamental structural ideas of his predecessors in such a way as to make them his own; and that Brahms's intense preoccupation with the problems of symphonic form was due to a realization of his debt, as he expressed it, to the "giant whose steps he always heard behind himself" — Beethoven. So, too, the works of the best symphonists of the latter part of the nineteenth and early years of the twentieth century owe much to the towering structures which preceded them; yet even a brief study of such representative works as Tchaikovsky's *Fifth Symphony*, Sibelius's *Second*, and Shostakovich's *Fifth* [1] will show that two of the composers, at least, were men of genius; Shostakovich has somewhat belied his great early promise.

TCHAIKOVSKY'S *Fifth Symphony* IN E MINOR

In this symphony, written twelve years after Brahms's *First Symphony*, we find the Russian composer achieving a unique uniformity of mood and structure through the employment of a theme common to all four movements, what he called a "motto theme." It is almost as though Tchaikovsky had said to himself: "In this symphony at

[1] The miniature scores of these works are available in the following editions: Tchaikovsky's *Fifth Symphony*, Kalmus Edition; Sibelius's *Second Symphony*, British Edition; Shostakovich's *Fifth Symphony*, Musicus Edition.

least I will rid myself of my tendency to rhapsodize [this composer was a severe self-critic] and will choose one theme around which my whole work can revolve. This symphony must and shall be homogenous." This is the theme he used:

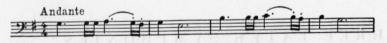

In carrying out his plans, Tchaikovsky employs the usual four movements, through all of which this theme runs like a dark thread through a gorgeous tapestry.

In the first movement there are two main subjects, the first (42–48), obviously influenced by the character of the motto theme, sad and reflective:

The second, in contrast, is full of brightness and vitality (116–120):

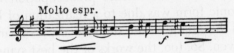

Two subsidiary themes are immediately introduced, the first (154–157):

the second (170–174):

The composer, in his development section, considers these equally as important as his main subjects; in fact, the introduction of so much thematic material robs the development of the particular importance it possesses in the Beethoven and Brahms works. But there are much brilliance and animation, with plenty of repetition of themes and those peculiar rushing passages so characteristic of this composer. Then the main and subsidiary themes are restated, the first in rather shortened form; suddenly, in the midst of the brilliant coda (which begins at 471), the first theme appears, the mood of the music grows somber and dies away in Tchaikovsky's mournful manner, down and down to lower strings and bassoon, on this melody.

The second movement — *Andante cantabile, con alcuna licenza* [2] — takes the form of a songlike romanza, the first section of which (1–65) is based on a lovely horn theme with string accompaniment (8–12):

The middle section is of a quicker character (66–107) with this theme, first given to the clarinet and then answered by the bassoon:

Moderato con anima

In the third section (108–157) of this song form, the first theme is assigned to the strings, with a charming wood-wind embroidery. Everything quickens and strengthens until the coda, when suddenly the motto theme is heard again, *fff* (159), breaking in upon the prevailing happy mood of the movement. From this point there is a decrescendo until the end, marked *pppp*.

The third movement is a graceful one in 3/4, to which the composer has given the name *valse*, based on this theme:

Allegro moderato

[2] Slowly, in a singing manner, with some license.

A sprightly, trio-like middle portion (73–144) stands out in fine contrast. After a restatement of almost exactly the same length as the first section, there follows a short coda of 52 measures, at the end of which occurs a weak citation of the motto theme in 3/4 time, its only appearance in the whole symphony which does not seem spontaneous.

In the finale the motto theme comes into its own; the impressive introduction to this last movement (1–57) is entirely based on it, in major, and we feel that this must have been the form of the origin of the theme. The movement grows clearer as it proceeds, as though "the heart had cast off a load of suffering and God's world shone out bright once more." The exposition is based on the following themes:

There is a development of some 120 measures and a restatement that is of approximately the same length as the exposition. The coda (426–565), the most important factor in the whole movement, heralds the final entry of the motto theme against a whirling woodwind background; the clouds lift, the skies clear in this grandiose setting. Here is a fine example of this composer's Byronic power of becoming momentous and eloquent on small provocation. Like the popular romantic poet, Tchaikovsky assumes on slight occasion a more tragic mien than the average Englishman does (to use Bernard Shaw's words) when he is going to be executed. Here the composer whips himself into a frenzy and proclaims this last utterance of his generative theme with tremendous power and impressiveness. Yet all the frenetic energy does not impress or move us as do the finales of the Beethoven and Brahms symphonies; in comparison, Tchaikovsky's seems too obvious and unmotivated.

Yet one need not pretend that this work is Jovian in order to enjoy it. It has its own color, due to consummate orchestral draftsmanship; it alternates romance and revelry; it delights in melancholy, yet in the end hope triumphs over despair. Tchaikovsky does not need to indulge in bizarre effects or violate accepted canons of form to make his work distinctive; yet he did not hesitate to use whatever means his muse seemed to require in order to secure the effect desired, regardless of custom or convention. A stirring work, and one that is bound to occupy an important place among late romantic compositions.

SIBELIUS'S *Second Symphony* IN D MAJOR

It is natural that a composer who wrote almost a century later than Beethoven should display a tendency to rebel against many of the conventionalities and clichés that had become an essential part of romantic expression. In many ways the seven symphonies of Sibelius are the record of such a revolt. In them Sibelius, a composer who kept himself isolated from the many fads and poses of his time, a man of incorrigible sincerity and real genius, gradually freed himself from what he felt to be the spirit of German dominance in music. The later symphonies, particularly the Fourth, Sixth, and Seventh, reveal this composer at the height of his individualistic expressive powers; the Second, written during his exuberant thirties, is a full, rounded expression of his virile talent, even though it contains obvious connections with the past. In it, as one of his ardent admirers says, Sibelius already shows himself a giant among men, composing with a seven-league stride that his fellows never knew or conceived, gifted with a fresh northern sense of beauty as well as a power of form denied "punier though wishful colleagues" (Olin Downes).

The name of this composer has become inseparably connected with Finnish nationalism. And quite rightly so, for his music is full of the spirit of the north, colored with an austere, often ascetic, hue, shot through with faërie fantasy, born of the same blood as the stirring northern sagas. There is a dark and somber character to much of the music Sibelius has written, a certain powerful, granitic strength and uncompromising austerity; with it all, however, is a sincerity and spontaneity not excelled by any of his contemporaries, a warmth of emotion all the more moving in that it is so well controlled.

This *Second Symphony* corresponds in its composer's career to the *Eroica* in Beethoven's or the Fourth in Tchaikovsky's; all three works represent their creators as young men girding their loins for the race ahead of them, fully conscious of their irrepressible genius and teeming with ideas. It shows many of the most characteristic

Jean Sibelius   *Photo, Davart*

traits of Sibelius's symphonic style: his choice of short fertile melodic fragments as thematic materials; his method of working these fragments into a full-sized theme that finally arrives as a supreme climax, rather than working them out on principles of exposition, development, and recapitulation; the use of peculiarly built whirring accompanimental passages, out of which coherent ideas suddenly crystallize; and the repetition of melodic ideas and rhythmic patterns, sometimes almost to the point of satiety.

Even in such an early work as this *Second Symphony*, we should not try to look for the ordinary structural patterns in Sibelius's writing. Although he follows the general ideals of symphonic form, the first movement is based upon the following generative fragments, without any hint of a first and second theme in the accepted manner:

1. A series of detached chords for the strings

2. A six-measure melody for the wood winds over a detached string accompaniment

3. A theme given out by the bassoons

4. An epic-like proclamation by the violins alone, as virile as one of the heroes in the *Kalevala,* Finland's great national poem

5. The most potent phrase of all, consisting largely of one high, long-held note for the wood winds, followed by a sort of shake, and a sudden drop of a fifth, thus:

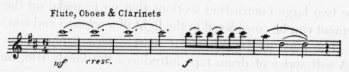

These fragments succeed each other simply, with no transitions or connecting materials; they are gradually combined and gather meaning, the whole musical fabric unfolding without break and mounting toward inevitable climax. Sibelius's constructive process here is one of gradual fusion of material, rather than the usual dissection and reassembling of themes; it can be felt more easily than analyzed and "bespeaks a full heart, magnificent fertility, an absorption which pervades all things and directs them to a single end."

Again in the second movement thematic snatches follow one another with poignant effect; they are dramatically contrasted and presented with a skill which never deviates from a single purpose, that of arousing expectation and of slow shaping toward a climax. Here are materials out of which the movement is made:

1. A sad tune for the bassoons

2. An intense dramatic bit in accelerated pace

3. A lovely lyric string theme

4. Another lyric bit, this time played by oboes and clarinets

The two large contrasting sections that go to make up the third movement can be considered in the light of a scherzo and trio movement. The pace of the scherzo is swift — *vivacissimo* — the time, 6/8. A soft series of drum taps introduces the lovely trio, built on this simple oboe melody:

Both sections are repeated with a change of orchestration, and then a dramatic transition leads into the *Finale*, in which Sibelius yields to orthodoxy, for there are two principal theme groups:

1.

Allegro moderato

2.

Development, with plenty of spinning, whirring accompanimental figures, follows; heading back to the restatement is a long-breathed, wonderfully sustained crescendo of 91 measures, after which the themes are dramatically reheard with magnificent accretion of instrumental power and color. A triumphant coda over a throbbing kettledrum bass brings the work to a clarion conclusion.

Coming from the composer's early period, this symphony is surprisingly effective and moving today, half a century after it was written, in spite of certain conventional idioms and derivations and a few close approaches to banality. For it speaks of things that eternally matter, with a greatness of manner and a sincerity of utterance that raise it high above so much of the music that has been written since. Its composer has shown himself to be completely independent of the cliques and schools that grew up all about him in the early decades of the twentieth century, cliques and schools that have sunk deeper and deeper into a morass of "chauvinism, self-deception, and evasion of emotional reality." Built firmly upon the past, with no aim of overthrowing the great traditions of art, this music nevertheless points steadfastly towards the future; its composer, like Dante, is a revolutionary by temperament but a conservative by opinion. Above all else, he is a man, at least in this work, who thinks clearly and feels deeply, who does not hesitate to say simple and sometimes obvious things in a simple and direct way. We may well leave judgment as to the result in the lap of the future.

SHOSTAKOVICH'S *Fifth Symphony*, OP. 47

Written for performance in celebration of the twentieth anniversary of the Republic of Soviet Russia, this important work was first heard in Leningrad on November 21, 1937. At that time its composer was 31 years old, and had a formidable number of compositions to his credit; he had come to the conclusion, "not acquired without travail, that music is not merely a combination of sounds arranged in a certain order, but an art capable of expressing by its own means the most diverse ideas or sentiments," as he himself put it [3] in an article written just before the performance of this symphony. "Working ceaselessly to master my art," he goes on to say, "I am endeavoring to create my own musical style, which I am seeking to make simple and expressive. I cannot think of my further progress apart from our socialist structure, and the end which I set to my work is to contribute at every point toward the growth of our remarkable country. There can be no greater joy for a composer than the inner assurance of having assisted by his works in the elevation of Soviet musical culture, of having been called upon to play a leading role in the recasting of human perception."

All of which accounts for the directness and simplicity of this symphony; Shostakovich does not hesitate to use, in the broadest of ways, the abstract historical forms hallowed by the past; neither does he hesitate to use, and very effectively, some of the newer devices of "modernism." The point is that, however he writes, he

[3] *La Revue Musicale,* December, 1936.

says something — he is a man with life and imagination and real
musical consciousness, not a mere conjurer of notes or designer of
tonal patterns. The design of this symphony is strikingly simple and
unaffected; there is nothing here that need bother anyone who is
willing to concede the prolonged use of dissonance as an effective

Musical Quarterly, G. Schirmer

Caricature of Shostakovich
By Kukriniksi (1942)

means of musical communication. In contradistinction to so many
of his contemporaries, Shostakovich has been wise enough to sim-
plify and clarify his style so as to meet the needs of the large mass
public for which he writes. The result is striking and impressive, if
the hearer is not too far removed from life to appreciate the earthy,
bourgeois tang of this music.

The first movement opens with a wide-jumping theme stated antiphonally between the high and low strings:

The second theme is lyric and expressive; it is a fine example of this composer's ability to write a tune of sustained melodic power:

There follows an extended development in which the tempo is quickened, the rhythms tightened, and the melodies made even more eloquent. With the restatement, the *largamente* mood of the opening theme is restored; the second theme is beautifully exploited by the wood winds over a throbbing string accompaniment. The end comes peacefully. The whole movement is taut and clear — there are only 305 measures in it — with little waste in thematic material or instrumental sonorities.

There is an ironic, gamin-like spirit to the second movement which has made it seem cheap to some ears. It is in the traditional scherzo form, all the elements of which are clearly discernible: after the opening allegretto section based on two themes, there comes a contrasting trio, and then the first part is repeated *da capo*. This vivacious dance movement serves as a perfect link between, and a necessary contrast to, the sustained mood of the first and third movements.

The third movement, marked *largo*, is one of slow melodic growth from simple beginnings that are again announced by the strings:

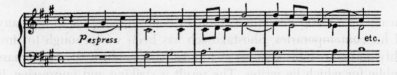

The mood of the whole is dark and brooding, as if the composer would reveal the melancholy searchings of his Russian soul; gradually more and more voices enter; the tension increases and then subsides as the ecstatic melodies are sung once more muted and in high register. A stab of harp and celesta color brings the movement to a close.

The theme of the last movement *rondo* is strongly Russian in flavor, an uncouth but buoyant march rhythm:

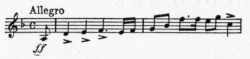

There is a slower section during which the lyric qualities of the earlier movements are recalled, and the whole winds up with an impressive and broadened reappearance of the rondo theme.

TOPICS FOR FURTHER DISCUSSION

Which of these three works makes the deepest impression on you? Why?

Can you trace any derivations in the works of the two later composers from the style of Tchaikovsky? If so, where?

One enthusiast regarding Sibelius calls him "the greatest symphonist since Beethoven"; another critic says that his music is "excellently put together by a man with nothing profound to say"; still a third maintains that his music does not come to grips with the problems of our own world, and so the attempt to set this composer up as the "great modern composer of our day" is certain to fail. How much truth do you think there is in these statements?

Speaking of the Shostakovich symphony, a recent critic has asked, "Who else among the contemporaries has composed a work lasting fifty minutes that is so consistently interesting and stimulating?" Can you answer?

DEFINITE SUGGESTIONS FOR READING

Lives of the Great Composers, Vol. III: Tchaikovsky (New York: Pelican Books)

THIRTY–TWO

THE ROCOCO AGE

CLASSIC AND ROMANTIC

The two eighteenth-century predecessors of Beethoven, Mozart and Haydn, are best understood if their music is heard in direct contrast with the later Romanticism. These three composers may be said to have been the first to show us the full glories of the modern art of music. Their compositions breathe much the same spirit — that of a deep understanding of the essential property of art — but there is a wide difference in the character of their work. Compare the *Fifth Symphony*, for instance, with the *C Major Symphony* of Mozart (No. 34) or the *Oxford Symphony* of Haydn. In place of the striving, the striking individualism, the intense feeling, the vivid and abrupt changes of mood that we find so constantly present in the Beethoven music, there is a certain serenity in Haydn and Mozart, a serenity of detachment from the realities of life, something that lies beyond its transient joys and sorrows. These eighteenth-century men seem largely concerned with the molding of their materials in the most artistic and well-balanced manner possible. The music of Beethoven delights because of its communication of ideas and emotions, to which we so readily and fully respond. There is in addition, of course, a sturdy and suitable structure which grows out of the emotional need of the composer's expression. With Haydn and Mozart, we cannot but feel that the position is reversed; our pleasure is first of all an aesthetic one, less connected with the outside world and more concerned with the adjustment of abstract ideas of proportion. The one style we call Romantic — the composer expressing his individual experiences, sometimes out of the white heat of his own crises, sometimes shaped by calmer reflection and intellectual manipulation; but, in any case, the music is always personal and impassioned. The other style we call Classic: here the composer's emotion seems cleared of circumstances, cleansed of personalities, assimilated and purified, an "emotion not only recollected in tranquillity, but also generalized from humanity." The American painter and writer on art, Kenyon Cox, has given an excellent description of the meaning of classicism in art. He said that "the classic spirit is the disinterested search for perfection, the love of clearness and reasonableness and self-control. It is also the love of permanence and of continuity. It asks of a work of art, not that it shall be novel and effective, but that it shall be fine and noble. It seeks not merely to express individuality and emotion but to express disciplined emotion and individuality restrained by law. It strives for the essential rather than the accidental, the eternal rather than the momentary."

THE EIGHTEENTH-CENTURY SPIRIT

A consideration of the difference in the periods in which these composers lived and worked will give an excellent idea of the reasons for these differences in their music. All three men were typical of their time: Beethoven a man of the nineteenth century; Haydn (1732–1809) and Mozart (1756–1791) of the eighteenth. Today, as we look back from the vantage point of the present, we can see these centuries in just perspective. The seventeenth century had been a period of brilliant activity, of intellectual, artistic, and material achievement; Europe was beginning to experience the full power of the tremendous forces which had been set in motion by the Renaissance. This century was a time of fierce and joyous pride in national life. Under Elizabeth, James I, Charles I, and Cromwell, and under Richelieu and Louis XIV, England and France became conscious of new powers and struggled towards new destinies. There were great discoveries in physical science: this was the time of Francis Bacon and his turning of the current of man's thought towards material things, of Galileo and his telescope, of Isaac Newton and his law of universal gravitation. New lands had been discovered and opened up, England reaching out towards India on the one hand and the New World on the other. There had come a complete revaluation of literature and art: it was the time of Shakespeare and Bacon, of Corneille and Molière, of Rubens, Rembrandt, Velásquez, and Van Dyck — these latter carrying on the traditions instituted by the

A Composer of the Eighteenth Century

Showing his chamber music to his friends. The
painting is ascribed to Robert Tournières, c. 1705.

sixteenth-century Renaissance painters. And last, but by no means
least, there had developed new and rather unaccustomed ideas of
religious tolerance and freedom. Music, during this time, had come
out from under the protection of the Church and had developed an
entirely new method of expression — that of the more personal
instrumental style. "At the end of the sixteenth century, a composer was a man who wrote church music in the accepted tradition
. . . but before the seventeenth century was very old, a composer
had almost as many fields in which to work as would be open to him
at the present time" (Buck).

ROCOCO ART

But there came an end to this glorious period. After all this enthusiasm, these strong opinions, these great discoveries, this tre-

mendous activity in the arts, and these many wars, there came complete exhaustion. The next century was a period of natural and inevitable reaction. After an epoch of great creative forces, it seems necessary for nature and man to recoup their strength and regain their balance. And so in this new century, the people, weary and disillusioned, no longer pursued their ideals of religious, political, and intellectual life. "There could be no wars of religion now, for men had not much faith in anything. The intellectual outlook was frank and tolerant, but not serious. Life was an art, to be

An Aspect of Mozart's Music in Architecture

Probably the finest example of Rococo in Europe — the Amalienburg in Munich, built 1734–1739 after plans by Cuvillies. Here are the molded curves and the facile ornaments of the eighteenth century at their best.

pursued gracefully by all who had the means to live like educated people" (Mowat). The strong feelings of nationalism had degenerated into political bickerings, the earlier enthusiasms for scientific discovery into a period of research. Instead of the universal curiosity and burning enthusiasms of the earlier time, artists of the eighteenth century reflect the grace and intelligence of their period. It was, of course, the era of the great French domination, and Louis XIV, the Sun King (who lived well into this century of which we speak), and his successor Louis XV became models for all Europe; their luxurious court at Versailles was the envy and pattern of every king, prince, and courtier. The society of this century was, as Strachey observes, the most civilized that history has ever known. Art, religion, intellectual activities, economic conditions — everything was organized and disciplined for the advantage of the absolute monarchs who ruled in the different European countries.

All the arts catered to the manifest desire of the times for the enjoyment of life in the most aristocratic manner possible; the century has come to be known as the Rococo period. In reality the art of the Rococo period derived from that of the earlier Baroque (discussed in a later chapter), being a graceful refinement and an aristocratic adaptation of its rich strength and buoyant vitality. Rococo architecture was of harmonious, gracefully flowing lines; the interior decorations, dainty in style, made use of gay draperies and formal furniture. These provided an ideal setting for the gorgeous dresses, formal wigs, and lace jabots affected by the *haute monde*. Against this gleaming background the polished and stilted manners of the period, the carefully stylized diversions and the witty, malicious conversations are easily understandable. Writers and composers paid less attention to spontaneous and inspired creation, and more to the development of craftsmanship and skill for the delectation of their princely patrons. Painters filled their pictures with distinguished figures in ravishing colors, ladies and gentlemen in glistening silks, or lovers ensconced in Fairy Islands of the Blest — dainty fantasies of luxurious idleness as well as of tender love. Sculptors, jewelers, wood carvers, iron workers, even chinaware makers catered to this passion for decorative grace. Everything and everybody, in so far as the creative world was concerned, combined to form a fitting setting for the existence of superlative luxury. In this ostentatious setting there was little tolerance for the bold expression of emotion in art.

Rococo Architecture at Its Best

The Residenz Theater in Munich, built by Cuvilliés in 1751–53. This almost perfect Mozart theater was destroyed during World War II.

But because this Rococo art of the eighteenth century was created to frame the social graces of the period, and so possesses a stylized, formal aspect, it should not be thought of as being only artificially conventional and pleasingly correct. The artists of the time used mediums of expression that were natural and logical for their purpose, and used these mediums with an almost unbelievable ease and fluency. But underneath all this seeming ease and natural complexity there exists a profound art; the effects that were attained were the results of the most skillful manipulation of materials. Accent and quantity and proper stressing of syllables; ornaments and scrolls and harmoniously curving lines; gilded scale passages, lovely in their thin airiness, lightly curving melodies, and exquisite harmonies — all were molded by the artists of the century into an art of real significance. And if we learn to know the achievements of one type of artist in this luxurious period, we can better understand the others. The writings of Pope and Collins will help us to appreciate the paintings of Watteau, Boucher, and Chardin. The creations of Cuvillies, Neumann, and the Brothers Asam are the architectural counterparts of the music of the younger Scarlatti and the youthful Mozart.

THE VIEWPOINTS OF TWO POETS

If we examine the treatments given similar themes by poets of this period and of the Romantic epoch, we can see these eighteenth-century characteristics very clearly. In his "Ode to Evening," William Collins (1721–1759) uses this manner of treatment, a manner that is most characteristic of the whole century under discussion:

If aught of oaten stop, or pastoral song,
May hope, chaste Eve, to soothe thy modest ear,
Like thy own solemn springs,
Thy springs and dying gales;

O Nymph reserved, while now the bright-haired sun
Sits in yon western tent, whose cloudy skirts,
With brede ethereal wove,
O'erhang his wavy bed:

Now air is hushed, save where the weak-eyed bat
With short shrill shriek flits by on leathern wing,

Or where the beetle winds
His small but sullen horn,

As oft he rises, 'midst the twilight path
Against the pilgrim borne in heedless hum:
Now teach me, maid composed,
To breathe some softened strain,

Whose numbers, stealing through thy darkening vale,
May not unseemly with its stillness suit,
As, musing slow, I hail
Thy genial loved return!

Shelley — an ardent Romanticist if there ever was one — thus expresses himself on the same theme:

I arise from dreams of thee
In the first sweet sleep of night,
When the winds are breathing low,
And the stars are shining bright.
I arise from dreams of thee,
And a spirit in my feet
Hath led me — who knows how?
To thy chamber window, Sweet!

The wandering airs they faint
On the dark, the silent stream —
And the Champak odors fail
Like sweet thoughts in a dream;
The nightingale's complaint,
It dies upon her heart
As I must on thine,
O! belovèd as thou art!

Oh lift me from the grass!
I die! I faint! I fail!
Let thy love in kisses rain
On my lips and eyelids pale.
My cheek is cold and white, alas!
My heart beats loud and fast;
Oh! press it to thine own again,
Where it will break at last.

It is easy to realize the comparative restraint, the insistence upon balance and clarity of structure, the deft manipulation of expressive means for their own sake found in the first poem, especially when placed in immediate juxtaposition with the second. But we can hardly say that the Collins ode lacks feeling because it is so restrained in expression and so balanced and clear in its structure, or because often the words are used just for the sound they convey. There is emotion in the first poem, certainly; but it is the emotion that has little to do with the immediate individuality of the writer, emotion that is cleared of the violent personality of the second writer. In the words already quoted, Collins's emotion is "recollected in tranquillity and generalized from humanity." In reading the first poem we are not so much impressed with the fact that we ourselves have felt exactly the emotion contained therein, as we are with "clearness, reasonableness, and self-control" so evidently present. When Romantic poetry or music is concerned with its intensity of personalized emotion, we are often tempted to say: "Why, that is exactly how I have often felt!" With the composers and artists of the Classic period, on the other hand, we have a sort of subconscious feeling that what they have expressed for us is the very essence of what humanity in general has experienced throughout its development.

LIST OF SUGGESTED MUSIC

Romantic Music

Fifth Symphony in C Minor   Beethoven
Third Symphony in E Flat Major   Beethoven
Symphony in C Major   Schubert

Classic Music

Symphony in C Major (Jupiter)   Mozart
Quintet in G Minor   Mozart
Symphony in G Major, No. 92 (Oxford)   Haydn
Quartet in D Major, Op. 64, No. 5 (Lark)   Haydn

TOPICS FOR FURTHER DISCUSSION

It is sometimes charged that a great deal of the music of the eighteenth century — even Mozart's — is too much according to formula:

that one familiar with it often can predict what is coming, since the same turns of phrase constantly recur. Discuss the weight of formalism in this period and its influence, as far as you have noted it in the above sense.

Jan Gordon, art critic of the London *Observer,* has said: "The product of love and leisure is almost always embellishment." Discuss this in connection with Rococo art.

The distinction customarily made between Classic and Romantic art is this: by *Classic* and *Romantic* we mean art in which emphasis is largely on design and emotion respectively. Is this true? If so, where would we place Bach?

Discuss the statement that every "Classicist" was a "Romanticist" when alive.

Discuss Lowell's definition of a classic — that which "maintains itself by that happy coalescence of matter and style, that innate and requisite sympathy between the thought that gives life and the form that consents to every mood of grace and dignity, and which is something neither ancient nor modern, always new and incapable of growing old."

DEFINITE SUGGESTIONS FOR READING

Music in History: The Eighteenth Century, General Backgrounds

THIRTY-THREE

MOZART AND HAYDN

A MIRROR OF THE EIGHTEENTH CENTURY

It is in the works of Haydn and Mozart, especially the latter, that we find the musical incarnation of the eighteenth-century spirit. Both these composers were affected by the intellectual and spiritual characteristics of the period in which they lived, and there is much in their music that suggests the airs and graces, the molded curves and facile ornaments of the eighteenth century. Yet we are coming to realize that there is much more than this mere suggestiveness of the elegancy of a minor age in their works, or they would have passed into oblivion long ago. Haydn is not merely an individual who wrote jolly, conventional, light-hearted, but rather meaningless music; and Mozart's hold on posterity is the result of far more than the limpid clarity and perfection of his style. Both these men were composers who were able to feel deeply as well as to write clearly: they were not merely periwigged "Classicists," buried under the patronage of dukes and bishops; they were living, sensitive individuals. Haydn, for all his rugged simplicity and straightforward spontaneity, has a depth of feeling in some of his slow movements that anticipated Beethoven. Underneath much of the intuitive grace, the melodic charm, and the refined perfection of Mozart's music we can surely feel a peculiar sadness which suggests that he, like Beethoven and Brahms who were to follow him, realized the tragic futility of all human activity — that he could feel the taste of death on his tongue, as he himself phrased it.

THE CLASSICAL COMPOSER AT WORK

Mozart's compositions group themselves naturally into two great divisions: first the "gallant" works, strongly eighteenth-century in pirit; and second, the greater compositions which transcend time, place, and circumstances. Much of his chamber music, his sonatas and concertos, his church music (strangely enough), his serenades, and some of his earlier operas belong to the first group. His great symphonies, notably those in G minor, E flat major, and C major, the

Wolfgang Amadeus Mozart

From a contemporary print

six quartets that he dedicated to Haydn, his *G Minor Quintet,* the operas *The Marriage of Figaro* and *Don Giovanni,* can be classed together in the second group.

No better introduction to the beauties of the works of the first type can possibly be found than the charming serenade *Eine kleine Nachtmusik,* written for performance at some courtly, out-of-door occasion. Holmes, one of the early Mozart biographers, has this to say of the Mozart serenades:

Sunday garden fêtes in the spring and early summer are peculiarly characteristic of life in Vienna, where the pleasure of the promenade and the enjoyment of the air and sunshine regularly succeed the observances of religion. In such a scene, where all the beauty, rank, and talent of the capital are assembled, the spirit of the season is irresistible. And there is the music. An orchestra is erected in some green walk among the trees; and the first sound is the signal to suspend conversation, to sit quietly, or to cluster round the musicians. . . . A style of instrumental music at once light and ariose — somewhat between the symphony and the dance, but calculated to give elegance and tenderness of sentiment to the promenaders — was at any time attractive to Mozart and among his easiest work. His serenades were not such as the starved lover sings, but imbued with all the genius of the South; in fact, when we consider the emotions aroused by his instrumental music, and by the *adagios* of his symphonies in particular, the imagination of the author may be compared to a Mohammedan paradise; for in no other element can such refined voluptuousness and elegance be conceived to originate.

The four short movements of this work well illustrate Holmes's description: this miniature symphony is frankly meant to delight the senses, and we should listen to it with this in mind.

The *Symphony in D Major* is another fine example of the gallant Mozart style. This astonishing work, sometimes called the *Haffner Symphony*, was written in the almost incredible time of two weeks, at a time in Mozart's life when his attention was largely occupied with other matters. He did it at the request of his father for the Haffner family in Salzburg, the town of his birth, during the summer of his twenty-sixth year. Six months afterwards, when Wolfgang was arranging for its rehearsal and first performance, he had so completely forgotten the contents of the score as to write to his father, "the new Haffner symphony has quite astonished me, for I do not remember a note of it. It must be very effective."

And very effective it certainly is, especially if we can listen to it interpreted for us by some Mozart specialist, Beecham or Bruno Walter, for instance. The slow movement again suggests the serenade style of "refined voluptuousness and elegant repose." The last movement, in rondo form, is full of high spirits and keen wit; but there is none of the vigorous boisterousness that we so often find in the last movement of the Haydn symphonies.

MOZART's *G Minor Symphony*

To turn to Mozart's *G Minor Symphony* from some of his earlier works is to realize the depth and range of his mind, whose ultimate richness was so far above the somewhat superficial Rococo graces of his time, as expressed in some of the works already discussed. It is amazing to consider what must have been his mental concentration and illumination in the summer of 1788, when within a couple of months he produced three of his greatest symphonies, each of them as different from the others, emotionally, as it could possibly be, works happy, noble, and troubled. Truly that "heart of fire and brain of ice" that Wagner speaks of as vital necessities for a composer were Mozart's.

There is a breath as of foreboding in the *G Minor Symphony*, a more somber feeling than that of the other two works in this group. It is music peculiarly meet for study in the waning days of the year, when the face of nature has changed from summer pride to autumn brooding. The dignity and power of nature are in the music, too, the dignity that suggests the unchanging processes of life, that in right contemplation are noble, however sad.

The orchestration suits the work's mood — strings, wood wind, and horns only. The blare of the heavier brass would be out of place. The gravity of the horns alone is required. It may be noted that although no clarinets are found in the first version of this work, they are used in the second which Mozart prepared. A note upon this will be found in the Philharmonia score.

FIRST MOVEMENT

Over a soft, impassioned pulsating viola figure is given out the first theme, *Allegro molto:*

In the second theme (44),

we may feel sweetness and a faint sadness, in a gliding chromatic movement. The magnificent dramatic life of the whole movement is lived in the spirit of the first theme only, with the interweaving of parts suggesting the complexity of life. A wistful dialogue for wind and strings (138) leads back to the recapitulation (164). Here the first theme is extended and there is an urgent coda (281), mounting upwards and ending on the heights of dramatic tension.

SECOND MOVEMENT

This is in regular "first-movement form," like the first and the finale. It may be that Mozart felt this form, with its possibilities of conflict and working-up of tension in the development, to be peculiarly fitted as the stage for his drama in music. The first theme of the *Andante* seeks comfort, and finds it within. Soon after the second subject has begun (at 37), there is a poignant chord (44) that hints at much behind the self-control of the opening. Throughout the movement the modulations, and the calling and answering of the themes, are emotionally suggestive and artistically masterly.

MINUET

Is there spiritual conflict here also? Its firmness is curiously austere, in the first part. The Trio (43) brings a softer mood, when strings and wind graciously bow to each other. The return of the first section, with its earnest, even stern urgency, emphasizes the feeling that Mozart has departed from the usual Minuet spirit because he so strongly felt the work as an organic whole. Between its four movements there is a rare consonance in moods and power.

FINALE

Restlessness, anxiety, a going to and fro in the mind, with searching of the spirit. Here is something of the first movement's imperiousness, in the sweeps of the strings and the chordal interjections of the wind. The first theme

enters at once, the second

at 71. Here again is the chromatic hint of noble melancholy that we found in the earlier movements. At 125 Mozart begins to work out his thoughts by declaiming the first in interrupted sentences, before settling down to tear the heart out of it in impassioned exhortation and the weaving of argument, moving masterfully from key to key and leaving the issue uncertain when he turns to the recapitulation (207). The change in the latter portion of the second theme (twice, at 251 and following) will not escape attention. It is as if at the last the composer sought to make even more urgent the poignancy of his thought.

Piano Concerto in D Minor

Nowhere is Mozart shown to better advantage than in his piano concertos; they were written during the busiest years of his short life, for his own use as soloist, and are excellent examples of his characteristic style. Perhaps the most popular of the twenty-five works in this form that he has left us is the *Concerto in D Minor,* K. 466. It belongs to a wonderful year of productivity, 1785, when its writer was twenty-nine, about the time when Haydn assured Mozart's father that his son was the greatest composer he knew. The key is a rather rare one with Mozart, and when used in his other works it seemed to signify to him drama.

FIRST MOVEMENT

Here is Romance, of a dark brooding type, as felt in the very first measures; the opening seems to suggest something menacing, and we think of the world of the *G Minor Symphony.* Just before the solo instrument enters another mood is suggested, that of pathos. The pianist's theme, when it does come in, contrasts sharply with what the orchestra has foreshadowed passionately. It is as if (Einstein puts it) "the orchestra represents an anonymous threatening power, and the solo instrument voices an eloquent lament." Much of the dramatic sense of conflict felt throughout this movement develops from the opposition of the orchestra and the solo parts. The end is quiet, but not peaceful.

Here are the principal themes:

1) Allegro
(Strings)

2) Allegro
(Wood Wind)

3) Allegro
(Piano)

SECOND MOVEMENT

Mozart entitles this, unusually, a "Romanze." There is something sweet, almost fragile, in it; and we find, for a time at least, amid the suave orchestration — strings, wood winds, and horns — the peace that seemed so unsure when the first movement's conflict ruled. But in the course of this Romanze, which is in rondo form (the gentle theme appearing at measures 1, 68, and 119), there is a return of the fierce romantic spirit of the first movement, in the strange middle section (measures 90–119). Here there are brief, tense, repeated passages in which the orchestration, instead of being extended, is concentrated into the wildness of a few instruments; remarkable craftsmanship is shown, in displaying the cutting, driving power of the reeds. In the last section peace reigns, the piano uttering a parting sigh.

THIRD MOVEMENT

The finale is again in rondo form, with the trumpets and drums restored, that had been omitted in the Romanze. Its principal theme begins:

Thus is recalled the intensity of spirit, and something of the passion, of the *G Minor Symphony*. The first contrasting theme is also in the minor, beginning:

The second of the contrasting themes sings happily in the major:

On its return this theme appears in the minor, and the sky is clouded. After the cadenza, the first idea is momentarily recalled, before the clouds finally roll away, the wood winds echoing the cheerful three-octave tune in sunny cordiality.

BERNARD SHAW ON MOZART

In one of the best descriptions of the Mozart style ever written, Bernard Shaw [1] says that nothing but the finest execution — beautiful, expressive, and intelligent — will serve for this music. The phrases look straightforward and clear, but a deviation of a hair's breadth from perfection shows up immediately, though the music

[1] *Music in London — 1890–1894* (London: Constable).

sounds so obvious that it seems as if anyone could do it. But it is "impossible to make an effect with Mozart, to work up an audience by playing on their hysterical susceptibilities. It is still as true as it was before the *Eroica Symphony* existed that there is nothing better in art than Mozart's best. We have had Beethoven, Schubert, Mendelssohn, Schumann, and Brahms since his time . . . but the more they have left the Mozart quartet or quintet behind, the further it comes out ahead in its perfection of temper and refinement of consciousness. In the ardent regions where all the rest are excited and vehement, Mozart alone is completely self-possessed: where they are clutching their bars with a grip of iron and forging them with Cyclopean blows, his gentleness of touch never deserts him: he is considerate, economical, practical, under the same pressure that throws your Titan into convulsions. We all in our barbarism have a relish for the strenuous: your tenor whose B flat is like the bursting of a boiler always brings down the house, even when the note brutally effaces the song; and the composer who can artistically express in music a transport of vigor and passion of the more muscular kind, such as the Finale to the *Seventh Symphony* of Beethoven, or the *Ride of the Valkyrie* of Wagner, is always a hero with the interpreter in music. . . . With Mozart you are safe from inebriety. Hurry, excitement, eagerness, loss of consideration are to him purely comic or vicious states of mind. . . . Give me the artist who breathes the true Parnassian air like a native and goes about his work in it as quietly as a common man goes about his ordinary business. Mozart did so; and that is why I like him. Even if I did not, I should pretend to; for a taste for his music is a mark of caste among musicians, and should be worn, like a tall hat, by the amateur who wishes to pass for a true Brahmin."

While it is hardly necessary to follow Shaw's whimsical suggestion and feign a liking and understanding of Mozart's music, this will gradually assume its proper place in the repertoire of the listening amateur if we give it a chance. Acquiring a taste for Mozart is an invaluable experience, if for no other reason than the sensing of the value of a consummate perfection of workmanship in art.

HAYDN THE PATHFINDER

It was Haydn who gave Mozart the form of the quartet and symphony that he was so quickly to make his own. We cannot remind ourselves too often that Haydn was the composer who first used the orchestra in its modern sense and who developed the general type of music which it was to play. Basing his work on the experiments carried out by earlier men (notably Carl Philipp Emanuel Bach, a son of the great Johann Sebastian Bach, and the various conductors of the orchestra at the ducal court at Mannheim), Haydn laid out

Franz Josef Haydn

From a drawing made in 1794

a plan for the symphony which we still use today — that of writing it in four movements, each with a different form. Particularly important was his scheme for the working out of a plan for the first movement — the sonata form, as we have come to call it. He it was who introduced the Minuet, a dance in great favor with court circles at the time, into the symphony as its third movement. The type of orchestration which he adopted after long experimentation has remained in general use up to the present: instead of arranging his orchestra as a general unit and giving parts rather indiscriminately to all the instruments, no matter what their individual tone might be, Haydn separated his band into groups (we call them "choirs"), each of them having a special significance in the make-up of the whole. And he uses these "choirs" according to their significance: strings alternate with wood winds for special dialogue effects, for instance, instead of always combining with them as they did in the orchestra of Johann Sebastian Bach; contrasts of timbre and tone are frequent, with many sudden changes and rather whimsical turns throughout the music. It was this general scheme which Mozart adopted, adding some instruments to it and polishing it up as to style and finish; Beethoven took it up in turn and passed it on to the later composers — Liszt, Berlioz, Wagner, and Strauss — for their further development. We could also call Haydn the father of the string quartet, for he chose the four instruments that are used in this combination and marked out for them a type of music well suited to the display of their essential traits.

Naturally when compared to the heaven-storming work of his followers, Beethoven and Brahms, or even the more perfect compositions of his friend and contemporary, Mozart, Haydn's writing sounds a bit uneven and experimental, especially in those passages which we call "bridge passages," uniting the themes in the various movements. He had not learned how to lead gradually and almost imperceptibly from one theme to another, as Beethoven knew so well how to do. Some of Haydn's phrases lack the concentrated perfection of Mozart's writing; but there is always a fresh, spontaneous quality about Haydn's work that makes it most acceptable to us today. Of Teutonic stock, he was brought up in a humble atmosphere abounding in Croatian and Hungarian folk songs with plenty of rhythm and gracious melody; and it was natural that he should introduce the idiom of these songs into his music. There is a certain sincerity and often a depth of feeling in his work that is suggestive of the great Romanticist, Beethoven. Haydn perhaps may have been somewhat more of a "common" man than was Mozart, but for that reason he is often a very likable one.

HAYDN'S *"Surprise" Symphony*

He shows this likable quality in a remarkable degree in his *"Surprise" Symphony,* to which the Germans gave the nickname *Paukenschlag* and the French, *Battement de timbales.* The "surprise" is not, to modern ears, much of a shock. It is just a loud chord suddenly interpolated in a soft part of the slow movement, supposed to wake up sleepy listeners, but in reality a bit of showmanship. We must remember that this symphony was designed for Haydn's London season of 1792, when he had to do everything possible to direct attention to his concerts.

FIRST MOVEMENT

The symphony, scored for flutes, oboes, bassoons, horns, trumpets, and drum in pairs, and the usual string parts, begins with his favorite slow introduction, a device he used so often and Mozart so rarely. The tone is grave, and the climbing chromaticism bespeaks the arrival of the Romantic age. The *Vivace* movement to which this is the preface has a first theme closely allied to that of the slow introduction's opening:

Its easy-going gaiety echoes some figurations from the introduction. Haydn has fun joining together his two themes: indeed, he is already developing ideas before the expected Development section is due. He seems to play a "false alarm" trick at measure 54, but it is just his way of leading out the second theme, which waltzes in at measure 69:

Very soon a third theme follows, restful, *dolce:*

And so he goes on to the Development (at measure 109), which, although it consists of less than fifty measures, has the usual delicious diversity of keys and contains some quite strenuous, even fierce, music. In the Recapitulation we find Haydn reaching his waltz theme earlier than before, in order to bring in some new development — a device characteristic of his methods of composing; and changed figurations in the accompaniment will be noticed, a new combination of thematic material (measures 196–200) and a feeling of his being about to work this into a long final coda. But the third theme duly makes its reappearance, to crown all with a benevolent farewell. The actual coda comprises but a few measures of definitive ending.

SECOND MOVEMENT

The slow movement consists of a set of variations on a tune that was then well known; the version nowadays familiar is set to the words "Ah, vous dirai-je, maman" (the plowman whistles this tune in Haydn's oratorio *The Seasons*).

The surprise comes at the sixteenth measure. In the first variation the decorative elements are simple, sufficient, and perfectly obvious. In the second comes a typical Haydn outburst, in the minor key, with the two halves of the tune treated quite differently. This, a frequent device in variations, makes what is called a "double." The variation ends with a tiny cadenza. In Variation 3, the strings and wood wind duet together, and the flute sings a new melody.

In the fourth there is more diversity: large chords and a broad swing mark its outer features, and a much milder tone its inner ones. The coda artistically carries on for a short time in the swashbuckling style; then there is a pull-up, as if a new section were to begin or (if this had been a concerto) as if a cadenza were to be inserted. But it is only one of Haydn's genial false alarms. Some sweet, new, forward-looking romantic harmonies delicately put the theme to rest.

THIRD MOVEMENT

The swinging, countrified *Ländler* spirit of the Minuet reminds us that Haydn was a man of the people. He neatly avoids squaretoedness in phrase lengths and shows a delightful amount of variety in his keys. The two sections of the Minuet (before the Trio comes) make a hearty little piece, complete in itself.

The Trio uses the same sort of running figure that we heard as the second part of the Minuet began, but it is now reversed — upside down. Bassoon and flute get their turn. This Trio is so shaped that it, too, is by itself complete, forming a short three-part piece of the "sandwich" order (which could be lettered A B A, the B bit being briefly developed into eleven measures, against the A's eight).

FINALE

This is in what we know as sonata-rondo form, partaking of the nature of both these forms; this is a very common structure for symphonic finales in the eighteenth century. Haydn begins lightly:

The orchestra comes in gradually as he develops this first idea right away. This development takes the place of what might usually be expected, some kind of bridge to the second theme, which enters at measure 75, demurely, accompanied by the twinkling figure from the start of the main theme:

Very quickly No. 1 is back again, for an extremely short visit; in the middle part of the movement there is a development along the lines of the first theme, in which string ejaculations are uttered in various keys, while the wind instruments leap about. At measure 140 Haydn feigns a Recapitulation, but the chase is still afoot, with new hedges to jump, the real Recapitulation coming in at measure 182. In this the first theme is cut short by ten measures, while the second gets short shrift too. The coda comes at measure 226, with deceptive quietness; in it there is one final scurry over hill and dale with a few final "Hollos!" before the wild chase comes to its end.

HAYDN'S HUMANISM

In the slow introduction to the *Clock Symphony* (a work also written for the London concerts of the impresario Salomon) we have an opportunity for observing the depth of feeling that has been suggested as characteristic of Haydn at times. This introduction is full of a grave beauty that is an excellent foil to the graceful theme which immediately follows it; the rest of the movement is in the usual sonata form. The second movement is that which gives the work its popular name, for the repeated chords of the accompaniment are very suggestive of the slow ticking of a clock. Over this is heard a sedately shaped melody of great charm, typically eighteenth-century music. The whole thing is especially human and understandable. After the usual Minuet, we come to the rapid last movement; here it will be interesting to try to determine the formal scheme used — is it sonata form or rondo?

HAYDN AND MOZART COMPARED

Sacheverell Sitwell in his little book on Mozart, a book that contains some strange inconsistencies, as well as much that is good, has a neat word to say as to the differences between the music of Haydn and that of Mozart — differences which are easier to feel than they are to describe. "If music is loved for its simple and pure qualities," he says,[2] "unmixed with introspection and self-analysis, the best of Haydn's symphonies are as beautiful as anything that the civilization of Europe has given us. Their clean, neat workmanship; the manner in which the simplest things of life are taken up and charged with humor and poetry; the grace and liveliness of his minuets; the speed and brilliance of the finales. Mozart is more delicate, less earthly; his perfection of beauty is to be found in the *andante* (the slow movement). There he has an angelic, a seraphic tranquillity; a peace in which, as it were, you could hear Haydn breathe. In the Minuet and Trio Haydn is always predominant; in the hands of Mozart the Minuet is very often the subject of a courtly and aristocratic sadness; with Haydn it is a true dance which touches the blood. The Trio grows out of it, not merely stands in contrast with it, and it sometimes has the character and force of a

2 From *Mozart* by Sacheverell Sitwell, quoted here by kind permission of Appleton-Century-Crofts, publishers.

Ländler or Viennese waltz; when the Minuet comes back again after the Trio, it is with the grateful comfort of music heard once more that might have gone forever."

Mr. Sitwell thinks, and with good reason, that the physical contrasts of the two men have a great deal to do with these differences: Haydn was a strong, peasant sort of man, robust, straightforward, with an unspoiled childhood back of him and the good chance of a strong maturity before him; Mozart's childhood had been spent playing at all the courts of Europe. His hectic life, the fact that he was always pressed for money, that he must have realized that his earthly course was to be soon run, give a nervousness and a sadness to much of his music, even as they add, of course, an aristocratic distinction and polish to it. The richness, quickness, and facility of his invention are inevitably felt in everything that Mozart wrote; they are the hallmarks of his inimitable style. Haydn went more slowly and for that reason very often goes more deeply and more convincingly into the emotions.

LIST OF SUGGESTED MUSIC [3]

C Major Symphony, No. 34   Mozart
Eine kleine Nachtmusik   Mozart
Symphony in D Major   Mozart
Symphony in G Minor   Mozart
Piano Concerto in D Minor   Mozart
Surprise Symphony   Haydn
Clock Symphony   Haydn

TOPICS FOR FURTHER DISCUSSION

Following on the section "Haydn and Mozart Compared," can you add some impressions of your own as to the clear distinctions between (a) the aims and (b) the styles of these composers? How far were

[3] The piano scores of the first four works in this list are available in the Breitkopf edition. Orchestral scores (miniature size) are in both the Philharmonia and the Eulenburg editions.

The piano scores of the Surprise Symphony and the Clock Symphony are in the following editions: Breitkopf, Universal, Schirmer (edited by Daniel Gregory Mason), Ditson (edited by Percy Goetschius) No. 1 (Surprise only).

The orchestral miniature scores are in the Kalmus editions: Surprise, No. 25; Clock, No. 106.

their aims determined by the differing circumstances of their life and work? This point, about the influence of a composer's circumstances upon his work, might be discussed in relation to others, both earlier and later than Haydn and Mozart.

What do you consider one of the strongest formal elements in Haydn's finales — one that is rarer in Mozart's?

By referring to the scores, compare the orchestration of the following: Wagner's *Götterdämmerung*, Beethoven's *Fifth Symphony*, Mozart's *G Minor Symphony*, Haydn's *Surprise Symphony*.

DEFINITE SUGGESTIONS FOR READING

Music in History: Franz Josef Haydn
"In Search of Mozart"

OPERA:

ITS VARIOUS STYLES

MOZART'S *Don Giovanni* AN EXAMPLE

Haydn and Mozart both wrote operas, Haydn eleven and Mozart twenty-two. Most of Haydn's were written for production in the little opera house of his patron's sumptuous establishment at Esterhazy, built by Prince Nicholas Esterhazy in an attempt to outdo the glories of the French kings at Versailles. They were entertainment music pure and simple, written in the conventional Italian style of the time and contributing little to the development of this popular form. Mozart's, leaving out the early boyish works written in Italy, not only summarize the best achievements of this style of writing up to their time but also start a new era, one which greatly influenced all those operatic writers who followed him. They comprise works in both the types then general: *opera seria,* treating mythological and heroic-historical subjects with the grace and elegance peculiar to their time and made up of long, florid melodic arias, recitative, and a few ensemble numbers; and *opera buffa* — light opera — which arose out of the desire to parody and lighten the serious character of grand opera. In order to understand their particular significance, it will be necessary to take a brief backward glance historically at the origins of this dramatico-musical form.

THE BEGINNINGS

The beginning of the art form that we know as *opera* — a peculiar hybrid born of the union of music and the drama — may be traced to the type of musical declamation used by the Greeks in reciting their poetry and in producing their great dramas. The modern opera as we know it came into being during the exciting days of the Renaissance through the endeavors of a group of Florentine noblemen. These musical amateurs, possessing the characteristic enthusiasm of the period for the culture of the Greeks, tried to write music in imitation of the Greek declamation; the result was a work that may be fairly said to have been the first opera — *Eurydice* by Peri and Caccini, produced in 1600. But long before that the eternal human passion for dressing up and enacting dramas (many of them containing bits of music) began to show the way towards a final union of the two forms. The medieval miracle and mystery plays contained music, and they must have turned the attention of composers toward a possible music-drama union. Italian soil was particularly fruitful, and when the madrigal had reached the great heights of its development and no more could be done in that direction, the influence of songs inserted into stage comedies, and of the *dramma pastorale,* permeated Italian thought about the stage in the sixteenth century. The intricate weavings of the music of the madrigals made their poetry of little account, and people were wanting fresh emotional interest in their music. Drama took hold of the imagination, and the solo voice, always beloved by the Italians, began to seek mastery. The solo song with lute accompaniment was very popular as a form of musical expression during the late sixteenth and early seventeenth centuries: Dowland's "Awake, Sweet Love" is a fine example of this new interest in music for the single voice. Harmony instead of counterpoint (that is, the thinking of music in vertical terms rather than in terms of horizontal weaving) had its chance; and the orchestra crept into being. Instead of thought in the mass, and singing in the mass, there was more and more interest in individual thought and performance. The round date 1600 is an easy one to remember, but the gradual growth of the idea of what we call opera during the whole sixteenth century must be kept in mind. There was no sudden birth.

Nearly all the composers of vocal music up to that time had been singers. Monteverdi, the first extensive prober of the possibilities of the new form, was almost the first composer who was not a singer. Some of his harmonies were wonderfully fresh, and he experimented valiantly with orchestration, using the heterogeneous collection of instruments that came to his hand. The form of the opera was of

The Opéra in Paris

The festive interior of one of the world's great opera houses

no importance at first — almost the whole work was written in a sort of recitative. Only gradually were the mechanics of this new union of drama and speech worked out. The *recitative* — a sort of tonal declamation in imitation of dramatic speech, with a very spare instrumental accompaniment — was found to be the best means for carrying on the dramatic action, while the *aria* — a set song with richer orchestral accompaniment — was used for displaying reflective emotion. The various solo voices were grouped into different combinations — duets, trios, quartets — while the chorus took a subordinate part. Characteristic themes were employed, and the orchestration devised so as to introduce dramatic effects.

THE EARLY DEVELOPMENTS

The great advances made by Monteverdi over the original ideas of Peri and Caccini may be realized by comparing such an aria as *Funeste piaggie* from the setting which they made of *Eurydice* ("Ye dismal hillsides, how lonely and sad you are without Eurydice") with Monteverdi's *Ecco purch' a voi ritorno* from his setting of the same story, called *Orfeo*. In this latter, which is sung as Orpheus realizes that his Eurydice will never return to him, we recognize a much greater freedom of melody and sense of dramatic strength. The great era of dramatic music begins with Monteverdi. The vanity of singers, fanned by popular applause, before long carried the vocal floriations which composers had introduced into their arias to great excesses. The singers were not content to sing what the composers had given them but had to enrich and embroider this with all sorts of vocal gymnastics and ornaments. The composers raged, but in vain; they had to give the public what it demanded, and the form of the opera became exceedingly popular. Opera houses were opened — at Venice in 1637, in London in 1656, and in Paris in 1669. From a recreation of the nobility, opera became the joy of the masses. Names we may remember in this Italian development of the early opera are, besides Peri and Caccini and Monteverdi, Cavalli, Cesti, Caldara, Stradella. And there were many others who were writing in this new mode.

EARLY DEVELOPMENTS OUTSIDE ITALY

Lully carried these new ideas to France, and started opera there under royal patronage. The French loved the ballet, and that soon played a strong part in their adaptation of the style. Early French operatic writers were not so brilliant as those of Italy, and there are fewer really distinctive names to remember, those of Destouches and Campra being among them.

Germany got the operatic taste from Italy, too, and opera houses were built in Hamburg and Vienna, with native composers to provide music for them. England developed her operatic ideas from the liking for the masque, that aristocratic entertainment of poetry, dancing, music, and scenic display that was cultivated before the Civil War. After the Restoration of Charles II (1660) we note, as an operatic landmark, Purcell's *Dido and Aeneas*. Handel, a German composer who lived in England and wrote Italian operas, composed a whole series of works for London, beginning with *Rodrigo* in 1706. He largely swamped English effort, but was not the man to realize the need for reform in the artificial, singer-dominated form he used.

Gluck was the one who attempted this Herculean task of making the opera a truer, more dramatic unity. Like Wagner, Gluck learned

as he went along, beginning in the Italian style, whose artificiality
he sought to leaven with finer art. He was in Vienna in 1746 when
he was just over thirty, and for sixteen years he developed mastery
of his medium in such works as *Alcestis, Orpheus, Paris and Helen,
Iphigenia in Aulis,* and *Iphigenia in Tauris.* The overture, from
being a movement dramatically unimportant and even unrelated,
became something to "prepare the audience for the action of the
opera, and serve as a sort of argument to it," as Gluck puts it. But
old habits were too strong, and after his death, Gluck's reforms did
not endure. No finer example of this composer's success in achieving dramatic feeling in his music could be found than the great
aria *Che faro senza Euridice* ("I Have Lost My Eurydice") from
Orpheus. It will be interesting to compare this with versions by
earlier composers.

Mozart wrote his first Italian *opera buffa, La finta semplice,* at the
age of twelve in Vienna; but it was during his three journeys to
Italy during the years 1769–1772 that his style came to fruition in
three operas commissioned for performance in Milan. Later works

Interior of the Theater of the Margrave of Bayreuth

Built in 1744 by the Italians, Galli and Biebiena, it is one of the best
Baroque interiors in Europe.

followed for production in Munich, Vienna, and Prague, for which music-loving city the greatest of his works, *Don Giovanni,* was written in 1787. No better representative of the Italian school at its best can be found than this opera, called by some critics the world's greatest work of art.

MOZART'S *Don Giovanni*

It deals with a more-or-less traditional story of Don Giovanni (Don Juan), a dissolute Spanish nobleman whose insatiable pursuit of women induces a life of crime, for which he pays with an untimely death at the ghostly hand of a man whom he has murdered. What makes Mozart's treatment of this not-too-subtle story the towering achievement it is, is the wonderful psychological portrayal of the various characters involved in the drama and his profound universal wisdom as to the forces which seem to motivate man's actions. All commentators agree that this unique work of genius combines the powers of drama and music to "depict the most fundamental and subtle relationships of life, religion, and morals."

It constitutes a standard work, perhaps more so than any other single opera, in the world's great opera houses; fortunately it has been wonderfully recorded by an ensemble that could be heard in few places today, carefully directed for musical and technical perfection. A fine idea of this work can be gained by following this excellent recording in its entirety or even in such a condensed version as we give here, a version which, although it leaves out some of the great ensemble scenes that give a festive contrast to the grim events, does show the styles of Italian recitative, aria, and duet at their best. The excellent translation, which closely follows the Italian original of Da Ponte, Mozart's librettist, is by Edward J. Dent, published by the Oxford University Press. It is by far the best English version available.

A CONDENSATION OF *Don Giovanni*

Libretto by Da Ponte　　　*Music by Mozart*

CAST OF CHARACTERS (in the order of their appearance)

LEPORELLO, servant to Don Giovanni, *Bass*
DONNA ANNA, betrothed to Don Ottavio, *Soprano*
DON GIOVANNI, licentious young nobleman, *Baritone*

THE COMMENDATORE, father of Donna Anna, *Bass*
DON OTTAVIO, friend of Don Giovanni, *Tenor*
DONNA ELVIRA, a lady of Burgos, deserted by Don Giovanni, *Soprano*
ZERLINA, peasant girl (*Soprano*), betrothed to
MASETTO, a peasant, *Bass*
Chorus of Peasants and Demons
The scene is laid in Seville of the seventeenth century.

ACT I
Leporello is discovered assisting his master in one of his many intrigues. Pursuing Donna Anna, daughter of the Commandant of the Knights of Malta, the young roué is interrupted by the Commandant and kills him. Anna's betrothed, Ottavio, swears vengeance.

Don Giovanni, meeting by chance an old flame, Donna Elvira, leaves her to Leporello, who reads her a list of his master's amours:

LEP.:
Pray allow me! Let me draw your attention
To this long list of names and addresses —
A complete list of all his adventures.
Take a seat, ma'am, and read with me,
Here you are, ma'am, come read with me.
Here is Italy, six hundred and forty,
Next comes Germany, more than two hundred,
France and Turkey have each over ninety,
Oh, but in Spain here, one thousand and three.
Here are country girls in plenty,
Ladies' maids and would-be ladies,
The nobility and gentry,
This for royalty the page is.
Handsome, ugly, high or humble,

All are women, all for him.
Hear him court one, carefully choosing
Words appropriate to her complexion:
If she's darkfaced, she'll be faithful;
Fair in color, kind and gentle.
In December plump he'll have them,
In July prefers them slender.
Is the lady like a Maypole,
Then he'll call her tall and stately.
When she's tiny, he calls her fairy.
Ev'n the elderly, those between two ages,
He'll find room for in these pure pages.
But his favorite form of sinning
Is with one who's just beginning.

Otherwise it never matters
Who she is or what's her name;
She need only be a female,
Don Giovanni plays his game!

Two peasants, Zerlina and Masetto, about to be married, appear with their friends. Giovanni, telling his servant to take the party to see his palace, is left with Zerlina and proceeds to woo her.

Duet: Don Giovanni and Zerlina

D.G.: You'll lay your hand in mine, dear,
Softly you'll whisper, "Yes";
'Tis not so far to go, dear,

Your heart is mine, confess.

Z.: What answer shall I make him?
My heart will not be still.
I'd love to be a lady;
Surely he means no ill.

D.G.: Come, then, my fairest treasure!

Z.: Masetto'll ne'er forgive me!

D.G.: I'll give you wealth and pleasure.

Z.: Surely you'll not deceive me?

D.G.: You'll come, you'll come!

Z.: I will!

BOTH: Where youth and love invite us,
With pleasure to delight us,
Of joy we'll take our fill!

As they are going off arm in arm, Elvira appears to denounce him. He tries to pooh-pooh her accusations to Anna and Ottavio, who suddenly appear, as those of a mad woman.

Masked, the two injured women and Don Ottavio gain admission to the festivity in the palace. From the room into which Don Giovanni has taken Zerlina are heard cries for help. Giovanni rushes out, pretending that Leporello is the guilty one. Though menaced by the whole company, Giovanni makes his escape.

ACT II

A street, with an inn. *Duet:* Don Giovanni and Leporello

D.G.: Now then, you rascal,
What's that you say?

LEP.: My lord, I tell you,
I will not stay!

D.G.: Oh, that's all nonsense!

LEP.: I'll stay no longer.

D.G.: Well, what's the matter?
Why will you leave me?

LEP.: Oh, nothing much, sir.
You nearly killed me.

D.G.: 'Twas only joking,
I've told you so.

LEP.: My lord, I'm serious,
I mean to go.

D.G.: No, then, you rascal,
Don't talk such nonsense!

	Why, what's the matter?
	'Twas only joking!
LEP.:	I give you notice,
	As from today, sir.
	No, no, no, no,
	I mean to go, sir!
	I beg to let you know,
	I'll not stay, sir,
	I mean to go.
D.G.:	Damn you, you rascal!
	What's that you say?
	Why, what's the matter?
	You shall not go.
LEP.:	My lord, I tell you,
	I will not stay.
	My lord, I'm very serious,
	I mean to go!

(He tries to go. Don Giovanni detains him.)

D.G.:	Leporello!
LEP.:	Did you speak, sir?
D.G.:	Come here, I've something for you, take it.

(Gives him money.)

LEP.:	What, sir?
D.G.:	Four gold pieces.
LEP.:	Thank your lordship. Just for this once I'll accept your condescension; but you must understand, sir, that a gentleman of parts like myself is not like a woman, to be seduced with money.
D.G.:	Say no more about that. Have you got parts enough to execute my orders?
LEP.:	If you'll have done with women.
D.G.:	Have done with women!

Have done with women? What next? You know they're as necessary to me as my food and drink are, or the air I'm breathing.

LEP.:	And you've the heart, sir, to deceive every one of them!
D.G.:	Because I love them! If to one I were faithful, how unfair to the others! Such is the extent of my amatory feelings, I love them all and sundry! But women have no head for mathematics, and my infinity they confuse with infidelity.
LEP.:	My lord, I am no scholar, but whatever you call it, it has no equal! Now, sir, what can I do for you?
D.G.:	Listen! Did you observe the waiting-woman of Donna Elvira?
LEP.:	No, sir.
D.G.:	Where were your eyes, man? 'Twas a rare piece of beauty, my worthy Leporello. With this fair damsel I shall now try my fortune. 'Tis getting dark now, and the thought has struck me, I might be more attractive in appearance if I were to put on your hat and cloak, sir.
LEP.:	May I ask the reason,

why you won't wear your own, sir?

D.G.: Women in service don't always look with favor on birds of noble feather. (*Takes off his cloak.*) Off with them, quickly!

LEP.: My lord, for several reasons —

D.G.: (*angrily*) Have done with you! I'll stand no contradiction!

(*They exchange cloaks.*)

Donna Elvira appears at the window. It gradually becomes dark.

Trio

D. ELV.: Ah, why do I remember
How fondly once I loved him?
He left me, the base deceiver;
To love him now were sin!

LEP.: Softly, my lord, and listen,
That voice is Donn' Elvira's.

D.G.: Ah, then I'll seize the moment.
Stand there while I begin.

(*He stands behind Leporello.*)

My own adored Elvira!

D. ELV.: 'Tis Don Giovanni calling!

D.G.: Yes, dearest, I am calling,
Your pity I entreat.

D. ELV.: Ah! what is this that moves me,
Moves me to listen to him,
Moves me so strangely to listen?

LEP.: Soon we shall see the woman
Fall at his very feet.

D.G.: Come down, my heart's desire,
Come down and I will show you
How madly I adore you,
If only you'll be kind!

D. ELV.: I'll not believe a word you say.

D.G.: Be mine, again!

D. ELV.: Not a word, sir!

D.G.: (*excitedly, almost in tears*) Or you'll kill me!

LEP.: If this goes on much longer,
Soon I shall burst with laughter.

* * * * *

D.G.: Truth in my heart you'll find!

D. ELV.: Too sorely I am tempted!

D.G.: How quickly she is tempted!

LEP.: Soon by his words she's tempted!

D. ELV.: Shall I be firm or follow?
Have mercy, have mercy, Heaven,
On my poor trusting heart!

(*She disappears from the window.*)

D.G.: She cannot choose but follow!

There's no one to surpass me
At playing such a part!

LEP.: All when he calls must follow;
Have mercy, have mercy, Heaven,
On her poor trusting heart!

D.G.: (*in great spirits*) Now, what d'you think of that?

LEP.: If you ask me, sir, I think you're worse than heartless.

D.G.: I think you are a blockhead. Listen a moment, she will be here directly; then you must run to meet her, talk to her in a whisper, so that she thinks 'tis my voice. Then do the best you can to get her away into a safe place.

LEP.: But, my lord —

D.G.: Dare you answer me?

LEP.: But suppose she discovers?

D.G.: Well, if she finds you out, 'twill be your own fault. Hush!
She's coming, now be wary!

(*He runs off to the side, leaving Leporello alone; Donna Elvira enters from the house, she advances to meet Leporello; Don Giovanni watches their movements from the side.*)

D. ELV.: Dearest, I'm coming.

D.G.: (*aside*) I'll watch what she will do.

LEP.: (*aside*) Here's a fine stew.

D. ELV.: So at last your stony heart has been melted by my tears and my prayers? You have repented, my dearest Don Giovanni, and to the woman you loved you're now returning?

LEP.: Yes, my dearest!

D. ELV.: If only you could know what misery, what suffering and anguish you have caused me!

LEP.: I caused you anguish?

D. ELV.: You did.

LEP.: My adored one! Can I bear to think of it?

D. ELV.: You won't desert me now?

LEP.: How could you ask me!

D. ELV.: You'll always be my love?

LEP.: Always!

D. ELV.: My very own!

LEP.: My very own! (*Aside*) This part has its attractions.

D. ELV.: How I love you!

LEP.: I worship you!

D. ELV.: I am all fire and flame for you!

LEP.: I'm burnt to ashes.

D.G.: (*aside*) They're growing rather too warm!

D. ELV.: And you will not deceive me?

LEP.: No, of course not.

D. ELV.: So swear to me.

LEP.: By this sweet hand I

swear it, I swear it by these kisses I print upon it.

D.G.: (*pretends to waylay them*) Your money or your life!

D. ELV.: O heavens!

LEP.: O heavens!

(*Elvira and Leporello run away.*)

D.G.: Your money or your life! I think the tide of fortune's turning. Where are we? There's a light in the window — now for some music!

Canzonetta

Look down from out your window, I now implore you,
O fairest of the fair, and hear my sighs!
Your favor grant to me, who stands before you,
Or here your own dear eyes will see me dying.
Though honey sweet lies hidden deep in roses,
Sweeter far is the honey your mouth discloses!
No longer, lady fair, to me be cruel,
Throw me one glance, I pray, my lovely jewel!
There's someone at the window; I can see her.
(*Blows kiss.*)

Masetto enters, armed with gun and pistol, followed by several armed peasants. He attempts to beat up Don Giovanni but gets drubbed himself. Zerlina comes in and comforts him:

Aria

If you will promise me not to mistrust me,
I have a remedy will make you well.
It will not hurt you, you're sure to like it,
But what its name is I shall not tell.
You may not ask for it, you cannot buy it,
It is a remedy no one will sell.
Where do I keep it? Would you know more?

(*Laying his hand on her heart*)

Feel what is beating here, there is my store.

(*Exeunt Zerlina and Masetto.*)

Ottavio and Anna reveal to Elvira that her beloved is a murderer. Ottavio renews his pledge to avenge the Commandant.

Giovanni leaps over the wall of a churchyard containing the statue of the Commendatore.

D.G.: (*laughing*) Ha, ha! Here's a fine place for a game of hide and seek! How bright the moon is! Why, 'tis clearer than daylight, just the night to go a-hunting for pretty little ladies! What time is it? I do not think it has yet struck eleven. I'm longing to know what the end of the story was, how Leporello fared with Donna Elvira, if he managed it nicely!

(*Leporello appears on the wall.*)

LEP.: (*aside*) I'm convinced that he meant to let me in for it.

D.G.: Why, there he is. Oh, Leporello!

LEP.: (*from the wall*) Who's that calling?

D.G.: Don't you know your own master?

LEP.: I wish I'd never known him.

D.G.: That's ungrateful!

LEP.: Oh, is that you? Beg pardon.

D.G.: What has happened?

LEP.: On your account I was nearly put in prison.

D.G.: Well, wasn't it an honor to be taken for me?

LEP.: My lord, I thank you!

D.G.: Come on, make haste, come here. I've got a good piece of news for you.

LEP.: What are you doing here?

D.G.: Come in and I'll tell you. I've had several adventures since you left me to talk to Donna Elvira, but I'll tell you them later; only the prettiest of all you shall hear.

LEP.: About a lady?

D.G.: Well, of course, 'twas quite a young thing, but she knew how to carry herself well, when I saw her. So I approached her, I took her by the hand; she wasn't willing, so I talked to her softly and she mistook me — can you guess?

LEP.: No, I can't.

D.G.: For Leporello.

LEP.: For me?

D.G.: For you.

LEP.: A compliment!

D.G.: It was she who took me by the hand then.

LEP.: Better and better!

D.G.: She caressed me, and kissed me, called me her dear Leporello, Leporello, her own love! I saw at once that she was one of your conquests.

LEP.: Oh, curses on him!

D.G.: I did not waste my chances, but then somehow she recognized me; called out — people heard her, and I had to desert her. As luck would have it, I climbed a wall and came down safe inside here.

LEP.: And you tell me this as a pretty sort of story?

D.G.: And why not?

LEP.: But suppose the lady were my own wife?

D.G.: Better and better! (*Laughs loudly*)

STATUE: Before tomorrow's dawn your laughter's ended.

D.G.: Who spoke then?

LEP.: Oh, that must have been some ghost from the other world who knows all about you.

D.G.: *(puts his hand to his sword, looks about among the tombs, and strikes at some of the statues)* Stop that fooling! Who is there? Who is there?

STATUE: Be silent, blasphemer! Leave the dead to their slumber!

LEP.: There, I said so!

D.G.: More likely 'tis some merry fellow trying to fool us. (*With indifference*) Ah! that must be the statue of the late Commendatore. Tell me what's that written below?

LEP.: Beg pardon, I'm not much of a scholar, especially by moonlight.

D.G.: Read, I tell you.

LEP.: *(reads)* "I wait in prayer and patience until my murderer by his own act is punished." Did you hear, sir? How dreadful!

D.G.: Ridiculous old gentleman! Tell him to come to supper with me this very evening.

LEP.: Are you mad? Can you think — oh, look, sir, how he seems to be glaring at us with his eyes! You'd almost think he heard you, that he was going to speak!

D.G.: Do as I say, or else I'll kill you and bury you as well, too.

LEP.: Oh, my lord, don't be angry! I'll do your bidding.

Duet

LEP.: *(to the statue)* To your most noble effigy, My lord Commendatore —
Oh dear, I'm all a-tremble, I cannot speak a word.

D.G.: Have done with you, do my bidding, Or I shall use my sword.

LEP.: Your whim is too capricious.

D.G.: A rather new sensation!

LEP.: It makes my blood run cold.

D.G.: The fellow's none too bold!

LEP.: My lord presents his compliments, If marble ears can hear them —
Oh, my lord, did you see him? The statue, it threatens with its eyes.

D.G.: Fool, I'll kill you!

LEP.: No, no, pray wait a moment!
My master asks your lordship —
'Tis he that asks, not I, sir —

To sup with him this night.

(*The statue nods its head.*)

Oh, good Lord, this is too dreadful.

He bends his head in answer.

D.G.: Don't talk such silly nonsense!

LEP.: But look, sir, just look, sir,

Look there yourself, I beg you.

D.G.: And what is there to see?

LEP.: He bends his head in answer,

As if he would say yes.

(*Imitates*)

The statue bends its head.

D.G.: (*to the statue*)

So speak then, if you're able,

Commendatore! You'll come to supper?

STATUE: Yes!

LEP.: I cannot stir for terror,

My heart within me falters,

For goodness sake, come quickly,

No longer let us stay!

D.G.: A strange adventure this is,

To ask a statue to come to supper!

I'll order him a fine meal,

So now we must away!

(*Exeunt*)

While Giovanni is getting ready for the feast, there enters Elvira, begging him to amend his ways. He is callous and refuses. As she goes away, she screams; going to see what is the matter, Leporello returns, dismayed, and shuts the door.

LEP.: Oh, my lord, for goodness sake,

Do not one step further take!

All in marble, 'tis the statue!

If you saw him you'd shiver as I do,

If you saw him looking at you,

Heard the noise his footsteps make,

Ta, ta, ta, ta!

D.G.: What does all this nonsense mean?

LEP.: Ta, ta, ta, ta!

D.G.: You are drunk, it seems to me.

(*Knocking heard at the door*)

LEP.: There, sir, listen!

D.G.: Someone's knocking! Open!

LEP.: (*trembling*) I dare not!

D.G.: Go and open!

LEP.: Ah!

D.G.: Quickly!

LEP.: Ah!

D.G.: Coward! Who's making this disturbance?

I shall go myself and see.

LEP.: I've seen quite enough, thank you, sir,

This is not the place for me.

(*Don Giovanni opens the door, Leporello hides under the table. Enter the Statue.*)

COMM.: Don Giovanni, you did
invite me
Here to supper, so bid
me welcome!

D.G.: 'Tis an honor unexpected,
But the best I can, I'll do.
Leporello, clear the table,
Get another supper ready!

LEP.: (*puts his head out from
under the table*)
Oh, my lord, oh, my lord,
This is like the Day of
Judgment!

D.G.: Go, I tell you.

COMM.: Nay, do not go!
They who taste the food
of angels
Eat no more the corrupt
food of mortals,
Far more grave the mes-
sage I bring,
Far more awful the fate I
shall show!

LEP.: I'm a-tremble as if I'd
the ague;
I shall meet with a ter-
rible fate.

D.G.: Pray continue, and tell
me what would you.

COMM.: Hear what I tell you before 'tis too late.

D.G.: So speak on, then, I
listen and wait.

COMM.: You bade me here to
supper,
I bid you now in my turn.
Come, answer me, come,
answer me,
Will you come with me
to supper?

LEP.: No, no, no, no!
Say you've another en-
gagement!

D.G.: Shall it be said of me then
A coward's part I played?

COMM.: Resolve me!

D.G.: I am resolved, sir!

COMM.: You'll come then?

LEP.: Sir, tell him no.

D.G.: I know what I'm doing,
I fear you not, I'll come.

COMM.: Give me your hand upon
it!

D.G.: There it is! My God!

COMM.: 'Tis cold?

D.G.: Not death itself were
colder.

COMM.: Think on your sins, repent them;
Your hour of doom ap-
proaches!

D.G.: (*vainly tries to free him-
self*)
I'll hear of no repentance;
Hence, gibbering ghost!
Avaunt!

COMM.: Think on your sins, repent them!

D.G.: You speak the words of
dotage.

COMM.: Kneel and pray!

D.G.: No!

COMM.: Kneel!

D.G.: No!

COMM.: Pray!

D.G.: No!

COMM.: To God!

D.G.: No! No!

COMM.: Your hour of grace is
past!
(*Sinks below. Flames ap-
pear.*)

D.G.: Trembling has seized on
every limb.
Can this be fear that now
I know?

Whence come those whirl-
ing gusts of flame?

That deadly acrid smell?

DEMONS *(from below)*:

Sinful has all your life
been;

Now take your sin's re-
ward!

D.G.: What are those shapes
which torture me?

What poison burns within
my veins?

And drags my brain to
madness,

And drags me down to
Hell!

LEP.: He writhes in deadly
torture,

And hideous voices call
him.

The ground before him
opens;

Down he must go to
Hell!

DEMONS: Sinful has all your life
been;

Now take your sin's re-
ward.

Come, then, come, then,

Take the reward of sin!

D.G.: Ah! They drag me down
to Hell!

[INTERCHAPTER]

OPERA:

ITS VARIOUS STYLES (*continued*)

DEVELOPMENTS OF THE 18TH AND 19TH CENTURIES

Working in Vienna a little after Mozart was Cimarosa, whose sense of perfection in comedy, as well as his likeness to Mozart's style, may be realized in the popular overture to his opera *The Secret Marriage,* produced in Vienna in 1792. In Italy, Rossini was the grand figure of the early nineteenth century, with Donizetti and Bellini as popular second and third strings. This style of writing culminates in the operas of Verdi, who was born in 1813, the same year as his great contemporary, Richard Wagner. Verdi's works divide naturally into two groups, the earlier, more popular operas such as *Rigoletto, Il Trovatore, La Traviata, La forza del destino,* and the mature *Aïda, Otello,* and *Falstaff.* A close student of Wagner's work, Verdi changed his style in his later works, the last two of which were written after he was seventy-five, employing a richer instrumentation and more dramatic treatment than in the earlier operas with their "salt-box-and-tongs" accompaniment and excessive insistence upon vocal display. Someone has rightly said that Verdi began his career as a composer of operas appealing to the taste of the period and ended it as a writer of works that will live for all time. Even in the mature works, however, it will be noticed that Verdi always keeps the voice supreme, with the orchestra furnishing a subordinate accompaniment — in complete contrast to Wagner's reversing of this process. It is not difficult to hear the Verdi operas; they are popular in every opera house in the world, and most of them have been recorded in full, so that the in-

[452]

quiring student may easily compare the various styles. These selections are characteristic of his mature style:

Credo; Ave Maria; Salce, Salce (Willow Song) from *Otello*

Sul fil d'un soffio etesio (From Secret Caves) from *Falstaff*

After Verdi the Italian traditions were taken up by Puccini, probably the most popular of all the Italian composers at the present time. His many works — the best known are *Manon Lescaut, La Bohème, Tosca,* and *Madam Butterfly* — abound in technical resource, dramatic invention, and power of emotional expression. They are tremendously effective works when seen upon the stage; whether or not we like them depends upon our taste for the Italian operatic conventions. In *Turandot,* which he left unfinished, he seemed to be moving towards new strength.

Mozart's *The Magic Flute* is generally conceded to be the first real German opera, that is, a work treated in the more dramatic, romantic style beloved by the Germans. Wagner, the greatest of all German writers of opera, said that *The Magic Flute* of Mozart laid the foundations and exhausted the possibilities of German opera, which is rather an overstatement in view of what he was to write himself later. Beethoven's one opera, *Fidelio,* has a noble theme (something rare in opera), and he made fine drama of it, human and tender. It was not until Weber that pure German opera found its prophet; and he, with his fine feeling for the German hearth and its affections in legendary heroism and romance, led directly on to Wagner. Weber's operas, *Der Freischütz, Euryanthe,* and *Oberon* (even though the last was written to an English text), may be said to be the first great German operas; Agatha's aria from *Der Freischütz, Wie nahte mir der Schlummer,* is a typical Weber aria.

THE OPERAS OF RICHARD WAGNER

It is impossible to treat adequately of Wagner's contributions to operatic literature in a few paragraphs; his greatest works, *Tristan und Isolde, Götterdämmerung,* and *Die Meistersinger,* transcend the limiting borders of operatic style and must be classified as among the greatest treasures of all music. Put briefly, Wagner was the great reformer of opera; and his ideal was to do away with those operatic traditions which he considered too artificial for real dramatic expression. In place of these accepted forms, he devised a

Photo by Hansa Luftbild

The Opera House at Bayreuth

Built by Wagner for the production of his operas

new one which he called the "music drama" and which in its dramatic elements was founded on the plays of Shakespeare and Schiller, and in its musical elements on the works of Bach and Beethoven. Theoretically the music, the drama, and the staging were of equal importance to his scheme, but in reality the music overshadowed everything else. In order to obviate the overimportance of the voice that was so disturbing an element in the older scheme, Wagner made the orchestra the chief exponent of his dramatic action, weaving its score out of the short and characteristic "leading motives" (*leitmotifs*) definitely associated with various dramatic situations. In fact, these motives in such works as *Götterdämmerung* and *Tristan und Isolde* are woven into such a poignant and expressive musical fabric and form such an eloquent commentary upon the ever-changing dramatic situation as to make the staging and singing almost superfluous.

The actors in these great works of Wagner's use a sort of declamation (*Sprechstimme*, he called it) which has striking dramatic power, but comparatively little musical interest. Consequently most of the operagoers of Wagner's day, as well as some of them today, were at a loss to comprehend the new form, listening, as they did, to the voice for their chief interest. It is the orchestra that tells Wagner's story, and in richness, variety, and impressiveness of effect his scores have never been equaled. He wrote his own librettos, using as subjects various Germanic legends, and these he changed and manipulated to suit his dramatic needs. These librettos may leave something to be desired from the dramatic point of view, for they are full of strange and unnecessary inconsistencies and are often couched in phraseology that is anything but clear. As drama, for instance, the four operas that constitute the cycle of *The Nibelung Ring* (*Das Rheingold, Die Walküre, Siegfried, Götterdämmerung*) are something of monstrosities, built upon motives that are not consistent and which have to be laboriously "explained" at length time and time again. They provide for an excess of dramatic action that sometimes becomes unmanageable, and demand cumbersome spectacular development that is difficult to make convincing. *Tristan und Isolde*, on the other hand, suffers from the absence of varied dramatic motives; it is only in *Die Meistersinger* that Wagner achieved a real balance between dramatic impulse and consequent action. But the more one hears these Wagner operas, the more he realizes that the only function of the libretto is to stimulate musical development, and provide a sustained musico-dramatic element that had never been thought possible before Wagner's time and has never been equaled since.

In Wagner's early works — *Rienzi, The Flying Dutchman, Tannhäuser*, and *Lohengrin* — there may be traced his gradual evolution from a devotee of the grandiose traditions of the German-Italian schools, through various experiments that gave more variety and refinement to his style, to the final achievements of his musical personality. His mature period begins with the first of the Ring cycle, *Das Rheingold*, and continues through the rest of that monumental series, to *Tristan und Isolde, Die Meistersinger*, and *Parsifal*, his last work. In all these, as he himself put it, he tried to get rid of the former mistakes in the form of opera in which the means of expression (the music) was the end, and the end to be expressed (the drama) was made the means. But, in spite of these intentions, the music became so much more important than any of the other elements in the fusion that today we go to the mature operas of Wagner to revel in their music and not because of their dramatic power. As time passes, we see Wagner more and more in correct perspective — as a musical figure of the most colossal proportions.

"He is one of those masterminds that belong to no time and no nation, whose work lives as one of the vital forces of civilization."

Since his death no one has arisen to carry on his work; there have been attempts to write in his style, but the results have been mostly unimportant. Humperdinck, in his two charming operas *Hänsel und Gretel* and *Königskinder,* uses the Wagner idiom with taste. Richard Strauss has written a number of works in a style peculiarly his own, achieving powerful effects without directly imitating the Wagnerian technique. The most important of these are *Salome, Elektra,* and *Der Rosenkavalier,* in which Strauss, an avowed admirer of Mozart, achieved a great and world-wide success.

THE DIFFERENCES OF OPERATIC STYLE

A brief word may well be given as to the essential differences between the several operatic styles, differences which should be taken into account when listening to the various works. We should not expect Wagnerian profundity of thought or greatness of inspiration in the Italian works; nor do we look for Italian simplicity and melodious grace in the German operas. From the very beginnings of the opera, Italians have loved melodic flow and provided opportunities for vocal display and sonority in their works, oftentimes at the sacrifice of dramatic sincerity and musical worth. The Germans, on the other hand, are a much more introspective people dramatically and have demanded above everything else sincerity and musical truth in their operas. Gluck summarized the requirements of opera in this fashion, a summary that has influenced all German writers in this genre — Beethoven, Weber, Wagner, and Strauss: "The true mission of the music is to second the poetry, by strengthening the expression of the sentiments and increasing the interest of the situations, without weakening or interrupting the action by superfluous means for tickling the ear or displaying the agility of fine voices." These requirements have been met in various ways, perhaps most successfully in Wagner's *Die Meistersinger,* an almost perfect equation between dramatic impulse and musical action.

FRENCH OPERA

The French taste in opera was originally borrowed from the Italians; early works stressed the importance of the spectacle and

"Here Comes the Part I Like Best . . . Where They Murder the Soprano."

An American cartoonist here depicts what he considers to be the typical reaction of his countrymen to opera — a social amenity beloved of the ladies, to which men are dragged against their will. As a matter of fact, however, statistics show that opera was more popular in the United States in the year 1950 than it had ever been before.

the ballet, but gradually there was evolved a definite national opera style. Lully realized the possibilities of the *recitative* as a dramatic factor, and made it an essential part in the development of the plot and not just a conventional link between arias and choruses. Rameau's works are now considered by the French to be the foundation stones of their operatic style; these contain more feeling and show much more constructive skill than do the operas of Lully. Gluck's reforms were mostly carried out in Paris and were the chief means by which the course of French operatic development was changed and rescued from Italian influences. The writers of opera during the Romantic period in France were men who were important enough in their own day, but most of their works have disappeared from the present operatic repertoire. Meyerbeer, a German Jew possessed of real genius, lived most of his creative life in Paris; he was clever enough to give the people what they liked, paying little attention to anything but his own immediate success. The lighter forms of opera writing chiefly engaged native talent at this time; men like Monsigny, Grétry, Gossec, Méhul, Boieldieu, Auber, Hérold, and Halévy developed the special characteristics of the *opéra comique* — comic, light opera that was not, as time went on, very different from *grand opera*.

Later important names in the development of French opera are Gounod, whose fame is largely the result of his opera *Faust,* whose languorous love music and sweet, cloying harmonies have made it one of the most popular operas ever written; Bizet, the genius who wrote *Carmen,* to many people an almost perfect opera; Saint-Saëns, who was equally at home in all forms, and whose *Samson et Dalila* has contributed two important arias to the repertoire of the operatic singer; Massenet, who has achieved great popularity both in Europe and in America for his heavily scented romantic style; Charpentier, composer of the realistic *Louise,* based on a story of life in Bohemian Paris; and, greatest of all, Debussy, whose *Pelléas et Mélisande* is a work that is absolutely *sui generis,* standing alone in its difficult, reserved beauty as the one great modern French opera.

OPERAS OF OTHER COUNTRIES

The Russians have produced some very powerful works written in a most distinctive style: operas like Moussorgsky's *Boris Godunov,* Borodin's *Prince Igor,* or Rimsky-Korsakoff's *Le Coq d'or.* Smetana's *Bartered Bride* stands, together with Weinberger's *Schwanda,* as representative of the Czech opera — works that are colorful and rhythmic, without being very important. The other nations, including the English-speaking ones, have never seemed to be fitted for the rather exacting demands of operatic thought and have not as yet produced any outstanding serious works in their various experiments with the form. Ballad opera was once very popular in England (*The Beggar's Opera* is the type), and in this line Vaughan Williams's *Hugh the Drover* is a modern production. But the most popular English operatic style is "Gilbert and Sullivan" — comic opera.

LATER OPERAS

We have already had something to say regarding the encouraging signs of operatic achievement during the second quarter of the twentieth century in the English-speaking countries. Benjamin Britten has been the outstanding figure in England, with his *Peter Grimes*, a real grand opera, the *Rape of Lucretia* and *Albert Herring*, which he calls chamber-operas, and his work for amateurs, *Let's Build an Opera*. In the United States Stravinsky and W. H. Auden began collaboration on an opera, *The Rake's Progress*, in 1947. New York has produced a number of significant works which the producers have hesitated to call operas because of the unfortunate distaste for that term on the part of the general public. But Weill's *Street Scene* and *Lost in the Stars* are essentially opera in a popular form — and good, vivid opera, too; while Menotti's little *opera buffas, Amelia Goes to the Ball* and *The Telephone*, and his more serious *The Medium* and *The Consul* show how it is perfectly possible to fuse the more traditional characteristics of Italian opera writing with the demands of the popular Broadway stage.

A LIST OF SUGGESTED SELECTIONS (all of them recorded)

"Hymn to Apollo"   Transcribed by Reinach

Very probably this transcription of one of the few authentic examples of Greek declamation-chant sung in translation does not sound to our ears the way it did to those of the Greeks of the first century B.C. It is impossible to reproduce these historical examples without such reproduction being affected by modern ideas and tastes. Nevertheless this Greek fragment suggests the general character of the means which the Greeks used for the musical projection of their poetry and drama.
Other examples are recorded by Decca.

"Awake, Sweet Love"   John Dowland

This is one of the best of the sixteenth-century solo-songs. Dowland, born probably in Ireland (1563), was a widely traveled cosmopolitan, and his compositions were known all over Europe.

Funeste piaggie from *Eurydice*   Peri

This is an example of recitative from the first opera ever written.

Lasciatemi morire from *Arianna*   Monteverdi

This shows Monteverdi's great improvement over his predecessors.

Ch'io mai vi possa lasciar d'amare from *Siroe*   Handel

Here is Handel's Italian style at its best.

Che faro senza Euridice from *Orpheus*   Gluck

Overture to *The Secret Marriage* [1]   Cimarosa

Overture to *The Marriage of Figaro* [1]   Mozart

Una voce poco fa from *The Barber of Seville*   Rossini

Una furtiva lagrima from *The Elixir of Love*   Donizetti

Komm, O Hoffnung from *Fidelio*   Beethoven

Agatha's aria from *Der Freischütz (Leise, leise)*   Weber

Caro nome from *Rigoletto*   Verdi
Ah, fors' è lui from *La Traviata*   Verdi
The Final Duet, Act III, *Aïda*   Verdi
"Willow Song" from *Otello*   Verdi
"Credo" from *Otello*   Verdi

These different Verdi selections give an excellent opportunity for comparing the characteristics of his early, middle, and late styles.

Addio di Mimi from *La Bohème*   Puccini
Un bel di vedremo from *Madam Butterfly*   Puccini

Overture to *Rienzi* [1]   Wagner
"Spinning Chorus" and "Senta's Aria"
from *The Flying Dutchman*   Wagner

[1] Orchestral selection.

Overture to *Tannhäuser* [2]   Wagner
Dich, teure Halle from *Tannhäuser*   Wagner
Prelude to *Lohengrin* [2]   Wagner
"Elsa's Dream" from *Lohengrin*   Wagner

This group of selections represents the earlier Wagner style.

Prelude to *Tristan und Isolde* [2]   Wagner
Prelude to *Die Meistersinger* [2]   Wagner
Prelude to *Parsifal* [2]   Wagner
Funeral March from *Götterdämmerung* [2]   Wagner
Wotan's Abschied from *Die Walküre*   Wagner
"Waldtraute's Narrative" from *Götterdämmerung*   Wagner
Isolde's "Love Death" from *Tristan und Isolde*   Wagner
Was duftet doch der Flieder from *Die Meistersinger*   Wagner
Wahn! Wahn! from *Die Meistersinger*   Wagner
Good Friday Music from *Parsifal*   Wagner

No better means for understanding the method employed in the later Wagner works of building up the score from a multitude of leading motives can be found than in such excerpts as these.

Monologue of the Marschallin and Presentation of
    the Silver Rose from *Der Rosenkavalier*   Strauss
"Salome's Dance" from *Salome* [2]   Strauss

Overture and Pantomime from *Hänsel
    und Gretel* [2]   Humperdinck

Ich bin der Schwanda from
    Schwanda, the Bagpipe Player   Weinberger

Coronation Scene and Death of Boris from
    Boris Godunov   Moussorgsky

"Hymn to the Sun" from *Le Coq d'or*   Rimsky-Korsakoff

"Aria of Khan Kontchak" from *Prince Igor*   Borodin
Polovtsian Dances from *Prince Igor* [2]   Borodin

Habanera, Seguidilla, and "Toreador's Song"
    from *Carmen*   Bizet

[2] Orchestral selection.

"Flower Song," "Jewel Song," and "E'en Bravest
Heart" from *Faust*   Gounod

Il sogno from *Manon*   Massenet
Il est doux from *Hérodiade*   Massenet

Depuis le jour from *Louise*   Charpentier

"Nay, Maccus, Lay Him Down" from
The King's Henchman   Deems Taylor

Four Sea Interludes from *Peter Grimes* [3]   Britten
Ride of Collatinus from *Rape of Lucretia*   Britten

"September Song" from *Lost in the Stars*   Weill

Overture to *Amelia Goes to the Ball* [3]   Menotti
"Monica, Monica" from *The Medium*   Menotti

TOPICS FOR FURTHER DISCUSSION

Why has opera been one of the most popular forms of music?

Why was Wagner never able to work out his complete union of drama, staging, and music?

What are the present-day ideas of the possibility of further development in the field of the opera?

Discuss the various reforms of Gluck, Weber, Wagner.

Why was Brahms never tempted to write an opera? What are the essentials of a good opera composer?

Summarize Wagner's contributions to the development of the opera.

[3] Orchestral selection.

THIRTY-FOUR

BACK TO BACH

BACH'S PLACE IN HISTORY

In the course of our backward historical survey, we have marked a number of definite "movements," each of them climaxing in the works of a single composer. We found, for instance, that nineteenth-century Romanticism — that mighty period of achievement — started with the symphonies of Beethoven and came to a close with the works following Wagner. In spite of the wealth of musical material found in the Wagnerian music-dramas, no one appeared able to develop their style much further. Seemingly Wagner exhausted the possibilities of his medium, and later developments had to take place in other directions — impressionism and so on. So it was with Mozart; his best works, together with those of the mature Haydn, mark the end of the period of eighteenth-century classicism and beyond them there was nothing to be said in that particular manner. The composer whose works we are now to study — Johann Sebastian Bach — likewise marks the end of an epoch, the so-called period of polyphony.

If we examine the music produced from the beginning of the Christian Era up to the time of Bach (the beginning of the eighteenth century), we will find that it divides itself naturally into two great categories. The first is that of monophonic music, comprising only a single melodic line without additional parts or accompaniment: all music up to, roughly, the ninth century was monophonic; and even after vocal part music or *organum*, as it was originally called, began to be developed by the Church some time between eight and nine hundred A.D., much of the popular music remained monophonic. Early part music was described by a twelfth-century theorist, John Cotton, as being a "combination of different sounds, appropriately executed by at least two singers in such a manner that, when one sounds the melody, the second colors it with other tones. At every point of rest the two meet either in consonance or in octave; this kind of singing is called *organum.*"

It was this second, polyphonic style which, starting thus simply, was developed and elaborated in instrumental and choral composition during the time between the twelfth and the seventeenth century and which culminated in the music of Johann Sebastian Bach.

A Lady Seated at the Virginals

Painting by Vermeer (1632–1675)

In it, as we have already said, all the parts contributed more or less equally to the musical fabric. After Bach there came still a third type of music — the homophonic, in which one voice or melody is prominent and is supported by an accompaniment that is mostly in chordal style. Practically all nineteenth-century music was written in this homophonic style, and it is thus by far the most familiar style to most listeners.

It is difficult to imagine a more adequately prepared composer genealogically or one more fortunately placed historically than J. S. Bach. Born in the center of Protestant Germany in 1685, he was descended from a long line of church and town musicians; it is a matter of record that, out of thirty-two of his sixteenth-century progenitors' descendants, seventeen were professional musicians. Sebastian Bach, as we have just said, completed the grandiose polyphonic structure that stretched, through Palestrina, clear back to the Middle Ages; he also foreshadowed the new harmonic style that was to take complete possession of the musical world that followed him. He was thus able, at an important turning point in music's history, to master two fundamentally different styles of composition; and he stands as a marvelous synthesis of the past and a symbol of things to come. Combine superb technical mastery, fortunate historical position, and outstanding strength of musical imagination with never-questioning religious faith, and you have the fundamental reasons for Bach's great supremacy as a composer.

He composed consistently from the days of his apprenticeship as a young teen-age organist to the very last days of his life. "I worked hard," he said once to someone inquiring as to the secrets of his genius; "if you are as industrious as I was, you will be no less successful." His tremendous output divides itself into definite categories, which may be conveniently labeled as

The Baroque Bach
Bach the Church Musician
Bach the Master of Musical Construction

THE BAROQUE BACH

The German historians like to say that Bach is the great man of the Baroque era; and they are certainly right in so far as one phase of his writing is concerned. Just as Haydn and Mozart were to a certain degree the musical representatives of the German Rococo period during which they lived, so some of the works of Bach suggest aspects of the earlier Baroque art out of which the Rococo developed, and of which it is a refinement. The desire for the expression of a buoyant and rich vitality in art may be said to be one underlying characteristic of this period. Stretching roughly from the beginning of the seventeenth century to the latter part of the eighteenth, the Baroque era takes its character largely from the grandiose Italian architectural constructions by which the Church, during the period of the Counter Reformation, endeavored to regain something of its lost prestige and power in the eyes of the world. It marks a period in European history strongly dominated by an upthrusting optimism never again equalled. No other period in man's existence has been more active in liberating his powers or in giving him the foundations upon which he has built his life ever since. It was a time of great intellectual curiosity, of an amassing of wealth and prestige in the hands of the powerful individual; and

RUBENS: *Mary with Christ and the Saints*

"In all Baroque art we find an inevitable leading on of our spirits, a piling up of effects, a magnificent ascent to a final and monumental climax."

it resulted in one of the richest and most vital outpourings of art of all kinds the world has ever seen.

Stimulated by the richness and magnificence of the Italian ecclesiastical creations, and catering to the rather satiated and cynical tastes of the time, architects and painters, landscape gardeners and sculptors over a good part of Europe worked in that grandiloquent manner of expression that we have come to know as the Baroque style. In all the great capitals of Europe, especially those of the southern countries, as well as in the numerous small principalities of Germany, building flourished; stimulated by the example of the Sun King at Versailles, the princely rulers desired to demonstrate their power of domain through costly and elaborate architectural creation, just as the Church had attempted to re-assert its glory and pomp through the creation of fanciful and highly decorated structures, built in the most eloquent and grand style imaginable.

It was a period of luxuriant strength, of colorful vitality, of almost overpowering magnificence of creative thought; and this spirit affected all phases of artistic activity. From his great predecessors — men like Reinken and Buxtehude in the north of Germany and Pachelbel in the south — Bach inherited this predilection for ponderous, flamboyant expression, and many of his great organ works unmistakably show its influence. Listen to such a youthful organ composition as his great *Toccata, Adagio and Fugue in C Major,* for instance, and you will hear what we mean. In its constant up-swirling phrases, the grand balancing of its parts, and the soaring architectural design of its musical form, this work may be said to be truly Baroque. Heard on an adequate and properly designed instrument, it is almost overpowering in its magnificence; as, indeed, are the *Toccata and Fugue in D Minor* and the *Fantasia and Fugue in G Minor.* Certainly there is a striking similarity of spirit between such works and those architectural creations of his time and country, the Residenz in Würzburg or the lovely little Asam Church of St. Johann Nepomuk in Munich.

In comparing these similar forms of different arts, our first impressions are those of the monumental impressiveness and tremendous sweep of creative power to be found in both. The architects of these impressive structures were men possessed not only of great imagination but also of superabundant technical powers. Their superb craftsmanship was equal to their vision. If we examine these Baroque architectural creations carefully, we shall find that their

The Grand Stairway in the Castle at Würzburg

One of the finest examples of Baroque art in Germany

imposing magnificence is made up of a wealth of meticulously executed detail: carefully balanced members, gracefully molded designs, majestic rhythmic patterns give significance and purpose to the whole. And in them all we find an inevitable leading-on of our spirits, a piling-up of effects, a magnificent ascent to a final and monumental climax that marks the true essence of the Baroque. In this phase of his creation, Bach was as truly a man of his epoch as were the architects Neumann, Bähr, and the Brothers Asam or the stage designers, the Bibienas.

In addition to the twenty-six preludes and fugues which he wrote for the organ, a number of other instrumental works should be included in this Baroque category. Prominent among these are the *Brandenburg Concertos*, each written for a different combination of instruments; with their tremendous vitality of expression and constant sustenance of creative energy, they are good examples of the decorated Baroque style, as are some of his clavier compositions, such as the *English* and *French Suites,* the *Goldberg Variations,* and the *Italian Concerto.*

Overlapping into this category may also be mentioned such choral works as the *St. Matthew Passion* and the *B Minor Mass;* their very length (each of them takes over three hours to perform) and their richly decorated, soaring architectural qualities make them monumentally impressive, as well as emotionally overwhelming, works. Charles Sanford Terry has called the *St. Matthew Passion* "the deepest and most moving expression of devotional feeling in the whole of musical literature"; certainly much of its emotional force is derived from the relentless Baroque intensification of the means used. The *B Minor Mass* is a more brilliant work, perhaps even more monumental, than the *St. Matthew Passion;* but its effect comes from the same underlying sublimity and structural grandeur.

BACH THE CHURCH MUSICIAN

The second phase of this composer's work will best be understood if we review briefly his career as a musical official in the service of the German Protestant Church. He was born in the small Thuringian village of Eisenach, a little town deeply steeped in the traditions of the German Reformation; his father was town musician as well as *Hofmusicus* to the local duke, Johann Georg. This Bach musical tradition had been maintained for generations; in fact, the association of the two terms, Bach and musician, was so close throughout Thuringia that a musician was usually called Bach, no matter what his family name happened to be. The members of this great family were noted for their sturdy piety as well as for their musical ability, and so it is no wonder that much of Johann Sebastian Bach's greatest and most characteristic work was done during the rather prosaic discharge of his duties as church organist and choir director. As Schweitzer put it: "Music was an act of worship with Bach; his artistic activity and his personality were both based on his piety. If he is to be understood from any standpoint at all, it is from this. For him, art was religion, and so had no concern with the world or with worldly success. It was an end in itself . . . for him the tones do not perish, but ascend to God like praise too deep for utterance." All his music was the natural expression of a belief acquired through generations of God-fearing, simple-living ancestors, sheltered from the ways of the world; and it was heightened by an unusually fertile imagination and a superb expressive technic.

Chorales

No better introduction to Bach could be found than that obtained from the chorales, for they were intimately associated with his career as a church composer and could have sprung from no other source. The Protestant Church had as one of its tenets the popularizing of its services, and so it encouraged the participation of the people in the liturgical part of worship. To this end the chorale or hymn was developed so that large congregations could sing in unison with great effect; the services did not have to depend upon the trained members of the choir, as had been the case in the older branch of the Church. The chorale goes back to the very beginnings of the Protestant faith, for Luther himself was a musician and poet of considerable ability, and is supposed to have written some of the earliest examples of this type of worship music. By Bach's time, some two hundred years later, there had been produced a great number of these fine, sturdy tunes (about five hundred in all), and one of his most significant contributions to musical literature was the reharmonizing and re-arranging of some two hundred fifty of these so that they would be effective for congregational singing with the accompaniment of the organ.

These Bach chorales represent in shortened form the same technical mastery that is evident in his greater works, as well as the inherent strength of emotional expression that is peculiar to them. They were set largely in the harmonic style (in distinction to the polyphonic style, which he employed so largely) and have a tremendous appeal for all kinds of listeners, learned as well as inexperienced. "Nothing in music is more wonderful, perhaps more surprising, than the power and grip which these chorales have over all classes of musical listeners and over the singers themselves. In all choirs . . . these simple, four-part harmonic compositions hold singers and listeners probably more strongly than any other form of art. The Bach chorale has, in fact and in the supremest degree, a religious and mystic effect upon the hearer that cannot be explained or analyzed." (Hannam) [1]

[1] From *On the Church Cantatas of Bach*, by permission of Oxford University Press.

Johann Sebastian Bach

This portrait was painted by the Dresden Court
Painter Elias Gottlieb Haussman in 1746. It is in the
Stadtmuseum, Leipzig. Bach holds in his hand a triple
canon in six parts.

At the end of this chapter will be found a short list of some of
the best of these chorales. Many of them can be found in any good
American or English hymnal; and complete editions with German
and English texts are readily available. In case you are not familiar
with them, listen to them carefully if you would penetrate to the
soul of Bach's expression. Even playing them on the piano gives
a hint of their spiritual beauty; but to appreciate their mighty
power, it is necessary to hear them sung by a large chorus or congregation.

Chorale Preludes

One of the most common forms of organ composition in Bach's time was the chorale prelude, formed by taking a melody of one of these chorales (which would be very familiar to the congregation) and weaving other parts about it in such a way as to bring out its beauty in the highest degree. These chorale preludes were meant for practical use in the church service and are, in reality, miniature tone poems embodying the spiritual character of the words of the chorale upon which they were based. Some of these are meditations uttered from the loneliness of the composer's soul; others are poems of praise, outbursts of joy and thankful gratitude for blessings received. They are a musical world in miniature, containing every possible emotion and manifesting all the powers of expression of which Bach deemed the organ capable. They differ in the richness of their expression from everything else he wrote.

An instructive way to realize the difference between the harmonic and the polyphonic way of writing music, as well as of getting acquainted with the great beauties of Bach's more intimate music, is to select a chorale and then compare it with the chorale prelude which Bach evolved from it. The interpretation of the chorale preludes, as indeed of all of Bach's organ music, is a matter of varying tastes. Those listeners concerned with historical accuracy and purity of interpretative style will insist that this music should be played only on the organ, and on an instrument that imitates the peculiarly bright, brilliant tone of the organs of Bach's day. Others, more interested in the musical and emotional significance of the music, will not object to its being transcribed for the modern orchestra, as has been so often done in recent years.

Something can be said on both sides of this argument. The purists are apt to forget that the tonal ideals and interpretative style of the music of one period can never be successfully re-created in another, later time if the music is to have any communicative vitality and meaning; too many changes have taken place in the meantime that are apt to make any such "pure" approach seem artificial and academic. On the other hand, contemporary transcribers sometimes exceed the limits of good taste and are inclined to make their arrangements unnecessarily fussy and romantic. The best way to resolve such an argument is to listen to the music in various interpretations and then decide which way of playing these masterworks is most appealing to your particular temperament. In view of the fact that Bach himself was an inveterate arranger and transcriber of his own as well as other composers' works, it can hardly be said that there is any one and only *true* way of interpreting him. Here are some chorale preludes readily available in recordings:

FOR ORGAN:

Wachet auf, ruft uns die Stimme (Sleepers, Wake! A Voice is Calling)

Taken from the cantata described later, the chorale is given out on one manual of the organ, against a dancing figure in the accompaniment and pedals. There is little doubt that Bach had in mind here illustrating the two lines of the chorale text:

Zion hears the watchmen calling
And on her heart deep joy is falling.

Christ lag in Todesbanden (Christ Lay in Bonds of Death)

There is a sense of joy and freedom in this music, suggestive of the solemn jubilation of the Easter season. The chorale tune is in the soprano, with accompaniment of triumph-motives in the other parts. A poetic interpreter thinks the fine pedal part was meant to symbolize the rolling away of the stone before the tomb. Bach's music is full of such rather naive, imitative effects.

Herzlich tut mich verlangen (Passion Chorale)

Based on a tune that was originally secular in character, this wonderful tune is used many times in the *St. Matthew Passion* and is here given that sense of deep longing that Bach expressed so often:

Lord, hear my deepest longing
To pass to Thee in peace,
From earthly troubles thronging,
From trials that never cease.

FOR ORCHESTRA:

Aus der Tiefe ruf' ich (Out of the Deeps I Call)

In this chorale prelude Bach makes use of a set of beautifully contrived variations to bring out the suppliant character of the words:

Out of the deeps have I called upon Thee, O Lord;
Hearken to my crying and let Thine ears be attentive to the voice of my supplication.

Each variation seems to accentuate the wonderful expressiveness of the words.

Wir glauben all' an einen Gott (We All Believe in One God)

No wonder that Bach, when he decided to write a chorale prelude upon the tune associated with these words, turned naturally to the fugue as his best means of expression. For no other method of treatment known at that time, or since, seems as adequate for the strong affirmative principle of Christian faith which underlay Bach's very existence. The fugue is a structural synthesis built out of a single idea; it grows entirely from one element, and nothing else could therefore be so suggestive of the idea of Oneness that pervades the words of this chorale. We can easily hear that the one short phrase heard at the very beginning, a phrase which Bach took from the opening measures of the chorale, permeates the whole structure of the fugue. It is heard in various parts and piles up to a tremendous climax, while through the bass stride giantlike progressions suggestive of the strength of the composer's faith.

SOME OUTSTANDING BACH CHORALES:

Den Vater dort oben (God in Heaven Almighty)
Wachet auf, ruft uns die Stimme (Sleepers, Wake! A Voice is Calling)

These are magnificent examples of an exalted religious expression.

Das alte Jahr vergangen ist (The Old Year Has Passed Away)

Ponders on the inscrutable flight of time and the mystic qualities of God.

Wenn wir in höchsten Nothen sein (When in the Hour of Greatest Need)

Jesu, Jesu, du bist mein (Jesus, Thou Art Mine)

Intensity of expression, almost unbelievable in such short pieces of music.

O Welt, ich muss dich lassen (O World, I Now Must Leave Thee)

A secular tune turned to religious use; full of tender feeling.

O Haupt voll Blut und Wunden (O Sacred Head, Now Wounded)

The most famous of the chorales; used many times in the *St. Matthew Passion*.

SOME OF BACH'S OUTSTANDING WORKS, LISTED BY PERIODS

The Baroque Bach

FOR ORGAN:

Toccata, Adagio and Fugue in C Major
Toccata and Fugue in D Minor
Fugue in G Minor (The Little G Minor)
Passacaglia and Fugue in C Minor

FOR ORCHESTRA:

Brandenburg Concerto No. 5 (for flute, violin, keyboard, and strings)

FOR HARPSICHORD:

Chromatic Fantasy and Fugue in D Minor

Nothing shows the advantage of the Equal Temperament (see next chapter) in keyboard music better than this harpsichord work, written c. 1720–3.

Bach the Church Musician

CHORALE PRELUDES FOR ORGAN:

Wachet auf, ruft uns die Stimme
Christ lag in Todesbanden
Herzlich tut mich verlangen

CHORALE PRELUDES TRANSCRIBED FOR ORCHESTRA:

Aus der Tiefe ruf ich
Wir glauben all' an einen Gott

DEFINITE SUGGESTIONS FOR READING

Music in History: The Sacred Music of Bach

J. S. Bach, by Schweitzer (New York: Macmillan), Reprint Edition, London, 1945. Chapter IX, pp. 151–70.

This book, written by one of the greatest men of our time and a recognized authority on the music of Bach, contains the best account of his life and work.

THIRTY-FIVE

B A C H (*continued*)

The best introduction for one not acquainted with the glories of the choral works which Bach wrote during the fulfillment of his duties as organist and choirmaster would be the study of one of the complete cantatas that he wrote for performance at the Sunday morning services of the Thomaskirche, Leipzig. No better cantata for this purpose could be found than the one composed for the twenty-seventh Sunday after Trinity: *Wachet auf* (Sleepers, Wake!), No. 140 in the Gesellschaft Edition of Bach's complete works. For, as one ardent admirer of this work has said, we cannot help but feel that in it the highest art, the deepest feeling, and the most exalted expression are united into a single composition.

The general constructional plan of this cantata is easily followed. It is based entirely upon one chorale, the words and music of which were written by a German pastor, Philip Nicolai, as the result of a deeply personal emotional experience. This chorale treats in a mystic way, very typical of its time (1599), the parable of the Wise and Foolish Virgins found in the Gospel of St. Matthew. Using the wedding scene of this story as a background, the hymn goes on to describe the coming of the Bridegroom, the Saviour, who invites the Bride, His Church, to her wedding. The text describes their meeting, the Bridegroom comforting the Bride and promising her eternal bliss, with a final hymn of praise sung within the gates of the New Jerusalem.

Like so many of the texts which Bach set to music, this hymn of Nicolai's seems to the present-day listener unnecessarily confused and mysterious. Much of this religious poetry (some of it might better be called doggerel) came out of the period of Germany's greatest suffering, the Thirty Years' War (1618–1648), when the whole country was overrun by the armies of Europe and was in complete ruin; "the only thing of the soul that survived was religion, in whose bosom poetry took refuge." No wonder that this poetry was sometimes overemotional and overnaive in its strained symbolism; we of today are more interested in it as the basis for the expression of Bach's great musical communication than we are in its theological connotations or its high-flown poetic extravagances.

A SPECIFIC EXAMPLE

The musical scheme (each of Bach's works in this field has its own design) of *Wachet auf* calls for the use of all three verses of Nicolai's hymn, presenting the tune in as many different ways. The first chorus treats it in a complex chorale-prelude-like style, the melody being given to the soprano and the other parts weaving wonderful contrapuntal lines around it; the last chorus is in simple chorale form so that the choir and congregation could join in its singing. Interpolated after verses one and two is a recitative and duet, to words thought to be by a contemporary poetaster (Christian Friedrich Henrici, who wrote under the pseudonym of Picander). These interpolated operatic-like numbers dramatize the union of Christ and His Church.

This introduction of operatic forms, such as the recitative, arias, and duet, into the religious works of Bach seems to many listeners of today a strange anomaly. Schweitzer explains it thus: "Protestant church music from the beginning of the seventeenth century to that of the eighteenth consciously and deliberately gave itself up to all the influences of both religious and secular music, from whatever source, without shrinking from or fearing anything new, animated only by a holy impulse of expounding the Gospel in music." And so it did not seem at all incongruous to Bach, and his predecessors in this field of church music, to incorporate boldly into their cantatas and "passions" the devices of the great Renaissance innovators in opera and of their later Neapolitan followers.

Bach, no great innovator in so far as the forms he used were concerned, followed along the paths of his predecessors: all educated people of his time, clerical as well as lay, had before their eyes, according to Schweitzer, the antique ideal of the religious drama; and none of them, even Bach, seemed conscious of how far their poetry and music were from attaining this ideal. The operatic elements in Bach's church compositions are simply the manifestation of a contemporary style which did not particularly concern him, although they may surprise some listeners today. We have to accept them as he did, if we are to get the beauty of his communication.

But how wonderfully he used them! The opening chorus of this cantata is filled with the excitement aroused by the sudden announcement of the coming of the Heavenly Bridegroom; its accompaniment quivers with animation and above it sounds the solemn tune in the soprano and the winding polyphony of the other three parts:

I

Chorus

Wachet auf! ruft uns die Stimme	Wake from sleep, hark, strikes the hour,
Der Wächter sehr hoch auf der Zinne.	The watchman calls high on the tower:
Wach auf, du Stadt Jerusalem!	Awake, awake, Jerusalem!
Mitternacht heisst diese Stunde;	Midnight strikes, hear, hear it tolling,
Sie rufen uns mit hellem Munde:	O hear the voice of warning rolling:
Wo seid ihr klugen Jungfrauen?	"Where are ye, O wise virgins, where?"
Wohl auf, der Bräut'gam kommt,	Awake, the Bridegroom comes,
Steht auf, die Lampen nehmt!	Awake and trim your lamps!
Alleluia!	Alleluia!
Macht euch bereit	For Him prepare
Zu der Hochzeit,	A feast most rare,
Ihr müsset ihm entgegen geh'n.	So go ye forth to meet Him there!

II

Recitative — Tenor

Er kommt, er kommt, der Bräut'- gam kommt! Ihr Töchter Zions, kommt heraus, sein Ausgang eilet aus der Höhe in euer Mutter Haus. Der Bräut'gam kommt, der einem Rehe und jungen Hirsche gleich	He comes! The Bridegroom comes! So, Zion's daughter, now rejoice! He comes from Heaven and hastes to greet thee within thy mother's house. The Bridegroom comes, erect and fleet as it were a nimble

auf denen Hügeln springt, und
euch das Mahl der Hochzeit bringt.
Wacht auf, ermuntert euch! den
Bräut'gam zu empfangen; dort!
sehet! kommt er hergegangen.

hart that on the mountain springs,
and here the wedding banquet
brings. Awake! and be prepared
the Bridegroom now to meet! Lo,
He comes! Go ye forth to greet
Him.

III

Duet: Soprano and Baritone

Wann kommst du, mein Heil?
Ich komme, dein Teil, ich komme!
Ich warte mit brennendem Öle.

When com'st Thou, my Lord?
Behold me, thine own!
I seek Thee with lamps brightly
burning.

Eröffne den Saal
Zum himmlischen Mahl.
Ich öffne den Saal
Zum himmlischen Mahl.
Komm', Jesu!
Ich komme; komm', liebliche Seele!

Throw open the hall,
Me to thy feast call!
I open the hall,
Thee to my feast call!
Come, Jesu!
I seek Thee, for Thee I am yearn-
ing.

IV

Chorale for Unison Tenor

(It is this number that Bach adapted for an Organ Chorale Prelude.)

Zion hört die Wächter singen,
Das Herz tut ihr vor Freuden
springen,
Sie wachet und steht eiland auf.
Ihr Freund kommt vom Himmel
prächtig,
Von Gnaden stark, von Wahrheit
mächtig,
Ihr Licht wird hell, ihr Stern geht
auf.
Nun komm', du werte Kron',

Herr Jesu, Gottes Sohn.
Hosianna!
Wir folgen All' zum Freudensaal
Und halten mit das Abendmahl.

Zion hears the watchmen calling,
And on her heart deep joy is fall-
ing.
She waits and watches, all alert.
Down from Heaven her Lord comes
glorious,
So full of grace, in truth victorious.

Her Star, her Light, illumes the
earth.
Thou'rt come Who wear'st the
crown,
Lord Jesus, God's dear Son!
Alleluia!
We follow all within Thy hall
To sup with Thee and heed Thy
call.

V

Recitative — Tenor

So geh' herein zu mir, du mir
erwählte Braut! Ich habe mich mit
dir in Ewigkeit vertraut. Dich will
ich auf mein Herz, auf meinen Arm
gleich wie ein Siegel setzen, und
dein betrübtes Aug' ergötzen. Ver-
giss, O Seele, nun die Angst, den
Schmerz, den du erdulden müssen;
auf meiner Linken sollst du ruh'n,
und meine Rechte soll dich küssen.

Come, enter in with Me, My
chosen bride that art! Since time
began to be thou art of Me a part.
I take thee to My heart. Upon
Mine arm, e'en as a seal, I set
thee, and will with love always entreat thee. Forget, beloved, all thy
grief and pain that lately hurt and
pressed thee! Upon My left shalt
thou bide, and with a loving heart
I kiss thee.

VI

Duet: Soprano and Baritone

Mein Freund ist mein!
Die Liebe soll nichts scheiden;
Ich will mit dir
In Himmels Rosen weiden,
Da Freude die Fülle,
Da Wonne wird sein!

O Friend, Thou'rt mine!
Thy love no power can sever.
With Thee in heaven's
Bright paths of joy I'll wander.
The fullness of joy
In my presence is Thine.

Und ich bin dein!
Die Liebe soll nichts scheiden;
Du sollst mit mir
In Himmels Rosen weiden,
Da Freude die Fülle,
Da Wonne wird sein!

Yes, I am thine!
My love no power can sever.
With Me in heaven's
Bright paths of joy thou'lt wander.
The fullness of joy
In my presence is thine.

VII

Chorale for Choir and Congregation

Gloria sei dir gesungen
Mit Menschen und englischen
Zungen,
Mit Harfen und mit Cymbeln
schon.

Gloria sing all our voices,
With angels all mankind rejoices,
With harp and strings in sweetest
tone.

Von zwölf Perlen sind die Pforten	Twelve bright pearls adorn the portals,
An deiner Stadt; wir sind Con- *sorten*	Where God has gathered His Im- mortals
Der Engel hoch um deinen Thron.	As angels round His glorious throne.
Kein Aug' hat je gespürt,	No eye has ever seen,
Kein Ohr hat je gehört	No ear has ever heard
Solche Freude.	The joy we know.
Dess sind wir froh,	Our praises flow,
Io, io!	Io, io,
Zum Gott in dulci jubilo.	To God *in dulci jubilo.*

(From Terry's and Drinker's translations.)

A few things may be noted: the third number, a dialogue between the Saviour and His Church, contains the strange symbolism we have mentioned. The two voices here converse in much the same manner as would a pair of lovers in an opera; the tender vocal parts are greatly enhanced by a violin counterpoint weaving in and around them. In the fourth number, the swaying, lilting, dancelike accompaniment was very likely suggested to Bach by the opening lines of this verse of the hymn; this accompaniment seemed to Spitta, Bach's first great biographer, like the "dance of souls in bliss." The chorale melody strikes almost dissonantly across this, as if it had little to do with it, suggesting the solemn cry of the watchmen sounding against the festive procession of the Bride- groom. The second duet is very gay and happy, the lovers cele- brating the complete harmony of their union. In the final chorus, the unadorned harmonization of the chorale suggests the proces- sion entering the festal hall where the wedding is to be celebrated, with the Foolish Virgins, left outside, in despair. Schweitzer main- tains that not until Berlioz do we meet dramatic pictorial music that is comparable to this.

St. Matthew Passion

The custom of performing a Passion, *i.e.*, an epic dramatic and musical setting of the story of the sufferings and death of Christ, was an exceedingly ancient one in the Christian Church. In the Reformed Church, performances of such Passions in German may be said to have begun in the latter half of the sixteenth century. By Bach's time these had become exceedingly elaborate, embracing the best of the forms introduced from the musical drama (*i.e.*, the recitative and aria) as well as the traditional devices of the chorus and chorale. Dr. Salomon Deyling, the head of the spiritual affairs of Leipzig during Bach's tenure as organist there, thus addressed his talented Cantor on this subject:

"On each Palm Sunday and Good Friday the history of the Passion of our Lord is made known antiphonally, according to one or the other of the Evangelists, exactly in accordance with the sacred writer's words. Who could improve on this? They must be sung, how else are they to be understood by all? But they must be sung by someone who can sing, namely by you [meaning Bach!]. And so that everything may sound well and be impressive, they must be musically sung and accompanied.

Your best singer, who can pronounce clearly and well, must sing the words of the Evangelist in recitative, and, in order to produce more impression of life and variety, the other persons of the story must be represented by other singers, and the Jewish people by a chorus. At the chief points of the story there will be pauses, during which, by means of an aria, the congregation shall lay to heart what they have heard; and that all of us shall be refreshed from time to time, there shall be well-chosen verses from all the known hymns, in which the congregation can join. Now, your business is to carry all this out in a connected and artistic manner!"

Which Bach proceeded to do. It is not known how many settings of the Passion story he made; two of them have come down to us complete, the Passions according to *St. John* (written for performance in the Thomaskirche, Leipzig, in 1723) and that according to *St. Matthew* (first performed on Good Friday, 1729). Both follow the same general scheme, but the latter is by far the more impressive and effective work, employing all the resources of musical art: a double, mixed-voice choir, a *ripieno* choir of sopranos, two complete orchestras and a double organ part. The words of the evangelist are sung by the traditional tenor; the words of Jesus are given to a bass, always accompanied by a string orchestra; the parts of the other persons connected with this tremendous drama (Peter, Pilate, Judas, etc.) are sung by solo voices. The words of the Jewish *turba* or crowd are given to the two choirs and are set polyphonically. In addition to the Biblical words, Bach used a text by Picander, especially written for him, for the accompanied recitatives, arias, ensemble numbers, and gigantic choruses.

Typical of the Baroque spirit of magnificence and splendor is the opening chorus, which Schweitzer feels to be a realistic description of a crowd moving excitedly about, crying as Jesus is led through the town to the Cross: "Come, ye daughters, help me mourn. . . . See the Bridegroom, like a lamb"; part of the crowd cries from time to time, "Whom? . . . How? . . . What?" while above the whole surging mass soars the lovely line of the *ripieno* choir singing the chorale: "O Lamb of God, Most Stainless":

Double Choir

Kommt, ihr Töchter, helft mir klagen;	Come, ye daughters, share my mourning;
Sehet! Wen? Den Bräutigam.	See Him! Whom? The Bridegroom Christ.
Seht ihn! Wie? Als wie ein Lamm.	See Him! How? A spotless lamb.
Sehet! Was? Seht die Geduld.	See it! What? His patient love.
Seht! Wohin? Wohin? Auf uns're Schuld.	Look! Look where? On our offense.
Sehet ihn! Aus Lieb' und Huld	Look on Him. For love of us
Holz zum Kreuze selber tragen.	He Himself His Cross is bearing.

The work should be heard, if possible, in its entirety; there are now a number of recordings available. But an idea of its dramatic impact is best gained from the section devoted to the description of Christ's final sufferings and death on the cross, beginning with the recitative

LXXI

Und von der sechsten Stunde an ward eine Finsterniss über das ganze Land, bis zu der neunten Stunde. Und um die neunte Stunde schriee Jesus laut, und sprach: "Eli, Eli, lama, lama sabachthani!" Das	Now from the sixth hour there was darkness over all the land until the ninth hour. And about the ninth hour Jesus cried with a loud voice, saying, "Eli, Eli, lama sabachthani!" That is to say, "My God,

ist: "Mein Gott, mein Gott, warum hast du mich verlassen!"
Etliche aber, die da standen, da sie das hörten, sprachen sie: Der rufet den Elias.

my God, why hast Thou forsaken me?"
Some of them that stood there, when they heard that, said:

Chorus

Der rufet den Elias.

He calleth for Elijah.

Recitative

Und bald lief einer unter ihnen, nahm einen Schwamm, und füllete ihn mit Essig, und steckete ihn auf ein Rohr, und tränkete ihn. Die Andern aber sprachen:

And straightway one of them ran, and took a sponge, and filled it with vinegar, and put it on a reed, and gave Him to drink. The others said, however:

Chorus

Halt, halt, lass' sehen, ob Elias komme, und ihm helfe.

Let be, let us see whether Elijah will come to save Him.

Recitative

Aber Jesus schriee abermal laut, und verschied.

Jesus, when He had cried again with a loud voice, yielded up the ghost.

Chorale

Wenn ich einmal soll scheiden,
So scheide nicht von mir!
Wenn ich den Tod soll leiden,
So tritt du dann herfür!
Wenn mir am allerbängsten
Wird um das Herze sein,
So reiss' mich aus den Ängsten
Kraft deiner Angst und Pein!

Be near me, Lord, when dying,
O part not Thou from me!
And to my succor flying,
Come, Lord, and set me free!
And when my heart must languish
In death's last awful woe,
Release me from mine anguish
By thine own pain and woe!

Recitative

Und siehe da, der Vorhang im Tempel zerriss in zwei Stück', von oben an bis unten aus. Und die Erde erbebete, und die Felsen zerrissen, und die Gräber taten sich auf, und standen auf viel Leiber der Heiligen, die da schliefen; und gingen aus der Gräbern nach

And behold, the veil of the temple was rent in twain, from the top unto the bottom, and the earth did quake, and the rocks rent. And the graves were opened, and there arose many bodies of the saints which had slept, and came out of the graves after His resurrection,

seiner Auferstehung, und kamen in die heilige Stadt, und erschienen vielen. Aber der Hauptmann, und die bei ihm waren, und bewahreten Jesum, da sie sahen das Erdbeben, und was da geschah, erschraken sie sehr, und sprachen:	and went into the holy city, and appeared unto many. Now when the centurion, and they that were with him, watching Jesus, saw the earthquake, and those things that were done, they feared greatly, saying:

Chorus

Wahrlich, dieser ist Gottes Sohn gewesen.	Truly, this was the Son of God!

THE *Mass in B Minor*

Nothing shows better the deep spiritual quality of so much of Bach's choral writing than some of the sections from the great *Mass in B Minor*. This is a work of tremendous proportions, set to the regular liturgical text in use in the Catholic Church, that Bach gradually composed during the maturest years of his life, from 1731 to 1737. Although many of its twenty-four sections were adapted from earlier works, it is difficult to imagine a more unified or more thoroughly inspired whole. It seems as though, as H. C. Colles has said, Bach in planning, composing, and adapting this work from the "treasures of his past experience and his present vision, resolved only to create a work which, though no temple made with hands should be large enough to contain it in its ritual, should rise 'to the height of this great argument.' We have to go outside music for the true parallel to the mystery of Bach's Mass, and we find it in Milton's composition of *Paradise Lost*," the writing of which, we must remember, likewise covered such a long period of time.

Fully to understand and appreciate the Mass takes a long time; the music must be placed against the background of Bach's great religious faith, as well as against the general Baroque ideals of the time. The great protagonist of this stirring piece is the choir: fourteen of its twenty-four numbers are choruses covering every phase of emotional expression, from the exaltation of the *Sanctus* to the gloom of the *Crucifixus*. These choruses are written in from four to eight parts and constitute the most substantial contribution ever made to this phase of musical art. The contrasting solos and duets are of much less interest to modern ears; they were conceived in the pure Baroque decorated style and must be listened to with this constantly in mind. As was his custom, Bach loved to combine, in some of these numbers, the solo voice with a solo instrument — such as the violin in the *Laudamus te* or the oboe in *Et in spiritum sanctum.*

If time does not allow for an immediate hearing of the whole Mass, listen to these sections at least:

XV

Et incarnatus est de Spiritu Sancto ex Maria Virgine, et homo factus est.

And was incarnate by the Holy Spirit of the Virgin Mary, and was made man.

Here the mood is one of solemn awe, tinged with fear, a mood far from the usual happy one of the telling of the Bethlehem story. It is simply a foretaste of the tragedy to come:

XVI

Crucifixus etiam pro nobis sub Pontio Pilato, passus et sepultus est.

And was crucified also for us under Pontius Pilate; He suffered and was buried.

In this *Crucifixus* a solemn, descending phrase in the bass is repeated over and over again, each time with more poignant harmonies, until at last the voices sink down at the end into a whisper at the words *sepultus est*. This darkness is broken by the electric shock of the *Et resurrexit,* coming from the whole choir and orchestra like a sudden "shaft of dazzling light which gradually spreads over all creation as the message of the resurrection is happily unfolded."

XVII

Et resurrexit tertia die secundum Scripturas, et ascendit in coelum, sedet ad dextram Patris, et iterum venturus est cum gloria judicare vivos et mortuos; cuius regni non erit finis.

And the third day He rose again according to the Scriptures and ascended into heaven; and sitteth at the right hand of the Father, and He shall come again with glory to judge both the quick and the dead. Whose kingdom shall have no end.

SOME OF BACH'S OUTSTANDING CHORAL WORKS

Cantatas:

Wachet auf! (Sleepers, Wake!), No. 140

Christ lag in Todesbanden (Christ Lay in Bonds of Death), No. 4

Likewise based on a famous chorale, this is another of the more than two hundred surviving Bach cantatas now recorded and thus available for general listening.

Du Hirte Israel, höre (Shepherd of Israel, Hear), No. 104

A cantata for the Second Sunday after Easter; "the delicate lyricism, ravishing harmony, and perfect grace of this work have an immediate effect upon an audience and make this one of the most suitable works for overcoming the common fear of Bach."

Lobet Gott in seinen Reichen (Praise Our God), No. 11

Motet:

Singet dem Herrn (Sing Ye to the Lord)

A motet was sung each Sunday at St. Thomas Church, Leipzig, at the beginning of the morning service. This is the best known of six of Bach's that have come down to us.

St. Matthew Passion
Mass in B Minor

THIRTY-SIX

BACH'S INSTRUMENTAL STYLE

There is still another aspect of Bach's life which we must consider: Bach, the servant of princes, producing music at a court of his period. His compositions belonging to this period have furnished the modern instrumental repertoire with some of its most significant numbers. In 1717 Bach entered the service of one of the many German princes of the time, Leopold of Anhalt-Cöthen, as master of the court music. He had no church duties at all but did have at his disposal a small orchestra; and it was only natural that he began to experiment with it during his six-year term. At Cöthen he wrote for a number of small instrumental combinations, including a somewhat limited (at least from the modern viewpoint) orchestra consisting of strings, drums, oboes and bassoons, horns and trumpets, to which his experimental mind caused him to add, on occasion, other instruments.

It was this sort of experimenting that produced a different orchestration in each of the six concertos he wrote on commission from the Duke of Brandenburg. The experience he gained in this orchestral writing stood him in good stead later at Leipzig, when he was called upon to furnish different kinds of orchestral accompaniments for his cantatas and Passions. To this Cöthen period belong also the English and French harpsichord suites — the distinctive titles of which point to slight differences in style between these sets of movements in dance form — as well as the four suites, or overtures, which he wrote for the orchestral combination mentioned above. The sequence of movements in these works follows the typical pattern of their time: an extended overture made up of a slow introduction and a fugue, plus a series of contrasted movements in idealized dance form. During the Cöthen period was also written the first part of that famous collection of preludes and fugues familiarly known as *The Well-Tempered Clavier*.

In all these instrumental works can be seen the particular aspect
of Bach's manifold musical nature that was concerned with, and
superbly mastered, the forms of musical construction. Certainly
no other composer has equaled him in this: he wrote freely and
naturally in the difficult forms current in his day — the invention,
the fugue, the partita — but we have no feeling that these gave
him any trouble whatever, even if some of the music he produced
in the process does not represent him at his greatest. He manipulated the texture of the fugue with an ease and fluency that is dis-
arming, to say the least; for the fugue is probably the most abstract
and difficult of all the types of construction developed during the
long course of music's history. We find over forty fugues scattered
through his organ works alone, and there are many others used
throughout his instrumental and vocal compositions. In his last
work, left unfinished at his death in 1750, *The Art of Fugue,* this
style of fugal and canonic writing may be said to have reached its
climax. Although written as a sort of treatise, the series of fugal
examples this work contains, based on one theme, seems fresh and
exciting two hundred years after it was first put on paper.

THE WELL-TEMPERED CLAVIER

His best-known collection of fugues is in *The Well-Tempered
Clavier,* a group of forty-eight preludes and fugues written to illustrate the advantages of a system of tuning which Bach favored, and
which he wished to see generally adopted. It may surprise the
average listener to know that the system by which the modern piano
is tuned, and on which our whole modern European music is based,
is not in strict accord with the natural system based on the scientific
relations between tones as worked out in the physicist's laboratory.
When this latter is used, the results do not meet the requirements
of composers as regards the need for freely modulating into any
key desired. A piece written in "just intonation," as this natural
system of tuning is called, will be dead in tune so long as it does
not try to wander too far afield from any one key. The scientific
reasons for this need hardly be gone into here, but may be found
in such a book as Redfield's *Music: A Science and an Art.*[1] The need
for a free interchange of keys being strongly felt by Bach's time, he
advocated dividing the octave into twelve equal semitones, each

[1] Tudor Publishing Co., New York.

of them slightly false according to the scientific standards as established in experiment, but giving a result that was entirely satisfactory musically in all keys.

To establish this "well-tempered" or compromise system of
tuning, Bach wrote this collection of two cycles of preludes and
fugues, each set going through all the major and minor keys, twenty-
four of each. This collection was designed to be played on any
suitable instrument that happened to be available, and not on the
clavichord alone, as is so often suggested by the rendering in care-
less translation of its German title as *The Well-Tempered Clavichord*. It is of great significance not only because of its qualities as
music, but also because of its establishing, once and for all time,
the advantages of equal temperament as a basis for writing music.

Any performance of *The Well-Tempered Clavier* in its entirety is
an epic undertaking, and it is not easy to find a performer constantly
equal to the task. Some years ago the great Swiss pianist, Edwin
Fischer, recorded all forty-eight works on the piano; also Isabelle
Nef, a French harpsichordist, and Wanda Landowska, the famous
Polish research scholar and harpsichordist, have accepted the re-
sponsibility of undertaking the complete work. Listeners may learn
much from these outstanding interpretations, despite the tendency
of Fischer at times to become somewhat dry, of Nef to muff occasional notes, and of Landowska to do rather unusual things sometimes beyond the printed page. Although Bach undoubtedly had a
logical, aesthetic scheme of placing these preludes and fugues
according to a stepwise progression of keys, almost any single prelude and fugue from this great collection may be heard with
pleasure and profit, since each is an entity in itself.

BACH'S HEALTHY WHOLENESS

Perhaps any attempt such as we have made at classification of
a composer's output is rather dangerous, for it presupposes the idea
that everything a man such as Bach wrote falls logically into one or
another pocket, which can be definitely separated and labeled. This,
of course, is not true, for many times the characteristics of one type
are found in works which generally belong to another. When we
say, for instance, that Bach was largely concerned with the problem
of form in one broad type of music he wrote, this does not necessarily mean that these formal works are devoid of expressive feel-

ing; many of the fugues in *The Well-Tempered Clavier* are full of emotional content, as we have suggested. Nor should such a classification be construed to mean that the works which fall within the second of our groups are lacking in structural strength — they are carefully and superbly put together.

Nevertheless, some such grouping is a help in understanding the seeming contradictions of Bach's genius. Many a person has been somewhat repelled by what he has called the mathematical aspect of Bach, without knowing anything about the emotionally moving chorale-preludes or the Passions; others have been so fascinated by the supreme perfection of Bach's structural form that they have neglected or perhaps not understood what may rightly be called his romantic characteristics; and certainly some of the interpreters who have gloried in the grandiloquent, Baroque aspect of Bach's writing have never paid attention to the still, small voice of his more intimate works. Thus is he really the universal composer.

Bach's supremacy lies in his ability to fuse the best of the earlier polyphonic styles (with which we deal in a later chapter) with the powerful Protestant influences of the Reformation, and the lighter rhythmic effects of the court and "gallant" music of the period. "He includes the past as well as much of the future. His contemporary Handel, at his Italianate best, is *par excellence* the composer of the late Baroque. This is a good thing to be, but Bach is that and much more." (W. H. Mellers: *Music and Society*)

Although there has been considerable questioning in the minds of some listeners as to the advisability of transcribing some of Bach's compositions for the modern orchestra, as Leopold Stokowski has so often done, there can be no doubt about the truth of this famous conductor's statement regarding the music of Bach and his reasons for wanting to make it popular:

The composer I go back to, always with renewed inspiration and deepest musical inspiration, is Bach. I think it is because he combines all the music of the past with that of the future. Even today he is a modernist: in the first and last choruses of his *St. Matthew Passion* the sequences of harmonies are so abrupt and impetuous they still amaze us, although our ears are accustomed to Bartók, Schönberg, and other contemporaries.

Bach's music is difficult in many ways. Often complex in harmony and concentrated in texture, it is not easy, from a technical standpoint, to play and record. But the greatest difficulty is to evoke its depth of feeling. When there is no feeling, when only the correct notes are played, it sounds meaningless and sterile. There are profound depths in this music, qualities which are eternal and universal. To express all of these demands the utmost striving on the part of the recording artist.

Bach's inner personality was a miraculous balance of hand, head, and heart. He was a master player of harpsichord, violin, cello, viola, and organ. His intellectual mastery of every phase of music has never been surpassed. The poetic inspiration and depth of feeling that came from his heart and that glow in his music lift it to the highest level of expression of all time. To encompass all of this and record it in permanent form, so that it may be heard anywhere in the world, requires the utmost sensitivity and the deepest understanding.

SOME OF BACH'S OUTSTANDING INSTRUMENTAL COMPOSITIONS (in addition to those already listed)

Suite No. 2 in B Minor (for flute and strings)

Overture
Rondo
Sarabande
Bourrée
Polonaise
Minuet
Badinerie (Playful)

Certainly one of Bach's happiest inspirations — graceful, gay, stately by turns.

Suite No. 3 in D Major (for two oboes, three trumpets, drums, strings, and cembalo)

Overture
Air
Gavottes
Bourrée
Gigue

Contains the world-popular Air, one of the most beautiful of Bach's lyric movements.

The Well-Tempered Clavier: Book One, First Eight Preludes and Fugues

The beginning of the so-called Old Testament of the musicians' Bible.

The Art of Fugue

Bach's last work, this has been well called a titanic monument of all musical — and human — achievement. Bach himself gave no specific performing directions for this music; it is available in several different instrumental arrangements.

DEFINITE SUGGESTIONS FOR READING

Music in History: The Secular Works of Bach
J. S. Bach, by Schweitzer: Chapters ix, x, and xv

THE ORGAN [1]

THE KING OF INSTRUMENTS

This will be a suitable place to consider Bach's great instrument, for which he wrote so much. A recent writer on musical subjects laments the fact that a modern performer on the organ is not regarded by critics and concert-goers as in the same artistic class as a Cortot, a Casals, or a Kreisler. "Lists of virtuosi in various branches of music invariably omit mention of the organist with the same regularity as the critic demurs from listening to his playing or treating his instrument with serious regard." Anyone familiar with the musical situation will readily confirm the truth of this statement and at the same time wonder why such things be. For the organ, one of the most ancient of instruments, has always been held in a certain esteem by music lovers: grand, sublime, impressive, inspiring — these are the adjectives which have been used from time immemorial in characterizing the tone of this King of Instruments. As an ancient writer puts it: "When its tones swell forth, there is no denying it, it is like the fiat of the Omnipotent." And a modern lover of the organ thus apostrophizes it:

Temple of Tone art thou! The shrine supreme
Of sound's mysterious powers and richest gifts,
God-given thought alone could have inspired
The human mind to frame so grand a work!
Great Organ — Monarch of all Instruments.

GEORGE ASHDOWNE AUDSLEY [2]

Why then the musical public's lack of interest? The writer quoted above suggests that the low standard of playing in vogue among

[1] Partly reprinted from *Disques* by permission of the publishers, H. Royer Smith Company.
[2] By permission of J. Fischer & Bro.

organists until recently has been largely responsible; but there are other and remediable causes for the lack of general interest in the organ and its music.

The impressive, soul-satisfying dignity of the organ's tone is a result of the manner in which it is produced, not by means of beating reed or vibrating string, but by metal and wooden pipes blown, as Emperor Julian described it in the fourth century, "by a blast that rushes up from a leathern cavern beneath their roots, while a mortal running with swift fingers over the keys that are their concordant rulers makes them give forth melodious sounds." In principle the organ is nothing more than a mechanical means for playing a Pan's Pipe or syrinx — one of the earliest of all instruments, consisting of tubes of varying lengths bound together in such a way that they could be blown upon by the player's breath. In the organ the air is supplied mechanically and its admittance to the pipes controlled by means of keys, one of them for each pitch produced. In order to produce varied qualities of tone, the pipes are made in different ways and whole sets of them, one for each note on the keyboard, used for certain qualities of tone desired. In order to build up a suitable ensemble these various sets of pipes are used together, so that oftentimes when a single key is depressed in a large organ it gives breath to as many as fifty or sixty pipes of different sorts all sounding the same note, or its octaves or other ratio notes.

A VARIED HISTORY

The broadly elevated character inherent in organ tone was early recognized by the Christians as being ideal for providing music in their services, and this in spite of its unfortunate associations in so far as they were concerned; for it had been used by the Romans for theatrical and gladiatorial spectacles. Ever since the fourth century, however, its most natural and fitting place has been in the church, especially since the magnificent interiors supplied by the early church builders were ideal places for the proper hearing of organ tone. As ecclesiastical architecture grew more and more magnificent and the church interiors vaster and vaster, those responsible for providing organs for these buildings experimented with various means for flooding their great churches with tone, and the organ's mechanism became more and more elaborate in order to provide adequate tonal resources. It was not until the seventeenth and early

The Sound-producing Mechanism of an Organ of Bach's Day

The Siebermann organ in the cathedral at Freiberg

eighteenth centuries that the development of the mechanics of organ building allowed the builders to attain their ideal in providing an ensemble completely suitable for their purpose. The organs of these years, in spite of crudities of mechanical control when compared to our modern instruments, were able to provide a rich, satisfying, thrilling tone which sounded to wonderful advantage in the resonant interiors available. And, as has always been the case in similar circumstances, composers were inspired to provide suitable music, once the instrument became capable of playing it. The organ of those days was an important, living, vital instrument in the sense that it hardly is today. Johann Sebastian Bach, one of the supremely great, was providing it with a repertoire which in extent and quality has never been equaled. It had arrived at a point of perfection in its tonal development that has not been greatly improved upon in the years since then, and it had the advantage of adequate and proper surroundings into which to project its glorious voice.

Since then the organ has fallen on rather evil days, especially as far as many instruments in America are concerned. Although most European builders have followed more or less closely the ideals of the eighteenth century in developing their instruments and have had the incalculable advantage of proper auditoriums for their organs, those following what has come to be known as the "modern trend" have forsaken the sunny fields of adequate, dignified tone and wandered astray into ear-tickling and sensation-mongering paths. This has been partly due to the small, stuffy, "parlor" churches which so many societies have seen fit to provide in order to secure homey, social surroundings for their services. Organ tone, because of its peculiar quality, demands a certain amount of reverberation — echo, to use an everyday term — to make it completely effective. And because this enlivening influence has been impossible in churches of wood and plaster, it was natural that the organ builders and players should turn their attention to effects that could come off in these unresonant surroundings. Soft, enervated tones, effects borrowed from the orchestra, string, wood-wind, and brass imitations, percussive, harp, and chime tones, all of them justifiable in themselves but only as subsidiary to essential organ tone, became the rule. Many of our present-day instruments are built up of a rather miscellaneous collection of these pleasing effects, and the glorious richness and dignified strength which should be provided above all things is likely to be forgotten. And, as was again inevitable, a school of organ composition suitable to these conditions has arisen, and we have the rather pitiable spectacle of the King of Instruments being called upon to discourse sobbing accompaniments or else to produce orchestra-like imitation unsuited to its natural dignity.

THE AUDITORIUM AN IMPORTANT FACTOR

The importance of the character of the auditorium into which an organ sounds cannot be overestimated. Technically speaking, the auditorium is an acoustical device of great importance to any instrument, orchestra, piano, voice, as well as organ. Its chief purpose in so far as music is concerned is to enable persons assembled to hear what occurs in it to best advantage. And the very fact that so many architects have been ignorant or perhaps negligent regarding the action of sound phenomena within confined spaces has given us so many very bad auditoriums. If these are not properly constructed, a resultant echo caused by the reflection of the sound pulsations from the various wall surfaces will so confuse the music being produced as to make it an unpleasant jangle of discordant elements, and thereby destroy its beauty. On the other hand, if every bit of reverberation is removed (as used to be done in a broadcasting studio) the music will sound lifeless and dead to the auditors who are somewhat removed from its source. This period of reverberation is more important for organ tone than for that of any other instrument; and a certain amount of echo, even an amount that would somewhat confuse other types of musical tone, is necessary if we are to get the power and thrill of the full organ as well as the beautiful floating quality possible from some of the softer tones. Those who have heard a properly designed organ speaking into a fine, large, resonant interior, playing the type of music really suited to the character of the instrument, know what organ tone should sound like. Unfortunately the coincidence of these necessary factors in the production of good tone is rare; and so many of us, critics as well as laymen, have never heard great organ music as it may sound, although we are surrounded on every side by instruments that are supposed to produce it. Practically every church in the country possesses one, they are being placed in many auditoriums in all the large cities, and the wailing tones of a certain species of them greet our ears almost continuously on the radio.

Fortunately architects, organ builders, and players are all seeing the light, and in recent years we have had some interiors that are almost ideal for sound; and there is a gradual but certain swing away from the rather theatrical ideals of tone appointments that have prevailed in recent years back to those of the classic period. Young players are coming to the fore, equipped with splendid technic and possessing high musical ideals, ready to take advantage of the changes which impend. Perhaps we are on the verge of a renaissance in organ music.

RHYTHM AND REPERTOIRE

There are two factors, however, that mitigate against the organ's becoming a popular instrument in the sense that the piano or the orchestra is one. The first of these is its essentially unrhythmic character. Organ tone by nature is broad, thick, rather unsuitable for any change in pulse; and there is an added difficulty for the organist who strives to maintain a good rhythmic flow in his playing — the mechanical obstacles he must overcome in obtaining accent, the chief means by which rhythm is attained. When a pianist wishes to accentuate a particular note, he does so by extra pressure on the key; the violinist obtains the same effect by a stronger pressure on his bow. But no such direct means are available to the organist. He has to resort to subterfuge, for the only ways he can produce accent are by suddenly increasing his tone by the addition of extra stops (an awkward mechanical feat), or by opening the shutters which enclose a group of pipes in a "swell box," thus swelling the tone at the particular place desired, or by breaking the flow of the music so as to give at least a suggestion of pulse. The continuously flowing, largely unaccented tone of the organ, lacking definite percussive quality, becomes confusing to those who are more familiar with orchestral or chamber music.

The other serious handicap of the organ is its lack of repertoire. Whereas instruments such as the piano, the string quartet, and the orchestra have had compositions written for them by such masters as Beethoven, Haydn, Brahms, Chopin, Schubert, Schumann, and so on — and in prodigious amounts — the organ has to fall back upon the works of two writers for its really *great* music: Johann Sebastian Bach and César Franck. And even in the case of these two men, the amount of music available is limited. Practically all the other great masters through a combination of circumstances left the organ severely alone. To be sure, Handel has left us some organ music, but like so much of his other work, it is outmoded today; Brahms wrote a few lovely things; Mendelssohn and Rheinberger (neither of whom by any stretch of the imagination could be called great) wrote their best music for the organ. The more recent Germans include Max Reger, who left behind a plethora of involved works interesting largely from the viewpoint of construction, and Karg-Elert, who has given us some well-written program music.

And there are the rather pretentious works of the modern French writers, men like Widor, Vierne, and Tournemire, who surround a few interesting pages with stretches of rather disappointing wastes. This limits the repertoire of the organist, unless he falls back upon transcriptions of music originally written for other instruments. A serious handicap, of course, and one which probably precludes the organ from becoming a concert instrument in the full sense of that term unless we come into an unexpected period of fecundity on the part of writers of organ music. Most of the great things that have been written for the organ are suggestive of its religious associations, and its place for many years will probably be in the church.

MECHANICAL PROBLEMS

The problems involved in the development of our modern organ have been three: (1) securing a satisfactory composite tone from a large number of pipes sounding together; (2) obtaining a satisfactory means of controlling the admittance of the air to the pipes by the mechanism of the keys; and (3) perfecting a satisfactory wind supply. All these problems were present in the organ of the Alexandrian, Ctesibius, which was built about 250 B.C. and had rows of bronze pipes controlled by slides connected to iron keys by ropes. They are still in process of development today, for our tonal ideas, as has been suggested, are in a state of flux, and the elaborate electrical mechanisms which have been devised for connecting key and valve controlling the admittance of air to the pipe are not satisfactory in every respect. The early organs in the cathedrals had large keys which were connected by means of ropes and shafts to slides or valves under the pipes; these slides or valves had metal springs to pull them shut when the pressure was removed from the key. Such a crude mechanism was in essence that of our modern organs, but was very difficult to manipulate because it had to work against the wind pressure ready to enter the pipes, and the only way the keys could be depressed was by striking them. And so organ players came to be known as organ beaters, a name they have not entirely lived down today. When more than one note at a time was to be played, a second beater was brought into action, and as can be readily imagined, harmony as we consider it today was quite impossible on these instruments. The providing of wind for these crude instruments was a formidable task; a Winchester chronicler thus describes the organ — an instrument of some four hundred pipes — in his cathedral: there were "ten each to one of forty slides, for which the wind supply came from twenty-six bellows in two rows at which seventy strong men did labor with their arms and covered with the effects of their efforts, yet did each incite his fellows to drive up the wind with all their might." Playing, blowing, and listening to the organ must have been equally strenuous!

In these medieval instruments, there was no way to prevent all the pipes grouped on the slide and controlled by a single key from sounding when that key was depressed; one had to have all or nothing. But in the sixteenth century a Dutch builder invented the "stop," a mechanism which controls the air supply to each set of pipes. If the player pulls out the little lever placed at the side or above the keyboard, the particular set of pipes governed by that lever will sound; if the lever is pushed in, the air supply to that set of pipes is shut off and they remain silent. The same mechanism, called by the same name, is in use today.

There came to be various divisions in the big cathedral organs, developed according to the demands upon them; each of these divisions was played by means of its own keyboard. Hence we have the two, three, four, or five keyboards or "manuals" in the present-day instrument. We still call one manual the *great,* meaning that the loud stops representing the old medieval organ are largely grouped on this manual. The *swell* division derives its name from the device already mentioned, invented in the early eighteenth century, by means of which the pipes are placed in a box fitted with shutters which can be opened or closed by a pedal, thus giving the organist a means for swelling or diminishing the tone. The *choir* organ is suggestive of the days when this group of pipes was placed at the back of the player (the Germans still call this division the *rückpositiv*) and used to accompany the choir; it consists of the softer stops and provides a pleasant contrast to the tone of the other manuals. The stops which are used *a solo,* that is, by having some particular quality of tone standing out from a softer accompaniment, are grouped on a fourth manual called the *solo* organ. The *pedal* was probably first developed in the fifteenth century and provides a sustained bass to the whole ensemble; this device was later supplemented by the development of an independent pedal organ with pipes of its own, most of them of large size and providing the deep bass which we always associate with organ tone.

The mechanism of this complex instrument for centuries consisted of delicately adjusted levers between the keys and the pipe valves, once the crude early slides and ropes were done away with. Later, because it required too much physical strength from the player's fingers to actuate this mechanism, engineers devised means of doing the actual work of pulling down the pipe valves by small pneumatic bellows. And at the present time the whole mechanism is controlled electrically, so that the organist's touch upon the keys actually completes an electric circuit which in turn actuates a small pneumatic motor regulating the wind supply to the pipe. All this has been so perfected that the response is practically instantaneous once the key is depressed. The problem of wind supply which once was such a troublesome one has likewise been satisfactorily solved; the modern organ is blown by large rotary fans actuated by electric motors, thus giving an absolutely steady, dependable supply of air.

THE ORGAN'S TRUE GLORY

The quality of tone emitted by the pipes depends upon the way they are constructed, their size, the proportion of length to diameter, the materials used, and so forth. This is where art enters the organ industry, for the designing and constructing of the various sets of pipes condition the tonal result of the whole instrument. Music lovers are apt to think of the organ builder as a sort of glorified mechanic; in reality he should be a consummate artist as well as a thorough craftsman. The tendency of modern builders until recently has been so to concentrate their attention upon the mechanical and electrical side of the organ's development as to neglect its tonal improvement. In other words, they became so fascinated with the means that they almost forgot the end for which all the mechanism exists — the production of a glorious blend of tone, brilliant without being harsh, thrilling without being overpowering, masterful and compelling, soothing and appealing in turn, the sort of tone which rightfully belongs to the organ and which cannot be obtained from any other instrument; the sort of tone which not only causes the thrills up and down the spine, but which as well leads closer to the Infinite. Rolland describes such an effect upon Jean Christophe when he hears his first organ music. He is in church with his grandfather; suddenly there is a deluge of sound from the organ. He does not understand or know the meaning of it; it is dazzling, bewildering, and he can hear nothing clearly. But it is good. It is as though he were suspended in mid-air like a bird; and when the flood of sound rushes from one end of the church to the other, filling the arches, reverberating from wall to wall, he is carried with it, flying and skimming hither and thither with nothing to do but abandon himself to it. This is the real glory of the organ, a glory that is *sui generis* but obtainable only through the necessary coincidence of instrument, auditorium, and player.

In spite of the fact that the days of its greatest glory have apparently departed, the organ has a definite place in the present scheme of the musical universe if we give it an opportunity for being treated as it should be treated. That is, if we place it where it sounds at its best, if we design it so that its full beauty becomes apparent and do not make it merely a collection of pretty-sounding devices, and if we play music on it that suits its real character. Then, in spite of its evident weaknesses and its limited repertoire, the organ will still maintain its place as an instrument worthy of the serious consideration of critics and music lovers.

THE BAROQUE ORGAN OF THE TWENTIETH CENTURY

There has been a recent revival of interest in the type of organ used at the time of Bach, the instrument for which he wrote his grandiose organ works. Organ builders have devoted a great deal of time and energy to studying the instruments in Europe that still survive from the seventeenth and eighteenth centuries, with a view to imitating their tonal qualities in modern organs. The results have been most interesting and, in some cases, very effective. The distinctive feature of these new-old organs (they are called Baroque because they imitate the instruments of that period) is not the massive, diffuse, romantic tone to which most present-day listeners are accustomed, but a brilliant, sparkling, light clarity hitherto unassociated with the organ. The music of Bach and his predecessors takes on a new quality when played on these instruments; it seems more alive, if less impressive; more rhythmic and lyric, if less colorful. These Baroque organs lend themselves to recording, and a number of Bach and pre-Bach recordings have been made by the different companies.

THE ELECTRONIC "ORGAN"

In recent years there have come into being various electronic tone-producing systems inaccurately called "electric organs." In these the tones are produced either by high-frequency oscillations of radio tubes or by certain electro-magnetic devices. Besides more or less faithfully reproducing the qualities of organ stops these electronic devices can produce indigenous sounds not obtainable from any other instrument. On account of their flexibility and comparative cheapness they have come into wide use in churches, as well as in homes and places of public amusement.

LIST OF RECORDINGS OF ORGAN MUSIC

The following recordings, representative of the best in organ music, were readily available at the time this list was prepared. Many other valuable recordings, formerly available, have been allowed to go out of print, and in the future additional ones will doubtless be added from time to time.

Chaconne in E Minor   Buxtehude
Prelude and Fugue in E and A Minor   Buxtehude
Fugue C   Buxtehude
Chorale Preludes   Buxtehude
  In dulci jubilo
  Vater unser im Himmelreich
  Ach Herr, mich armen Sünder
Concerti (6) *for Organ*, Op. 4   Handel
Concerto 13 in F: *Cuckoo and Nightingale*
  (Organ and Orchestra)   Handel
Concerti (2) *for Organ and Orchestra in C Major*   Haydn
Simon   Haydn
Prelude and Fugue in B Flat Major   Haydn
Prelude on the *Ave Verum Corpus* (K.618)   Mozart
Adagio for Glass Harmonica (K.356)   Mozart
Sonatas for Organ and Strings   Mozart
Prélude, Fugue and Variations, Op. 18   Franck
Pièce héroïque   Franck
Fantasie   Franck
11 Chorale-Preludes, Op. 122   Brahms
Toccata from *Symphony No. 5*   Widor
Marche pontificale from *Symphony No. 1*   Widor

The following numbers, played by the great Bach authority Albert Schweitzer, are of special interest to all lovers of organ music. All are by Johann Sebastian Bach.

Preludes and Fugues

Prelude and Fugue in G
Prelude and Fugue in G Minor
Prelude and Fugue in C
Prelude and Fugue in A Minor
Prelude and Fugue in C Minor
Prelude and Fugue in E Minor
Prelude and Fugue in F Minor
Fugue in G Minor (Little)
Toccata and Fugue in D Minor

Chorale Preludes

Christum wir sollen loben schon
Liebster Jesu, wir sind hier
Mit Fried' und Freud'
Christus, der uns selig macht
Da Jesus an dem Kreuze stund
O Mensch, bewein' dein' Sünde gross
O Lamm Gottes unschuldig
Sei gegrüsset, Jesu gütig
An Wasserflüssen Babylon
Schmücke dich, O liebe Seele
Jesus Christus unser Heiland
Erschienen ist der herrlich' Tag

THIRTY-SEVEN

THE GERMAN-ENGLISH HANDEL

Careers more different than those of Bach and his great Baroque contemporary, George Frederic Handel [1] (1685–1759), can hardly be imagined. Born within a few miles of each other in Germany, these two great giants of the period never met. There are some strong contrasts in their careers: Bach came, as we have seen, from a long family line of musicians; Handel's father was a barber-surgeon, who did not wish his son to become a professional musician. Bach never became interested in the popular, courtly form of opera, and his vocal lines, when he did use them in his church music, partake almost of the character of instrumental music; since Handel was well trained both in Germany and in Italy in the field of operatic writing, and achieved his first great success with opera, it is natural that his writing assumed a lyric, vocal character that delighted the listeners of his day (as well as those of later times). Handel became a great operatic-oratorio composer and producer in London, known and revered everywhere for his great success in that metropolitan center; Bach hardly ever traveled beyond the borders of his native Thuringia in Germany and was known, if he was known at all, as an organ virtuoso rather than as a composer. Today it is Bach's music that is popular the world over, while Handel's is, outside of a very few works, hardly known at all.

HANDEL'S CAREER

After finally obtaining his father's permission to study music in Halle, his native town, Handel entered the university there as a law student. But after his eighteenth year he gave himself over to music, going to Hamburg in 1703 and playing in the opera orches-

[1] This was the form of his name that he adopted after settling in England.

[506]

tra there; he went to Italy in 1706, visiting all the principal cities. He absorbed the Italianate ways of composing to such a degree that he was able to write an opera for Venice, which in many ways was the real home of Italian opera. Coming first to London in 1710, he settled down there permanently a few years later, composing and producing several Italian operas a year with varying degrees of success, against a dangerous opposition on the part of the native musicians.

A man possessed of the utmost tenacity, great bravery, and an overwhelming fecundity of ideas, Handel pursued his exciting career in London through all sorts of vicissitudes and misfortunes that would have broken a less determined spirit. After writing several dozen operas, he tried his luck with English oratorios, when fashions and tastes changed. At first these oratorios were given only during the Lenten season, but they became so popular that Handel wrote and produced work after work in this style, nearly twenty in all. Between the parts of these oratorios, the composer would perform his organ concertos with great success; and his latter years, beginning with the *réclame* of the first Dublin performance of *Messiah* in 1741, were triumphant ones, although darkened by ill health and final blindness.

Handel was a quick worker and gave most of his time and tremendous energy to the production of music, not being bothered by social demands or family obligations. The result was a tremendous amount of vital, energetic, and thoroughly likable music. There is much of it in the fresh, open-air, forthright English style of his talented predecessor Purcell (1659–1695). Although on occasion Handel could penetrate as deeply as Bach, he does not consistently or even often do so. That is one reason why his operas do not hold the stage today; another is their unusual, unreal librettos and the fact that they call for a type of singing no longer fashionable. Of his oratorios, few are sung today outside *Messiah*, which is still the standard war-horse of village choirs and metropolitan choral societies throughout the English-speaking world. Handel's orchestral concertos are less often heard than Bach's, though in their lighter way they can take a place by the side of his contemporary's *Brandenburg Concertos*.

Messiah remains, and will probably always remain, Handel's best-loved work, embodying in its massive choruses, beautiful solos, and its fine orchestral backgrounds an affectionate and intimate

London in Handel's Day

Painted by his contemporary, Canaletto (1697–1768). In the river may be seen two barges similar to those for which Handel wrote the Water Music.

portrayal of the Christ story through its three phases — birth, death, and resurrection. It has its weaknesses as well as its moments of great strength; it is typically Baroque and fully Christian at one and the same time. To be convinced of this, one has only to listen to such a thoroughly graceful, beautifully decorated, and completely successful (vocally speaking) recitative and aria as the very first one, given to the tenor:

Comfort ye, my people, saith your God; speak ye comfortably to Jerusalem and cry unto her that her warfare is accomplished, that her iniquity is pardoned. The voice of him that crieth in the wilderness: "Prepare ye the way of the Lord, make straight in the desert a highway for our God."
Every valley shall be exalted and every mountain and hill made low: the crooked straight and the rough places plain.

Compare this with the terrific emotional intensity of such a chorus as the second one in the Second Part:

Surely He hath borne our griefs and carried our sorrows! He was wounded for our transgressions: He was bruised for our iniquities; the chastisement of our peace was upon Him.
And with His stripes we are healed.

And above all is the majestic dignity of the great *Hallelujah*, about which he himself said: "Whether I was in my body or out of my body when I wrote it, I know not. God knows."

Hallelujah: for the Lord God Omnipotent reigneth.
The kingdom of this world has become the kingdom of our Lord, and of His Christ; and He shall reign for ever and ever.
King of Kings, and Lord of Lords, Hallelujah!

THE CONCERTI

Though some of this music may have been in his mind before he began to write it, he composed this oratorio in three weeks, utilizing here and there pieces he had written for other purposes. His orchestration of it did not take that long, for this art was not yet thought to be of equal importance to choral and vocal writing. His set of twelve *concerti grossi*, mentioned above, were written in

1739 in the incredibly short space of a month, less time than it would take for a good copyist to write them out. It is said that at the beginning of his compositions he would write out all the parts in full; as he proceeded, he would, in his impatient haste, drop first one part and then another, ending up with just the bass alone, as a hint for what the other parts would be. Before he finished one piece he would begin another, sometimes working on two or three at the same time.

His instrumental style may be best observed in these *concerti grossi*, all of them written according to the accepted formulas of the time: an alternation (perhaps opposition is a better word) of a small solo group of instruments and a larger orchestra. These *concertino* solo parts were, in Handel's case, always performed by two violins and a cello; the *tutti* or full orchestra was a body of strings divided into first violins, second violins, violas, violoncellos reinforced by the double bass. This seven-part texture was enriched and tied together by a keyboard instrument (the harpsichord), from which the composer conducted the performance of the music.

Typical of the whole set, each one of which has its own organizational pattern, is the last, No. 12, in B minor, consisting of four main movements with a short *largo* introduction to the last. The first solemn overture-like movement contains a constant alternation of the tutti and the concertino; the second is lively, with long stretches for the solo instruments; the third is a song-like aria, which, if compared with the air from Bach's *Third Orchestral Suite*, will show the difference between the lyric style of these two great composers. This aria is followed by the two decorated variations, called in the parlance of the time a *double:* in it the concertino and the tutti play together. After a short slow introduction, comes the final movement, a four-part, light-hearted fugue, in which again the concertino and the tutti play together.

All twelve of these concertos are different, filled with the utmost variety of material and means. All in all, they represent Handel at his very best: the grand master of Italianate song style, the skilled improvisator, the mind teeming with fertile ideas. They show, like the rest of this composer's works, that, generally speaking, Handel is easier to absorb than Bach. But he hardly ever stands up to his contemporary in range or depth, in lasting power or in philosophical insight. Which does not mean, however, that he has not written some magnificent music, typical of its time, and teeming with forceful strength.

SOME REPRESENTATIVE HANDELIAN COMPOSITIONS

Messiah

Available in several good recordings, this should be studied in its entirety by those wishing to know Handel's varied characteristics.

Concerti Grossi, Numbers 1 to 12

These are available in a magnificent performance by a group of chamber-music players conducted by Adolf Busch.

Water Music Suite
Royal Fireworks Music

Music written by Handel for special occasions; now generally played in modernized orchestral versions. Wonderful, Baroque-styled writing, in real *pomposo* vein.

Arias from Operas and Oratorios:

Sound an Alarm (Tenor) from *Judas Maccabeus*
O Sleep! Why Dost Thou Leave Me (Soprano) from *Semele*
Hear Me, Ye Winds and Waves (Bass) from *Scipione*
Ombra mai fu (Tenor) from *Serse*
    (Popularly known as Handel's *Largo;* see pp. 90–91.)

DEFINITE SUGGESTIONS FOR READING

Music in History: Handel the Magnificent
A *Portrait of Handel* in Romain Rolland's *Essays in Music,* Reprint Edition (New York: Allen, Towne and Heath, 1948)

THIRTY-EIGHT

PRE-BACH

A GOLDEN AGE

As has already been remarked, this is not a history of music but rather a gleaning from the specially attractive fruits of the historical orchard. And although we have covered in this selective way about two and a half centuries, how much there remains ungleaned! But before closing even such a brief summary as this, it will be necessary that we say something about the period that was pre-Bach — roughly a matter of some nine centuries. The history of music is absurdly short, compared with that of most other arts. We know next to nothing of art music before about 800 A.D.; and for about six of these nine pre-Bach centuries composition can scarcely be said to have existed. But the period from about 1400 to the time of Bach (who was working soon after 1700) covers a wonderful amount of fine music — so much that we call part of it music's "golden age."

THE EARLIEST ART MUSIC

Let us see briefly what music was doing during the troubled ages that we call "medieval." We must remember how filled with disturbances these were, how plagues and famines, crusades and wars, wasted man's substance and confused his will. The chart at the end of this chapter shows only the important events in music's development during this time; the background of these ages of confusion should be grasped through reading some such account as that given in Wells's *Outline of History*, so that we may realize what little chance the arts had. With this fact we must associate another, that of music's youthfulness. Where is the music to compare with the literature and sculpture of ancient Greece? We know practically nothing about it, but it cannot have had anything like the same developed form.

We can deduce that present-day music had two principal origins: that of plainsong and that of folk song — sacred and secular sources. The developments from these followed concurrent paths, but it is much easier to trace those of ecclesiastical music, since its written records are so much more plentiful. In the earliest days of the Christian Era church music must have been influenced by contributions from ancient Greek and Hebrew sources that had come down to the early Christians through tradition. From such materials the Christian musicians wove unison melodies having small vocal compass (called plain chant or plainsong), set to the words of the liturgy used in the services of the Church. Each of these melodies was written according to one of the "modes" used by the Greeks. These unisonal chants have come to be known as "Gregorians," from St. Gregory, who sorted and ordered them for practical use during the sixth century.

It was a long time before the idea of singing in two parts at once occurred to the church musicians. The final results were primitive enough, being achieved through melodies sung in two pitches at once — in fourths and fifths. This was the practice in A.D. 900, before modern notation was used. *Organum,* as this process was called, had its theorists, among whom we chiefly remember the monk Hucbald, one of those remarkable Flemings who later were to blaze the trail for the "golden age." Organum started as parallel movement between the two lines of melody, and developed into the more elaborate oblique and contrary forms — one part at first going always in the same direction as the other; then, after all manner of experiments that must have seemed bold and exciting at the time, going a way of its own. Guido d'Arezzo, some time after 1000 A.D., wrote about it and showed how to write the music down surely and (as far as it went) scientifically. What we now call two-part counterpoint (two independent melodies combined) became the thing in church singing; but it must have been dull, for there was no "time" as we understand it — no variety of rhythm in the parts. Experiments with the rhythm of *words* were fruitful, and there was established the basic triple time that for so long held sway. Various subtleties developed which we cannot go into in such a general treatment as this, and there were rather wild shots at freedom of parts, as when one part sang a simple bit of melody and another "discanted" above it.

So composition was born with, probably, a great many happy

accidents among the laborious fittings of words and notes. Not until about 1300 did musicians find how delightful a change it would be to have two-time. About this period some of the variation experiments and queer combinations became rather scandalous — at least Pope John xii thought so, for in 1322 he ordained a simpler style of church music. The tune was again copied exactly by the singers, but at the octave and third, as well as the fifth, above. This made for a richer type of music, in "common chords" we would say. But it was not enough for composers, who began to find charm outside the walls of the Church. One such little part-song is a marvel for its time — the round *Sumer is icumen in,* which belongs to 1280 or early in the fourteenth century. It sings of open-air springtime joys, and there probably was a great deal of other secular music like it. What a pity that this has disappeared, leaving us with only an inkling of the freer, more "human" music which developed outside the Church!

MADRIGALS AND CHURCH MUSIC

English-speakers like to hail John of Dunstable as one of the first really free composers who provided all his own parts, instead of taking a church theme and working upon it. But though the English may have started it, the Flemings, energetic, inventive, exploratory, brought about the first glories of composed music in the way of madrigals and church music. Dufay, Josquin des Prés, Di Lasso, and others developed counterpoint into a lovely art. Listen to one or two works of theirs (many have been recorded and, since the early works of these composers are rather infrequently sung, these recordings are the best means we have for becoming acquainted with them); primitive they may sound, but who shall say that they are short of perfection of their own kind?

The new delight spread over France, Spain, Italy, and into England. The last had a magnificent group of composers of this type of music, from Tallis through the long-lived Byrd and Morley, Weelkes, Wilbye, to Orlando Gibbons. The Flemings carried their art to Italy, and the composers in residence in that land of beauty clarified and intensified it; up to the time the Italians made this music their own there was still a great deal of dusty scholasticism in it. Perhaps it is not without significance that democracy was just beginning to work out its destiny, too; the Church dominated, but

Instrumental Band of the Bavarian Hofkapella

Orlando di Lasso is shown at the clavier.

life was flourishing outside its command. Palestrina it was who brought this music to a pinnacle, always under the auspices and guiding hand of the fatherly Church. Palestrina felt with the Church that music's function was not only to cheer men's minds, "but also to guide and control them." In that sentence we have the key to the medieval view of music, but the key must not be thought of as too harshly turning in what we moderns may regard as the excessively massive lock of that time. There entered the oil of mysticism to smooth its turning.

MYSTICISM IN MUSIC

This aspect of the age has been admirably treated in Daniel Gregory Mason's chapter on "Palestrina and the Age of Mysticism" in his book, *Beethoven and His Forerunners*. It will suffice here to suggest that much of the mysticism of that time, though it aspired nobly, had not reached that conception of the spirit which Dean Inge has defined as "the attempt to realize in thought and feeling the immanence of the temporal in the eternal and the eternal in the temporal." We remember the sixteenth-century revival of intense mysticism in Spain and Italy, and recall the names of St. Teresa and St. Catherine of Siena. In the midst of much earthly misery — of war, famine, plague — men turned, passive, to the Church for comfort, not so much in this life as in that to come. Man was vile; his appetites must be subdued, mortified. Nowadays we believe that a fuller understanding of psychology shows where this kind of mysticism, though it might produce much holiness, went wrong, for it tended to mortify the *mind* as well; but it had its intense beauties, not the least of them the music of Palestrina, leading away from human affairs towards the Infinite. Only if we try to bring ourselves in imagination into the devout, submissive spirit of the time will we be able to understand something of the meaning of Palestrina's gently flowing, harmonious, acquiescent music, supreme as it is in this selfless, exalted kind. We remember, too, the basilicas and cathedrals in which this music was sung — the architecture a soaring counterpart of the aspiring music.

After this mounting, the art of music had to come down to the valley before other peaks could be ascended. Bach, as we have seen, soared, too, but it was on the wings of man's endeavor. In Palestrina the heavenly ones reach down to succor helpless man; in Bach, man, aware of himself and of his task, girds on his sword and aspires to the highest.

SOLO SONG EMERGES

The complexities of this woven choral music were considerable. Other ways of thought, now developing, demanded greater flexibility and humanity in music. Before the end of the sixteenth century, even whilst Palestrina was penning his masterpieces of contemplative devotion, composers were turning to the greater freedom of solo writing; and this led on to the great new form of *opera*. We considered its development, which had as a center date (roughly) 1600, in another chapter.

Turning to Germany, we find a strong influence for the simpler solo type of music in Luther and his ideas as reforming the Church. We have already suggested that these made unison singing popular. Schütz (born in 1585) belongs to the century just before Bach; he composed Passion music which was greatly strengthened by his feeling for drama. Opera and oratorio, then, were the important new forms of music in the seventeenth century.

The chart on page 523 puts into tabular form, in chronological order, the historical developments up to this time.

LIST OF SUGGESTED MUSIC

The only way to obtain an accurate idea of these pre-Bach developments is by hearing good musical illustrations of the various periods. Fortunately this is not so difficult as it might seem, for the recording companies have provided a number of fine records of this early music. Some of these have been brought together in collections, thus making them readily available for the student. By far the best of these are the magnificent *2000 Years of Music* edited by Dr. Curt Sachs and issued by Decca in the United States and Parlophone in England, and the *Columbia History of Music* (Vol. i), by Percy Scholes. Many of the records listed below have been taken from these sets; other record numbers have been given in order to facilitate the finding of these rather unusual records. Records from the Decca collection are marked * and those from the *Columbia History of Music* ♯. AS refers to *L'Anthologie sonore* (International).

The Traditional Sources of Gregorian Chant:

* Hymn to Apollo, the Sun-god; written by Mesomedes in the second century B.C. The scale used in this Greek chant corresponds to

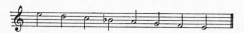

There is a restricted vocal range; the rhythm depends upon the words.

* Kaddish, Abodah, Selection from the Book of Esther; Jewish **chants.**

These are very suggestive of the chants in use in the Jewish ritual of the present day. The text of some of them has come down to us from the eighth and ninth centuries B.C. Notice the recitative-like character of the Esther selection.

Victor 7343   Graduals: *Qui sedes* (Seventh Mode)
  Dirigatur oratio mea
    (Seventh Mode)
  Christus Factus Est
    (Fifth Mode)

Solesmes Choir

Fortunately it is possible to hear really artistic recordings of Gregorian chant made under the most favorable auspices. Many records have been made by the choir of the Abbey of Solesmes, near Cambrai in France, whose monks have for a century made a study of the proper method of singing this chant. These records are especially recommended to the student.

The Beginnings of Part Music:

♯   Plainsong with organum: *Veni Sancte Spiritus* (about tenth century)

The vocal lines here run in exact parallel, the tenor holding the Gregorian melody, the bass singing a fourth below it. Soprano and alto duplicate tenor and bass an octave higher, the whole thing thus being a consecutive series of 4ths, 5ths, and octaves.

♯   *Mira lege* (eleventh century)

Here the music is in two parts, the lower carrying the plainsong, and the upper weaving a much freer part than in the preceding example.

*   *Congaudeant Catholici* (about twelfth century)

A pilgrims' song from Santiago de Compostela; its summons is that the faithful shall rejoice together: Let the Heaven-bound citizens be glad in sweet songs this day and hasten to the holy altar. The Latin words run:

Congaudeant Catholici,
Letentur cives celici
Die ista.

Haec est laudabilis,
Divina luce nobilis
Die ista.

Clenus pulchris carminibus,
Studeat atque contibus
Die ista.

Ergo caventi terminus
Benedicamus Domino
Die ista.

This illustrates a plainsong melody arranged note against note in two-part organum; above this weaves a graceful and loving descant melody of greater individuality, the whole forming a complex and exhilarating polyphony.

♯ Secular part song: *Sumer is icumen in* (thirteenth century)

This is a lilting spring song which is so written as to make a canon for four voices, with two extra bass repeating a phrase which gives support to the whole. The result is a most effective manipulation of simple material and seems to be far ahead of contemporary sacred music. The words, modernized, are:

Summer is a-coming in, Ewe now bleateth after lamb,
Loud now sing cuckoo; Loweth after calf the cow;
Groweth seed and bloweth mead, Bullock starteth, buck now verteth,
And spring the woods anew. Merry sing cuckoo!

AS Two Dances from the Middle Ages

These short instrumental pieces have been transcribed into modern notation from thirteenth-century English manuscripts. They show how unlike the popular music of the Middle Ages was to that of the Church. Here there is a strong pull toward regular rhythmic pulse and a definite feeling of key. The orchestra used, consisting of flute, reed, and drum, is a far cry from the modern dance band, but the rhythmic urge it gives to the music is very similar. (The record containing these dances is AS No. 16; the two included are Nos. 1 and 3 on the first record side.)

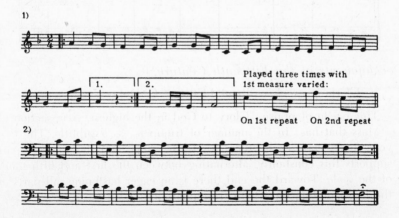

3) **Counterpoint (probably added later)**

Dance Tune

Developments of the Fifteenth Century:

*   *Gloria in excelsis* (about 1450)   G. Dufay

This paean of praise, "Glory to God in the highest," is a section of a Mass that has "In the manner of trumpets" as a subtitle. The two voice parts copy each other closely in canon, and the trumpet part supports this constantly, alternating between the first and fifth tones of the scale. Toward the end there is an eager hastening, all parts at the finish uniting on a high triumphal close.

*   *Et incarnatus est* (about 1500)   Josquin des Prés

This extract from the Mass *Ave Regina Coelum,* filled with a deep brooding and a sense of mystery, perfectly interprets the spirit of the words: "He was conceived . . . of the Virgin Mary and made man." This little gem has been called the most moving thing in early music.

Sanctus from *Missa Papae Marcelli*   Palestrina

These are the words transfigured by Palestrina's setting: "Sanctus, sanctus, sanctus Dominus Deus Sabaoth, Pleni sunt terra et coeli gloria tua. Hosanna in excelsis." (Holy, holy, holy, Lord God of Hosts, Heaven and earth are full of Thy glory. Hosanna in the highest.)

AS   *Sanctus* and *Agnus Dei* from the Mass
       Le bergier et la bergère   Orlando di Lasso

"Sanctus, sanctus, sanctus Dominus Deus Sabaoth, Pleni sunt terra et coeli gloria tua. Hosanna in excelsis." (Holy, holy, holy, Lord God of Hosts, Heaven and earth are full of Thy glory. Hosanna in the highest.)

"Agnus Dei, qui tollis peccata mundi, miserere nobis." (O Lamb of God, that takest away the sins of the world, have pity upon us.)

The title denotes the habit of composers of that time of taking a secular melody around which to weave a sacred movement.

AS   *Omnia tempus habent* (Motet)   Carlo Gesualdo
AS   *Moro lasso* (Madrigal)   Carlo Gesualdo

Madrigals — contrapuntal compositions set to secular words — were written concurrently with compositions for the Church by the masters of the sixteenth and seventeenth centuries, Flemish, French, Italian, German, Spanish, and English. Of these the Italians were perhaps the greatest, with the English composers a close second. Gesualdo, who lived from about 1560 to 1613, wrote madrigals which, because of their peculiar use of chromatic harmonies, sound modern. This is an excellent illustration of his style.

♯   *As Vesta was from Latmos Hill Descending*   Weelkes
♯   *The Silver Swan*   Gibbons

English composers of the Renaissance were among the most important of the time. The first of these two madrigals is from a collection of 1601 dedicated to Queen Elizabeth by twenty-nine different composers. Each sings the praise of this glamorous queen in his own way. Weelkes's six-part madrigal is a setting of the following words (note the — to our ears — peculiar artificiality of the sentiments expressed):

As Vesta was from Latmos hill descending,
She spied a maiden Queen the same ascending,
Attended on by all the shepherds swain,
To whom Diana's darlings, running down amain,
First two by two, then three by three together,
Alone their goddess leaving, hasted thither;
And mingling with the shepherds of her train,
With mirthful tunes her presence did entertain.
Then sang the shepherds and nymphs of Diana:
"Long live fair Oriana!"

The Silver Swan is a simpler type of composition, much less elaborately woven and containing poignant feeling. This five-part madrigal, one of the last specimens of that form composed in England, was published in 1612:

The silver swan who, living, had no note,
When death approached unlocked her silent throat;
Leaning her breast against the reedy shore,
Thus sung her first and last, and sung no more:
Farewell, all joys; O death, come close mine eyes;
More geese than swans now live, more fools than wise.

TOPICS FOR FURTHER DISCUSSION

In the music of which modern composers do you find the closest analogue to the medieval spirit of mysticism? Do you think such a spirit is likely to grow in music of the immediate future?

Many people do not find quite satisfying the reasons generally given for the decline of the madrigalian style. Do you? Which of the reasons do you consider most important, and the most suggestive as to the path that music was next to take?

Why do so many modern performances of the music of Palestrina, Di Lasso, and Victoria leave the listener cold? What are the conditions necessary for an adequate interpretation of these works?

SUMMARY OF HISTORICAL DEVELOPMENTS [1]

Music of Antiquity	The practice of music in the ancient civilizations — Egyptian, Hebrew, Greek, and Roman.
Early Christian Era to about 800 A.D.	One-part vocal music; a single melody with no accompanying parts.
Medieval Age: 800–1450	Organum: Melodies running in parallel parts. Descant: Gradual substitution of more independent parts and greater freedom of rhythm. Counterpoint: The evolution of involved part writing with much use of imitation between the parts. Polyphony: The perfection of the contrapuntal art in the fugue.
The Renaissance: 1450–1600	New ideas of homophony and instrumental style introduced; study of chords and "vertical" music. Evolution of opera and oratorio.
The Seventeenth Century	Gradual adapting of the older contrapuntal styles to the new medium of instruments and the development of instrumental forms (suite, and so on) climaxing in the works of Bach (1685–1750) and his perfecting of fugal art.
The Classic Period: 1700–1800	The development of the instrumental forms of the sonata, symphony, quartet. Music essentially homophonic in style (one chief melodic line with a harmonic accompaniment). Works of Haydn and Mozart.
The Romantic Period: 1800–1900	Romantic composers: Beethoven through Wagner. Gradual evolution of program music. Nationalism. Impressionism as the last manifestation. Strauss and the tone poem. Songs.
Modern Era: 1900–	Realism, etc. Polytonalities, polyrhythms, atonality, and so on. Smaller intervals than half tones. New instruments.

[1] The dates of the periods are only rough approximations, for there is much overlapping; and they are meant to refer to musical, not historical, developments.

A LIST OF COMPOSERS

In order that the reader may have a comprehensive understanding of the various composers and their works we have prepared the following list, giving the names of the principal creative artists in music in chronological order, suggesting the chief characteristics of their music, and occasionally mentioning their most important works.

The Renaissance

JOSQUIN DES PRÉS   *c.* 1450–1521

Josquin, the first composer in the history of the art whose music is interesting to modern ears, wrote a great deal of church music.

GIOVANNI PIERLUIGI DA PALESTRINA   1525–1594

The greatest of all Italian Renaissance composers, Palestrina devoted his whole life to the service of church music. There is a mystic detachment to his Masses and motets that makes them quite individual.

ORLANDO DI LASSO   *c.* 1530–1594

One of the most cosmopolitan of composers, Di Lasso wrote in many styles and in different countries. Unfortunately, not much of his music has been recorded.

TOMÁS LUIS DE VICTORIA   *c.* 1540–1611

The music of Victoria, the greatest of the Spanish composers, has a peculiar depth of feeling and wealth of color, in contrast to that of his Italian contemporary, Palestrina. He confined himself to church music entirely.

WILLIAM BYRD   1542–1623

Sometimes called the English Palestrina, Byrd was the outstanding figure in an important English school of the Renaissance. He wrote in all forms and styles.

CLAUDIO MONTEVERDI   1567–1643

He excelled as a writer of both contrapuntal madrigals and the new-style operas. His works in the latter form are the first successful compositions in this difficult and complicated medium.

Seventeenth and Eighteenth Centuries

HENRY PURCELL   *c.* 1659–1695

A writer of outstanding religious as well as secular music, Purcell is considered one of the greatest of English composers. His misfortune was to have lived at a time when music was no longer cultivated in England as in the Renaissance. Perhaps his best-known work is the opera *Dido and Aeneas.*

ARCANGELO CORELLI   1653–1713

Corelli was one of the earliest writers of violin music.

FRANÇOIS COUPERIN   1668–1733

A French counterpart of Sebastian Bach, Couperin *le Grand* (as he was called in distinction to the other members of his family) wrote a great deal of fine instrumental music.

ALESSANDRO SCARLATTI   1659–1725

DOMENICO SCARLATTI   1685–1757

Father and son, these two have great names in Italian music. The first was famous for his operas, the second for his harpsichord music.

JOHANN SEBASTIAN BACH   1685–1750

One of the most famous of all composers, Sebastian Bach wrote in practically every form then in use, except opera. He is known chiefly for his organ and church music.

GEORGE FREDERIC HANDEL   1685–1759

The possessor of a direct, vigorous style, Handel wrote operas and oratorios in abundance, as well as a great deal of fine chamber music, concertos, suites, and so forth.

CHRISTOPH WILLIBALD VON GLUCK   1714–1787

One of the great reformers of opera, Gluck is the earliest composer whose operas still hold the stage. His lovely *Orphée et Eurydice* is his best-known work.

FRANZ JOSEF HAYDN   1732–1809

A pioneer in orchestral and chamber music, Haydn said a great deal that is still interesting to modern ears. He wrote in every form; his symphonies and chamber-music works are chiefly heard today.

WOLFGANG AMADEUS MOZART   1756–1791

Probably the greatest genius among all composers, Mozart, beginning at the age of five, wrote an unbelievable amount of great music during his short lifetime. This includes some of the world's greatest operas and symphonies.

LUDWIG VAN BEETHOVEN   1770–1827

Standing at the crossroads between the eighteenth and nineteenth centuries, Beethoven is probably known to more people than any other single composer. Successful in all forms, except perhaps opera, he is best known for his magnificent series of nine symphonies.

The Romantic Composers

CARL MARIA VON WEBER   1786–1826

One of the earliest nationalist composers, Weber is known today for his operas, the first successful German works written in that genre.

FRANZ SCHUBERT   1797–1828

The greatest of the lyricists, Schubert is known today principally for his unequaled songs and a few symphonies. But he wrote a great deal in other forms.

HECTOR BERLIOZ   1803–1869

Berlioz was an outstanding French composer and pioneer in the development of the modern orchestra and music written for it. The *Symphonie fantastique* is his best work.

FELIX MENDELSSOHN   1809–1847

He was a talented Romantic composer with strongly Classic leanings.

FRÉDÉRIC CHOPIN   1810–1849

Unlike most composers, Chopin confined himself to writing music of one type, that for piano. In this particular field he excelled.

ROBERT SCHUMANN   1810–1856

One of the most characteristic Romantic composers, Schumann excelled in writing music for the piano — he loved to "dream with the pedal down," as someone put it. Some good songs and a few chamber-music works, in addition to his piano compositions, are still played.

FRANZ LISZT   1811–1886

Although he wished to be known to posterity as a composer, Liszt's reputation rests on his unusual ability as a virtuoso pianist. There is a tinseled element in much of his music that has not contributed to its lasting qualities.

RICHARD WAGNER   1813–1883

Wagner is the greatest of all opera composers. His name is one of the most outstanding in all music. Paderewski called Wagner's opera *Die Meistersinger* one of man's greatest creative achievements, and most unprejudiced listeners would agree with this pronouncement.

GIUSEPPE VERDI   1813–1901

The outstanding composer of Italian operas, Verdi was very prolific, and many of his best works are still popular — a good proof of their quality.

CÉSAR FRANCK   1822–1890

A Belgian composer, Franck lived almost all of his life in Paris. He is chiefly famous for his symphony and some good chamber music; although he was an organist and a devout churchman, some of his organ and church music is inferior in quality.

ANTON BRUCKNER   1824–1896

Bruckner was an Austrian composer whose complex scores are not too well known outside his native land.

JOHANNES BRAHMS   1833–1897

A doughty and valiant Romantic who excelled in his symphonies (of which he wrote four) and orchestral works, Brahms composed in practically all the other forms except that of opera.

MODESTE MOUSSORGSKY   1839–1881

He is the most individual of the Russian nationalists. His great opera *Boris Godunov* must always remain the outstanding work of its kind.

PETER ILICH TCHAIKOVSKY   1840–1893

The fervor, passion, and peculiar melancholy of this composer's music will always endear him to large numbers of people. His six symphonies (particularly the last three) and a few other orchestral works are best known, although Tchaikovsky composed in many different forms.

ANTON DVOŘÁK   1841–1904

This genial Czech composer wrote a great deal of interesting and colorful music, not all of it, perhaps, of prime significance.

NICHOLAS RIMSKY-KORSAKOFF   1844–1908

Rimsky-Korsakoff was a creator of highly colored, Oriental-hued Russian music.

EDWARD ELGAR   1857–1934

Elgar first succeeded in bringing his native England out of the musical doldrums in which she had drifted since the Renaissance.

GUSTAV MAHLER   1860–1911

Mahler was an extremely talented composer with a sensitive, tortured soul. His music shows Romanticism in decline.

CLAUDE DEBUSSY   1862–1918

The greatest of the impressionists, Debussy wrote music which at its best has not been excelled for delicacy of imagination and utmost refinement of expression. He has had few followers.

RICHARD STRAUSS   1864–1949

The great German follower of Wagner, Strauss was a man who carried the latter's Gargantuan orchestral developments to their ultimate conclusion. Strauss wrote mostly program music, and one great opera.

FREDERICK DELIUS   1863–1934

A self-taught, highly imaginative English impressionist, Delius wrote a few things that could have been done by no one else.

JEAN SIBELIUS   1865–

Still a much disputed figure, Sibelius has remained aloof from the rest of the world and has been content to express himself in a most individualistic manner. The results have often been impressive.

SERGEI RACHMANINOFF   1873–1943

Equally famous as composer, conductor, and pianist, Rachmaninoff has written some interesting, if not very individual, music.

ARNOLD SCHÖNBERG   1874–1951

Starting his composing career as a lush Romanticist, Schönberg is known today chiefly for his experiments in atonal writing. Some of his pupils have succeeded in this style better than did he.

MAURICE RAVEL   1875–1937

Ravel was the most sophisticated — and sometimes superficial — of the impressionists. His genius was equally at home in orchestral music, piano music, and opera.

MANUEL DE FALLA   1876–1946

Falla was an outstanding Spanish impressionist.

ERNEST BLOCH   1880–

Bloch's music is filled with the fervor and eloquence of the Jewish spirit. He has long been a citizen of the United States.

IGOR STRAVINSKY   1882–

Stravinsky is a sad example of a talented composer who was once a genius. His best work was written before the first World War.

SONG

FOLK SONG

We have just shown that the history of art music may be said to have begun somewhere around 1500. Folk music — the popular music that was evolved by the people themselves because of their desire to express their own feelings and describe their own interests — had probably existed from the earliest historic times. For human beings have always loved to give vent to their fundamental instinct for expression by means of dance and song. The ancient Hebrews and Egyptians, the later Greeks and Romans, the barbaric German tribes of the early Christian era, the common serfs and the brave knights of the Middle Ages, all have had their own songs and ballads. At the very time that the foundational principles of the art of musical composition were being slowly developed under patronage of Church and State, the people of the fifteenth, sixteenth, and seventeenth centuries were composing their own songs of love, of work and play, of religion. Some of these songs were the products of poets and composers entirely forgotten; some the composite result of various collaborators. All of them have been handed down from generation to generation and, since there was no direct way of writing them down, only the best have survived. The result of a long evolutionary process, the folk song thus has a sense of finality and an eternal quality possessed by no other music. These simple products of unknown masters represent in miniature the same results that were achieved later by the more sophisticated composers; for unconsciously the creators of these folk songs constructed them according to principles of design and balance, and gave them depth of feeling and universality of thought. Using materials found at hand, and expressing the ideas of the people who gave them birth, folk songs and dances utter the racial feelings and show the different characters of all the nations.

Throughout the entire history of music, serving as a fructifying and stimulating influence for some of its most impressive developments, there is woven this colorful thread of folk music. Naturally a great deal of it has disappeared in the course of the centuries. There must have been, for instance, a great deal of folk music composed by such peoples as the Spaniards and the Irish during the Middle Ages; but this has all been lost, although we have a number of manuscripts of the troubadours and the trouvères that were written down during the same period. But there have come down to us a great many examples of this art of the people that were composed centuries ago — no one knows in every case just how many. In more recent times these have been written down, collected, and arranged; there are hundreds of these folk songs and dances, most of them strongly characteristic of the different races. We have work songs, play songs, dances for many different occasions, patriotic hymns, lullabies and children's songs, religious songs (which have definitely influenced the more sophisticated church music), drinking songs, funeral songs, narrative ballads, epic legends, and, of course, love songs.

THE UNIVERSAL APPEAL OF FOLK SONG

The late Charles V. Stanford, writing for the first volume of *The Musical Quarterly*, has given us a fine panegyric on the universality of folk music.[1] He said in part:

"There is no diet so life-giving and so life-preserving as the natural outpouring of the songs of the soil. They have the sanctity of age coupled with the buoyancy of youth. As far as art work can be, they are in their nature immortal. Their claim to immortality is founded on the spontaneity of utterance and their inherent simplicity. There is no flummery or sophistication about them. They do not scruple to be coarse and are not ashamed to be refined when the sentiment and the environment demand. How well and truly they represent the spirit and the tendencies of a nation is obvious even to the least tutored ear."

According to Stanford there have been three main streams of European folk songs: Celtic, Slavic, and Germanic. Included in the Celtic races would be the Highland Scots, the Irish, the Welsh, the

---

[1] "Some Thoughts Concerning Folk-Song and Nationality," Charles Villiers Stanford, *The Musical Quarterly*, April, 1915 (New York: G. Schirmer).

Cornish, and the Breton. The Slavs would include such people as the Russians (Great Russia, White Russia, and the Ukraine); the Czechs (Bohemians, Moravians, and Slovaks); the Jugoslavs (Serbs, Croats, and the Slovenes); the Poles; the Lithuanians; the Bulgarians; and some of the Rumanians. The Germanic songs include those of Austrian origin and are closely allied to those of England. Then there are lesser strains: the Hungarian, the Scandinavian, the Italian, and the French.

A PRACTICAL METHOD OF BECOMING ACQUAINTED WITH FOLK SONGS

There is no better way of becoming acquainted with the rich literature of the folk song than through the fine examples that have been recorded by the various phonograph companies. It must be remembered that the folk song and the art song have to some extent interfused, some folk tunes, almost always originating in the countryside, having been taken up by the townspeople and popularized through drawing-room and stage performance. On the other hand, some folk tunes, for instance those of the shanty type sung by merchant seamen, have occasionally originated as art music of a lowly kind, such as sailors might hear in taverns and music halls and then adapt to their own uses. Those who wish to go into this fascinating subject of popular song will find it necessary to distinguish broadly between three types: first, the pure folk tune, generally transmitted through the generations without having been written down; second, the nontraditional, amateur, homemade ballad in folk style — the type, for instance, that goes with many of Burns's Scots songs and Moore's Irish verses, and the American cowboy ballads; third, the pure drawing-room or music-hall ditty, such as "The Roast Beef of Old England" or "Drink to Me Only with Thine Eyes," often mistakenly classed among folk songs.

THE ART SONG

Thus song has been a universal means for the communication of feeling and of ideas, and the simple folk songs have played a large role in the development of music. Many of the greatest composers have given attention to the song as a medium for expression, and a consideration of the art or consciously composed song is of

Luca della Robbia: *The Young Singers*
In the Opera del Duomo in Florence

importance to the student who wishes to get a comprehensive idea
of the world's music. And some description of the various types of
voices — the means by which song is produced — will be of great
help in this. Professor Redfield has suggested in his book *Music: a
Science and an Art* that in the final analysis all music is but singing, or at least singing and dancing. For instruments are but artificial voices, developed for use when we have no natural voice, or
for more power when our natural voices are too weak, or to provide us with voices more to our liking as to compass and tone color.
The theories as to the origin of music may be as antithetic as those
of Fétis, who defines music as the art of moving the emotions by
combinations of sound, and of Herbert Spencer, who considers

music as a form of expression arising from the reflex action of the vocal organs under emotional stress. But all authorities agree that song was probably the earliest form of human music. And we know that as soon as music became a conscious art it was associated with speech, and that drama and poetry were early used with music. The movements and rhythms of the dance were used to supplement it, and instruments were developed to provide accompaniments. The universal prevalence of instrumental music at the present time should not lead us to forget that the whole development of the first sixteen centuries of music was along vocal lines. By 1700 the Church had developed a perfection of singing that has ever remained as one of the art's chief glories. We have already sketched the way in which this church music developed. Let us turn aside to see how freely song was used outside the influence of the Church.

EARLY SECULAR SONGS

Church song was for a long time less progressive than secular song. In the ninth and tenth centuries churchmen encouraged minstrels to perform sacred plays, at first in villages and then in church. Latin, used at first, in time gave place to English. (Many of these old "mystery" and "miracle" plays have been revived.)

Music outside the Church followed its own path, cherished largely by minstrels, troubadours, trouvères, and minnesingers. History, too, was bound up and propagated in the narrative ballads of the bards. Minstrels were lowborn or highborn; the latter class (trouvères and troubadours, in France) were educated, and most of them were trained musicians. As education in those days centered upon the abbeys, their music showed very strongly the influence of the Church, on the one hand, and of the people among whom their songs became popular, on the other. These songs of the troubadours and trouvères are probably the first composed songs that we have that are of importance; many of them have survived and are worthy of study. The minnesinger was the German counterpart of the French troubadour. Tannhäuser was a minnesinger — you remember his story, and the contest of song, in Wagner's opera. Later came the mastersingers, burgher musicians, and these also Wagner celebrated in an opera. The themes of the French songs of this period deal largely with topics such as love and chivalry; the

German writers included a contemplation of nature and her beauties. There are lovely subtleties here which we cannot pursue.

THE INFLUENCE OF THE OPERA

Any discussion of the history of art song must include a word about the use of the voice in early opera, in sixteenth-century Italy, when instrumental music was little cultivated. The early writers of opera learned how to write effectively for the voice, and the arias from the operas of Monteverdi and Carissimi showed the way for later improvements. Unfortunately the cultivation of the solo song, as opposed to the complexities of the madrigal style of the time, led inevitably to one of music's permanent banes — the excessive glorification of the soloist. These singers from the very beginning tried to improve upon the ideas of the composers, decorating them with inventions of their own. Caccini, one of the earliest writers of opera, has deplored the way in which his pieces were "torn and altered." The liberties of singers, he said, were such that he considered it necessary to have his music printed in order to show what he had written.

We dealt more extensively with opera, the new form that Caccini and his contemporaries were seeking, in an earlier chapter. Now we review briefly the other events in the development of song as an art form. The so-called lute airs, songs written for a solo voice with lute accompaniment, were extremely popular on the continent and in England in the Tudor period; Dowland, through these, succeeded in turning the attention of musicians to the possibility of using the song as an individualized form of expression, although it was not until the time of Schubert that the song can be said to have come into its own. Practically all the important composers from Dowland to Schubert wrote songs — men like Scarlatti, Purcell, Bach, Handel, Mozart, and Beethoven; but they incorporated them in their operas, oratorios, and cantatas. Bach wrote only two separate songs aside from those difficult arias contained in his great church works; Mozart wrote a few, and Beethoven still less. But in no case did these men think of the song except as an incidental, unimportant form, chips which might fall from their workbench while they had been engaged in important works. Exceptions to this universal neglect of the song at this period are the beautiful early Italian arias of such composers as Giordani, Pergolesi, Caldara, and Marcello.

LATER DEVELOPMENTS

With Schubert begins a new epoch, for he was above all else a writer of songs. Possessing an instinct for pure melody that flowed as easily as water gushes from a spring, he wrote song after song with perfect balance and coherence between the words and the music. He raised the song from a place of obscurity to one of the great historic forms of musical expression and laid the secure foundations upon which his successors — Schumann, Franz, Brahms, and Wolf — built so well. Carl Loewe wrote some stirring narrative ballads; Schumann incorporated a more elaborate and poetic piano accompaniment into his songs; Liszt gave us a few magnificent songs that are not known so well as they should be; Brahms's songs, according to many critics, represent him at his best. Robert Franz and Hugo Wolf concentrated their creative activity almost entirely upon songs. The intense German Romanticism of Franz has caused his songs to become dated; the greatness of Wolf's songs, however, transcends all periods and times, and his works stand as the high-water mark in song literature. Extremely difficult to interpret, and requiring an imaginative power possessed by few singers, these songs are not heard so frequently as they deserve. Grieg's pure lyricism displays itself beautifully in his songs. Richard Strauss's best songs, the product of his earlier years, stand among the greatest in the literature. Writers of French songs — César Franck, Debussy, Fauré, Duparc, and Ravel — have produced some works of great beauty, and the Russian writers — Moussorgsky, Rimsky-Korsakoff, Gretchaninov, and Rachmaninoff — have contributed a number of gorgeously colored songs of deep feeling to the repertoire of the artist. Modern English and American writers have composed some excellent songs which, if not of the highest rank, deserve the attention of vocalists.

WHAT IS THE VOICE AND HOW DOES IT WORK?

Redfield, in the book already mentioned in this chapter, shows that the voice differs in no important respect from other instruments as a device for producing the successive pulsations in the atmosphere that reach our ears as tone. The piano hammer starts the string in vibration; as the string vibrates it causes condensations and rarefactions of the air which travel to the listener's ear as fast as they are produced. This pulsing of the atmosphere gives us the sound of the piano string. So with the clarinet reed fluttering back and forth between the air cavity in the player's mouth and that within the clarinet, or the trombone where the air from the player's lungs escapes between his tightly stretched lips, causing them to vibrate and so produce the successive condensations and rarefactions in atmosphere. The human voice resembles most closely such an instrument as the siren, for two folds of muscles are drawn towards each other and withdrawn, and air is passed across them from the lungs; they vibrate, and the sound is produced by the cutting of the air current into regular puffs, as in the ship's siren. These weak vibrations need reinforcement or resonance, comparable, broadly, to the air column that exists within the body of the clarinet, the French horn, or the trombone. In the case of the voice this resonance is given by the air cavities above the vocal cords; and any practical singer will testify that the quality of the tone he produces depends to a great extent upon the combination of these resonance chambers — (1) larynx to top of throat, (2) the mouth, and (3) the passage continuing from the throat up behind the nose.

The actual mechanism, then, by which the voice is produced is part of the individual who plays the instrument, which fact accounts for the intimate, personal quality that it is possible to inject into vocal music. Truly, a lovely voice is the most appealing of all instruments, but it is impossible always to hear it at the best advantage, for the conditions of the singer's instrument depend not only upon his physical well-being, but upon his mental attitude as well. And there is a further handicap which must be overcome by the singer — the lack of definite and practical instruction in the way his instrument should be used. A clarinet player may take his clarinet to a teacher, and because clarinets are all alike, receive exact information as to how to manipulate it under different conditions of blowing, fingering, and so forth, to produce the tones desired, whereas no two voices are ever exactly alike, since nature never repeats exactly the same conditions as to size of vocal muscles, resonating chambers, and so on.

It is likewise manifestly impossible to detach the instrument while it is in the act of producing tone, but two inventions have in turn enabled us to become much surer about what happens when we sing. One was the laryngoscope (invented by Manuel Garcia, 1805–1906), an arrangement of mirrors for examining the action of the vocal folds. The other is the method of applying X rays to singing, first expounded and illustrated in Evetts and Worthington's *The Mechanics of Singing*. Even so, it is difficult to teach singing, when we consider that almost all such tuition must take place in the absence of scientific instruments and that, after all, the instruments show only what happens, not how to manipulate the organs. It is little wonder that there are still so many varied theories of voice training. A definite treatment is F. C. Field-Hyde's *Art and Science of Voice Training* (Oxford Press, 1950).

The voice mechanisms of men and of women are exactly alike except as to size; the vocal cords of men are larger, and naturally the male resonating cavities are larger than those of the female. Hence there is a difference in pitch between the voices of the sexes, the average difference being about an octave. All sorts of voices have been developed among both men and women singers: women who have small vocal folds are sopranos, those with larger ones sing alto; men whose vocal folds are small are tenors, those with larger muscles have bass voices.

THE TYPES OF VOICES

If the physical conditions are suitable, a soprano voice is often able to soar clear and high, and if this natural facility is trained so as to execute all sorts of "bravura" passages — trills, turns, and rapid series of runs — we call the voice a *coloratura*. These acrobatic types of voices are not so popular today as they once were, perhaps because the general musical taste is of a somewhat higher level; but technical skill of any kind is always able to excite admiration, and coloratura sopranos will probably always enjoy a certain amount of popularity. Such operatic numbers as *Una voce poco fa* from *The Barber of Seville* (Rossini) or the Mad Scene from *Lucia* (Donizetti) serve to display this kind of voice. If a light, high soprano is suited to a fluent melody in which deep sentiment can be expressed, we call that voice a *lyric soprano*. "Solvejg's Song" from Grieg's *Peer Gynt* and the "Song of India" from Rimsky-Korsakoff's opera *Sadko* are good examples of purely lyric songs. A soprano voice that is a little lower than the coloratura and is useful in opera because of its rich quality and wide range of emotional color is called a *dramatic soprano*. Listen to a good soprano in such operas as *Aïda* or *La Vestale*, and you will become familiar with the velvety quality and the dramatic intensity that a good voice of this kind possesses. But you will also notice that the vocal quality is often of much greater interest to the audience than is the music sung!

A voice lying midway between soprano and alto is called a *mezzo-soprano*. The voice that has the lowest range and the deepest quality among women singers is the *contralto* or, as it is usually abbreviated, the *alto*. Like the baritone in men's voices, this is well adapted for lament or other emotional expression; but its greatest handicap is that its repertoire is decidedly limited. Composers seem to have given their most brilliant inspirations to sopranos, since so much of the dramatic and lyric expression has been inspired by the young heroine, whereas the alto voice is characteristic of the older woman and consequently not so popular, although it is capable of a much wider range of human experience. Onegin singing Brahms's *Sapphic Ode*, or Branzell, Schubert's *Death and the Maiden*, or Schumann-Heink *Der Erlkönig* will give you an idea of the glories of the alto voice.

The highest and lightest tenor voice is known as the *lyric tenor*, a voice that is apt to become tiresome because of its overinsistence upon sentimentality. Von Bülow certainly had lyric tenors in mind when he made his famous quip: "A tenor is not a voice — it's a disease." And yet it seems to have been, and still is, a necessary disease. Wagner gave all his principal roles to dramatic tenors (who have a somewhat lower range and a rounder, fuller quality than the lyric tenors), in spite of the fact that the standards of singing in his time were probably no better than they are in ours. The tenor of heroic proportions is called a *tenore robusto;* the Germans use the term *Heldentenor*, heroic tenor. It is hardly necessary to cite examples of lyric tenor songs — they are numerous and very well known; unfortunately many of the sticky Irish ballads and sentimental mother songs have been perpetrated by this type of singer. Fine examples of dramatic tenor songs are the "Prize Song" from Wagner's *Die Meistersinger* (if sung by a good voice — the chances are unfortunately against it) or *In fernem Land* from the same composer's *Lohengrin*. An excellent robust tenor solo is the ever-popular *Celeste Aïda* from Verdi's opera. Italian composers and singers know how to make the most of this style.

Of all voices, male or female, the baritone has the greatest range of possibilities. A *lyric baritone* has much the same range as the *tenore robusto* but possesses more of a bass quality, especially in the lower voice. To appreciate the completely satisfying quality of this kind of voice, listen to a program by such a favorite singer as John Charles Thomas or Schlusnus, representing, as it does, all types and sorts of songs. A *bass baritone* is lower in range than the lyric baritone and has a heavier quality. The *basso profondo* has the lowest voice in range, and the deepest in quality; the Russians seem both by birth and training to have produced the best of these voices. Chaliapin, the great singing actor, is an outstanding example; he can be heard on many fine records, notably in the "Aria of Khan Kontchak" from the opera *Prince Igor* and the "Song of the Viking Guest" from Rimsky-Korsakoff's *Sadko*.

VOCAL COMBINATIONS

Single voices are often used in combination: in duets, trios, quartets, quintets, and so forth. The chorus, a grouping of a large number of voices singing the various parts under the direction of a conductor, corresponds within limits to the effectiveness of the instrumental orchestra. Duets usually comprise contrasting voices — tenor and baritone, soprano and alto, and so on. They are a favorite form of expression with the Italian opera writers; witness the great pact duet from Verdi's *La forza del destino,* or the impressive final duet sung against a choral accompaniment in the last scene from the same composer's *Aïda.* The effect of the latter is gained by fusing voices of similar quality. The trio is somewhat of an unwieldy form in comparison with the duet or the quartet, and consequently has never become very popular. The quartet must always remain the most used of the smaller vocal ensembles, for it contains all the parts necessary for full harmony. The popular American term "harmonizing" means singing in quartet, and we hear constantly all sorts of this combination of voices, good, bad, and indifferent, mostly the last. To sound well together, four voices must have sympathetic blending qualities, each voice supplementing and complementing the others. The most artistic combination is the mixed quartet — soprano, alto, tenor, and bass; the most popular, the male quartet — two tenors and two basses (sometimes with an alto in place of one of the tenors).

A *cappella* singing — that is, singing after the fashion of a choir, without accompaniment — is to the minds of many music lovers the most supremely satisfying form of musical expression. And there is reason for such an opinion, for the intimate appeal of the human voice to which we have already referred suffers no diminution when a large number of singers is heard together. There is a charm in the blending of the various parts as they interweave one with the other, constantly separating and then flowing together again, as well as a striking purity and beauty of well-tuned chording not found in every kind of music. In *a cappella* singing we have the possibility of a purity of intonation that gives the music an appeal something like that of the string quartet and makes us realize how much of a compromise the tempered scales of the keyboard instruments are. Hearing a good choir sing dead in tune (and fortunately there are many such opportunities) should convince the most skeptical of us that the advantages are not all on the side of equal temperament (see Glossary), even though the employment of such a scheme has made possible our modern instrumental music.

THE LISTENER'S REPERTOIRE OF SONGS

In preparing a repertoire of songs for the listener we are faced with a peculiar difficulty due to the fact that the form associates music so closely with words. In writing a song, the composer is first concerned with the words; from them he draws his inspiration for music, and out of them the musical structure grows naturally and inevitably. So, in interpreting a song, the artist must strive above all things to emphasize the meaning of the words and should make his rendering of the music a means to that end. Unfortunately for English-speaking peoples, most of the world's great songs have been written to texts in other languages, and so in listening to them music lovers lose a great deal of the effect intended by the composer. Two courses are open to English-speaking audiences: the words of the original can be translated and sung in English by the artist, thus making the meaning of the song clear enough but often doing violence to the composer's association of text and music; or the listener can familiarize himself in advance with a translation of the original text and thus approximate the general meaning of the song as he listens to the artist sing it in the original language. In the latter course the intimate connection between the verbal and musical phrases is lost. In any case, if the hearer is to realize the great beauty of mastersongs, he must by some means familiarize himself with the meanings of their words. All the songs in this list have been recorded.

ART-SONG REPERTOIRE

Songs of the Troubadours and Trouvères

Blondel de Nesle: *A L'entrant d'esté*
Perrin d'Angicourt: *Quand voi an la fin d'estey*
Thibaut of Navarre: *L'Autrier par la matinée*
Adam de la Halle: *Or est Baisrs en la Pasture*

Songs of the Minnesingers

Walter von der Vogelweide: Palestine Song
Meister Rumelant: *Ob aller mynne*

Early Opera and Cantata Airs

Monteverdi: *Oblivion soave* (*L'Incoronazione di Poppea*)
     Maledetto, sia l'aspetto
Carissimi: *Vittoria, Mio Core*

Elizabethan Lute Songs

Dowland: Come Again, Sweet Love
    Come, Heavy Sleep

Other Art Songs

Lully: *Bois épais* (*Air d'Amadis*)
A. Scarlatti: *Son tutto duolo*
Purcell: Dido's Lament (*Dido and Aeneas*)
    I Attempt from Love's Sickness to Fly
J. S. Bach: *Aus Liebe will mein Heiland sterben* (*St. Matthew Passion*)
     Bist du bei mir
Handel: I Know That My Redeemer Liveth (*Messiah*)
    Oh Sleep! Why Dost Thou Leave Me? (*Semele*)
    Where'er You Walk (*Semele*)
Mozart: *Das Veilchen*
    Alleluia
Haydn: With Verdure Clad (*The Creation*)
   Rolling in Foaming Billows (*The Creation*)
Beethoven: Creation's Hymn
     Adelaide
Schubert: *Der Erlkönig*
    Der Wanderer
    Die Winterreise (Cycle)
    Der Doppelgänger
    Du bist die Ruh'

	Am Meer
	Der Tod und das Mädchen
Loewe:	Der Erlkönig
	Edward
	Archibald Douglas
Schumann:	Die beiden Grenadiere
	Frauenliebe und Leben (Cycle)
	Du bist wie eine Blume
	Mondnacht
Liszt:	Du bist wie eine Blume
	Die Lorelei
Franz:	Im Herbst
	An die Musik
Wolf:	Verborgenheit
	Anakreons Grab
	Heimweh
	Das Ständchen
	Auf einer Wanderung
Grieg:	Solvejg's Song
	The Nightingale
Brahms:	Sapphische Ode
	Immer leiser wird mein Schlummer
	Feldeinsamkeit
	Von ewiger Liebe
	Auf dem Kirchhofe
Franck:	La Procession
	Panis Angelicus
Richard Strauss:	Morgen
	Ständchen
	Traum durch die Dämmerung
	Zueignung
	All' mein' Gedanken
Debussy:	Chansons de Bilitis
	Fêtes galantes No. 1 and 2 (6 songs)
Fauré:	Au cimetière
	L'Horizon chimérique
	La Bonne chanson
Duparc:	Chanson triste
	Testament
	Soupir
Ravel:	Shéhérazade:
	La Flûte enchantée
	L'Indifférent

Mahler: *Ich atmet' einen Lindenduft*
Ich bin der Welt abhanden gekommen
Moussorgsky: Song of the Flea
Songs and Dances of Death
Gretchaninov: The Mournful Steppe
Rachmaninoff: Oh! Do Not Sing Again
Griffes: By a Lonely Forest Pathway
Carpenter: The Sleep That Flits on Baby's Eyes
Serenade
Vaughan Williams: *On Wenlock Edge* (Cycle)
Warlock: Fair and True
Piggesnie
My Own Country
Britten: *Holy Sonnets of John Donne* (Cycle)

A WORKING LIST OF USEFUL BOOKS

The standard reference work for any extended investigation in music is the multi-volumed *Grove's Dictionary of Music and Musicians* (Macmillan). For somewhat briefer reference there are several one-volume cyclopedias, the most useful being (in alphabetical order): Apel's *Harvard Dictionary of Music* (Harvard University Press), Scholes's *Oxford Companion to Music* (Oxford University Press), and Oscar Thompson's *International Cyclopedia of Music and Musicians* (Dodd, Mead).

Books which describe or analyze numerous specific works include O'Connell's *Victor Book of the Symphony* and *The Victor Book of Overtures, Tone Poems and Other Orchestral Works* (both published by Simon and Schuster), of an easily readable nature; *The Symphony,* edited by Ralph Hill (Penguin Books) contains brief analyses of a large number of works; Bernard Shore's *Sixteen Symphonies* (Longmans) has longer descriptions of some of the most popular things; Tovey's seven volumes of *Essays in Musical Analysis* are famous for their scholarly treatment and occasional humorous sidelights (Oxford University Press); Veinus's *Victor Book of the Concerto* (Simon and Schuster) treats of the best-known works in this field. The standard American reference works in so far as annotated programs are concerned are the bound volumes of *The Boston Symphony Programme Notes* (Symphony Hall, Boston, Mass.) by Philip Hale and John N. Burk.

In chamber music the fullest study of composers' styles and individual works is W. W. Cobbett's two-volume *Cyclopedia Survey of Chamber Music* (Oxford University Press). A description of the history and development of this purest style of music is Ulrich's *Chamber Music: The Growth and Practice of an Intimate Art* (Columbia University Press); a much shorter sketch, well illustrated, is Hyatt King's *Chamber Music* (Wyn).

In addition to the one-volume general survey of the history of music against the background of its time mentioned throughout this book, McKinney and Anderson's *Music in History* (American Book Company), there may be mentioned among the dozens of different approaches Curt Sachs's factual *Our Musical Heritage* (Prentice-Hall: published in England by Dobson as *A Short History of World Music*) and Alfred Einstein's *Short History of Music* (Knopf). Láng's scholarly and extensive *Music in Western Civilization* (Norton) makes a good reference book. Nef's *Outline of the History of Music* (Columbia University Press) well justifies its title.

For the lovers of opera there is the excellent well-packed, brief Penguin book, *Opera*, by E. J. Dent; at the opposite extreme in bulk is the two-volume *Short History of Opera* by Grout (Columbia University Press). Upon *The Opera and Its Future in America* (Norton) Herbert Graf of the Metropolitan Opera, New York, has written with authority. Without doubt, the best books on the stories and plots of operas are the three by Ernest Newman: *Stories of the Great Operas and Their Composers* (Putnam); *Wagner Operas* (Knopf); and *More Stories of Famous Operas* (Knopf). Upon the specialized subject of *Opéra Comique* there is the little illustrated book so entitled by Martin Cooper (Wyn).

For ballet the most useful storybook is Beaumont's *Complete Book of Ballets* (Putnam); Haskell's *Ballet* (Penguin) gives the amateur briefly all he needs as a guide to the art.

Lives of composers are to be found in several collections, the best of which are Weinstock's *Men of Music* (Simon and Schuster); *The Stream of Music* by R. A. Leonard (Doubleday); and the three-volume Penguin *Lives of the Great Composers*. Some of the most useful books on individual composers' lives may be noted: *Bach*, by S. and M. Grew (Dutton); *Handel*, by Weinstock (Knopf); *Haydn*, by Geiringer (Norton); *In Search of Mozart*, by Ghéon (Sheed and Ward); Sullivan's *Beethoven* (Penguin); *Schubert*, by Kobald (Knopf); *Brahms, His Life and Work*, by Geiringer (Oxford University Press); O. Thompson's *Debussy* (Dodd, Mead), a standard work; Roland-Manuel's *Ravel* (London: Dobson), translated into English. Then there is a *Life of Tchaikovsky* by Weinstock (Knopf) and, upon contemporary Russian work in general (including that of such men as Shostakovich, Khachaturian, and Prokofieff), there is Gerald Abraham's *Eight Russian Composers* (Oxford University Press). Contemporary music and its makers have been provocatively reviewed by Constant Lambert in *Music Ho!* (Penguin). The American scene has been crisply surveyed by Virgil Thomson in his *State of Music* (Morrow), and a useful little book on *Music in England* has been produced by Eric Blom (Penguin). The standard work on American composition is Howard's *Our American Music* (Crowell), and a comprehensive work on jazz in Blesh's *Shining Trumpets* (Knopf).

Two simple books on form and its significance are Abraham's *Design in Music* (Oxford University Press) and J. Raymond Tobin's *How to Understand Musical Form* (Boosey, Hawkes). Reliable guides to the technical problems of acoustics are Lloyd's *Music and Sound* (Oxford University Press) and Redfield's *Music, A Science and an Art* (Knopf). Some of the arguable aspects of aesthetics are discussed in the following: O'Neill, *The Relation of Art to Life* (Routledge); John Dewey, *Art as Experience* (New York: Minton, Balch; London: Allen & Unwin); Schoen, *The Psychology of Music* (Ronald); Vernon Lee, *Music and Its Listeners* (New York: Dutton; London: Allen & Unwin).

Finally, these books will be valuable to those making a collection of records: Moses Smith, *The Select Record Guide* (Macmillan); Kolodin, *New Guide to Recorded Music* (Doubleday); Hall, *Records, 1950* (Knopf); and *The Jazz Record Book* (A. S. Barnes). Most comprehensive of all is Clough and Cuming, *The World's Encyclopaedia of Recorded Music* (London: Sidgwick & Jackson).

GLOSSARY

This glossary is not meant to be a detailed dictionary, but a list of terms that music lovers are likely to come across. A good cheap pocket-sized book giving additional information is Baker's *Pronouncing Pocket-Manual of Musical Terms* (New York: Schirmer; London: Chester); and a Penguin *Music Dictionary* can be had.

Absolute music. Music which is sufficient in itself, and does not depend on literary or other outside associations. (See Chapter Nine.)

A cappella (It., "in church style"). Music written for unaccompanied singing, or without independent accompaniment.

Accelerando (It.). Accelerating, getting gradually quicker. Its opposite is *ritardando, q.v.*

Accidental. A chromatic sign not found in the signature but introduced in the course of the piece.

Accompaniment. A part added to the leading melody or part in order to support and enrich it.

Acoustics. That branch of physics which treats of the phenomena and laws of sound; the sound-affecting qualities of an auditorium.

Adagio (It., "slow, leisurely"). A slow rate of movement. See scale of speeds at end of Glossary.

Ad libitum (L., "at will"). The performer may employ a tempo or an expression that suits his pleasure. Sometimes used to signify that a passage may be omitted if desired.

Air. (*a*) A melody of sufficient interest to stand alone without accompaniment.

(*b*) A self-contained solo movement from a larger work.

Alla breve (It.). A composition in 4/4 (common) time executed by counting two beats to the measure, hence doubly fast.

Allargando (It.) Gradually growing slower and broadening the time.

Allegretto (It.). Moderately fast; diminution of *allegro*. See scale of speeds at end of Glossary.

Allegro (It., "merry, quick"). A brisk rate of movement sometimes qualified by *non troppo* ("not too much"), or increased by the terms *assai* ("very") or *molto* ("much"). See scale of speeds at end of Glossary.

Andante (It., "going, moving"). A moderately slow rate of movement which has the implication of moving along or flowing. Sometimes qualified by such terms as *sostenuto* ("sustained") or *con moto* ("faster"). Commonly applied to the slow movement of a sonata or a symphony. See scale of speeds at end of Glossary.

Animato (It.). Spirited, with animation.

Anthem. A sacred choral composition of moderate length; usually based upon Biblical text.

Antiphonal. Music in which groups of performers answer each other. Most often applied to choral music.

Appoggiatura (It.). A musical ornament consisting of a single note introduced as a suspension before any note of a melody.

Arco (L., "bow"). A direction for bowed instruments to resume bowing after a *pizzicato* (plucked) passage.

Aria (It., "air"). A composition for solo and instrumental accompaniment, taken from a work such as an opera or an oratorio.

Arpa (It.). Harp.

Arpeggio (It.). A chord in which the notes are played one after the other instead of all together.

Art Music. "Created" music of high purpose, in contrast to traditional folk music and "popular," ephemeral music.

A tempo (It., "in time"). At the original rate of speed; used after a change of pace.

Atonal. Having no fixed key; not centering on any single key.

Ballet. A dance performed as an artistic unit, usually employing a dramatic thread or story.

Bar. A vertical line dividing measures on the staff and indicating that the strong beat falls on the note immediately following. The proper emphasis on this strong beat is what creates the rhythmic pulse or flow in music. To the English the term "bar" means "measure."

Baroque (Fr., "irregular or bizarre"). A term generally used in art history to signify the style of art prevailing during the late sixteenth, the seventeenth, and part of the eighteenth century and characterized by the use of grandiose and contorted forms. By association it is often applied to music of the same time, especially to that of Bach's general period.

Bass. The lowest register in voices or instruments. The lowest part of a composition.

Batterie (Fr.). The group of percussion instruments in the orchestra.

Beat. In acoustics, the sudden reinforcement of sound, occurring at regular intervals and produced by the interference of sound waves of slightly different periods of vibration. In music, the regularly recurring and periodically accented pulse which constitutes a unit of measurement in music; in practical use, the term is made to refer to the time value of the basic unit within a measure (such as the quarter note in 4/4 time) or the motion of the hand, baton, and so on, used in marking such units.

Ben, bene (It.). Well. *Ben marcato,* well marked.

Berceuse. A cradle song or lullaby.

Binary. A two-part form, A–B; see Chapter Thirteen. Sometimes confusingly applied to the form A–B–A, as having only two separate subjects.

Bourrée. A dance of French or Spanish origin, in rapid tempo, 2/4 or 4/4 time, frequently employed as a movement of the classical suite.

Cacophony. The dissonant effect produced by sounds which are so combined as to be displeasing to the ear.

Cadence. The series of notes or chords through which a melody or harmony is brought to a temporary or final close. Various types of cadences used have different degrees of finality, the greatest being the *authentic cadence,* that progression of the chord on the dominant to the chord on the tonic (V–I).

Cadenza (It.). An ornamental passage in a concerted work in which a soloist displays his virtuosity. Occasionally it contains fine craftsmanship, but in general, especially when expanded into a lengthy fantasia designed for technical display, it is the curse of the concerto.

Canon. A form in which a melody begins in one part and is exactly copied by one or more parts at a given distance. A good example is the opening of the Finale of Franck's violin and piano *Sonata.*

Cantabile (It.). Singable; in a singing or vocal style.

Cantata. Originally a sung work, as opposed to a played one ("sonata"). Now means a secular or sacred work for soloist(s) and chorus, usually with orchestral accompaniment.

Cantilena (It., "a little song"). A tuneful, songlike flowing passage on an instrument or for a voice.

Cantus firmus (L., "fixed chant"). A given melody or plainsong tune to which other parts are to be set according to rule.

Caprice. Whim or fancy, hence a composition (instrumental) in free form, distinguished by originality in harmony and rhythm.

Cembalo. A name given to many keyboard instruments in musical history.

Chaconne. An instrumental piece consisting of a series of variations over a ground bass. Differs from the traditional *passacaglia* in that the bass theme may occur in an upper voice.

Chamber music. Compositions written for a small concert room, to be played by a small musical organization. See Chapter Nineteen.

Chant. A liturgical vocal melody. See also *Gregorian.*

Chorale [sometimes spelled *choral* (Ger.)]. A hymn tune of the Lutheran church, slow and dignified.

Chord. A simultaneously sounding group of two or more notes of different pitch. Chords can be built upon any note of the scale, their character depending upon their constituent notes.

Chorus. A body of singers, or a composition for them.

Chromatic ("colored"). Largely including, or moving by, half tones. Opposed to *diatonic, q.v.* Also used to mean containing notes foreign to a given key.

Classicism. The style of composition in which the strongest emphasis is laid upon formal beauty coupled with feeling (as distinguished from *Romanticism, q.v.*).

Clavichord. A precursor of the piano; a keyboard instrument in which the strings are struck by small brass tangents operated by the keys.

Clavier ("keyboard"). A word used colloquially for whatever keyboard instrument was fashionable; at one period it meant the harpsichord, later the pianoforte. To the Germans it meant the clavichord.

Clef. A sign (formerly a letter) put at the start of a line of music, to fix the name and pitch of one note, from which all others are reckoned.

Coda ("tail"). A concluding phrase or section rounding off a piece.

Concert overture. A separate orchestral piece, usually in sonata form, and not infrequently programmatic.

Concerto. A work for one or more soloists and orchestra.

Concord; consonance. Sounds which by themselves give a sense of completion.

Continuo, sometimes called *Thorough Bass.* The accepted manner of accompanying nearly all music during the seventeenth and eighteenth centuries. The composer wrote his bass part with figures which showed the harmonies to be employed, in a sort of musical shorthand. These were carried out by a cembalo (keyboard instrument), usually a harpsichord or organ, thus providing a gentle harmonic background to the whole. In order to insure a good foundation, the bass line was usually strengthened by a violoncello, viola da gamba, or other suitable instrument.

Counterpoint ("note against note"). Used to refer to a type of composition made up of various simultaneously sounding musical lines. Also known as *polyphony.*

Countersubject. In a fugue, the counterpoint stated in continuation of the *subject,* while the answer is being given in another voice.

Courante. Early French dance in triple measure and lively tempo. Frequently found in the classic Suite, as the second of its four cornerstone movements.

Crescendo. See *dynamics.*

Cyclic form. A scheme of construction in which certain ideas reappear in various movements. Franck and D'Indy were fond of it.

Czardas (csardas). A Hungarian popular dance consisting of the contrasting "Lassu" (slow and impassioned) and "Friss" (lively).

Da capo [D.C.] (It., "from the head"). Repeat from the beginning.
  Da capo al fine. Repeat from the beginning to end (*i.e.,* "fine").
  Da capo al segno. Repeat to the sign (:S:).

Decrescendo. See *dynamics.*

Descant (discant). The first attempts at polyphony with contrary motion in the parts, as opposed to *organum,* in which parallel motion was the rule. Now used to mean a free part added to a principal melody.

Development. The building up of the thematic material in a work after it has been expounded. See *Sonata form.*

Diatonic. Pertaining to, or designating, the standard major and minor scales made up of tones and semitones, as distinguished from *chromatic,* made up entirely of semitones.

Diminuendo. See *dynamics.*

Dissonance. Sounds which require progress into others in order to give a sense of completion.

Dominant. The fifth tone of the major or minor scale. *Dominant chord.* A chord having the dominant note as its root (dominant triad, dominant seventh, dominant ninth).

Duet; duo. Composition for two performers.

Dynamics. Of, or pertaining to, the scheme of tonal power used in interpreting music. The following abbreviations are in common use for designating various volumes of tone:

fff	*fortissimo assai*	As loud as possible
ff	*fortissimo*	Very loud
f	*forte*	Loud
mf	*mezzoforte*	Moderately loud
mp	*mezzopiano*	Moderately soft
p	*piano*	Soft
pp	*pianissimo*	Very soft
ppp	*pianissimo assai*	As soft as possible
fp } pf }	*forte piano* or *piano forte*	A quick transition from loud to soft, or soft to loud
sfz	*sforzando*	A sudden increase of tone, applied to single notes
rfz } rf }	*rinforzando*	A sudden increase of tone, applied to musical phrases
cresc	*crescendo*	A gradual increase of tone
dim decresc	*diminuendo* *decrescendo*	} A gradual decrease of tone

Enharmonic chords. Chords differing in notation but alike in sound.

Ensemble ("together"). A term applied to any group of executants, and to the art or effect of their playing together.

Entr'acte. Interval between acts; hence a light instrumental composition or short ballet, for performance between acts of a theatrical performance.

Episode. In general, a term applied to those portions of a musical work which connect portions of greater significance. In the fugue, it represents a digression from the principal theme, interpolated between the statements of the latter. In such large works as symphonies and quartets, episodes may be said to be synonymous with *bridge passage; i.e.,* they perform the function of furnishing musical continuity between main theme sections.

Étude (Fr., "study"). Frequently designed for particular technical difficulties; many are intended for concert performance, *e.g.* Schumann's *Études symphoniques.*

Euphony. The acoustic effect produced by sounds so combined as to please the ear.

Exposition. The first section of a movement in sonata form, in which the themes are "exposed" or set forth. See *Sonata form.*

Fantasia. A composition free in form and feeling.

Figure. An easily recognizable pattern of notes.

Finale. The last movement of an extended work. Sometimes given as the title to a separate piece, suitable to conclude a concert.

Flat. The character ($\flat$) which lowers by a semitone the pitch of a note before which it is placed.

Folk music. Music which comes from the folk and becomes traditional with them.

Form. The element in music that is concerned with its scheme of architecture or design. Without some formal scheme music would result in meaningless incoherency.

Fugue ("flight"). A contrapuntal composition which is made up of a characteristic sectional treatment, through imitation, of at least one main subject or phrase.

Fuoco (It.). *Con fuoco:* with fire; *i.e.,* forcefully and fast.

Gavotte. An early French dance in strongly marked quadruple time, beginning on the third beat. Frequently employed as a movement of the classical suite.

Gigue. An early dance in rapid tempo and in triple or compound time. In the classic suite it is usually the last movement.

Glee. An English invention of the eighteenth century: an unaccompanied vocal piece for (usually) four males.

Glissando (It., "slide"). In piano music, playing with the nail of one or more fingers, producing a very brilliant scale; *glissando* on bowed instruments demands a flowing, unaccented execution of a passage.

Grace note. A nonessential note as an embellishment, generally designated in small notation.

Grave (It.). Slowly and solemnly. See scale of speeds at end of Glossary.

Gregorian. The form of liturgical chanting ordained by Pope Gregory the Great (Pope, 590–604), and ever since widely used. See Chapter Thirty-Eight.

Harmonics (*Harmonic overtones*). Additional notes produced when a fundamental sound is generated. They give to a sound its individual character. Also flutelike tones produced on stringed instruments by touching the string lightly with the finger.

Harmonization. The arrangement of tones so as to create chordal harmony.

Harmony. The science of manipulating chords. Also used of the music produced by such manipulation.

Harpsichord. See Interchapter: The Piano.

Homophony. Music in which one part stands out and the others accompany, mainly in chord effects. The music is thus formed vertically, as opposed to *polyphony*, where the parts move horizontally.

Imitation. The contrapuntal device of employing a melodic or rhythmic figure in one voice which has been stated in another.

Incidental music. Music played during the incidents and intervals, but not the whole course, of a dramatic work.

Instrumentation. The choice of instruments for a composition. ("What is the instrumentation of Haydn's *Surprise Symphony?*" "Strings, with two each of flutes, oboes, bassoons, trumpets, horns, and drums.")

Intermezzo. A short piece intended, or suitable, for an interlude.

Interval. The pitch distance between two tones; in England, between two notes.

Intonation. Quality of tone; also, truth of pitch; also, the beginning of chanting in *plainsong*.
Just intonation is tuning by exact mathematical ratios; the opposite procedure is called tuning by *temperament* — tempering the wind, as it were, to various shorn lambs of intervals, so as to make them work tolerably well in all keys. *Equal temperament* is the modern method of tuning.

Introduction. A preliminary section.

Kapellmeister (G., "chapel master"). Generally applied to the director of music in eighteenth-century choirs, often in princely houses. Now used in Germany to mean a conductor at the theater or concert hall.

Key. The particular system of tones and semitones built upon a selected tone (the *tonic*) as a basis. The keynote or tonic thus becomes the first note of the scale and provides the name of the key, such as D major or C minor. The term *key* is also used for the black and white digitals of the keyboard.

Larghetto (It.). Slightly faster than *largo*. See scale of speeds at end of Glossary.

Largo (It.). Slowly and with dignity. See scale of speeds at end of Glossary.

Ledger line. A short line used for scoring notes above or below the staff.

Legato (It., "bound"). Smooth.

Leitmotiv (Ger., "leading theme"). In dramatic music, an identifying theme associated with a particular character, mood, or situation, and usually accompanying its reappearances.

Lento (It.). Slow. See scale of speeds at end of Glossary.

Libretto. The "book" of words of an extended choral composition, such as an opera, a cantata, or an oratorio.

Lied (Ger., "song"). Strictly used of the great number of art songs by German composers; most fittingly sung in German.

Madrigal. A secular, contrapuntal vocal work, usually in linked sections, originally sung by a few voices to each part. See Chapter Thirty-eight.

Major. As applied to scales, a pattern of seven steps (eight sounds), consisting of tones and semitones, the latter occurring between the third and fourth and seventh and eighth steps. A major interval is one semitone greater than a minor. Major chords and keys are those in which major intervals predominate.

Marcato (It.). Marked, *i.e.*, each note played with emphasis.

Mass. Musical setting of the Roman Catholic Eucharist.

Mastersinger. German bourgeois member of a medieval musical guild; successor to the *Minnesinger, q.v.*

Mazurka. A Polish national dance in triple time and moderate tempo, with variable accents on the third beat.

Measure (*bar*). A rhythmical unit of two or more beats.

Melody. Any agreeable and familiar series of notes. See Chapter Eight.

Meter (*Metre*). Any specific scheme of rhythm, determined by the number and length of the notes it contains.

Mezzoforte (It.). Moderately loud. See *Dynamics*.

Mezzopiano (It.). Moderately soft. See *Dynamics*.

Minnesinger (Ger., "love singer"). The German counterpart of the *troubadour, q.v.*

Minor. As applied to scales, the pattern of seven steps consisting of tones and semitones, the latter either between the second and third, fifth and sixth, and seventh and eighth steps (harmonic form); or between the second and third and seventh and eighth steps ascending, and the second and third and fifth and sixth steps descending (melodic form).

Minuet. An old French dance in dignified 3/4 rhythm. It is conventionally found as the third movement of the classic symphony. As an art form it is usually a double minuet with contrasted sections, the first section repeated after the second (trio).

Mode. Strictly, any mode or manner of arranging tones and semitones to form a scale. Generally, the term refers to the ancient scales used for both religious and folk music.

Modulation. The process of going from one key to another.

Motet. A religious counterpart of the *madrigal, q.v.*

Motive. A brief theme or figure, either an integral part of a larger theme or the generating idea out of which the theme develops.

Movement. A piece complete in itself, forming part of an extended work.

Music drama. Wagner's name for his operas.

Mute. A means of mechanically damping resonance of tones.

Natural. The character (♮) which contradicts a sharp or a flat.

Nocturne ("night piece"). Usually a piece of subdued, poetic feeling.

Note. The written or printed symbol for a tone.

Nuance. A shade of difference in tone color, tempo, or degree of force.

Obbligato (It., "indispensable"). An accessory part written for a particular instrument: as a violin part, additional to the piano accompaniment of a song.

Octave. A series of eight consecutive diatonic tones; also the interval between the first and eighth of such a series.

Opera. A play set to music that is nowadays usually, though it was not invariably, continuous.

Opus ("work"). A conventional word used by composers in numbering their works, as an *opus number.*

Oratorio. The sacred counterpart of opera, but invariably without stage appurtenances.

Orchestration. See *Instrumentation.*

Organ point (*pedal point*). A tone sustained in one part (usually the bass) while harmonies are executed in other parts.

Organum. The earliest attempts at harmonic or polyphonic music in which two or more parts progressed in parallel motion (fifths, fourths, and octaves).

Overtones. See *Harmonics.*

Overture. An instrumental prelude to a choral work. See also *Concert overture.*

Passacaglia. An early Italian dance in triple time and stately movement — with a ground bass. An instrumental composition in such form.

Pavan. A slow, stately dance of Italian or Spanish origin.

Phrase. A musical clause composed of two or more motives.

Piano (It.). Softly. See *Dynamics.*

Pianissimo (It.). Very softly. See *Dynamics.*

Pizzicato (It.). Plucked (of strings).

Plainsong (*plain chant*). The music of the early Christian centuries; based on modal scales. Rhythm and tempo were governed by word accent; sung in unison.

Polka. A lively round dance in 2/4 time originating in the early part of the nineteenth century as a peasant dance in Bohemia.

Polonaise. A dance of Polish origin in 3/4 time and moderate but animated tempo.

Polyphony. See *Counterpoint.*

Portamento. A smooth gliding from one tone to another, more deliberate than *legato*, actually (though rapidly) sounding intermediate tones. Banal except when artistically employed.

Prelude. An introductory section or movement. A *chorale prelude* is a polyphonic instrumental treatment of a chorale. See Chapter Thirty-four. The prelude to an opera is usually called the *Overture.*

Presto (It.). Very fast. See scale of speeds at end of Glossary.

Program music. Music based on some scheme of literary or associative values, evoked by means of sound. See Chapter Nine.

Quartet. Group of four executants. Also, the music they perform.

Quintet. Group of five executants. Also, the music they perform.

Recapitulation (*restatement*). The third section of a movement in sonata form, in which the themes are presented as at first.

Register. Section of an instrument's compass, characterized by a distinctive quality of tone.

Requiem. Mass or service for the dead. Also used of a memorial choral work.

Resolution. The process of discords progressing to concordance.

Rhapsody ("a stitching together"). A title borrowed from literature, originally meaning an epic poem. In music, a declamatory type of piece, in free form.

Rhythm. Generally speaking, the regular recurrence of like features in an artistic composition. The placing together of music's elements so as to ensure progression and shape. Recurrent pulses or patterns.

Ripieno. The "replenished" parts played in *concerti grossi* by the whole orchestra, not just the *concertino* of the few solo instruments. Used also of a choral body (as in Bach's *Passion*).

Ritard., ritardando (It.). Gradual slowing of tempo.

Rococo (Fr.). A florid and ornamental style characteristic of the eighteenth century. Often applied to music of that time. See Chapter Thirty-Two.

Romanticism. A style of composition in which the strongest emphasis is upon the personal expression of poetic sentiment, as distinguished from *Classicism, q.v.*

Round. A vocal *canon* (*q.v.*) at the unison or octave.

Rubato (It., "robbed"). Practically, the opposite of robbery, since time borrowed in one part of a phrase is replaced in another part of it; or a whole phrase might be slightly hurried, and the next slightly slowed. A characteristic element in the performance of most romantic music: to be sparingly used in older works.

Saraband. A stately dance of Spanish or Oriental origin in slow tempo and triple time. Its place in the *Suite,* as the slowest movement, is before the *gigue.*

Scale. A succession of tones in some arranged order, used as the basic material for writing a piece. The modern scales developed out of the *modes, q.v.*

Scherzo ("a jest"). A type of third-movement form, a development of the *minuet,* introduced into the symphony by Beethoven.

School. A group of musicians animated by ideas held in common or using common principles of structure.

Score. The parts of the various voices or instruments laid out beneath one another. *Short score* puts more than one part on each stave; *open score* gives each part its own stave. A *vocal score* gives all the voice parts of, say, an opera or an oratorio, together with, as a rule, a two-stave accompaniment, compressed from the orchestral score. A *piano score* of such a work would be on two staves only but would often show where the voices come in.

Semitone. A half tone.

Sequence. The repetition in succession of a melodic figure at different pitch intervals.

Serenade ("evening song"). Applied to suites of light music suitable to be played in the open air.

Sextet. A composition for six executants. Also, the music they perform.

Sharp. The character ($\sharp$) which raises by a semitone the pitch of a note before which it is set.

Siciliano. A dance of the Sicilian peasants, a kind of pastoral in moderately slow tempo and 6/8 or 12/8 time, frequently in a minor key.

Signature. The signs set at the head of the staff at the beginning of a piece of music. *Key signature:* The chromatic sign or signs (sharps or flats). *Time signature:* The figure or fractional sign indicating the measure.

Signs. Certain symbols are commonly used by composers for conveying performing directions. The ones most frequently used are:

⋅ ⋅ ⋅	Staccato
⌒	Slur or Tie
⊂	Crescendo
⊃	Decrescendo
tr	Trill
⌢	Hold
𝄆 ⫶ ⫶	Repeat

Sonata form. A misleading term for which *first-movement form* is perhaps better substituted. A *sonata* is the whole work for one or more soloists, in several movements, each having its own form. The form of the first movement is that in three sections, of which the first (Exposition or Statement) sets forth the thematic material, usually in two chief "subjects" or tune groups, in contrasted keys; the second (Development) works out and builds up this material; and the last (Recapitulation, or Restatement) brings back the tune material (in the *tonic key*) — in the earlier sonatas, pretty much as at first, but in later practice (Beethoven's, *e.g.*) often with some further treatment towards the end.

Song form. A term derived from the classic procedure of alternating two or more contrasted sections; probably originating in the simple contrasts of ideas in the song. Many slow movements of sonatas and symphonies are in song form.

Sostenuto (It.). Sustained.

Staccato. Detached or separated; a style of performance in which the notes or chords are more or less abruptly disconnected, as opposed to *legato, q.v.*

Staff. The five parallel lines used in modern notation.

Statement. See *Exposition.*

String quartet. Two violins, viola, and violoncello. Also, applied to the music played by these executants.

Style. A characteristic manner of expressing ideas.

Subject. A tune or theme.

Suite. A set of pieces either centering upon some general subject (*e.g.,* Grieg's *Peer Gynt* suite), or made up of contrasting but associated rhythmical styles (*e.g.,* Bach's suites based upon old dance forms).

Symphony. A *sonata* for orchestra.

Syncopation. A temporary displacement or shifting of the normal beat or accent of a piece of music. Sometimes applied to music which contains this device.

Technic; technique. All that relates to the purely mechanical part of musical performance. Mechanical training, skill, dexterity.

Temperament. System of tuning instruments so as to allow modulation without the use of a large number of pitch distinctions. See *Well-tempered.* Certain adjustments are made so as to get rid of physical inaccuracies in the intervals between certain notes.

Tempo. Time. Mostly used to mean "pace."

Ternary. Having three sections. Used of A–B–A form.

Tessitura (It.). The "lie" of a passage — its position in the compass of the instrument or voice.

Theme. A tune or subject.

Timbre (Fr.). Tone color or characteristic.

Timpani. Kettledrums.

Toccata. "Touch piece" — one designed to display brilliance of execution.

Tone color. A term borrowed from painting to denote the varied qualities of tone.

Tonic. The keynote of a scale. *Tonic chord.* A chord having the tonic note as its root.

Transition. Used of passages which lead from one principal idea or key to another.

Transpose. To put into a different key or position on the staff.

Tremolo. Quivering or fluttering; in singing, a tremulous, unsteady tone, caused by improper breath or muscular control; on bowed instruments, an effect produced by the very rapid alternation of down bow and up bow; on the piano the rapid alternation of the tones of a chord.

Triad. A three-note chord: root, third, fifth.

Trill. The even and rapid alternation of two tones a major or a minor second apart; the lower tone is the principal note, the higher the auxiliary.

Trio. Three performers, or the music they perform. Also, the middle, contrasting section of a *minuet* or a *scherzo.*

Troubadour. High-born minstrel in medieval France (Provence, *c.* 1100–1300). See Post Chapter: Song.

Trouvère. The Northern French counterpart of the *troubadour;* also included minstrels not highly born.

Unison. A tone of the same pitch as a given tone; also, a higher or a lower octave of the given tone.

Variation. A new presentation of a musical idea. The *theme and variations* is one of the oldest of musical forms; it is a "dinner of one sort of fish served up in many courses," each having a little different cooking and sauce.

Vibrato (It.). A foul form of ululation fantastically imagined by most of its users to add beauty to singing or playing. Subtly used by an artist, it is a legitimate means of heightening emotion.

Virtuoso. A superlatively equipped executant.

Vivace (It.). Vivaciously.

Well-tempered. Equally tuned. Applied to keyboard instruments tuned so that music in all keys can be played upon them.

Whole-tone scale. A scale moving by full tones: from C it comprises C, D, E, F sharp, G sharp, A sharp (or B flat), C.

Wood wind. The group of wood-wind instruments in the orchestra, as opposed to the brasses.

A Scale of Speeds

Largo } Lento }
Grave } — Adagio } — Andante-Allegretto-Moderato-Allegro } —Presto-Prestissimo
Vivace }

Slow   Fast

BIOGRAPHICAL LIST

OF COMPOSERS

PRONUNCIATION

Mᴀʀᴋɪɴɢꜱ: ā in lāte, ȧ in chȧotic, â in câre, ă in făt, ä in fär, á in lást, a in sofá; ē in mē, ê in rêturn, ĕ in mĕt, ḙ in quiḙt, ẽ in uppẽr; g in get; ī in fīne, ĭ in tĭn; ᴋ = ch in German *ach;* ṇ = ng, ɴ = ng in its effect (nasal) on the preceding vowel, but is not itself sounded; ō in nōte, ȯ in ȯbey, ô in fôr (same sound as aw in saw), ŏ in nŏt, ô̦ in sô̦ft, ö (set lips as if to say oh, but then say ĕ as in met, keeping the lips fixed in the first position); ōō in schōōl, ŏ͞o in wŏ͞ol; ₮ħ in ₮ħine; ū in tūne, ŭ in nŭt, û in bûrn, u̇ in su̇bmit, ü (set lips as if to say oo as in boot, but then say ee as in beet, keeping the lips in the first position); (ʹ) indicates the heavily accented syllable, (ʹ) indicates the syllable with secondary accent.

Adam de la Halle (ă·däɴʹ dü lä äl), b. Arras, 1238?; d. 1288. A prominent trouvère; master of the chanson.

Albeniz (älʹbă·nēthʹ), Issac, b. Camprodon, Spain, 1860; d. 1909. Spanish composer of note who reproduced the rhythms and other characteristics of Spanish popular music.

Arensky (a·rĕnʹskḙ), Anton, b. Novgorod, Russia, 1861; d. 1906. A prominent Russian composer-pianist of the Tchaikovskyan rather than the extreme nationalist school.

Bach (bäᴋ), Carl Philipp Emanuel, b. Weimar, Germany, 1714; d. 1788. Son of J. S. Bach; a pioneer of the sonata form and symphonic orchestration.

Bach, Johann Sebastian, b. Eisenach, Germany, 1685; d. 1750. The greatest composer of the polyphonic period, and one of the greatest of all time.

Balakirev (bäʹlä·kēʹrĕf), Mily, b. Novgorod, Russia, 1836; d. 1910. A pianist and composer; one of the Russian "Five."

Bartók (bär'tŏk), Béla, b. Transylvania, 1881; d. 1945. Modern Hungarian nationalistic composer and pianist.

Bax (băks), Arnold, b. London, 1883. English neo-romantic composer with Celtic sympathies.

Beethoven (bā'tō·vĕn), Ludwig van, b. Bonn, Germany, 1770; d. 1827. One of the greatest of all composers, especially in the realm of symphonic and chamber music. Historically he welded together the "Classical" and self-conscious "Romantic" periods.

Bellini (bĕl·lē'nē), Vincenzo, b. Catania, Sicily, 1801; d. 1835. Prominent Italian opera composer.

Berg (bärg), Alban, b. Vienna, 1885; d. 1936. Modern atonal theorist and composer; pupil and follower of Schönberg.

Berlioz (bĕr'lĕ·ôs'), Hector, b. Côte Saint André, France, 1803; d. 1869. A pioneer of program music.

Bizet (bē'zĕ'), Georges, b. Paris, 1838; d. 1875. Well-known French opera composer.

Bloch (blŏĸ), Ernest, b. Geneva, Switzerland, 1880. Modern Jewish composer of distinction, whose music epitomizes the history and aspirations of his race.

Boccherini (bŏk'kă·rē'nē), Luigi, b. Lucca, Italy, 1743; d. 1805. Prolific Italian composer, especially of chamber music.

Borodin (bŏr'ŏ·dĭn'), Alexander, b. St. Petersburg, 1834; d. 1887. One of the Russian "Five"; he utilized folk music in his scores.

Brahms (brämz), Johannes, b. Hamburg, Germany, 1833; d. 1897. One of the greatest composers of all time; combined romantic expression with classic form.

Bruch (brŏŏĸ), Max, b. Cologne, Germany, 1838; d. 1920. A talented German composer, excelled in choral music.

Bruckner (brŏŏĸ'nēr), Anton, b. Ausfelden, Upper Austria, 1824; d. 1896. Symphonic composer of great facility.

Busoni (bŏŏ·zō'nē), Ferruccio, b. Empoli, Italy, 1866; d. 1924. Pianist and composer of great influence on modern music. Transcribed and arranged many of Bach's organ works for the piano.

Buxtehude (bŏŏks'tĕ·hŏŏ'dĕ), Dietrich, b. Helsingborg, Sweden, 1637; d. 1707. Eminent organist and composer who influenced Bach's early career.

Byrd (bûrd), William, b. London, 1542; d. 1623. One of the greatest of Elizabethan madrigal composers.

Caccini (kă·chē'nē), Giulio, b. Rome, 1558; d. 1615. One of the pioneer opera composers. Collaborated with Peri in writing *Dafne*, the first opera ever produced.

Carpenter (kär'pĕn·tēr), John Alden, b. Park Ridge, Ill., 1876; d. 1951. Successful American composer in many forms.

Casella (kä·sĕl'lä), Alfredo, b. Turin, Italy, 1883; d. 1947. Prominent modern Italian composer.

Chadwick (chăd'wĭk), George Whitefield, b. Lowell, Mass., 1854; d. 1931. American composer in the classic style.

Chaminade (shȧ'mē'nȧd'), Cécile, b. Paris, 1861; d. 1944. French composer in the lighter forms.

Charpentier (shȧr'päɴ'tyä'), Gustave, b. Dieuze, Lorraine, 1860. French composer famous for one opera — Louise.

Chausson (shŏ'sôɴ'), Ernest, b. Paris, 1855; d. 1899. Pupil of César Franck and composer of distinguished individuality.

Cherubini (kā'rōō·bē'nĕ), Maria Luigi, b. Florence, Italy, 1760; d. 1842. A composer of the contrapuntal period, successful in both operatic and sacred forms.

Chopin (shŏ'păɴ'), Frédéric, b. Warsaw, Poland, 1810; d. 1849. The most individual and popular composer for the piano. Confined his work almost entirely to this instrument.

Coleridge-Taylor (kōl'rĭj·tā'lēr), Samuel, b. London, 1875; d. 1912. English Negro composer.

Corelli (kŏ·rĕl'lĕ), Arcangelo, b. Imola, Italy, 1653; d. 1713. Violinist and composer; founder of violin style and technic.

Couperin (kōō'pĕ·răɴ'), François (surnamed le Grand), b. Paris, 1668; d. 1733. Most eminent of a famous family of composers. His music is full of Baroque grace and charm.

Cui (kü·ē'), César, b. Vilna, Russia, 1835; d. 1918. One of the Russian "Five"; wrote in many forms, but his vocal works are his best compositions.

Czerny (chĕr'nĕ), Karl, b. Vienna, 1791; d. 1857. A pupil of Beethoven; eminent pianist and pedagogue.

Debussy (dē·bü'sē'), Claude Achille, b. Paris, 1862; d. 1918. Founder of the school of impressionism in music, and one of the most individual composers.

Delibes (dē·lēb'), Léo, b. St. Germain-du-Val, France, 1836, d. 1891. Popular ballet composer.

Delius (dē'lĭ·ŭs), Frederick, b. Bradford, England, 1863; d. 1934. An important English composer.

Diaghilev (dyä·gē'lĕf), Sergei Pavlovich, b. Novgorod, Russia, 1872; d. 1929. Founder of the famous Russian ballet which bore his name; commissioned the writing of many modern ballets, including the best works of Stravinsky.

D'Indy (dăɴ'dē'), Vincent, b. Paris, 1851; d. 1931. Most famous pupil and follower of César Franck, and one of France's leading composers.

Dohnányi (dō'nän·yĕ), Ernst von, b. Pressburg, Hungary, 1877. Hungarian pianist, conductor, and composer. His compositions are conserva-

tive and individual in style, carrying on the romantic traditions of th
nineteenth century, not the least attractive element being a tincture o
Brahms's spirit.

Donizetti (dō'nĕ·dzĕt'tĕ), Gaetano, b. Bergamo, Italy, 1797; d. 1848
Popular opera composer.

Dukas (dü'käh'), Paul, b. Paris, 1865; d. 1935. French composer of consid
erable attainment, especially successful in the larger symphonic forms

Dvořák (dvôr'zhäk), Anton, b. Mühlhausen, Bohemia, 1841; d. 1904
Leading Bohemian composer; lived several years in America.

Elgar (ĕl'gär), Edward, b. Worcester, England, 1857; d. 1934. The leadin₤
composer of modern England.

Falla (fä'yä), Manuel de, b. Cadiz, 1876; d. 1946. Spanish composer o
opera and ballet, showing folk and nationalistic influences.

Foster (fŏs'tĕr), Stephen Collins, b. Pittsburgh, Pa., 1826; d. 1864. Creato
of the American Negro popular song.

Franck (frängk), César, b. Liége, Belgium, 1822; d. 1890. France's mos
important modern composer.

Franz (fränts), Robert, b. Halle, Prussia, 1815; d. 1892. Master of Germaı
lied.

Gibbons (gĭb'ŭnz), Orlando, b. Cambridge, England, 1583; d. 1625. ₳
leading English madrigal composer.

Glazunov (glä'zŏŏ·nôf'), Alexander, b. St. Petersburg, 1865; d. 1936
Popular Russian composer.

Glinka (glĭng'kä), Michael, b. Smolensk, Russia, 1803; d. 1857. Pioneeı
Russian nationalistic composer.

Gluck (glŏŏk), Christoph Willibald von, b. Weidenwang, Upper Palatinate
1714; d. 1787. An operatic reformer of importance.

Goldmark (gŏlt'märk'), Karl, b. Keszthely, Hungary, 1830; d. 1915. Popu
lar composer in many forms.

Gounod (gŏō'nō'), Charles, b. Paris, 1818; d. 1893. Popular opera com
poser.

Grétry (gră'trē'), André Ernest, b. Liége, 1741; d. 1813. Important French
opera composer.

Grieg (grēg), Edvard, b. Bergen, Norway, 1843; d. 1907. Outstandin₤
Scandinavian composer.

Handel (hăn'd'l), George Frederic, b. Halle, Prussia, 1685; d. 1759. Wel
known for his classic forms and styles, especially his oratorios.

Harris (hăr'ĭs), Roy, b. Oklahoma, 1898. Important American composer

Haydn (hī'd'n), Franz Josef, b. Rohrau, Austria, 1732; d. 1809. Innovatoı
of classic form; father of the symphony and sonata form.

Hindemith (hĭn'dĕ·mĭt), Paul, b. Hanau, Germany, 1895. Facile composer in modern style.

Holst (hōlst), Gustav, b. Cheltenham, England, 1874; d. 1934. Modern British composer.

Honegger (hŏn'ĕg'ēr), Arthur, b. Havre, 1892, of Swiss parentage. Lively exponent of advanced, piquant tastes. Enjoys using counterpoint.

Humperdinck (hŏŏm'pĕr·dĭngk), Engelbert, b. Bonn, Germany, 1854; d. 1921. A talented composer and follower of Wagner; famous for his opera *Hänsel und Gretel.*

Josquin des Prés (zhŏs·kăn' dē·prä'), b. Burgundy, 1450?; d. 1521. A pioneer in vocal polyphonic music.

Kodály (kō·dä'ē), Zoltán, b. Kecskemét, Hungary, 1882. Modern Hungarian composer and arranger of folk music.

Lasso (läs'sŏ), Orlando di, b. Mons, Belgium, 1530?; d. 1594. Great master of sacred as well as secular polyphony.

Leoncavallo (lā'ŏn·kä·väl'lŏ), Ruggiero, b. Naples, 1858; d. 1919. Popular Italian opera composer.

Liszt (lĭst), Franz, b. Raiding, Hungary, 1811; d. 1886. World's greatest piano virtuoso and successful composer in many forms, especially the symphonic poem.

Loeffler (lĕf'lēr), Charles Martin, b. Mühlhausen, Alsace, 1861; d. 1935. Alsatian-American composer in the modern style.

Lully (lü'lē'), Jean-Baptiste, b. Florence, 1632; d. 1687. Important pioneer in opera; developed the overture and introduced the brass into the orchestra.

MacDowell (măk·dou'ĕl), Edward A., b. New York, 1861; d. 1908. Well-known American composer.

Mahler (mä'lēr), Gustav, b. Bohemia, 1860; d. 1911. Conductor and composer of symphonies, many of which are fantastic in conception.

Malipiero (mäl·ē·p'yä'rŏ), Francesco, b. Venice, 1882. Distinguished modern Italian composer.

Mascagni (mäs·kän'yĕ), Pietro, b. Leghorn, Italy, 1863; d. 1945. Popular composer of Italian opera.

Mason (mā's'n), Daniel Gregory, b. Brookline, Mass., 1873. Grandson of Lowell Mason and distinguished teacher and composer.

Mason, Lowell, b. Medfield, Mass., 1792; d. 1872. Pioneer American teacher and composer.

Massenet (mä's'nĕ'), Jules, b. Montaud, France, 1842; d. 1912. Popular composer of French opera.

Mendelssohn (mĕn'dĕl·sōn), Felix, b. Hamburg, 1809; d. 1847. Talented composer in many forms.

Meyerbeer (mī'ĕr·bār), Giacomo, b. Berlin, 1791; d. 1864. Creator of spectacular and popular operas.

Milhaud (mēl'ō), Darius, b. Aix-en-Provence, France, 1892. One of the modern French group known as the "Six."

Monteverdi (mŏn'tå·vâr'dĭ), Claudio, b. Cremona, 1567; d. 1643. Pioneer of modern harmony and homophonic style.

Morley (môr'lĭ), Thomas, b. England, 1557; d. 1603? Well-known Elizabethan madrigalist.

Moussorgsky (moō·sôrg'skĕ), Modeste, b. Karev, Russia, 1839; d. 1881 Extremely nationalistic Russian composer.

Mozart (mō'tsärt), Wolfgang Amadeus, b. Salzburg, 1756; d. 1791. Perhaps the greatest natural genius music has ever known, and a prolific composer throughout his short life.

Nicolai(nē'kŏ·lĭ), Karl Otto, b. Königsberg, Germany, 1810; d. 1849. Gifted operatic composer.

Offenbach (ŏf'ĕn·bäк), Jacques, b. Cologne, 1819; d. 1880. Popular composer of light operas.

Paderewski (pȧ'dĕ·rĕf'skĕ), Ignace Jan, b. Podolia, Poland, 1860; d. 1941. Renowned Polish pianist, composer, and statesman.

Paganini (pä'gä·nē'nĕ), Niccolo, b. Genoa, Italy, 1782; d. 1840. One of the greatest violinists in history; composer of many melodies which were later transcribed by others.

Palestrina (pä'lås·trē'nä), Giovanni Pierluigi da, b. Palestrina near Rome, 1525; d. 1594. The greatest and most important composer of the vocal polyphonic period.

Peri (pä'rĕ), Jacopo, b. Florence, 1561; d. 1633. The composer of *Dafne*, the first opera, in collaboration with Caccini.

Prokofieff (prō·kō'fē·ĕf), Serge, b. Russia, 1891. Prominent Russian modernistic composer.

Puccini (poō·chē'nĕ), Giacomo, b. Lucca, Italy, 1858; d. 1924. Popular Italian operatic composer.

Purcell (pûr'sĕl), Henry, b. London, 1659?; d. 1695. One of England's greatest composers.

Rachmaninoff (räк·mä'nĕ·nŏf), Sergei, b. Onega, Russia, 1873; d. 1943. Outstanding composer-pianist.

Rameau (rȧ'mō'), Jean Philippe, b. Dijon, France, 1683; d. 1764. One of the important men in the development of French opera; wrote more than twenty operas.

Ravel (rȧ'vĕl'), Maurice, b. Ciboure, France, 1875; d. 1937. Modern composer of many works in the manner of Debussy.

Respighi (rĕs·pē'gĕ), Ottorino, b. Bologna, Italy, 1879; d. 1936. Accomplished modern Italian composer.

Rheinberger (rīn'bĕrg'ēr), Josef, b. Liechtenstein, Germany, 1839; d. 1901. Eminent organist, teacher, and composer.

Rimsky-Korsakoff (rĭm'skĕ·kôr'sȧ·kŏf), Nicholas, b. Novgorod, Russia, 1844; d. 1908. A leading Russian composer with a distinct feeling for the Oriental style.

Rossini (rŏs·sē'nĕ), Gioacchino, b. Pesaro, Italy, 1792; d. 1868. Popular Italian opera composer.

Rubinstein (rōō'bĭn·shtīn), Anton, b. Bessarabia, 1830; d. 1894. Brilliant pianist and popular composer.

Saint-Saëns (săn'säns'), Charles Camille, b. Paris, 1835; d. 1921. Distinguished French composer.

Sarasate (sä'rä·sä'tȧ), Pablo de, b. Pamplona, Spain, 1844; d. 1908. Great violinist and minor composer.

Scarlatti (skär·lät'tĕ), Alessandro, b. Trapani, Sicily, 1659; d. 1725. Pioneer in opera; advanced monodic composition.

Scarlatti, Domenico, b. Naples, 1685; d. 1757. Son of Alessandro; developed harpsichord style and technic.

Schmitt (shmĭt), Florent, b. Blamont, France, 1870. Modern and original French composer, trained in the impressionistic school.

Schönberg (shön'bĕrк), Arnold, b. Vienna, 1874; d. 1951. One of the outstanding representatives of extreme modernism in music; founder and leading exponent of atonalism.

Schubert (shōō'bĕrt), Franz, b. Vienna, 1797; d. 1828. One of the great natural geniuses of music; had a prodigious output throughout his tragically short life.

Schumann (shōō'män), Robert, b. Zwickau, Saxony, 1810; d. 1856. Important early romanticist; possessed novel ideas as creator, interpreter, and critic of music.

Scriabin (skryȧ·bĭn'), Alexander, b. Moscow, 1872; d. 1915. Important Russian composer with unusual and often fantastic ideas.

Shostakovich (shŏs·tȧ·kō'vĭch), Dmitri, b. 1906. Russian composer, neoromantic, original. One of the Leningrad group, developing from Rimsky-Korsakoff. Has written both symphonies and operas.

Sibelius (sĭ·bä'lĭ·ōōs), Jean, b. Tavastehus, Finland, 1865. Well-known and extremely talented nationalistic Finnish composer.

Sinding (sĭn'dĭng), Christian, b. Kongsberg, Norway, 1856; d. 1941. Well-known Scandinavian composer.

Smetana (smĕ'tä·nä), Bedrich, b. Leitomischl, Bohemia, 1824; e. 1884. Distinguished Bohemian composer.

Spohr (shpōr), Louis, b. Brunswick, Germany, 1784; d. 1859. Violinist, teacher, composer.

Strauss (shtrous), Johann, Jr., b. Vienna, 1825; d. 1899. The "waltz king"; wrote over 400 waltzes.

Strauss, Richard, b. Munich, 1864; d. 1949. Distinguished composer in many forms, especially eminent as a song and symphonic composer.

Stravinsky (strà·vĭn'skē), Igor, b. near Petrograd, 1882. One of the leading modernists, especially significant as a composer of ballets and symphonic works.

Taylor (tā'lēr), Deems, b. New York, 1885. Distinguished American composer of operas and symphonic works.

Tchaikovsky (chĭ·kôf'skē), Peter Ilich, b. Votkinsk, Russia, 1840; d. 1893. Eminent romantic Russian composer.

Thomas (tŏ'mä'), Ambroise, b. Metz, 1811; d. 1896. Successful composer of popular French operas.

Vaughan Williams (vôn wĭl'yămz), Ralph, b. Wiltshire, England, 1872. Individual and talented leading British composer.

Verdi (vâr'dē), Giuseppe, b. LeRoncole, Parma, 1813; d. 1901. Greatest Italian opera composer, master of vocal melodic writing.

Vivaldi (vē·väl'dē), Antonio, b. Venice, 1676?; d. 1743? Violinist and composer of distinction.

Wagner (väg'nēr), Richard, b. Leipzig, 1813; d. 1883. The greatest dramatic composer of all time, replacing the old-fashioned opera with music drama.

Weber (vā'bēr), Carl Maria von, b. Oldenburg, Germany, 1786; d. 1826. Important German composer, especially in the field of opera; influenced Wagner's early career.

Weinberger (vīn'bĕrк·ēr), Jaromir, b. Prague, 1896. Writer of picturesque operas, the most famous of which is *Schwanda*. Now a resident of the United States.

Widor (vē'dôr'), Charles Marie, b. Lyons, France, 1845; d. 1937. Distinguished French organist, teacher, and composer.

Wieniawski (vyĕ'nyäf·skē), Henri, b. Lubin, Poland, 1835; d. 1880. Brilliant violinist and composer for the violin.

Wolf (vŏlf), Hugo, b. Styria, 1860; d. 1903. One of the immortal masters of German lieder.

Wolf-Ferrari (vŏlf'-fĕr·rä'rē), Ermanno, b. Venice, 1876; d. 1948. Popular opera and song composer.

INDEX